Psychopathology and Personality Dimensions

In the *World Library of Psychologists* series, international experts present career-long collections of what they judge to be their finest pieces – extracts from books, key articles, salient research findings, and their major practical theoretical contributions.

In this fascinating collection, Professor Gordon Claridge charts the development of a model of mental health that blurs the line between madness and sanity; conditions such as schizophrenia and other forms of psychosis are seen as dimensions of 'normal' personality and temperament rather than separate abnormalities. Working with, and influenced by, the late Hans Eysenck, Claridge is celebrated for evolving research on personality and psychological disorders into a revised view of the spectrum of psychotic traits. The concept of schizotypy, re-evaluated by Claridge, sees mental illness not as a pathology suffered by a few, but as the end of a continuum experienced by us all. *Psychopathology and Personality Dimensions* brings together some of the author's most influential publications on the topics of schizotypy and psychoticism, personality disorders, and the use of drug techniques to investigate normal and abnormal individual differences.

Interspersed throughout with specially-written retrospectives by Professor Claridge, looking back at his work and contextualising where it sits in the wider literature, the collection illustrates a radical and influential model of mental illness that continues to resonate today. This book is an essential resource for all those interested in the field of personality and psychological disorders.

Gordon Claridge is Professor of Abnormal Psychology at the University of Oxford Department of Experimental Psychology, an Emeritus Fellow at Magdalen College, and a Fellow of the British Psychological Society. Over an exceptional career spanning nearly sixty-five years, and as a past President of the International Society for the Study of Individual Differences, he has been at the forefront of research around the theme of schizotypy, investigating the major psychological disorders.

World Library of Psychologists

The *World Library of Psychologists* series celebrates the important contributions to psychology made by leading experts in their individual fields of study. Each scholar has compiled a career-long collection of what they consider to be their finest pieces: extracts from books, journals, articles, major theoretical and practical contributions, and salient research findings.

For the first time ever the work of each contributor is presented in a single volume so readers can follow the themes and progress of their work and identify the contributions made to, and the development of, the fields themselves.

Each book in the series features a specially written introduction by the contributor giving an overview of their career, contextualizing their selection within the development of the field, and showing how their thinking developed over time.

Psychopathology and Personality Dimensions: Selected Works of Gordon Claridge
By Gordon Claridge

Reasoning, Rationality and Dual Processes: Selected Works of Jonathan St B T Evans
By Jonathan St B T Evans

The Assessment, Evaluation and Rehabilitation of Everyday Memory Problems: Selected Papers of Barbara A. Wilson
By Barbara A. Wilson

Philosophy and History of Psychology: Selected Works of Elizabeth Valentine
By Elizabeth R. Valentine

Developmental Transitions across the Lifespan: Selected Works of Leo B. Hendry
By Leo B. Hendry

Psychopathology and Personality Dimensions
The Selected Works of Gordon Claridge

Gordon Claridge

LONDON AND NEW YORK

First published 2018
by Routledge
2 Park Square, Milton Park, Abingdon, Oxon OX14 4RN

and by Routledge
711 Third Avenue, New York, NY 10017

Routledge is an imprint of the Taylor & Francis Group, an informa business

© 2018 Gordon Claridge

The right of Gordon Claridge to be identified as author of this work has been asserted by him in accordance with sections 77 and 78 of the Copyright, Designs and Patents Act 1988.

All rights reserved. No part of this book may be reprinted or reproduced or utilised in any form or by any electronic, mechanical, or other means, now known or hereafter invented, including photocopying and recording, or in any information storage or retrieval system, without permission in writing from the publishers.

Trademark notice: Product or corporate names may be trademarks or registered trademarks, and are used only for identification and explanation without intent to infringe.

British Library Cataloguing in Publication Data
A catalogue record for this book is available from the British Library

Library of Congress Cataloging in Publication Data
A catalog record for this book has been requested

ISBN: 978-1-138-28761-7 (hbk)
ISBN: 978-1-315-26821-7 (ebk)

Typeset in Times New Roman
by Swales & Willis Ltd, Exeter, Devon, UK

To the study participants and research collaborators without whom the works reprinted here could not have been written

Contents

	Acknowledgements	ix
	List of works reprinted	x
1	Hans Eysenck's contribution to our understanding of personality and psychological disorders: a personal view GORDON CLARIDGE	3
2	The relationship between incentive, personality type and improvement in performance of imbeciles GORDON CLARIDGE AND NEIL O'CONNOR	17
3	Sedation threshold, personality, and the theory of neurosis GORDON CLARIDGE AND CAPTAIN REG N. HERRINGTON	29
4	Why drug effects vary GORDON CLARIDGE	47
5	The relative influence of weight and of "nervous type" on the tolerance of amylobarbitone sodium GORDON CLARIDGE	64
6	Animal models of schizophrenia: the case for LSD-25 GORDON CLARIDGE	72
7	Covariation between two-flash threshold and skin conductance level in first-breakdown schizophrenics: relationships in drug-free patients and effects of treatment GORDON CLARIDGE AND KENNETH CLARK	99

8	LSD: a missed opportunity? GORDON CLARIDGE	109
9	The schizophrenias as nervous types GORDON CLARIDGE	122
10	Theoretical background and issues GORDON CLARIDGE	143
11	The factor structure of 'schizotypal' traits: a large replication study GORDON CLARIDGE, CHARLES MCCREERY, OLIVER MASON, RICHARD BENTALL, GREGORY BOYLE, PETER SLADE AND DAVID POPPLEWELL	158
12	The Oxford-Liverpool Inventory of Feelings and Experiences (O-LIFE): further description and extended norms OLIVER MASON AND GORDON CLARIDGE	169
13	Schizophrenia risk and handedness: a mixed picture GORDON CLARIDGE, KENNETH CLARK, CAROLINE DAVIS AND OLIVER MASON	183
14	Creativity: a healthy side of madness GORDON CLARIDGE AND NEUS BARRANTES-VIDAL	192
15	Psychotic traits in comedians VICTORIA ANDO, GORDON CLARIDGE AND KEN CLARK	205
16	Old thoughts: new ideas: future directions GORDON CLARIDGE	214
	References	223
	Index	249

Acknowledgements

For their help in facilitating the reproduction of the papers printed here thanks are due to the following: John Wiley; Oxford University Press; Elsevier; Routledge; Blackwell; Royal College of Psychiatrists; Sidestone Press; and Karen Langdon at the Oxford University Radcliffe Science Library.

I would also like to thank Russell George, editor of this book series, for offering me the opportunity to produce my collected works; and to editorial assistants Liz Rankin and Alex Howard, for their patient help in getting the volume into production.

Lastly, I have much appreciated the unfailing guidance given to me in the final proof checking stage of the manuscript by Caroline Watson of Swales & Willis.

Works reprinted

Claridge, G. (2016) Hans Eysenck's contribution to our understanding of personality and psychological disorders: A personal view. *Personality and Individual Differences, 103*, 93–98.

Claridge, G. S. & O'Connor, N. (1957) The relationship between incentive, personality type and improvement in performance of imbeciles. *Journal of Mental Deficiency Research, 1*, 16–25.

Claridge, G. S. & Herrington, R. N. (1960) Sedation threshold, personality, and the theory of neurosis. *Journal of Mental Science, 106*, 1568–1583.

Claridge, G. (1970) Why drug effects vary. In G. Claridge *Drugs and Human Behaviour*. London: Allen Lane, Chapter 5, pp. 123–146.

Claridge, G. S. (1971) The relative influence of weight and of 'nervous type' on the tolerance of amylobarbitone sodium. *British Journal of Anaesthesia, 43*, 1121–1125.

Claridge, G. (1978) Animal models of schizophrenia: The case for LSD-25. *Schizophrenia Bulletin, 4*, 186–209.

Claridge, G. & Clark, K. (1982) Covariation between two-flash threshold and skin conductance level in first-breakdown schizophrenics: Relationships in drug-free patients and the effects of treatment. *Psychiatry Research, 6*, 371–380.

Claridge, G. (1994) LSD: A missed opportunity? *Human Psychopharmacology, 9*, 343–351.

Claridge, G. (1972) The schizophrenias as nervous types. *British Journal of Psychiatry, 121*, 1–17.

Claridge, G. (1997) Theoretical background and issues. In G. Claridge (ed) *Schizotypy: Implications for Illness and Health*. Oxford: Pergamon, pp. 3–18.

Claridge, G., McCreery, C., Mason, O., Bentall, R., Boyle, G., Slade, P., & Popplewell, D. (1996) The factor structure of 'schizotypal' traits: A large replication study. *British Journal of Clinical Psychology, 35*, 103–115.

Mason, O. & Claridge, G. (2006) The Oxford-Liverpool Inventory of Feelings and Experiences (O-LIFE): Further description and extended norms. *Schizophrenia Research, 82*, 203–211.

Claridge, G., Clark, K., Davis, C., & Mason, O. (1998) Schizophrenia risk and handedness: A mixed picture. *Laterality, 3*, 209–220.

Claridge, G. & Barrantes-Vidal, N. (2013) Creativity: A healthy side of madness. In B. D. Kirkcaldy (ed), *Chimes of Time*. Leiden: Sidestone Press, pp. 115–130.

Ando, V., Claridge, G., & Clark, K. (2014) Psychotic traits in comedians. *British Journal of Psychiatry, 204*, 341–345.

Claridge, G. (2015) Old thoughts: New ideas: Future directions. In O. Mason & G. Claridge (eds) *Schizotypy: New Dimensions*. London: Routledge, pp. 217–227.

Commentary

It might seem strange to open this collection – intended to span works produced over a long career – with a paper that was, at the time of this writing, my most recently published. The paper forms part of a journal special issue assessing the contribution to psychology of the late Hans Eysenck, commemorating the 100th anniversary of his birth. To some readers the choice might appear especially odd, even irritating, in perhaps signalling that the later pieces to be reproduced will merely constitute yet another eulogy of Eysenck. The assumption (and the annoyance), while understandable, are unfounded. But let me first clear up one or two facts about Eysenck. As those who lived through the period when he was active in psychology – or know its history – will realise, Eysenck was an extremely controversial figure. He was argumentative, challenging of received ideas, and often ready to espouse scientifically dubious or socially divisive causes. He has been the subject of at least one critical recent biography (Buchanan, 2010) and a caustic evaluation by his own psychologist son (Eysenck, M., 2013). There are some who would like to see him assigned to a dustbin of flawed geniuses who practised a form of psychological scientism that is best forgotten – as did the British Psychological Society which snubbed him throughout his lifetime and has largely done so since. This, despite efforts by some admirers to revive Eysenck's work for a younger audience: notably Corr (2016) writing, pointedly, in the present tense!

Why, then, the opener here? One clue lies in the title of this book. The first paper to be reproduced was an invited piece assessing Eysenck's contribution to abnormal and normal personality psychology; exactly chiming with the subject matter of the present volume. Beyond that, however, there are other sound reasons for giving the paper such prominence here. As indicated in the title of the article, it was written very much from a personal point of view, reflecting the fact that from an early stage in my career – indeed as an undergraduate student – I came under Eysenck's influence, theoretically and practically, eventually as one of his employees. Of course this adds no legitimacy to the ideas he imparted to me or to any version of them that I adopted in my own subsequent work. On the contrary it might even serve to undermine them, extrapolated from the opinions about his interests in less savoury areas of knowledge that came eventually to define his reputation. In his defence I would argue that these were aberrations that unfairly overshadow appreciation of what was the genuine core of his life's work, namely his research on normal and abnormal psychology – a dedicated interest that lasted throughout his career, dating from the time when he was forced as an alien to work in a British military psychiatric hospital. It was from there that he began to formulate a theory of the psychological disorders and personality that was to revolutionalise our understanding of those fields, doing so in a single insight that was, in my opinion, a mark of genius. The theory he proposed brought together three principles that had never before been considered in conjunction with one another. These were that: (a) human variations can be described dimensionally, even in their abnormal forms; (b) psychological disorders represent pathological transformations of normal personality; and (c) some at least of the variations observed can be accounted for by biological, including genetic, factors. I was so moved by this formulation when I heard it as an undergraduate that, in one form or another, it was to shape my thinking for the whole of my career.

Finally, there is one other reason why the paper is well-placed to open this collection. The autobiographical narrative form in which it is written allows the reader to trace the evolution of my research from its early beginnings: first actually working directly on Eysenck's theory, then moving on to investigating topics distant from his ideas but where remnants of his influence can still be discerned. The piece can therefore act as a useful template, signposting themes taken up in the later papers reproduced here.

1 Hans Eysenck's contribution to our understanding of personality and psychological disorders
A personal view

Gordon Claridge

In his lifetime Hans Eysenck was such a controversial figure that any comment on his work is bound to be touched by individual bias; even the serious academic research discussed here, let alone his ventures into socially divisive topics and fringe areas of science. His ideas about personality were contentious and evoked strong opinions, even from those of us who knew and worked with him. It is appropriate to let an autobiographical theme run through this paper, in order to explain how Eysenck influenced my own thinking and my eventual conclusions about his contribution to personality theory and abnormal psychology. I have already covered part of the topic in several previous publications (Claridge, 1981, 1983, 2009a) and fully in an earlier *Festschrift* to Eysenck (1997). Given the lighter touch of the present piece, consulting, especially, the last of those papers will help the reader fill in details of evidence and arguments about the various themes to be introduced (Claridge, 1997a).

I first encountered Eysenck in the early 1950s when, as an undergraduate in the Psychology Department at University College London, I took his lecture course on personality. Even to my naive student eye it was obvious that the Department was not at the best place in its previous and subsequent prestigious history. I was aware that the famous – eventually to become infamous – Cyril Burt had just retired and the place had the taste of a collection of leftovers, spiced up by large dollops of Hullian learning theory, which seemed pointlessly irrelevant to the human psychology I had gone to university to study. I was probably on the point of dropping out. For good or ill Eysenck saved me from that fate.

Eysenck's lectures were a revelation. With the lucidity and confidence that we all came to recognise as the hallmark of his public presentational style, he laid out an approach to individual differences that seemed awesomely complete: a statistically derived account of the descriptive features (dimensions) of personality; an explanation of their underlying biology, accessible through laboratory investigations (In my enthusiasm I obviously failed to notice his heavy reliance there on learning theory concepts and methodology!); and a connection to psychological disorders, envisaged as merely extreme positions on personality dimensions. In that last part of his theory he was foreshadowing his eventual vehement dismissal of the medical model (Eysenck, 1960), a stance that evoked much furore among the psychiatric profession but the arguments for which were already obvious to disciples such as myself – reflected in my scepticism about the content of a parallel series of lectures I was attending on mental 'diseases', given by a clinical psychiatrist.

Despite considerable shifts in my research interests over the years, the power of this 'Eysenck epiphany' has lasted a lifetime and traces of it still pervade my thinking; especially about the dimensionality of personality and spectrum approach to disorder, and a belief that biology and genetics must play some part in shaping these variations. (Nothing new there to some contemporary observers but easy to forget that Eysenck pioneered both ideas in the modern era.) I have assimilated alternative perspectives, but that has always required a curious kind of *effort* not demanded by the Eysenck dogma. I sometimes liken the phenomenon to the experience I have noticed in lapsed Roman Catholics among my friends and colleagues: try as they might they can never fully shake off the last vestiges of their faith.

Eysenck's influence on my thinking – and eventually my perceptions of the flaws in his work – were reinforced when he took me on as a research assistant. My remit was to test out in psychiatric patients the 'causal' part of his theory, *viz.* using laboratory measures to explore correlates of the psychological disorders that formed the 'criterion groups' allegedly defining the end points of introversion–extraversion (I–E): anxiety based neuroses (dysthymics, as Eysenck called them) for introversion; and, for extraversion, various forms of hysterical disorder, as well as psychopathy. Neuroticism (N), being an orthogonal dimension and therefore assumed to be similarly high in both clinical groups, was not at the time considered relevant; predictions from the theory were solely about differences between the extreme manifestation of I–E.

A further word about dysthymia–hysteria, the clinical manifestation, according to Eysenck (1957b), of extreme introversion and extraversion. The introverted end was unproblematic in being defined by a recognisable and relatively homogenous group of neurotic disorders. This was less true at the extraverted end, as eventually proved to be the case in subsequent thinking about those conditions, both within and outwith Eysenckian theory. Psychopathy was later hived off to define the third, psychoticism (P), dimension (Eysenck & Eysenck, 1976). Meanwhile 'hysteria', because of its dubious sexist connotations, dropped out of psychiatry altogether. The ragbag of disorders previously denoted by the term 'hysteria' remained in the psychiatric classification, to be spread diagnostically across other abnormal reactions to stress: somatoform and dissociative. In the research discussed below, using the old nomenclature – that also included a category of hysterical personality disorder – and bundling in psychopathy as well, made the 'extraverted disorders' group quite mixed, diagnostically: they were often labelled 'hysterico-psychopaths' for the purpose of data analysis and reporting. To anticipate slightly, it actually turned out that there were very few differences between the various subgroups on important experimental measures, suggesting that the heterogeneity across that half of the sample was not as marked as might have been feared.

Despite the fact that Eysenck had promoted his theory as an explanation of *both* normal introversion–extraversion *and* clinical dysthymia–hysteria, a comparison had never been properly made of the two criterion groups. Work attempting to connect the personality and clinical domains had been confined, albeit with a vigorous debate, to questionnaire studies (McGuire, Mowbray, & Vallance, 1963; Sigal, Star, & Franks, 1958; Slater, 1960; Storms & Sigal, 1958). Results there were ambiguous and Eysenck judged – to my good fortune – that a comprehensive laboratory based investigation of the questions raised was necessary.

The setting for the research was unusual and deserves mention. My job was based not in the Institute of Psychiatry but, by special arrangement with the army, at the Royal Victoria Military Hospital, Netley near Southampton. There, freed from the constraints of actually working in the IoP Psychology Department and away from Eysenck's eagle eye, I established an outpost where I was free to do what I liked – and did: pursuing lines of research not immediately connected with testing his theory of neurosis. That 'unofficial' research involved studying an extra group of psychotic patients, unconnected at the time to the main hypotheses about neurosis and personality disorder. The work is not relevant to the present discussion, though it did introduce me to the topic of psychosis and eventually, among other things, shaped my thoughts about Eysenck's psychoticism dimension, returned to later. The whole programme of research at Netley – as it was known for short – was published in my book *Personality and Arousal* (Claridge, 1967).

Netley, now demolished, was a unique hospital, ideal for the research contemplated. As well as a ready supply of easily matched healthy controls, it offered patients covering all of the diagnoses necessary for the research. Referring back to my earlier remarks, it is worth noting the particular availability of patients falling into the category of hysteria, especially those with the now defunct diagnosis of conversion hysteria. Reportedly infrequently seen at that time in civilian *psychiatric* practice, such individuals were very common in the military setting. Patients covered the whole range of expression of that once commonly diagnosed syndrome of pseudo-neurological disorder; *viz. psychogenic* blindness and deafness, anaesthesia and partial paralysis of limbs, and fugue (amnesic) states. Importantly – especially for that particular patient subgroup – all of the participants were young fit men, having been screened on entry to the army for obvious physical complications. Furthermore, the way the military services processed their psychiatric casualties meant that patients when tested were generally free of, or on minimal, medication.

The battery of behavioural procedures administered covered a wide variety of laboratory measures then regularly employed in Eysenck's department to examine individual differences. They included tests of perception (e.g., Archimedes spiral after effect), motor performance (serial reaction time and Stroop interference), and auditory vigilance. To which we added a group of psychophysiological measures: EEG indices and tests of drug response. Among the latter the most salient – and figuring large in later research explicating certain features of Eysenck's theory – was the sedation threshold. This was a procedure used to determine individuals' tolerance of sedative drugs by injecting them intravenously with a barbiturate (commonly amylobarbitone sodium), continuing the infusion until they reached a defined end-point of loss of consciousness. It was introduced into psychiatry as a diagnostic tool by the American clinician Shagass (1954), who used EEG changes as his criterion for the threshold of sedation. Subsequently, in the 1950s and early 1960s there was a flurry of research on the technique, both by Shagass himself and by others exploring alternative criteria for determining the sedation threshold. Among them, at Netley, a psychiatrist colleague and I introduced a simple behavioural criterion (Claridge & Herrington, 1960).

Summarising the part of the work conducted at Netley on neurosis, two facts stood out. The first was that there was very good support for the predicted difference between the two criterion groups of anxiety based (dysthymic) patients and hysterico-psychopaths. (As noted above, there were few, if any, differences on objective laboratory measures among the subgroups of patients making up that diagnostically broad category.) The effects were especially evident for tests like auditory vigilance and sedation threshold, where dysthymics proved to have a significantly better vigilance performance and greater tolerance of the depressant drug (higher sedation threshold) than hysterico-psychopaths. The drug finding, incidentally, was scarcely a novel discovery since it had already been demonstrated by Shagass on a substantial sample of patients (Shagass & Jones, 1958). Still, it pleased Eysenck that his causal theory had been vindicated!

The other main finding from the study did not fit in with Eysenck's dysthymia–hysteria story. Since according to theory the neurotic criterion groups were merely abnormal counterparts of introversion–extraversion, comparing them should have nothing to do with N; being independent of I–E the latter logically should have had no influence, even in clinical populations. This proved manifestly not true in our research, where factor analysis of the psychophysiological data demonstrated what we identified as two distinct components of 'arousal', and led us to conclude that at the causal level *both* I–E *and* N contributed to dysthymia–hysteria, as an interaction between the two dimensions. At an individual test level, this was dramatically illustrated in some highly replicable findings on drug tolerance differences to be found among non-clinical subjects, assessed for I–E and N. The results came from studies examining both nitrous oxide tolerance (Rodnight & Gooch, 1963) and ones using the regular barbiturate (sedation threshold) procedure (Claridge & Ross, 1973; Claridge, Donald, & Birchall, 1981).

In all of those experiments samples were subdivided into high and low scorers on the neuroticism scale. It emerged that I–E was related to sedative drug tolerance in opposite directions in the two subgroups of N. There was higher tolerance in neurotic introverts compared with neurotic extraverts, thus paralleling the patient data. But quite the reverse was true in low N subjects; in that case it was *extraverts* who had the greater tolerance. These findings were damaging for Eysenck's theory, not only because of the novelty of the crossover effect itself, but also because it undermined his general prediction about the expected relationship between I–E and biological measures. Pointedly so, given the special 'drug postulate' he had deliberately introduced to connect personality study to psychopharmacology: the proposal was that psychoactive drugs could be used as a special experimental tool to explore the biological correlates of introversion–extraversion (Eysenck, 1963).

In his book *The Biological Basis of Personality*, Eysenck (1967) acknowledged the possibility of interactions between I–E and N and recommended that data sets be routinely examined for such effects using so-called 'zone analysis'. This proposed comparing the performance scores for individuals subdivided according to the four combinations of I–E and N. At the same time he revamped his biological model, bringing it more into line with Western thinking and terminology about the nervous system. Pavlovian nervous typological theory had served him well – and it is instructive to remember that he had relied on it to pioneer the application of biology to the understanding of human personality. But its language was quaint and the constructs ambiguous and difficult to apply. It was time for it to be abandoned even in the face of continuing attempts to retain connections to the Pavlovian and neo-Pavlovian schools of thought (see Nebylitsyn & Gray, 1973).

Unfortunately, neither the methodological nor the conceptual changes Eysenck brought to his thinking produced much that was new in understanding personality differences. Zone analyses of data hinted that an explanation of the I–E/N interaction might lie in inverted-U effects (Claridge et al., 1981; Eysenck, 1967). But that was about all and zone analysis disappeared into a dusty box of procedures never to be opened again, except on occasions such as this. And the new model of the 'conceptual nervous system' (acknowledgment to Hebb, 1955) elucidated little. The suggestion was that I–E reflected variations in ascending reticular (ARAS) arousal and N differences in limbic system activation. While this looked impressively 'neurophysiological' it proved to be more descriptive than explanatory.[1]

My personal view is that Eysenck's 1967 book marked the end of his novel contribution to our understanding of individual differences, as envisaged within his original two-dimensional framework. This is not to say that the book is without purpose. On the contrary, it should be read by anyone who has doubts about possible biological and behavioural genetic involvement in healthy and unhealthy personality: it contains a vast amount of evidence still relevant to current debates. And work inspired by the I–E/N formulation certainly rumbled on; for example in applications to medical topics such as smoking and lung cancer (see Nias, 1997). But what ultimately killed off Eysenck's own message was the revision to his theory suggested by Jeffrey Gray (1981). Gray's proposal for two alternative dimensions of anxiety and impulsivity – drawn diagonally across I–E and N – made clinical sense. The scheme indicated a more explicit connection to disorder, at least on the anxiety side, and suggested a more obvious way of mapping the descriptive features onto a possible underlying biology. In particular, Gray's reinforcement theory – anxiety and impulsivity representing sensitivity to, respectively, punishment and reward – seemed neater and less messy than Eysenck's own formulation. The recent history of research within the 'Eysenckian school' has, therefore, essentially been a history of pursuing and elaborating on Gray's theory – see Pickering et al. (1997) and other papers in this issue.

Irrespective of the judged success or otherwise of that later work, the form of the Gray revision – and its subsequent versions – and the language in which they are couched raises an important question that needs to be addressed here. How far are such formulations theories of personality, in the full sense of the word? The issue can be articulated as a distinction between *temperament* and *personality*, one that in the adult field has not often been explicitly debated (though see Claridge, 2006; Claridge & Davis, 2003; Strelau & Zawadzki, 1997). Temperament is generally regarded as the 'simpler' construct, reflecting emotional and motivational differences, grounded in quite genetically determined biological processes, readily observable in animals as well as in humans. The term has been more often applied in a developmental context, as a way of characterising apparently constitutional differences among children; giving rise to such formulations as the three-dimensional EAS scheme presented by Buss and Plomin (1984) who explicitly used strong heritability as a necessary criterion for a trait to be considered temperamental.

Judged in that light Eysenck's theory and derivatives of it – and others in the same genre (e.g., Zuckerman's, 1979, sensation seeking model) – are, in my view, more than anything accounts of temperament. Tracing Eysenck's theory to its origins makes this obvious, where key parts of his thinking were shaped by the ancient theory of temperaments: as a basis for defining his descriptive dimensions and, at the causal level, by drawing upon Pavlov's nervous type explanation of it, developed in his studies of dogs. Subsequently, in a sleight of Hans at which in argumentation he was notoriously adept, Eysenck tried to persuade us that his theory offered a comprehensive account of behaviours in many domains, even beyond strict personality differences, including social and political attitudes. Yet, as his 1967 revision reminds us, it remained at bottom (*sic!*) an account of psychological functions driven from below by relatively low brain structures. The impression (and perhaps the intention) given was that biology rules in a determinist, reductionist sense.[2]

Does this matter? It could be argued not, if pure temperament theories can elucidate behaviours that might be strongly determined by underlying hereditary traits and, therefore, seemingly 'biological' in nature. In the abnormal field, primary psychopathy comes to mind (Hare, 1993; Viding, 2004). However, even there, understanding of behaviour can benefit from insights that more fully formed accounts of personality can provide. For example, the almost universal child abuse and neglect found in psychiatric patients is a factor that pure temperament theories are ill-equipped to deal with, because of the limited scope of their constructs. A researcher who has recognised this fact is Cloninger (2006) with his formulation of personality that proposes a two-layered structure: *temperament*, containing motivational elements, like novelty seeking, familiar in other similar theories; and *character* made up of higher order psychological traits, such as self-directedness and cooperativeness. Cloninger gives a fairly obvious example of the advantages of this scheme. Take two individuals, both high in novelty seeking and low in harm avoidance, but differing in self-directedness and cooperativeness. In the absence of the modulating effect of the relevant character traits the person might be destined to become a criminal; in their presence, they might become, as he puts it, a 'daring explorer, inquisitive scientist, or acquisitive banker' (*sic!*).

One further point before moving on from Eysenck's two-dimensional theory. It and its later revisions were most successful when trying to explain *anxiety* – whether as personality or temperamental trait or as psychiatric state or disorder. There are good reasons for that. Among the descriptors found in psychology and psychiatry anxiety is the simplest and most basic, its psychophysiology most transparent, and its underlying brain mechanisms relatively straightforward. From an 'Eysenckian' perspective it scarcely mattered whether one tried to examine it by manipulating introversion and neuroticism or by pursuing Gray's anxiety continuum: individuals in the low E/high N quadrant invariably behaved and behave as predicted. The place of anxiety in psychological disorders is correspondingly uncomplicated. Indeed some expressions of it, like simple phobias, can be understood as conditioned responses, needing no recourse to the cognitive accounts to which Eysenck was somewhat averse, and treatable by simple exposure procedures. The same cannot be said of other disorders; for example some forms of antisocial behaviour, as well as what used to be labelled hysterical personality, possibly now overlapping with borderline personality disorder, itself a difficult condition to fathom. Most complicated of all, of course, are the psychotic disorders and in an attempt to explain those Eysenck had to move beyond his two-factor model. His speculations there actually constituted two distinct theories, developed years apart.

The first version (Eysenck, 1952b) was simply an extension of the two-dimensional theory, to include a third orthogonal dimension of psychoticism, comparable to N, intended to cover features that all psychotics had in common, with I–E explaining differences among them – as found in, respectively, schizophrenia and manic-depression (now bipolar disorder). It was arrived at by rejigging, through factor analysis, Kretschmer's (1925) earlier single dimensional model of schizothymia–cyclothymia. As a basis for making empirically based statements about the psychoses the formulation proved fairly useless, partly because of the blunt nature of the experimental methods available at the time it was proposed. But it did disclose two important theoretical issues. One was the idea, pioneered by Kretschmer, that even serious mental illnesses could fall on dimensions extending into normal personality. The other was the notion of unitary psychosis: that manic-depression and the schizophrenias were not categorically distinct conditions, but overlapped descriptively, and probably aetiologically. These two propositions, and especially the latter, were extremely controversial when Eysenck wrote about them and it is only in recently years that both have come to be accepted (Marneros & Akiskal, 2007).

When Eysenck did eventually return to psychoticism, he did so with a very different theory about it – and a questionnaire to measure it (Eysenck & Eysenck, 1975). Development of the P-scale, the research surrounding it, and controversies about its theoretical underpinning now define a debate about psychoticism very different from that stimulated by the original theory. It is impossible to discuss that debate without reference to the topic of 'schizotypy', a largely separate research movement in abnormal psychology that over many decades has also been devoted to trying to dimensionalise psychosis, especially schizophrenia. (For recent coverage see

Mason & Claridge, 2015; and *Schizophrenia Bulletin*, 2015.) Several viewpoints are represented in that research, sometimes with marked differences of opinion between them. But all agree that Eysenck's psychoticism concept sits uneasily with current models of the schizophrenia spectrum.

There are two related problems, one empirical, concerning the P-scale, and the other theoretical. Both are grounded in the notion that, as a personality descriptor, 'psychoticism' refers to antisocial, tough-minded, impulsive, aggressive traits. This is clearly evident in the items in the current P-scale and as stated formally in Eysenck's final statement about the nature of psychosis (1992b). The latter is certainly a dimensional model. It also contains an element of the unitary idea contained in his original theory, proposing that schizophrenia and bipolar disorder fall on the same continuum and, therefore, overlap. But the characteristic – antisociality – underlying that continuum and linking healthy personality to both forms of psychotic disorder is not one that most clinicians would recognise as a salient unifying feature.

Our own research investigations into the psychosis spectrum have indicated a possible way of rescuing Eysenckian psychoticism and its offspring, the P-scale (Claridge, 2015). Arguing that schizotypy is too limited a construct, we have suggested that it should be expanded to enclose bipolar disorder as well, embracing a unitary view of psychosis and related personality features. In support we quote questionnaire evidence for a fourth personality component over and above the three factors of cognitive disorganisation, perceptual aberration and anhedonia normally used to define schizotypy. The extra factor co-varies with those other components but is loaded separately on cyclothymic/bipolar traits, P-scale items and borderline personality. Taken in conjunction with the evidence in the clinical domain for a schizophrenia/bipolar overlap, this would argue the case for a broader personality equivalent corresponding to 'psychoticism' as Eysenck originally conceived of it, in his first theory.

It is intriguing to speculate why, in forming the later version of his psychoticism theory, Eysenck reached the conclusion he did on the topic. One view might be that he was continuing the mode of thinking he was comfortable with about the causes of other individual differences. As noted several times here, this had a bias towards motivational/emotional explanations, referred to relatively lower order brain mechanisms. And indeed this was also the case with psychoticism, as shown in the fact that its defining features were ascribed to aggression and aggressiveness. The explanation was endorsed by Gray (1973) and continued by his followers (Corr, 2010; Pickering et al., 1997). Judging this, it is true that emotional features are part of psychosis, notably in bipolar disorder – but also in schizophrenia, as flattened affect or dysregulation of mood driving, for example, paranoia. But in the schizophrenias, especially, cognitive mechanisms play an overriding role in the disordered behaviour, an element that Eysenck seemed unable or unwilling to bring directly into his theorising.

What, then, can we conclude about Eysenck's contribution to the field reviewed here? It scarcely needs stating that in academic psychology he was the foremost personality theorist of the 20th century. The very breadth of his contribution guaranteed that, combining as it did ideas about personality description, biological influences on individual differences, and connections to abnormal psychology. On all of those fronts he drew, of course, upon the writings of others: Pavlov, Kretschmer, Jung, to name a few. But that is almost always the case with innovation and takes nothing away from his unique intellect. Not unusually, the same qualities made him highly focussed on his work – and sometimes too convinced about the correctness of his own ideas. Change occurred slowly (and reluctantly), as in the two-dimensional theory, and never properly at all in the three-dimensional model: his notions about psychosis and psychotic traits remained flawed to the end. I have intimated frequently why that might have been: biological explanations that were doubly reductionist – primitive brain biology and not admitting into the discourse anything that smacked of the mentalistic.

On the purely abnormal side, some of the weakness in Eysenck's work can be ascribed to his lack of clinical experience and exposure to patients. He came to the topic as an unworldly academic. This led him to some conclusions that were out of step with the clinical reality. One sign was an oversimplistic view of the connection between personality and psychological disorders. He viewed the latter, defined as 'criterion groups', as *merely* end-points on the quantitative dimensions of normal individual variation: he made no apparent distinction between traits and symptoms, between personality and illness. This limited the capacity of his theories to deal with what are often qualitative shifts in the transition from one to the other, and the dynamics of such change. A small but significant early example is the case of conversion hysteria, as dissociative disorder was once named. According to the Eysenckian model, conversion hysterics should fall fairly and squarely in the high E/high N quadrant. Yet in the Netley study described earlier they did so only on experimental measures. On questionnaires they tended to be lower than expected on E and N; some patients I tested actually had zero neuroticism scores! A probable explanation of this lies in the phenomenon of *belle indifference*, the tendency for individuals dissociating from stress to, literally, 'convert' their anxiety into a bland unconcern, and focus on the somatic nature of their symptomatology. Eysenck's theory was not well placed to handle such dynamics.

The most blatant example of Eysenck's clinical naivety of course was his conceptualisation of psychosis and psychoticism. It is intriguing to speculate where that came from. Influenced by North American usage of 'psychotic' and 'psychopathic', the former often being wrongly used as a synonym for the latter? Buying into popular misconceptions, fuelled by lurid media reporting, of schizophrenics (in particular) as mad axe killers – not realising that psychotic violence is rare and generally triggered by abnormal cognitions such as delusions or hallucinations? As it is, the legacy is that 'psychoticism' is still too loaded a term to use as a descriptor for psychosis risk, at least in the European literature.

Stepping briefly outside the theory itself, to consider other contributions Eysenck made to the field under review, we should not forget the enormous influence he had on the work of other psychologists, worldwide. Very often it was merely through making available excellent, reliable and well-validated questionnaires: MPI, EPI,

EPQ – in junior and adult forms. (Here it is good to place on record Eysenck's generosity in turning a blind eye to his loss of royalties as investigators in their thousands made their own copies of the official versions.) Apart from Cattell's 16PF and the MMPI, the Eysenck scales had few rivals, a situation that only changed with the appearance of the 'Big 5' OCEAN questionnaire, which has now become more popular, especially in North America. But not after much criticism of it by Eysenck (1992a) in reply to Costa's claim that his five factors provided a more complete account of personality than his rival's three (Costa & McCrae, 1992). The argument was part of a wider discussion that ensued asking how many personality dimensions there, indeed, are. The debate was and is fruitless, largely depending on the vagaries of factor analysis – and the old adage about it: 'what you put in is what you get out'. In some quarters it finally nose-dived into absurdity with the contention that there is only *one* dimension of personality (Rushton & Irwing, 2008).

Within Eysenck's own department, in its heyday research on his ideas was a veritable industry, pursuing almost every corner of experimental psychology for evidence of the correlates of introversion–extraversion and neuroticism. Almost all experimental phenomena, in their individual variations, were up for grabs as possible indicators of 'nervous typological' differences between participants. Anecdotes of two memorable events from that period will perhaps illustrate the fever of the endeavour – and reveal something of Eysenck's personality. At one point I had occasion to tell him that I needed a tape-recorder to run some of the experimental tests I was planning to use in my research for him. Without ado he marched me off to Camberwell Green and bought one out of his own pocket – or so it seemed to me at the time, ignorant of grants and such. A sign of his informality, his generosity, his sense of self-importance? Probably a mixture of all three. The other experience was – potentially at least – more traumatic. Eysenck had suggested that, as one of the experimental procedures I might include in my test battery for Netley, was the assessment of Bidwell's ghost: measuring the effect of presenting a brief white flash after a primary visual stimulus, say red, so that all one sees is the after-image (green). At the time Eysenck had a graduate student – a young Japanese man – studying the phenomenon and I was told to go and discuss the test procedure with him. What I didn't realise was the hidden agenda: that the only way in which I could proceed was to remove to Southampton the whole of the Bidwell's ghost equipment – a complicated piece of apparatus that the student had spent months building and without which his own research was doomed, or at the very least considerably delayed. I approached the meeting with trepidation. True to his nation's traditional form of greeting the man merely bowed and impassively nodded. Losing my nerve and envisioning a kamikaze scenario (or worse) I backed off (literally) and went to tell Eysenck the news. He just shrugged, despairing at or sympathising with – who can tell? – his new research assistant's tendermindedness. As far as I am aware Bidwell's ghost never was assessed in psychiatric patients, at least in Eysenck's department.

In his 1967 book, Eysenck explained the reasoning behind his strategy of mining the experimental psychological literature for procedures, like Bidwell's ghost, for testing out his theory. There he drew attention to the 'two faces of psychology'. One, the classic form, concentrates on group effects, usually assigning any individual differences to error variance. The other sees those same individual differences as a concern in their own right, to be explained according to variations in the biological processes assumed to underlie the measure of interest. For Eysenck in his Pavlovian phase this meant manipulating the excitation–inhibition construct and, post-1977, arousal and activation.

Then, of course, there were the books he edited, giving others the chance to report their research findings or review evidence over a wide range of topics. Most notable perhaps were the two editions of his *Handbook of Abnormal Psychology* (Eysenck, 1960, 1973). Massive volumes, probably rarely consulted nowadays, but deserving attention from anyone interested in the history of differential and abnormal psychology; produced in an exciting era when non-medical investigators were trying to establish an experimental psychopathology, often arguing with one another other, with the psychiatrists for whom it was intended, and the non-experimental, clinical psychologists who disagreed violently with Eysenck for his soulless theorising.

I started this paper on a personal note and will end it on one. I kept my notes from Eysenck's undergraduate lectures for many decades. Indeed, if I searched long enough I could probably still find them in the jumble that is my office. The fact is of no real significance and says nothing about Eysenck's impact on the wider scene of personality and psychological disorders. Nevertheless I find it deeply satisfying. How many psychologists can say of their former professors that the truths imparted to them more than half a century ago still play on their minds!

Notes

1 The model was also, in terms of brain mechanisms involved, rather 'low level'. Which was ironic, given that the theory Eysenck had originally adopted was, by Pavlov's own prescription, a theory about the properties of the *higher* nervous system.
2 This is not of course an argument about biological as against non-biological explanations in psychology. As the existence of cognitive neuroscience demonstrates, brain research is now capable of demonstrating neural correlates of the most subtle mental processes. That does raise significant philosophical questions; but of an entirely different order from that discussed here.

Further reading

Claridge, G. (1997). Eysenck's contribution to understanding psychopathology. In H. Nyborg (Ed.), *The scientific study of human nature: Tribute to Hans Eysenck at eighty* (pp. 364–387). Oxford: Pergamon Press.

Commentary

The remaining papers reprinted are organised according to a somewhat untidy mixture of the thematic and the chronological. Mostly the latter but, because some topics preoccupied me for longer than others and took me along previously unplanned routes of research disconnected from the original purpose, some themes were pursued over many years. This is particularly true of my work on drugs, a topic which, as shown later, I studied and wrote about in several contexts. However, the paper presented next, written in the late 1950s, is firmly anchored at the beginning of my career.

The paper describes a study of personality (or more strictly temperament) in severely intellectually impaired adults housed in several institutions in the UK. The latter fact alone helps to date the article (such places have long since been demolished – or turned into luxury flats!); but more significant is the use of the word 'imbecile' in the title. This deserves comment.

In retrospect it is difficult to believe now that such demeaning descriptors as 'imbecile' – and 'idiot' – formed part of an official medical nomenclature for classifying what was then generically called 'mental deficiency' or 'mental retardation'. Rooted in a 19th-century intellectual tradition of genetics – and often eugenics – the terminology reflected a pessimistic view of certain less well-endowed members of society, assumed to be biologically challenged beyond hope. Alternative labels were equally pejorative: cretin, ament, moron, retard, feebleminded, subnormal, mongol. It was not until the second half of the 20th century that an attempt was made to find a more considered terminology. Even this was not unproblematic, being subject to what has been called the 'euphemism treadmill'. For a discussion of this process it is instructive to read the Wikipedia entry on 'intellectual disability':

> This [euphemism treadmill] means that whatever term is chosen . . . it eventually becomes perceived as an insult. The terms *mental retardation* and *mentally retarded* were invented in the middle of the 20th century to replace the previous set of terms, which were deemed to have become offensive. By the end of the 20th century, these terms themselves had come to be widely seen as disparaging, politically incorrect, and in need of replacement.
> (Wikipedia, 29/08/2016)

The introduction of intelligence tests and the concept of the IQ at the beginning of the 20th century did not, ironically, help matters much. True, they offered a metric for classifying severity differences in intellectual disability: 0–20 idiots, 21–50 imbeciles, 51–70 high grade (morons). At the same time, they constrained perceptions of such individuals and their capabilities, reinforcing the gloom about their prospects in everyday life and trapping them in the vast institutions to which they were consigned.

There were however some, mainly psychologists, who challenged that received wisdom and sought new ways of conceptualising and managing mental deficiency. It was my privilege to work with such a group and the paper presented here is a small contribution to their effort. The paper reports work that formed part of my PhD at the London University Institute of Psychiatry, attached to the MRC Social Psychiatry Research Unit which was located in the grounds of the Maudsley Hospital. The key figure for me there was Dr Neil O'Connor who took me on as his research student. O'Connor is now better known for his work, with Beate Hermelin, on idiot savants (Hermelin & O'Connor, 1983); but in the early days his research focused on exploring ways of rehabilitating and improving the lives of the inmates in the large institutions for the 'mentally deficient'. The work was part of a movement among some psychologists and psychiatrists at the time to change the subculture of such places. Part of it involved the opening of industrial-style workshops in which patients could be employed on real-life work contracted from local employers: simple tasks, such as folding boxes, for which they could earn money. The initiative questioned the validity of the long-established existence of the institutions as closed, self-sufficient places in which patients would certainly be employed, but according to an occupational therapy model – working in the kitchen or gardens, or making things such as boots and clothing for the use of the patients themselves. The new workshops – which were also opened in some hospitals for the mentally ill – were intended to, hopefully, prepare inmates for life outside the institution.

As an experimental psychologist, Neil O'Connor's particular contribution to that effort – and the remit for my PhD – was to explore factors affecting the workshop performance of participants, in a pseudo-laboratory setting. To that end we set up mock hospital workshops to which individuals (for the record, with a mean IQ around 30) would come daily to perform a repetitive task consisting of inserting pegs into small holes on a board. The main hypotheses tested related to group effects such as the influence on daily performance of motivational factors like regular encouragement and the setting of daily goals. As described in the accompanying paper, I also examined individual differences in response to those variables, having noted considerable within-sample variations in temperament, which I thought, might be relevant. The influence of Eysenck is obvious here; but not just because of the way of thinking about psychology he had inculcated in me as an undergraduate. By now, as Head of Department of the Institute of Psychiatry Psychology Department, he was my formal PhD supervisor. (Because Neil O'Connor was not a registered member of the university he could not fulfil that role, even though he was my day-to-day advisor.)

Ahead of this early paper a few personal recollections are worth recording, to illustrate what it represents beyond the purely academic, as an enjoyed phase in my career. Working in the area gave me probably as much satisfaction as any experience since; partly because of the 'characters' I met in my research and as a nursing assistant while working in several hospitals to help fund my studies – inmates, almost always cheerful, housed in soulless institutions (smelling of disinfectant) that have now thankfully disappeared from the landscape. Also because of my association with Neil O'Connor, an Australian psychologist of immense talent, with a dry sense of humour and a quirky side to his personality. Two memories of him remain with me. Both relate to being taken by him in his car to the hospital outside London where we did our experiments. The vehicle – a Ford Popular – had a very narrow wheelbase, which perfectly fitted the tramlines that criss-crossed south London at that time. Routinely Neil would locate the car into these tramlines and let go of the steering wheel while he opened his morning mail. Even more impressively he would occasionally erratically veer off the main road to deposit bundles of political leaflets on the doorsteps of houses in various side streets, leaping in and out of his car without a word and zooming back on to our route (I was to learn later that like several of his colleagues at that time he was a fully paid-up member of the Communist Party).

Finally, the Social Psychiatry Unit deserves mention, as a small friendly community run with great informality. Memorably, it was housed in a Nissen hut next to the Maudsley Hospital tennis court, a place visited by Hans Eysenck, at the same time every day without fail. There was no escaping him!

2 The relationship between incentive, personality type and improvement in performance of imbeciles[1]

Gordon Claridge and Neil O'Connor

Introduction

In a review of some relevant studies of learning among defectives, McPherson (1948) notes that ability in complex learning situations is generally predictable from mental age, although she adds the proviso that, even so, subjects with relatively homogeneous intellectual ratings do not perform uniformly in such situations. With very simple tasks this relationship between mental age and ability to improve may not hold at all. Gordon (1953), for instance, after a preliminary analysis, concludes that the ability of imbeciles to improve on a simple manual dexterity task cannot be positively identified with intelligence, a finding confirmed by Claridge (1956). Similarly, Woodrow (1940) with normals, found almost zero correlations between intelligence test scores and rate of gain on simple performance tasks.

Gardner (1945) has suggested, in fact, that intelligence tests do not tap some latent abilities in the mentally defective; that differences in their speed of learning may be due rather to personality factors. That there may be a systematic relationship between learning ability and personality was a concept proposed by Pavlov (1927), who distinguished, among dogs, a number of nervous types, differing in the ease with which they were conditioned. The Pavlovian concept of nervous types has recently been reinterpreted by Eysenck (1955a) in the light of current personality and learning theory. Eysenck's suggestion is that extraverts and introverts differ in respect of their position on a continuum of excitability-inhibitability, extraverts showing a predominance of inhibitory potential, and therefore conditioning slowly, introverts showing a predominance of excitatory potential, and therefore conditioning quickly.

In a number of group learning experiments carried out with imbeciles and reported elsewhere (Claridge 1956; O'Connor and Claridge 1955), the wide individual differences in improvement found did not appear to be associated consistently with tested intelligence, and, following Eysenck's hypothesis, it seemed that they might be more meaningfully related to personality differences.

This approach presented in itself a number of initial problems, for little systematic consideration had hitherto been given to the personality of the severely subnormal individual. One of the few discussions of possible differences in personality among individuals at this level of defect is that by Tredgold (1952), from an essentially observational point of view. He suggests that imbeciles may be divided into "excitable" and "apathetic" types. Of the low-grade mental defective he says, "Probably the majority of them are best described as phlegmatic, being apathetic, indifferent and comparatively un-excitable; but there are many who are excitable and demonstrative . . ."

Some approximation to the dimension of extraversion-introversion is clearly apparent in Tredgold's distinction and his concept of excitability-apathy appeared to provide a good starting-point for an analysis of individual differences in the improvement of imbeciles.

The problem of measurement was itself an obstacle, since most of the current personality tests, especially of the questionnaire type, which appeared to be relevant to the aims of the study were, for obvious reasons, unsuitable. What was more important, however, results obtained in this way were likely to be invalidated, once we went beyond a middle range of intelligence, as we were bound to do in dealing with the imbecile. In order to overcome some of these difficulties a rating scale was developed which covered various aspects of excitability and which appeared to relate realistically to the kind of behaviour expected in the imbecile.

Construction and application of the rating scale

The first step involved in the construction of the rating scale was to select a number of related areas of behaviour which, it was estimated, would reflect various aspects of excitability-apathy in the imbecile. These were Emotionality level, Aggressive behaviour, Activity level, Variability of work activity, Verbal activity, Sociability, Inter-personal response, Amenability, and Predictability. Each of these aspects, or items, was then scaled along a five-point scale. The procedure followed in scaling each item was to draw up concrete descriptions of typical behaviour in five graduated steps from one extreme of the activity to the other. In the preliminary form, then, the scale consisted of nine items, each being graduated along a scale from A to E, with each step defined.

In order to refine the scale to some degree at least, the preliminary version was tried out on a sample of imbeciles, twenty-one male and twenty-one female patients being rated by at least two independent judges, who were the Charge Nurses or Sisters on the wards of the patients concerned. An item analysis appropriate to this type of scale was then carried out on the data, according to the technique described by Slater (1956). The set of weights finally extracted by iteration suggested that some modification to the scale was necessary, since some responses to particular items appeared to be contributing little to the total scale. In these cases responses were either discarded or, where appropriate, combined with adjacent responses, the final scale consisting of nine items, seven of which were graded on a four-point scale, and two on a five-point scale. Each item was presented to the judge on a separate card.

In the group learning experiments, 155 imbeciles—97 males and 58 females—had been used as subjects and all of these were rated on the scale by at least two independent judges, who were their appropriate Sisters or Charge Nurses. The procedure used in all cases was as follows:

The rater was interviewed and the purpose of the study explained to him. He was then given a list of the patients he was being asked to rate together with the first card (Emotionality level). After he had read the alternative statements relating to Emotionality level he was asked to state which of these statements most closely described the first patient on the list and this was noted by the interviewer. This procedure was repeated until all the subjects under consideration had been rated for Emotionality level, when the second card (Aggressive behaviour) was presented, and all subjects rated for this trait, and so on for all the nine cards.

The sum of the nine weights appropriate to the statement chosen from each card was regarded as a subject's Excitability Score. Since in all cases where the rating scale was used two ratings were obtained for each subject, two such total scores were secured and the mean of these was regarded as the final estimate of a patient's excitability.[2]

Results

(a) *General considerations.* Of the total number of patients rated for excitability the males were distributed over three, and the females over two, hospitals. The mean and standard deviation for the three samples of male imbeciles were as follows:

Hospital	Number of subjects	Mean Excitability Score	S.D.
Ma	39	86.03	42.42
Da	18	93.00	43.21
Mi	40	89.48	45.74
	97	88.74	44.05

Similar data for the two samples of females were as follows:

Hospital	Number of subjects	Mean Excitability Score	S.D.
Ma	40	94.32	49.92
Da	18	92.89	53.25
	58	93.88	50.96

The mean Excitability Score for males and females combined was 90.66, S.D. 46.83. There seemed to be a surprising agreement in terms of mean score and distribution among the various samples, despite the fact that a number of raters had been involved, and the scale from this point of view, at least, appeared to be satisfactory and to represent a reliable estimate of the subject's excitability. The correlation[3] of the scale with intelligence was found to be non-significant, the value for "r" between I.Q.[4] and Excitability Score being +0.10 (N = 115).

All the subjects rated had taken part in one or more of the group learning experiments cited previously. Here they had received daily trials of an hour, and sometimes half-an-hour, on a simple manual dexterity task, which involved the insertion of small scutcheon pins on a perforated board. The task, termed the Nail-frame, is described fully by Gordon (1953). Subjects had worked either under non-incentive (Control) conditions or under the incentive of Goal with Encouragement, where they were encouraged to reach a goal based on their previous performance.

Because of the variety of conditions under which the original learning experiments had been carried out, the separation of the numerous effects operating was difficult, especially since the number of subjects working under equivalent conditions at the same state of practice was often small. Where possible, however, data from several experiments were combined in order to increase the reliability of the resulting correlations. This seemed justifiable since the various samples did not appear to differ greatly with respect to other variables, such as intelligence level, and experimental conditions in the separate studies were highly standardised.

The data were considered in two parts: improvement under non-incentive and improvement under incentive conditions. Each of these will be described in turn.

(b) *Improvement under non-incentive conditions.* The relationship between excitability and improvement was first examined using the data from an experiment which had been concerned with sex differences in the behaviour of imbeciles. An examination of improvement scores for the first ten (hourly) trials of this experiment suggested that imbeciles who were rated as apathetic, that is, had low Excitability Scores, improved during this early period of learning more than did those rated as excitable. Males and females did not appear to differ in this respect, the correlation between Excitability Score and absolute improvement over the first ten trials for males and females combined being -0.56 (N = 18), which is significant at the 0.05 and closely approaches the 0.01 level of confidence.

This preliminary finding suggested that further investigation was worthwhile and it was possible, by combining the data for several studies, to increase the reliability of the results. Forty-eight subjects had worked under non-incentive conditions for at least ten hourly trials from the beginning of learning.

The percentage improvement during this period was calculated for each subject and these scores correlated with excitability. As a result of this the initial findings were confirmed, the correlation between Excitability Score and percentage improvement being -0.41 (N = 48), which is significant at the 0.01 level of confidence. The correlation between Excitability Score and starting level was, on the other hand, non-significant, "r" being $+0.14$ (N = 48).

Where data based on trials of an hour's length had been used, the relationship between excitability and learning seemed, therefore, to be relatively clear-cut. Some data were also available based on shorter trials of half-an-hour, and similar correlations between Excitability Score and improvement were computed on this data. Here it was possible to consider, not only whether the earlier findings were confirmed, but also whether the relationship between personality type and learning still held at later stages of practice. The following correlations were found at various stages of practice under non-incentive conditions:

Trials 1–4	Trials 5–20	Trials 21–37
–0.30	–0.16	–0.44*

N = 20 in all cases. * Significant at the 0.05 level.

It is apparent from this that the findings based on the longer working period were not clearly defined. There did at the same time, however, appear to be a consistent tendency at all stages of practice for inert imbeciles to show the greater amount of improvement when given no external incentive force.

(c) *Improvement under incentive conditions.* Less data were available on the effects of incentives during the early period of learning and, because of the variety of conditions involved in the learning experiments, the combining of data was not possible. However, a number of interesting and consistent trends emerged from the separate consideration of each study. Where the hourly trials had been used the correlation between Excitability Score and improvement during the "learning period" was +0.26 (N = 20), which is not significant.

In an experiment where the shorter (half-hourly) trials had been employed the following correlations were found at each stage of practice under incentive conditions:

Trials 1–4	Trials 5–20	Trials 21–37
+0.44*	+0.29	+0.07

N = 20 in all cases. * Significant at the 0.05 level.

There appeared, therefore, to be a slight but consistent tendency for the relationship obtaining under non-incentive conditions to be reversed, excitable individuals improving rather more under incentive conditions than apathetic individuals. Results were not clear-cut enough to make possible any definite conclusions regarding these effects, but, at the same time, it certainly could not be said that the significant relationship between apathy and improvement found under non-incentive conditions was confirmed. This in itself seemed to indicate that at least the minimum conclusions could be drawn that the inferior ability of excitable imbeciles to improve could be offset by the use of special incentives.

With this conclusion in mind, the possibility was then considered that excitable and apathetic subjects may differ in their reaction to the removal of incentives after they had had experience of them. Some data were available on this point from an investigation reported upon previously (Claridge, 1956). Here a number of subjects had been changed from incentive to non-incentive conditions after twelve trials. A perusal of individual scores during the post-change period of this experiment revealed that most excitable subjects showed a tendency to decline, while apathetic subjects continued to improve following the removal of the incentive. The correlation between Excitability Score and rate of improvement during this period was –0.64 (N = 10), which is significant at the 0.05 level.

Discussion

From the results reported here there appears to be suggestive evidence that (a) differences in the personality of imbeciles may be described in terms of excitability and (b) these differences may be related to corresponding differences in their improvement on a repetitive motor task as well as to their response to incentives.

As operationally defined, the excitable defective is emotionally labile, restless, distractable, and socially responsive. The apathetic imbecile, on the other hand, may be said to be emotionally inert, plodding, persistent, and socially unresponsive. It seems possible that the differences demonstrated here in the behaviour of imbeciles of these two personality types are due to differences in the extent to which they will, under certain conditions, develop factors which are likely to inhibit, rather than facilitate, improvement.

It has, of course, long been recognised that prolonged repetition of the same response will produce a tendency for that response to be inhibited. On repetitive motor tasks, where performance will be spread over relatively long periods, this may be accompanied by other behavioural signs such as loss of motivation, reported fatigue, and so on. Individual differences in susceptibility to these effects have been noted among normal industrial workers and that these differences may be related to personality factors was suggested by Wyatt and Langdon (1937) who pointed out that loss of motivation in industry may be greater among extraverts than introverts.

The present work with imbeciles appears to confirm this result, since an inert imbecile might be said to improve much longer, or alternatively "fall-off" less quickly, on a repetitive task than does an excitable imbecile. Two facts support this finding. First, it is noticeable that such effects were more apparent the greater the amount of repetition required, i.e. the longer the length of trial. Secondly, it is also significant that this superiority of the inert imbecile was nullified, indeed almost reversed, when a stimulus (i.e. an incentive) was applied which, it might be supposed, served to dissipate the factors leading to the failure of the excitable subjects to improve. The occasional restimulation, by means of periodic encouragement, of the incentive effect of a goal is probably also important in this respect, if we follow the conclusion of Mace (1935) that, in order to be effective rewards must be spaced throughout the period of practice. Similarly, it is in keeping with the view of Hebb (1949) that, in order that the persistence of motivation in any one direction may be maintained, it needs continually new content or new stimulation, such as a change of set.

The work of Eysenck (1955a) referred to earlier, provides a possible theoretical basis for explaining the behaviour of subnormal individuals of different personality types in learning situations of this kind. At the same time it suggests the possibility of a link with motivational theory. Certainly, it might be said that the present evidence with imbeciles working on a repetitive motor task presents facts which are, at one and the same time, facts of learning and facts of motivation. Such evidence confirms, perhaps, the need for a conceptualization of motivation within the same context as other behavioural and neural events, in much the same way as that suggested by Hebb (1949). Defined in this way the two correlated behavioural phenomena, for example, of motivational "fading" and performance decreases, which both in the normal and in the defective appear to be associated with personality factors, could ultimately be related more meaningfully to learning variables such as inhibition, in the manner suggested by Eysenck (1955a) following Pavlov.

While the present work with imbeciles can only be regarded as exploratory in this direction it suggests a possible fruitful line of approach to problems of learning, motivation and personality in general, and more specifically to the behaviour problems of the severely subnormal.

Summary

As a result of the failure of tested intelligence to predict differences in the improvement of imbeciles on a repetitive motor task, it was suggested that these differences could be related to differences of personality, conceived in terms of excitability-apathy. Using this concept as a starting-point for an investigation of the individual differences found in some previous group learning experiments, a rating scale was developed covering nine correlated aspects of excitability. Ninety-seven male and 55 female imbeciles were rated for this trait and the resulting scores correlated with their improvement under either incentive or non-incentive conditions.

Significant negative correlations between Excitability Score and improvement suggested that inert imbeciles improved more than excitable ones when given no external source of motivation. Correlations with improvement under the incentive of Goal with Encouragement were low but consistently positive, while there was a significant tendency for excitable imbeciles to decline more than inert imbeciles when this incentive was removed.

It was suggested that the results provided a basis for a link between the approach to motivation as a central neural process and the current linking of personality and learning theory.

Acknowledgments

The authors wish to express their indebtedness to Dr. J. F. MacMahon and Drs. A. D. B. and A. Clarke of the Manor Hospital; to Dr. G. J. Bell and Dr. G. M. Tucker of Darenth Park; and to Dr. R. J. Stanley and Dr. H. C. Gunzburg of Monyhull Hospital, who kindly provided facilities for the research.

Notes

1. The research described in this article was carried out for the Social Psychiatry Research Unit of the Medical Research Council.
2. The Excitability Rating Scale is given in the Appendix.
3. All correlation coefficients reported in this paper are Product Moment.
4. I.Q., in all cases, was estimated by means of Form L of the 1937 version of the Binet.

Appendix

EXCITABILITY RATING SCALE*

Weighted Score		Item I. Emotionality level
0	A.	Is a placid patient who rarely gives recognisable signs of emotion.
9	B.	Is normally a cheerful patient who has few extreme changes in mood.
22	C.	Is an excitable patient who is easily pleased or cast down.
25	D.	Is "hysterical" and liable to frequent outbursts of temper or sullenness at minor things.

Item II. Aggressive behaviour

0	A.	Always remains passive in encounters with other patients.
9	B.	Can be roused, but usually only under extreme circumstances.
17	C.	Sometimes becomes aggressive, but usually only in quarrels, when upset by others.
26	D.	Sometimes has outbursts of violence against other patients for no apparent reason.

Item III. Activity level

0	A.	Would sit all day if left alone.
1	B.	Is slow, but gets things done with occasional prodding.
15	C.	Is active and gets things done at a reasonable speed.
17	D.	Is restless and extremely quick in movement.
29	E.	Is so jerky and overactive that this interferes with what he/she is doing.

Item IV. Variability of work activity

0	A.	Will continue repeating the same task until moved on to another.
14	B.	Seems to want to complete a task before starting on the next.
16	C.	Often starts a new job before he/she has finished the previous one.
24	D.	Extremely distractable, so that the job is never finished.

Item V. Verbal activity

0	A.	Speaks only occasionally or when spoken to.
11	B.	Speaks spontaneously and will carry on short conversations.
19	C.	Will talk at some length whenever there is an opportunity.
24	D.	Talks incessantly and often without meaning.

Item VI. Sociability

0	A.	Is completely solitary and almost always sits in a corner away from the other patients.
5	B.	Is usually seen with only one or two special friends, but tends not to mix with other patients in the ward.
9	C.	Has a number of friends and mixes with most of the other patients in the ward.
25	D.	Is frequently seen with someone different and is into everything that goes on.

Item VII. Inter-personal response

0	A.	Is completely unmoved by visitors to the ward and will not answer when they speak to him/her.
6	B.	Will show some interest in visitors but will answer only briefly when spoken to.
20	C.	Will wave to visitors when they enter the ward and answer freely when spoken to.
31	D.	Will rush excitedly towards visitors and often engage them in conversation.

Item VIII. Amenability

0	A.	Always obeys passively and without comment if asked to do something
9	B.	Usually does most things he/she is asked to do with apparent willingness.
17	C.	Seems to like to do things to please people and sometimes offers spontaneously.
25	D.	Tends to be intractable, often grumbling and sometimes refusing outright to do things when asked.

Item IX. Predictability

0	A.	Remains steadily the same for long periods, so that it is always easy to tell how he/she will respond to the approaches of others.
14	B.	Usually responds as expected to the approaches of others, since there is little variation in his/her response.
18	C.	Has the usual periodic ups and downs, but it is relatively easy, knowing his/her mood, to guess how he/she will react.
26	D.	Only when you know him/her well can you tell what the response will be to other people.
30	E.	Varies very rapidly in response to others, so that it is impossible to tell whether he/she will be hostile or friendly when approached.

*Rater is asked to choose the statement, A.B.C.D. (E), from each item which most closely describes ratee.

Subject's excitability score is the total of the weighted scores for one statement chosen from each of the nine items.

Commentary

I mentioned earlier how rewarding my exposure to 'mental deficiency' had been, working with enthusiastic research colleagues in settings that were, by the standards of the time, enlightened. How different when I subsequently moved on to become a professional clinical psychologist in a typically vast Victorian-built institution in north London. Patients as engaging as ever, of course, but their environment gloomy and without hope and disinterested medical staff more concerned with maintaining the physical health of the charges under their care than with efforts at social rehabilitation. As the sole and first appointed relatively junior clinical psychologist in the place there seemed no possibility of putting into practice the things I had learned in my research. In a self-professed vain attempt to at least assess the extent of the problem I spent most of my days interviewing and testing the intelligence of selected patients. One case in particular stands out: a man who was admitted to the hospital in the late 19th century having been found wandering apparently homeless in the London streets. I tested his IQ as 110! His admission to the hospital had clearly been a mistake, but explained by the overlapping and arbitrarily defined functions of mental institutions and the Poor Law hospitals that existed of the time. Of course, even if we had tried to place him in the outside community he would not have survived after suffering more than sixty years of incarceration. But discovering him – and I know there were others – somehow underscored my despair at the system I was working in.

One other event stays in my mind. The hospital housed the only full-sized fire engine in the sector at that time, in the charge of a professionally trained fire officer. The man was a slightly wild individual who would carry out hair-raising fire drills in the vehicle around the hospital grounds; in between calling the doctors to task (there were no lay administrators in those days!) for failing to comply with fire regulations. One of these was the installation of an open gas fire in the waiting room to my office. Meeting with him about this led to regular discussions about my work, my previous research, and my increasing pessimism at establishing a rehabilitation programme for the hospital. I soon discovered he was a man whose enthusiasms went far beyond matters fire-related: instead someone who expressed great compassion for the patients, as he railed against the failure to do anything to improve their lot. For the brief time I was in the job I had at least found – albeit from an unusual source – one ally (and friend) who understood.

It was with a mixture of relief and regret that one day I received a phone call from Hans Eysenck offering me a job. After a brief interview with the famously laconic professor – I opened most of the conversations and did most of the talking – I was appointed as one of his research assistants.

The earlier paper with which I introduced this collection summarises that part of my subsequent career working for Eysenck: my physical location, not in the Institute of Psychiatry itself, but in a military hospital in Southampton, and how that shaped my research and ideas; Eysenck's instruction to test out his personality theory in psychiatric patients; the increasing shift of that research towards psychophysiology; and the special interest in the use of drug techniques to explore the biological correlates of individual differences in normal and abnormal personality. It is with the last of these themes that the next series of papers is devoted.

The centrepiece of my early work on drugs was the 'sedation threshold', originally described by Shagass (1954). Sometimes given other labels – such as 'sleep threshold' or 'GSR-inhibition threshold' – the procedure's rationale was the same, differing only in the method used: to establish a person's tolerance of sedative drugs, usually some form of barbiturate. By its very nature the procedure was drastic, almost always involving the intravenous infusion of the chosen drug up to some point of lost or impaired consciousness. This feature requires comment.

By current standards of ethical practice the procedure would have been a non-starter: it is doubtful whether any ethics committee would now approve of its use, certainly in the context of personality or psychiatric research. It has the taste of unpalatable scientific and professional practice from a distant past age, non-dissimilar to that evoked by the term 'imbecile' in our earlier discussion: used without thought in the 1950s and 1960s, yet now startlingly inappropriate. Yet sedation threshold research was conducted at the time on a wide scale. And I would argue, at the risk of incurring the wrath of pernickety ethical revisionists, to great scientific effect – revealing important information about individual biological differences that could not be easily discovered in any other way. In this regard there is one further point worth making.

Although attracted to psychophysiology as a methodology I was aware of its flaws, and one in particular. Psychophysiology relies for its success on being able to infer significant insights in central nervous functioning from changes in relatively minute peripheral biological signals; signals that may be subject to influences irrelevant to the behavioural or psychological phenomena of interest. Take electrodermal activity. Although if properly measured its 'psychogenic' component is assumed to predominate, its observed level fluctuates according to several influences like room temperature, exact siting and size of the electrodes, and, as some prominent psychophysiologists fretfully argued, the exact chemical constituent of the electrode jelly! These sources of error could seriously compromise interpretation of data and sometimes lead to non-replication of results across experiments. (Some such measures were better than others, however. An example that comes to mind is variation in the amplitude and frequency of fairly easily definable brain frequencies, such as the EEG alpha rhythm; though doubts remain about more fine-grain derived indices like evoked potentials.) My enthusiasm for techniques like the sedation threshold was driven by a belief that such procedures swamp the 'noise' contained in more conventional psychophysiological methods, revealing more of the true co-variation between the biological and the psychological. Partly addressing this point with particular reference to the sedation threshold, and well worth reading for its clear and erudite exposition of the issues, is an Appendix contributed by Herrington to my book *Personality and Arousal* (Claridge, 1967) which brings together the research carried out in that early 'Eysenckian' phase of my career. Reg Herrington was the psychiatrist colleague and friend with whom I developed a new version of the sedation threshold technique, which I later went on to use with several other medical colleagues.

My work on the sedation threshold is represented here by three papers. The first describes the index of barbiturate tolerance Herrington and I devised, based on assessing a participant's performance on a simple arithmetical task (digit-doubling) while receiving a continuous intravenous injection of amylobarbitone sodium. Vindicating the use of the test, we reported the very significant – and predicted – differences that could be established between categories of psychiatric patients forming what Eysenck called his psychiatric 'criterion groups' that defined introversion–extraversion. The paper also summarises some of the other salient findings reported in my 1967 book, involving some performance tasks administered alongside the sedation threshold. As will be seen, a coherent pattern of correlations was observed, generally supporting our research aims – at least empirically. Theoretically things were less satisfying. Re-reading the paper again I get an embarrassing sense of imaginative but highly speculative *post hoc* thinking, juggling several hypothetical constructs to explain the data. In retrospect it is easy to see why.

The work was carried out at the cusp of a burgeoning optimism about the possibility of establishing a biological basis for key features of psychological functioning. The literature was full of references to notions like 'arousal' and 'activation' and to brain circuits such as the limbic system and the ascending reticular activating system (Duffy, 1962); and Hebb (1958) was writing about the 'conceptual nervous system'. On the individual differences side Eysenck was at the forefront – indeed a pioneer – of this movement. The problem was that he had chosen to couch his account of the brain in the quaint language of Pavlovian physiology, with a terminology unfamiliar to most Western readers: excitation-inhibition, protective inhibition and so on. Such concepts rarely figured in the equivalent Western models but were prominent in Eysenck's explanations of experimental data. The accompanying paper illustrates this (I was at the time still in thrall to Eysenck's Pavlovian-style theory and only later abandoned it. As did he!). Once I had brought my thinking more into line with Western models, understanding and explaining the sedation threshold fell more neatly into place.

3 Sedation threshold, personality, and the theory of neurosis

Gordon Claridge and Captain Reg N. Herrington

Introduction

For many years it has been observed that individuals differ in their tolerance of depressant drugs. In everyday life differential susceptibility to the effects of alcohol is that most commonly observed and this fact led to McDougall's early theorizing (1929) about drug tolerance and personality. Also at this time Pavlov, in dogs, recorded differences in drug sensitivity in his various temperamental types. However, the first attempt to measure individual differences in drug tolerance was made by Shagass (1954), who proposed the concept of "sedation threshold". This was defined in terms of the amount of sodium amytal required to bring about certain behavioural and other changes in the individual, the threshold itself lying somewhere between the state of complete wakefulness and that of complete sedation. Two methods of determining the threshold were employed by Shagass. First, the point of onset of slurred speech gave an approximate estimate of its position. Secondly, a more accurate determination was made by means of EEG changes, specifically the point at which inflexion occurs in the amplitude curve of induced fast frontal activity.

In his original paper (op. cit.) Shagass reports that the sedation threshold correlates positively and significantly with ratings of tension in psychoneurotics. Later, Shagass and Naiman confirmed a revised hypothesis that sedation threshold was correlated with the level of manifest anxiety, rather than tension, this relationship being shown to hold in both normals (1955) and neurotics (1956). In the latter paper the authors also report the ability of the sedation threshold to discriminate between various groups of diagnosed neurotics, anxiety states having high and hysterics low thresholds, with mixed neuroses intermediate. This finding was later confirmed on a much larger group by Shagass and Jones (1958), the respectively high and low thresholds of anxiety states and hysterics being explained partly by the different levels of manifest anxiety found in these two classes of neurotic. Finally, Shagass and Kerenyi (1958) report that, in addition to its relationship with anxiety, sedation threshold is also correlated with introversion, the significance of the previous results being considered in terms of a personality syndrome of obsessionality-hysteria.

These findings corroborate a simultaneous but independent prediction by Eysenck (1955a) that hysterics, being characterized by higher levels of cortical inhibition than anxiety states, should respond more quickly to depressant drugs, which he has suggested (1957a) are inhibiting in nature. The discovery of a measurable threshold of sedation may be said, therefore, to have had important implications, both for the practical problem of diagnosis and treatment in psychiatry, as well as for the general theory of neurosis. Unfortunately, however, although recently a Danish worker, Nymgaard, has reported (1959) positive findings using EEG methods, attempts by workers in this country to duplicate Shagass's results have rarely been successful.

Eysenck (1957b), for example, reports difficulty in corroborating the findings on sedation threshold. Similarly, Ackner and Pampiglione (1958) found that in at least two-thirds of their cases it was difficult, or even impossible, to define a threshold, in terms either of slurred speech or of EEG changes. In those cases where a measure was determined no relationship with rated anxiety was found, while the mean sedation chresholds of anxiety states and hysterics were identical. Following an attempt to assess the objectivity of Shagass's methods, Thorpe and Barker (1957) conclude that the onset of slurred speech is quite unsatisfactory as an indicator of the sedation threshold. More successful was Laverty (1958), who was able to discriminate extraverted and introverted neurotics and normals and also demonstrated a slight increase in extraversion under the effects of sodium amytal. At the same time he reports that there was difficulty in many cases in assessing the sedation threshold from slurred speech.

It is clear then that, although the concept of sedation threshold may be regarded as an important one, an alternative method of measuring such individual differences in drug tolerance is desirable, if it is to be considered a useful tool for diagnostic and research purposes. The aim, therefore, at the beginning of the investigation reported here was to develop a method of measuring sedation threshold which was less subjective than the slurred speech index, but which could, unlike EEG methods, be easily administered and scored. Having done so, a number of important issues arose.

The first clearly relates to the ability of the measure to discriminate between groups of diagnosed neurotics. It is probable, for example, that the failure of Ackner and Pampiglione (op. cit.) to find differences between anxiety states and hysterics was due, rather to the uncertain nature of their sedation threshold measure, than to the lack of a real difference between these two groups. A more reliable index would be expected to confirm the findings of Shagass that the sedation threshold is low in hysterics and high in anxiety states or, as we shall call them here, dysthymics. Normals would be expected to have thresholds falling between those of the two neurotic groups.

The second problem concerns the relation of the sedation threshold to the general personality traits underlying dysthymia and hysteria. As already noted, both anxiety and introversion have been considered in this respect. According to Eysenck's original analysis of personality (1953) extraversion-introversion is the main dimension differentiating hysterics and dysthymics. It should follow, therefore, from his later predictions (1957a) with regard to the effect of depressant drugs, and, of course, the work of Shagass and Kerenyi (op. cit.), that sedation threshold will correlate negatively with a measure of extraversion. At the same time, the findings of Sigal, Star and Franks (1958), and later of Claridge (1960), have indicated that hysterics are not as extreme on extraversion as was at first thought and, in addition, tend to have lower scores than dysthymics on a neuroticism scale. Since this is clearly relevant to the link which has been suggested between anxiety and sedation threshold, it might be expected that the latter would correlate positively with a measure of neuroticism as well as, of course, with a measure of manifest anxiety itself. Indeed, in making these predictions it was hoped that the correlations in this part of the study would help to elucidate the personality determinants of and, therefore, the psychophysiological processes underlying, sedation threshold.

This point serves to introduce the third issue, which concerns the significance that the concept of sedation threshold undoubtedly has for contemporary psychological theories of behaviour, particularly recent activation or arousal theories of drive (Hebb, 1955; Malmo, 1959), as well as Eysenck's postulate of a link between central inhibition and dysthymia-hysteria. The relation of the arousal concept to Eysenck's theory of neurosis has been considered in a previous paper (Claridge, 1960), where, after an intensive investigation of the behaviour of neurotics, it was concluded that differences between dysthymics and hysterics in drive level probably accounted for some of the inter-group differences in performance on perceptual and motor tests. A factor analysis of the data from this study did in fact reveal a factor recognizable as one of drive and having loadings on a neuroticism scale.

More recently (Claridge, 1961a), this hypothesis has been confirmed and a modification to Eysenck's theory suggested, to the effect that there may be in dysthymics and hysterics an effective shift in the excitation-inhibition balance assumed to underly the dimension of introversion-extraversion. The hypothesis proposed is that the excitation-inhibition balance and the level of arousal are linked in such a way that upward or downward changes in the latter will be reflected in a parallel shift in the excitation-inhibition balance. Thus, it is further hypothesized that in hysteria a decrease in arousal levels occurs resulting, other things being equal, in a more rapid growth of inhibitory processes than would be predictable from the hysteric's position on the introversion-extraversion continuum. A corresponding delay in the growth of inhibition would be expected from the heightened arousal level which it is proposed occurs in dysthymia.

In the previous studies quoted above no independent measure of arousal was forthcoming, although three sources of evidence were considered to point to anxiety as an important determinant of arousal differences in neurotics. These were (*a*) the finding, noted above, that hysterics and dysthymics differ in "neuroticism", together with the traditionally held view that the hysteric, in contrast to the dysthymic's heightened manifest anxiety, is characterized by the so-called "belle indifference" resulting from his "conversion" of anxiety; (*b*) the link found between performance, arousal level, and measures of the autonomic activity associated with anxiety (Malmo, 1957); and (*c*) the finding, such as that of van der Merwe (1948) that hysterics and dysthymics differ on such measures.

Clearly relevant in this context is the likelihood of a positive relationship between anxiety and sedation threshold, since it suggests that the latter may be a good index of arousal level. If so, it would be expected to bear systematic relationships with those aspects of performance on objective tests which may be considered to reflect the level of behavioural arousal or drive. Additionally, since it has been suggested that the excitation-inhibition balance, and therefore the relative proneness to inhibition, is partially dependent on arousal level, it would be anticipated that sedation threshold would tend to be negatively correlated with measures of inhibition.

The aim, therefore, of the study reported here was fourfold and may be summarized as follows: (1) to develop a simple, reliable index of the sedation threshold; (2) to determine the extent to which this measure differentiated hysterics, normals, and dysthymics; (3) to determine the relationships between the sedation threshold and various measures of personality; (4) to investigate the relationship between the sedation threshold and a number of measures from objective performance tests, in order to clarify some of the issues arising from the postulate that excitation-inhibition is an underlying concomitant of dysthymia-hysteria.

Selection and description of subjects

For the two patient groups consecutive untreated neurotic admissions between September and December, 1959 were selected where the psychiatrist in charge of the case could make a definite diagnosis of anxiety state or hysteria. Cases of immaturity were not included. Patients with evidence of brain damage, those with addiction to drugs or alcohol, and those subsequently shown to be psychotic were rejected. In each of the neurotic groups there were fourteen male and two female patients.

The normal control group consisted of sixteen volunteers, of whom fifteen were male and one female. All were engaged on various duties in the hospital, including that of nursing orderly, clerk, storeman, and laboratory technician.

The means for the three groups on age, weight, and Matrices I.Q. are shown respectively in Tables 3.1, 3.2 and 3.3. Only on age was there an overall significant difference between the groups, dysthymics being just significantly older than both hysterics and normals, although the latter two groups did not differ on this variable. The tendency for dysthymic reactions to present later than hysterical syndromes is thus reflected in the present sample, but this was not considered important, since Shagass and Jones (op. cit.) have shown that there is no correlation between sedation threshold and age.

Table 3.1 Mean age (in years) for each group

	Dysthymics	Normals	Hysterics
Mean	27.91	23.67	23.78
S.D.	5.987	4.559	4.916

F-ratio: 3.239, p < 0.05.
t-tests: Dysthymics *v.* Hysterics, 2.176, p < 0.05; Dysthymics *v.* Normals, 2.234, p < 0.05; Hysterics *v.* Normals, 0.058, N.S.

Table 3.2 Mean weight (in pounds) for each group

	Dysthymics	Normals	Hysterics
Mean	149.88	142.56	155.50
S.D.	13.042	20.860	21.943

F-ratio: 1.742, N.S.

Table 3.3 Mean matrices I.Q. for each group

	Dysthymics	Normals	Hysterics
Mean	111.31	113.25	106.25
S.D.	14.358	10.542	9.093

F-ratio: 1.472, N.S.

Experimental procedure

Sedation threshold

The sedation threshold was assessed in terms of the effect of sodium amytal on a simple task of attention. The stimulus material consisted of a tape-recording of random digits, relayed to the subject through earphones. While receiving a continuous intravenous infusion of sodium amytal at the rate of 0.1 G/min., the subject was required to respond by doubling the digits, which occurred regularly at intervals of two seconds.

The digits were grouped on a score sheet into blocks of five and the errors recorded were then plotted against blocks, giving graphs of the form shown in Figure 3.1. The threshold was taken as the point midway between the last two blocks with less than 50 per cent error and the first two blocks in which errors exceeded 50 per cent. In the majority of cases these blocks were consecutive. The amount of drug administered at this point was determined from a chart relating blocks to drug received and this dosage corrected for the weight of the patient, giving the threshold in terms of mg./Kg.

The onset of slurred speech was not related to the threshold as measured in this way, though other behavioural changes consistently preceded the end-point. This was heralded by a raising of the voice with increase of muscle tension, soon to be followed by relaxation and noticeable slowing of the reaction time, leading to perseveration before the end-point was reached.

Psychological tests

In order to obtain estimates of the relevant personality traits two questionnaires were administered to each subject. These were the Maudsley Personality Inventory (MPI), giving estimates of extraversion (E-scale score) and neuroticism (N-scale score), and the Taylor Manifest Anxiety Scale (MAS). Two objective performance tests were also administered.

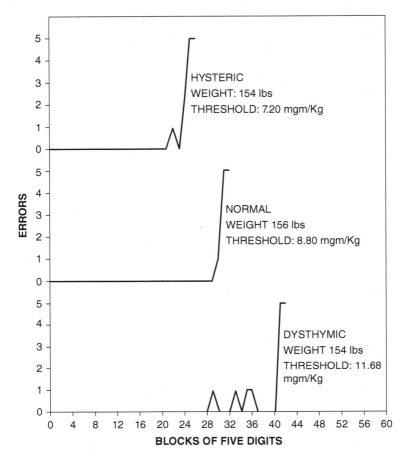

Figure 3.1 Typical sedation threshold curves: one subject from each group.

The first was a five-choice serial reaction time task. It consisted of a display panel set at 15 degrees from the vertical and containing five lights placed two inches apart in a horizontal row. In front of each light and in the horizontal plane was a key five inches long and approximately one inch wide. In operation the subject is required to press the key corresponding to the light which is lit at any one time, thus extinguishing it and illuminating another light to which a further response is made and so on. The order in which the lights were illuminated was a random one over a series of 50, except that no light appeared twice in succession. The subject's responses were registered on a simple counter, the score being recorded for each minute of the work period. The schedule followed in the present study consisted of a period of ten minutes' continuous performance, followed by a rest of five minutes and a further period of practice for one minute.

A consistent pattern of performance shown by most subjects on this test (Venables, 1959) is a gradual decline in performance level during the first five minutes, then an increase in speed during the second five minutes of practice. Following the rest the usual reminiscence effect appears, in the form of an abrupt rise in performance level. The four major measures which can usefully be extracted from the test are those of starting level, rate of initial fall-off, total number of errors, and reminiscence change. The underlying variables which are probably reflected in these measures have been outlined elsewhere (Claridge, 1961b) and will be considered only briefly here.

It has been suggested that starting level reflects the drive or arousal level of the subject and, as such, has been shown (Claridge, 1961a) to differentiate hysterics and dysthymics, the latter performing at a significantly faster rate than the former. In the present experiment it would be predicted, therefore, that this measure would correlate positively with sedation threshold, if, as we have suggested, the latter is an index of arousal level.

Changes in performance subsequent to the beginning of the test may be said to be due to the onset of inhibitory processes, the accumulation of inhibition being expected, for instance, partly to account for the initial fall-off in level which occurs. Also contributing to this decline is the onset of gaps in performance, which have been shown (Broadbent, 1958) to occur in this type of task. The approach taken by the present authors is that these gaps serve partly to dissipate previously accumulated inhibition and, therefore, themselves serve as an index of inhibition. A reliable overall measure of such gaps has been found to be errors or incorrect responses on the test, the assumption being that, even though a response is made, inhibition *centrally* accumulated will be partly dissipated in the same way as during the less frequent gaps which occur without a simultaneous error. Any inhibition undissipated at the end of the test should be reflected in the reminiscence measure.

In view of the hypothesis presented earlier relating arousal to excitation-inhibition, it would be expected that sedation threshold would correlate negatively with these three measures of inhibition, viz. rate of fall-off, total errors, and reminiscence. A complicating feature, however, is that, in terms of the *absolute* degree of inhibition induced by performance, the differential response rate associated with different arousal levels may tend to cancel out any effect which changes in arousal level may have on the rate of inhibitory growth *per unit response*. Thus, in the paper previously cited (Claridge, 1961a) hysterics tended to show *less* fall-off in performance than dysthymics, while the two groups did not differ on either reminiscence or errors. By partialling out the effect of differential performance levels results more in line with expectation were forthcoming. It may be anticipated, therefore, that the present hypothesis with regard to sedation threshold and inhibition will have to be interpreted with these findings in mind.

The second performance test used was the Archimedes Spiral. Here the subject is asked to fixate a rotating spiral for a given length of time and to report on the duration of the subsequent after-image which occurs when the spiral has ceased. The direction of rotation experienced as the after-image is always opposite to that obtaining during the stimulation period. In the present study a single-throw

180 degree spiral was used, four trials being given. In each trial the spiral was rotated for one minute, alternately clockwise and anti-clockwise, with a rest of one minute between trials. The mean of the four scores thus obtained was taken as a measure of the subject's performance on the test.

The processes underlying the spiral after-effect are unclear, although Eysenck (1957b) has argued that its length is inversely proportional to the amount of inhibition produced by the persistence of excitation after the spiral has ceased rotating. A similar explanation, leading to the same predictions, but taking into account the inhibition produced during the stimulation period itself, was proposed by Claridge (1960), who was able to show that dysthymics have significantly longer after-images than hysterics and, further, that the spiral after-effect was positively loaded on a factor of drive. Despite the lack of certainty about the underlying processes involved, it seems reasonable to assume that this phenomenon is in some way related to the balance between excitation and inhibition obtaining at the end of the period of stimulation, whether it is held that the after-effect itself is a persistence of excitation or a reflection of the inhibition existing at this point. It was possible to predict in the present experiment, therefore, that sedation threshold would be positively correlated with the spiral after-effect.

Results

Group differences in sedation threshold

As anticipated, there were marked differences between the three groups on the sedation threshold measure. It can be seen from Table 3.4 that the mean threshold for dysthymics was significantly higher than that of either normals or hysterics, while the latter two groups were differentiated at a lower, but still very acceptable, level of confidence. Typical sedation threshold curves are shown in Figure 3.1, where are plotted, for comparison, the results for three subjects of equivalent weight, one subject being from each group.

One aspect of the results which should be noted is the general tendency for the thresholds, as measured in this study, to be higher than those reported by Shagass and his co-workers. EEG changes would, of course, be expected to precede changes at the behavioural level and, in addition, in the method used here it is probable that the task had a slight alerting effect on the subject. Nevertheless, it is clear that the two methods produce comparable results.

Table 3.4 Mean sedation threshold (in mg./Kg.) for each group

	Dysthymics	Normals	Hysterics
Mean	10.18	7.86	6.43
S.D.	1.608	1.313	1.774

F-ratio: 21.837, $p < 0.001$.
t-tests: Dysthymics *v.* Hysterics, 6.544, $p < 0.001$; Dysthymics *v.* Normals, 4.049, $p < 0.001$; Hysterics *v.* Normals, 2.496, $p < 0.02$.

Sedation threshold and personality

In Tables 3.5, 3.6 and 3.7 are shown the mean scores for each group on the MAS and the E and N scales of the MPI. Product moment correlations between sedation threshold and these three measures were calculated over the total group of 48 subjects. The correlation between sedation threshold and the E-scale was –0.271, which was not significant. Both the N-scale and MAS were found to correlate significantly with sedation threshold, the values for r being +0.355 ($p < 0.05$) and +0.383 ($p < 0.01$) respectively. It is interesting to note, however, that within the normal group only a significant correlation was present between extraversion and sedation threshold, the value for r here being –0.524 ($p < 0.05$).

While the predicted relationship with extraversion is thus partly confirmed, the results for the total group indicate that sedation threshold is associated more directly with the level of manifest anxiety and general neuroticism than with the personality dimension of introversion-extraversion. This change in emphasis away from extraversion is perhaps further evidence, similar to that quoted earlier, of the over-riding role played by factors associated specifically with neurosis

Table 3.5 Mean M.A.S. score for each group

	Dysthymics	Normals	Hysterics
Mean	17.00	6.25	13.69
S.D.	3.774	3.699	5.860

F-ratio: 21.903, $p < 0.001$.
t-tests: Dysthymics v. Hysterics, 1.990, $p < 0.1$; Dysthymics v. Normals, 6.464, $p < 0.001$; Hysterics v. Normals, 4.474, $p < 0.001$.

Table 3.6 Mean E-scale (M.P.I.) score for each group

	Dysthymics	Normals	Hysterics
Mean	18.31	31.50	24.62
S.D.	8.169	7.575	8.366

F-ratio: 10.120, $p < 0.001$.
t-tests: Dysthymics v. Hysterics, 2.152, $p < 0.05$; Dysthymics v. Normals, 4.499, $p < 0.001$; Hysterics v. Normals, 2.346, $p < 0.05$.

Table 3.7 Mean N-scale (M.P.I.) score for each group

	Dysthymics	Normals	Hysterics
Mean	36.62	19.12	31.19
S.D.	7.631	8.392	11.092

F-ratio: 14.354, $p < 0.001$.
t-tests: Dysthymics v. Hysterics, 1.624, N.S.; Dysthymics v. Normals, 5.235, $p < 0.001$; Hysterics v. Normals, 3.610, $p < 0.001$.

when abnormal groups are included in the study of extraversion. That the relationship between sedation threshold and the processes underlying anxiety are not, however, completely uncovered by the present findings is suggested by the fact that, despite the overall correlations with both N and MAS, the hysteric group, while having higher scores than normals on both questionnaires, emerge with significantly lower thresholds. This is presumably due to the fact that the questionnaire measures do not entirely reflect the changes occurring at the onset of neurotic breakdown and in this respect the need for objective measurement of the autonomic activity involved may be emphasized. Nevertheless, there seems to be sufficient evidence in the present findings to allow us to accept the hypothesis that sedation threshold measures differences in arousal level arising as a result of variations in the degree of manifest anxiety.

Performance tests and sedation threshold

(a) *Serial reaction time.* As pointed out previously, four measures from this test were investigated, viz. starting level, fall-off during the first five minutes, total number of errors, and reminiscence change. The first two of these measures were obtained by calculating the coefficients of linear regression on each subject's scores during the first five minutes (trials) of the test. This gave two measures, the coefficient "b" representing starting level, and the coefficient "a" representing mean change per trial or rate of fall-off.[1] The group means for each of the four measures taken from the five-choice test are shown in Table 3.8.

The correlation between sedation threshold and the "b" coefficient was found to be +0.366, which is significant at the 0.05 level (d.f. 46). Thus, the assumption that starting level on this test reflects the general drive or arousal of the subject was justified, in so far as sedation threshold may be said, from our conclusions in the previous section, to be an index of this variable.

In view of this correlation it was apparent that the analysis of the relationship between sedation threshold and measures of inhibition was to be a complex one, since, as pointed out earlier, it was likely that the high rates of response associated with high arousal had led to greater absolute amounts of inhibition being accumulated at some stages in the test, even though, as hypothesized, the rate of inhibitory growth, or amount produced per response, may be reduced under heightened arousal.

It was not unexpected, therefore, that the correlation between the "a" coefficient and sedation threshold was negative, the value for r being -0.173 (N.S.). In order to investigate the relationship between sedation threshold and *relative* fall-off the effect of differences in starting level was partialled out, the correlation between "a" and "b" being -0.481 ($p < 0.01$). The resulting partial r had a value, however, of exactly zero, thus not confirming, for this sample, the tendency previously reported (Claridge, 1961a), for the more poorly aroused hysterics to show relatively greater fall-off than dysthymics. There were two possible explanations for this lack of relationship between sedation threshold and relative fall-off: either we were incorrect in our hypothesis that arousal level and rate of

Table 3.8 Five-choice test: mean score on four measures for each group

	Dysthymics	Normals	Hysterics
(i) Coefficient "b" (Starting Level)			
Mean	90.14	82.34	77.51
S.D.	15.412	11.331	12.499
F-ratio: 3.530, p < 0.02.			
t-tests: Dysthymics *v.* Hysterics, 2.632, p < 0.02; Dysthymics *v.* Normals, 1.625, N.S.; Hysterics *v.* Normals, 1.007, N.S.			
(ii) Coefficient "a" (Rate of Fall-off)			
Mean	−1.22	−0.12	−0.23
S.D.	1.954	1.451	1.713
F-ratio: 1.993, N.S.			
(iii) Reminiscence			
Mean	13.00	13.88	12.94
S.D.	9.434	8.901	9.473
F-ratio: 0.048, N.S.			
(iv) Errors			
Mean	11.12	8.63	19.88
S.D.	10.705	8.748	20.524
F-ratio: 2.563, N.S.			

inhibitory growth are inversely related; or some other factor was operating to cancel out the expected effect.

The reminiscence measure was therefore examined. The correlation between reminiscence and sedation threshold proved to be −0.135, a lack of correlation which is reflected in the mean reminiscence scores for the three groups (see Table 3.8). It was apparent from this that, although the more highly aroused subjects performed at a significantly faster rate, the absolute amount of inhibition accumulated during the test was identical with that of the slower, less aroused subjects. In order for this to occur the amount of inhibition produced per unit response must have been greater in the poorly than in the highly aroused subjects, thus confirming the original hypothesis.

How then do we explain the negative findings on fall-off, which seem somewhat paradoxical? Reference to Figure 3.2 suggests a likely explanation.

Seen clearly in this figure is the abrupt initial decline characteristic of the test. By the second half of practice this decline has become minimal, although the increase in speed expected at this point fails to appear in the present sample. It seems possible that all subjects proceed from the beginning of the test towards a stabilization of the balance between excitation and inhibition, the point of equilibrium occurring after about five or six minutes. The rate at which this proceeds is determined principally by the absolute number of responses made at the beginning of the task when inhibition is negligible; hence the correlation between "a" and "b" coefficients. Since high arousal prompts the subject to start at a higher

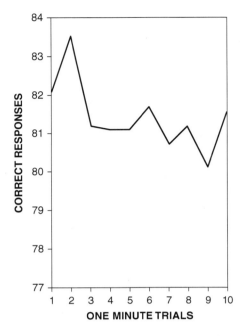

Figure 3.2 Serial reaction time: mean performance curve for 48 subjects.

level, the absolute amount of inhibition accumulated in the earlier stages of the test will probably be greater than in poorly aroused subjects and hence have a greater decremental effect on performance, i.e. produce greater fall-off. As this greater amount of inhibition begins to reduce response rate so the absolute amount of inhibition produced will decrease until a point is reached where both high and low arousal subjects are accumulating the same absolute amounts of inhibition. The response rate during the test is thus modulated in order to keep inhibition at a minimum level appropriate to the degree of arousal present. Since, as seems to be the case, heightened arousal reduces the amount of inhibition produced per response, this allows the subject to continue performing during the later stages at a higher level without producing by the end of the test a greater amount of inhibition to be dissipated in reminiscence.

One of the factors which allows inhibition to be kept at a minimum in the way proposed is the occurrence of gaps or errors in performance, which we have suggested serve the purpose of partly dissipating inhibition. The analysis of performance gaps is perhaps usefully considered in terms of Kimble's "critical level" principle. Briefly, he has suggested (1949) that inhibition builds up until it reaches the level of positive drive, or critical level. At this point a short pause occurs so that inhibition can dissipate sufficiently to allow correct performance to continue. Re-interpreting this analysis and applying it to the present data, it would be expected that a combination of low critical level (arousal) and the faster inhibitory growth rate associated with it would result in more frequent errors in poorly aroused subjects than in those with high arousal levels. This was confirmed by a significant correlation between sedation threshold and the measure of total errors, the value for r being -0.395 ($p < 0.01$).

The weight of evidence from this part of the study undoubtedly points to a confirmation of the hypothesis that there is a relationship between arousal and central excitation-inhibition, such that the relative proneness to inhibition is reduced where the level of arousal is high, and vice versa. One fact which does emerge, however, is the difficulty of obtaining adequate measures of inhibition. By using a self-paced task we unwittingly allowed the subjects to adjust their response rates so as to minimize inhibition, and so cancel out individual differences on all measures of this variable, except, significantly, that one which was itself involved in the maintenance of the excitation-inhibition balance. That there should have been a tendency in all subjects to maintain equilibrium in this way is not surprising, in view of the frequent operation of homeostatic processes at other levels of behaviour. Indeed, homeostasis is inherent in the concept of a balance, within the nervous system, between excitatory and inhibitory mechanisms.

(b) *Archimedes spiral.* In Table 3.9 is shown the mean spiral after-effect for each group, together with significance levels for the inter-group differences. A relatively high correlation was found between the spiral after-effect measure and sedation threshold, r being $+0.456$ which, for 48 subjects, is significantly beyond the 0.01 level of confidence. This result is also shown graphically in Figure 3.3, where it can be seen that there is a clear separation, without overlap, between the two neurotic groups, the normals falling in a roughly intermediate position.

We have already considered the two alternative explanations of the spiral after-effect, viz. that it is either a persistence of excitation after the spiral has ceased rotating, or that it reflects the amount of inhibition existing at the end of the stimulation period. The first is the simpler explanation, since it accounts directly for the greater after-effect shown by subjects with high arousal. However, it seems more likely that the spiral after-image arises as a result of inhibition generated during the prior stimulation. It is of interest, therefore, to reconsider, in the light of the theoretical approach developed here, the probable course of events occurring during performance on the spiral test.

Table 3.9 Mean spiral after-effect (in seconds) for each group

	Dysthymics	*Normals*	*Hysterics*
Mean	18.79	11.41	8.85
S.D.	5.093	4.125	3.767

F-ratio: 22.576, $p < 0.001$.
t-tests: Dysthymics *v.* Hysterics, 6.476, $p < 0.001$; Dysthymics *v.* Normals, 4.808, $p < 0.001$; Hysterics *v.* Normals, 1.668, N.S.

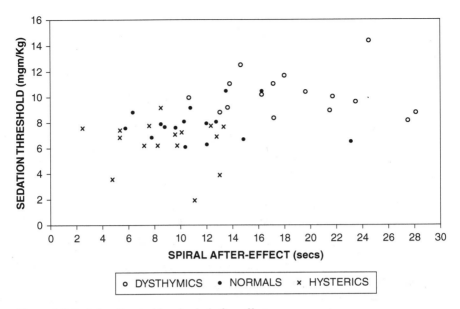

Figure 3.3 Sedation threshold and spiral after-effect.

Stimulation with the rotating spiral clearly serves, in effect, to disturb the balance of excitation-inhibition. Simultaneously with this increased excitation, inhibition is presumably generated, this tending to oppose and therefore to reduce the excitation level. Since the initial disturbance should be greater in highly aroused subjects and since, as shown in the previous section, the tendency to produce the opposing inhibition will be correspondingly reduced, the total amount of excitation developed throughout the stimulation period will be higher in these subjects than in those with low initial arousal. In keeping with this the total *absolute* amount of inhibition induced, and therefore the after-effect, will be greater in highly aroused than in poorly aroused subjects. To put the argument more crudely, the greater the absolute disturbance of equilibrium the greater will be the time required to recover.

It is apparent from this that, although the amount of physical stimulation on the spiral test is identical for all subjects, the same assumption cannot be made in the case of the central effects of this stimulation which are critically related to the balance between excitation and inhibition, and hence arousal level, in much the same way as was found to be the case on the serial reaction time test discussed previously.

Discussion

In so far as on sedation threshold the three groups in this study were clearly differentiated in the predicted direction, the results may be said to support Eysenck's theory of dysthymia-hysteria. Thus, the greater tolerance of sodium amytal found in dysthymics links his postulate that depressant drugs are inhibiting in nature with the hypothesis that the excitation-inhibition balance is weighted towards the positive (excitatory) side in anxiety states, while the opposite is true of hysterics.

Not entirely consistent, however, with this theory, but supporting previous results quoted earlier, is the finding that, while within the normal group the sedation threshold is predictable from the degree of extraversion present, this relationship fails to hold in the neurotic group, where manifest anxiety appears to be a more important determinant of the susceptibility to the effects of barbiturates. This, together with the findings from the objective performance tests, supports the hypothesis proposed at the beginning of this paper that a shift occurs in the excitation-inhibition balance of dysthymics and hysterics.

We have already suggested that this shift is attributable to changes in neurotics in the level of arousal and it is appropriate, therefore, to consider at this point the implication that arousal theory undoubtedly has for the problems under discussion. It is particularly relevant in the present context since neurophysiological evidence clearly relates arousal to anxiety and to differential susceptibility to depressant drugs.

Hebb (1955), for example, relates arousal to the activity of the ascending reticular formation and it is known that heightened activity of the mesencephalic (adrenergic) component of this system is accompanied by both EEG and behavioural arousal (Bradley and Elkes, 1957). Its activation has been demonstrated in physiological drives (Dell, 1958) and can be inferred clinically from the raised plasma-adrenaline (Weil-Malherbe, 1955) and fast low voltage EEG patterns (Lindsley, 1951) found in dysthymics. Since barbiturate anaesthesia initially and most markedly affects the activity of the reticular formation (King, 1956; Arduini and Arduini, 1954; French et al., 1953), increased activity of this system should be reflected in increased tolerance of sedation.

The neurophysiological evidence that relatively long-term changes in the state of arousal are feasible may be paralleled at the behavioural level by the finding of Shagass (1958) that a decrease in sedation threshold accompanies a reduction in the anxiety symptoms of the dysthymic neurotic. Comparable increases in the thresholds of remitted hysterics appear not to have been reported, although an investigation of this would be of considerable interest. That such changes would occur seems feasible if the behavioural aspects of hysterical conversion of anxiety are taken in conjunction with the fact that both descending and ascending effects are present in reticulo-cortical relationships.

Clinical and experimental evidence, both psychological and physiological, thus supports the contention that a link may be possible between arousal theory and Eysenck's inhibition theory of personality. To attempt a detailed integration of these two approaches at the moment would involve going far beyond the available facts. Particularly necessary is a more thorough investigation, in both normals and neurotics, of how measures of arousal in terms of autonomic functioning are related to the sedation threshold. The possibility of such a relationship is considered by Gellhorn (1957) in his discussion of hypothalamic imbalance and cortical excitability; its relevance to the problem of dysthymia-hysteria, and introversion-extraversion, is suggested by van der Merwe's findings (op. cit.) that anxiety states tend towards sympathetic and hysterics towards parasympathetic predominance in their autonomic reactions.

For the present it seems useful to consider the excitation-inhibition balance proposed by Eysenck as the complex result of an interaction, on the one hand, between subcortical and cortical influences and, on the other hand, between, at each of these levels, positive excitatory effects and the negative opposing (inhibitory) effects which psychologists have found it necessary to postulate and which physiologists in recent years have been able to demonstrate at some levels of central nervous integration (e.g. at the cellular level as discussed by Eccles (1958)). The ascending activating effect of autonomically-linked arousal mechanisms is thus just one factor which may be thought of as influencing this excitation-inhibition balance[2] and therefore performance. By emphasizing the importance of some of the possible underlying processes associated with neuroticism, this approach helps to account for the discrepancies found in recent studies relating dysthymia-hysteria to the personality dimension of introversion-extraversion.

In conclusion, it is perhaps pertinent to return to the point from which this study started, namely the sedation threshold. The importance of the latter as a research tool has certainly been vindicated, since it has been possible to uncover by this technique individual differences in nervous functioning which are meaningfully related to both human performance and personality. Indeed, the results as a whole may be said to have underlined the fact, already recognized by Eysenck, that the interrelated fields of psychopharmacology and personality hold a key place in the search for the laws underlying not only human behaviour in general, but also its normal and abnormal variations.

Summary

In this paper a new method of measuring the "sedation threshold" was described. Confirming previous work, sedation thresholds were found to be significantly higher in dysthymics than in hysterics, while a normal control group had a mean threshold falling between those of the two neurotic groups. Correlations calculated over the total group indicated that sedation threshold was correlated significantly and positively with measures of manifest anxiety and general neuroticism. A significant correlation with extraversion was found only when the normal group was taken separately. It was suggested that sedation threshold measures differences in arousal level arising from variations in manifest anxiety.

The relationship was then examined between sedation threshold and performance on two objective tests: Archimedes spiral and a five-choice serial reaction time task. On the latter sedation threshold was correlated significantly with starting level and negatively with errors, while reminiscence was identical in both high and low arousal subjects. This indicated that, despite leading to a higher response rate, heightened arousal did not induce greater absolute amounts of inhibition but in fact reduced the growth rate of inhibition. A positive correlation between sedation threshold and the spiral after-effect was also reported.

A link was suggested between arousal theory and Eysenck's inhibition theory of personality, the differences between hysterics and dysthymics being explained in terms of a shift, due to changes in the state of arousal, in the excitation-inhibition balance underlying introversion-extraversion.

Acknowledgments

The authors wish to acknowledge the co-operation of Colonel J. McGhie, Commanding Officer at the Royal Victoria Hospital, Netley.

The work of one of us (G. S. Claridge) was made possible by a grant from the U.S. Army (Grant No.: DA-91-591-EUC-1136).

Notes

1 To avoid confusion it should be pointed out that the more negative the value for "a" the greater the degree of fall-off. Negative correlations between "a" and other variables should, therefore, be interpreted with this in mind.
2 While in this paper emphasis has been laid on the positive relationship between efficiency of performance and arousal level, the authors are not unaware that at excessive arousal levels a reversal of this relationship may occur, giving rise to the U-shaped functions commented upon by a number of psychologists, including Duffy (1957), Malmo (1959) and Hebb (1955). This is quite consistent with the approach taken here if it is assumed that minimal inhibition may interfere with, rather than facilitate, performance on some tasks. This is particularly so on complex tasks, where U-shaped functions are most likely to appear, and where the inhibition of irrelevant stimuli may be essential for efficient performance.

Commentary

Virtually all biological theories of personality assume that some part of the observed individual variation is of genetic origin and in the early days considerable effort was expended to establish this. In the absence of modern techniques of genetical analysis the methodologies were necessarily those of behavioural genetics: in its simplest form monozygotic (MZ)/dizygotic (DZ) twin comparisons, or in attempts to disentangle environmental and heritable influences, the more complex techniques of biometrical genetics (Hay, 1985). The opportunity to pursue this genetics line on personality differences arose after my colleagues and I were given access to a twin register at the University of Glasgow to where I had subsequently moved. In the twin study we carried out – eventually published as a jointly authored book (Claridge, Canter & Hume, 1973) – we administered a variety of personality, cognitive and psychophysiological tests, including the sedation threshold. Choice of the sedation threshold in this context requires some explanation.

Even by the lax ethical standards of the day, recruiting non-clinical volunteers from the general population gave us pause for thought and presented something of a practical challenge; hence the necessarily small sample we were able to test. In the latter regard I continued to put my faith in the viability of the 'drastic' methodology I outlined earlier. Certainly in parallel we did study more conventional psychophysiological measures: electrodermal response, heart rate, EEG alpha rhythm (Hume, 1973). But my money was on the sedation threshold! As the next paper shows, I was not disappointed. In the paper – in which I present the main findings in the context of other data on genetical analyses of individual differences in drug response – it is clear that the sedation threshold stands out as a strong contender for such an index. This despite, as will be seen in the paper, a certain ambiguity that hangs over the data. On the one hand, the MZ/DZ comparison demonstrated overall a highly significant genetic effect. So much so that where MZ pairs resembled each other they did so to an astonishing degree, in terms of difference in the dose of drug required to sedate them. On the other hand, two MZ pairs in the sample showed an enormous difference in sedation threshold, presumably due to extraneous effects we found difficult to determine.

4 Why drug effects vary

Gordon Claridge

Some time ago a friend of mine was conducting an experiment on the effects of a common psychotropic drug on reaction time. At the end of the experiment, just as the subjects were leaving the laboratory, one of his colleagues happened to pass by. Noticing that one of the subjects looked extremely drowsy he later inquired casually how the experiment had gone and which sedative or tranquillizer was being used. He received the reply, 'That was no sedative; that was amphetamine.'

Paradoxical drug responses of this kind illustrate the difficulty of rigidly classifying psychotropic drugs as depressant, stimulant, tranquillizing and so on. For practical purposes it may be useful to do so, because it provides the psychopharmacologist with a shorthand description of the effects typically produced by different drugs. Whether a drug has its usual effect on a particular occasion will, however, depend on a number of factors which modify its normal action. Often the response to a drug will be greater or smaller than expected. Sometimes it may even be entirely opposite to that predicted, as in the case of the subject I have just described. The reason for this variability is easily understood if one realizes that a drug is just like any other stimulus applied to the organism, its purely pharmacological action interacting with the many other influences that are affecting behaviour at the same time. We have already seen how powerful these non-pharmacological influences can be in the case of the placebo response. In this paper we shall see how chemically active drugs do not always behave as they should and why their effects vary considerably from one individual or one situation to the next.

Although we shall be concerned here mainly with non-pharmacological factors it should be remembered that the drug itself can also give rise to a good deal of variability. The dose administered will clearly play an important role, though the effects produced may not always be a simple function of dosage. Some depressant drugs, for example, may have excitant properties at low doses, or at critical doses that are different for different individuals. The correct average dose to produce a predominantly depressant effect in a group of subjects therefore has to be chosen with care. Another pharmacological factor of some importance is the manner in which the drug is given, that is whether it is administered orally or by injection. Drugs given by injection will reach their peak effect very quickly and, dose for dose, induce more profound and immediate changes in behaviour.

By comparison, those taken by mouth will be absorbed much more slowly, their effects accumulating gradually over a period of time.

In most drug experiments, of course, the dose and route of administration is standardized and the variation in response observed is mainly due to other factors. These non-pharmacological influences can be divided into two types. First, there are those that arise from the situation in which the drug is given, including any expectations induced in the subject about the possible effects of the drug; and secondly, there are those that are due to the individual characteristics of the experimental subjects, such as undue sensitivity and either temporary or permanent resistance to the drug's action.

The potency of psychological influences on drug response has been demonstrated in a number of experiments designed in such a way that the normal effect of a drug is deliberately distorted by giving misleading information to the experimental subjects. Thus a group of subjects may be given a stimulant drug, such as amphetamine, and, with a suitably persuasive spiel, prepared to expect the effects normally produced by depressant drugs. The subjective and objective physiological changes that occur will be in the 'depressant' direction, reports of tiredness and slowness being much commoner than in subjects who are told the truth about the drug they have taken. If no instructions are given about the effects anticipated, then the pharmacological action of even a relatively large dose of a drug may disappear. This was recently demonstrated in a study carried out by Dr Frankenhaeuser and her colleagues in Stockholm (1964). They studied the reactions of subjects under three experimental conditions. Under one condition the subjects were given a placebo and told it would have the typical sleep-producing effects of a depressant drug. Under the other two conditions they were given 200 mg – a fairly high dose – of pentobarbital, but in one case they were told to expect the normal depressant effects and in the other that the drug might or might not have any effect at all. Various measurements were taken, including reaction time and ratings of subjective feelings under the three treatments. It was found that, despite the dose administered, the drug only had a consistently significant effect when it was combined with the appropriate suggestions beforehand. When given with neutral instructions its action was rather weak, the placebo by comparison being somewhat *more* effective in producing feelings of sleepiness.

In some situations, even though the subject may know the kind of drug he has taken, he may be motivated in such a way or to such a degree that he is able to overcome its effects. No doubt many a merry reader will have experienced the utter sobriety that comes over one when a sudden emergency arises requiring rapid action; as, for example, when a party guest is taken ill. On such occasions the subjective experience may actually be one of remarkable clear-headedness during the period of crisis, as though the alcohol consumed previously had actually speeded up mental processes more than usual. Is this possible? Certainly it has been shown in experimental situations that, if the incentive to perform is strong enough, then the typical slowing effects of depressant drugs may actually be reversed. This was demonstrated in a study carried out in the United States on the effect of pentobarbital on reaction time under different incentive conditions (Hill *et al.*, 1957).

The subjects were a group of former morphine addicts who, as a strong incentive, were offered a shot of morphine immediately after carrying out the experimental task. With this to motivate them the subjects given pentobarbital actually performed faster than usual, the drug apparently acting on this occasion as a stimulant. On the other hand, when only a weak incentive was offered – a morphine injection at some later date – the drug had its more usual depressant effect of slowing down reaction time.

Deliberately manipulating the individual subject's motives or expectations is one way, then, in which drug effects can be enhanced, diminished, or reversed. Other important influences will arise from the natural setting in which the drug is taken. If several people in a group take the same drug, then each person's response to it will act as a stimulus to other members of the group. This interaction may bring out features of the drug's action that are not apparent in people taking the drug alone. It is well-known that the solitary drinker rarely experiences the party spirit. He just gets more and more morose. The influence of social interaction on drug response is by no means confined to human groups, but can also be demonstrated in animal colonies. Thus, a very small dose of amphetamine given to a colony of mice may cause a significant increase in group activity, even though the same dose may have no detectable effect on the behaviour of an individual animal tested in isolation. Comparable effects have also been produced by administering depressant drugs. A dose of barbiturate which will normally heavily sedate a single animal may actually make a colony of mice much more active.

Group-interaction effects on human drug response have been studied in some ingenious experiments which have tried to isolate the separate influence of pharmacological and social factors. In some of these experiments small groups of, say, four subjects are used. On some occasions all of the group members will be given the same drug, either a stimulant or a depressant. Alternatively, drugs having opposing pharmacological effects will be given to different people in the same group, half of them being given a stimulant and the other half a depressant drug. As one might expect, when everyone in the group takes the same drug, its effects on behaviour tend to be exaggerated by the additional stimulus of social interchange within the group. Either the drug's normal action is magnified or its effects reversed. However, if drugs of opposite type are used in the same group of people they may cancel each other out. Thus, a person receiving a stimulant, for example, may not experience its usual effects when he is required to interact with someone receiving a depressant drug. This dilution of drug action has been named, rather appropriately, the 'wash-out' effect.

A particularly neat example of the kind of experiment just described is one carried out by Dr Starkweather at the University of California (1959). He was interested in the effect of giving different drug combinations to people working in pairs on a simple psychological task. The task was one called the trail-marking test which consists of numbers and letters scattered randomly over a page. The subject was required to join the numbers and letters in alternating sequence, joining 1 to A, A to 2, 2 to B, and so on. His score was the time taken to complete the test. The basic design of the experiment involved testing each subject individually both before and after an interval during which he cooperated with another subject on a modified version of the trail-marking test. In this modified form the test was adapted so that two people could do it together, each member of the pair being given half the information necessary to complete the task. Each was able to communicate his 'moves' to his opposite number by a system of coordinates which allowed him to indicate the direction and length of the lines drawn to connect particular letters and numbers. This schedule of individual and cooperative testing was repeated at weekly intervals for seven weeks. For three of the sessions all of the subjects were given placebos. For the remaining four they received either phenobarbital or amphetamine. On the drug days during cooperative testing the subjects were paired off in one of three ways. Sometimes both members of a pair were on the depressant, sometimes both on the stimulant, and sometimes one person was on the stimulant and his partner on the depressant. The effect of these different drug combinations was measured by seeing how subsequent performance on the individual version of the trail-marking test compared with that before the interaction experience.

Before carrying out this experiment Dr Starkweather made certain predictions about its outcome. These are shown in Figure 4.1. A fairly straightforward prediction could be made about the drug effects before the subjects were allowed to interact with each other. As seen in the left half of the diagram, it was simply predicted that performance would be worse, that is the task would take longer to complete, on phenobarbital than it would on amphetamine. It was anticipated that, after interaction, performance would change in the directions shown on the right side of Figure 4.1. Where both members of a pair had been on the same drug it was expected that the normal drug effect would be exaggerated, sedated subjects becoming even slower and stimulated subjects becoming faster. When partners had been on opposite drugs it was thought that a 'wash-out' effect would occur, performance afterwards changing to some intermediate level. The actual results are shown in Figure 4.2. Performance before interaction was as predicted, phenobarbital subjects taking significantly longer to complete the task than amphetamine subjects. After interaction, however, performance changed in a quite unexpected manner. As can be seen in Figure 4.2, pairing off two subjects who were on the same drug actually caused the normal drug effect to be reversed. This was true of both the stimulant and the depressant drug. Thus, stimulated subjects, who showed fast performance on the first testing, were slowed to the level of depressed subjects after working with someone who was also on the stimulant. Similarly, subjects on the depressant were not, as anticipated, slowed down further by working with a depressant partner. On the contrary they were speeded up to the stimulant level. The effect of pairing off people who were on different drugs was also rather unexpected. On this occasion a 'wash-out' effect did not occur. Instead, subjects on the depressant who worked with a stimulated partner were slowed down and those on the stimulant who worked with a depressed partner were speeded up. In all cases, then, the differences in performance after interaction were related, not to the drug the subject himself had taken, but to the drug his partner had taken. A partner who took amphetamine consistently slowed

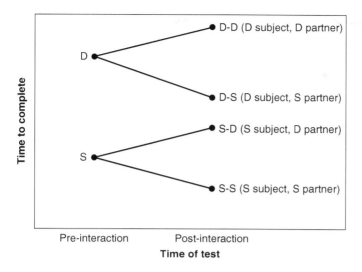

Figure 4.1 Diagram showing the predictions that were made before an experiment on the effects of interaction between subjects on either a depressant (D) or a stimulant (S) drug. Before interaction D subjects were expected to be slower than S subjects. It was thought that these differences would be exaggerated after subjects had interacted with someone on the same drug. In subjects on opposite drugs performance scores were expected to come together, producing a 'wash-out' effect (see text). Figure 4.2 shows the actual results of the experiment.

Source: Reproduced by permission of J. A. Starkweather.

down the person he worked with, while a partner on phenobarbital had the effect of speeding up his opposite number. This was true whatever drug the subject himself took and even though before interaction he had shown a typical drug response. This experiment illustrates very well how, in some situations, one's own response to a drug may depend, not so much on its direct pharmacological action, as on the perception of other people's behaviour with whom one is interacting. Or, as Dr Starkweather rather whimsically comments, if we look at it the other way round, perhaps it is the doctor who should take the drugs in order to influence his patients!

Let us turn now to the other important source of variability in drug response, namely the variation that arises from within the individual himself. That people differ widely in their sensitivity to drugs will be obvious to anyone who has relieved the monotony of a cocktail party by observing the reactions of his fellow guests. Some of this variation can be put down to factors of a temporary nature, since even the same person will react differently to the same drug given on different occasions. For example, the nearness and size of his last meal will help to determine how rapidly the drug is absorbed into the blood-stream and hence allowed to reach the brain. The presence of another drug in the body may also be

52 *Gordon Claridge*

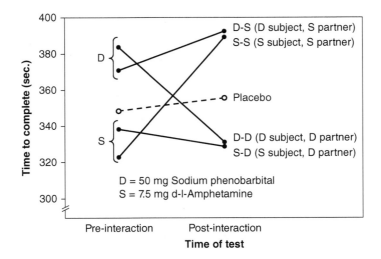

Figure 4.2 Results of an experiment on the effects of interaction between subjects on either a depressant (D) or a stimulant (S) drug. Differences in the performance of D and S subjects before interaction were as expected (cf. Figure 4.1). After interaction these differences were reversed in pairs on the same drug (D-D and S-S), subjects on the depressant now being quicker than those on the stimulant. Interaction between subjects on different drugs (D-S and S-D) produced the opposite of a 'wash-out' effect.

Source: Reproduced by permission of J. A. Starkweather.

important, one drug often intensifying the effects of another; as in the dangerous combination of barbiturates and alcohol. Another important variable is transient fatigue, which may make the person temporarily more sensitive to a drug than he would otherwise be. A less obvious factor is the individual's mood which will act as a touchstone for the social influences on drug response already described.

Apart from these random fluctuations within the same person, differences between people occur because of a variety of relatively permanent individual characteristics, many of which are purely physical. Weight, for instance, may be important because it is related to the volume of circulating blood, which helps to determine the concentration of drug reaching the brain at any one time. It is for this reason that for clinical purposes weight, or some index taking account of weight, is used as a rough guide to the dose of drug to be administered. For the same reason in experimental studies, instead of giving all subjects the same amount of drug, the dosage is often corrected so that each person receives a quantity proportional to his body weight. Another closely related physical characteristic is the body type, whether the person is fat or thin. Some drugs have a proclivity for fat, attaching themselves, as it were, to fatty tissue in the body and being released gradually from it over a period of time. In a very plump person, therefore, the time-course over which such drugs act will be altered compared with someone of more modest build. Both weight and body type will, of course, be related to age and sex, so that each of these will also indirectly affect the drug response. Physical health may be a further source of individual variability, someone with brain damage, for example, being particularly sensitive to psychotropic drugs. Another factor of some importance is the degree to which the person has built up a tolerance for the drug through previous experience with it or with a related class of drug.

To what extent do the factors mentioned so far account for individual variability? Unfortunately, they only go a little way towards it, though they do give the psychopharmacologist some guide to the sort of variables that have to be controlled for in designing drug experiments. Even in the technically perfect or near-perfect experiment, however, there will still be a very wide range of response to the drug among the subjects taking part. These individual differences can be a nuisance, of course, if the investigator is trying to establish an average drug effect, though in recent years psychopharmacologists have become more interested in them for their own sake. It is becoming more and more obvious that most of the variation observed among people taking drugs is due to intrinsic differences in their psychological, or more strictly I should say their psychophysiological, make-up. Although systematic investigation of this idea is only just beginning, the notion is really a very old one. Even in the late nineteenth century one French doctor wrote with confidence:

> It is a well-established notion that all subjects do not offer the same susceptibility to the action of medicaments and poisons. In respect of alcohol, Lasègue has specially insisted upon the differences of aptitude for intoxication: he remarked that if there are insusceptibles to alcohol there are also those, on the contrary, who are extremely susceptible to it, and suffer very rapidly its sad effects; they are alcoholizable.
>
> (Féré, 1899)

Who, however, *are* the 'alcoholizables'? Most of the research on this problem has been founded on another everyday observation, namely that susceptibility to drug effects is in some way related to personality. Several people have put forward this view, including the famous psychologist William McDougall. In the nineteen-twenties he voiced what has been the most popular hypothesis, namely that, in the case of alcohol at least, it is the introvert who is most resistant, extraverts being the ones who 'suffer very rapidly its sad effects'. In more recent years a similar theory has been proposed by Professor Eysenck who has suggested that introverts have a greater tolerance of all depressant drugs but are more affected by stimulants than extraverted people. Eysenck has based his views partly on those of the Russian physiologist Pavlov who, like most scientists working with drugs, noticed considerable variability in the response of dogs during conditioning experiments. Pavlov was particularly interested in the effects of caffeine and, to account for the individual variation in response to this drug, he proposed that there were different 'types' of nervous system which corresponded to differences in temperament.

Eysenck has applied a modern version of this nervous-type theory to man in order to explain why introverts and extraverts differ in their reactions to drugs.

There are several ways in which the psychopharmacologist can study the relationship between personality and drug response. One way is to administer a standard dose of some psychotropic drug, assess its effects by means of a number of psychological and physiological tests, and then see whether individual differences on these measures are related to scores on personality rating scales or questionnaires. In a series of studies of this kind an American psychologist, DiMascio, and his colleagues have isolated two broad personality types who differ in their response to a variety of psychotropic drugs. These have been named Type A and Type B personalities, respectively. People of Type A are described as practical, sociable and assertive extraverts with low anxiety and athletic body build. Type B people, on the other hand, are of slender body build, are more introverted and obsessional, have high anxiety and tend to inhibit rather than express their feelings.

In one of his early experiments DiMascio studied the response of these personality types to two different kinds of tranquillizer, phenyltoloxamine and reserpine (Klerman *et al.*, 1959). All of the subjects were given a battery of psychomotor tasks, including serial addition, tapping, and a test of visuomotor coordination. Physiological reactions to the drugs were measured by recording changes in heart rate, respiration, skin temperature, and muscle tension. Overall the two drugs had somewhat different effects. Phenyltoloxamine had a sedative/hypnotic action, both on psychomotor performance and on subjective mental state. Reserpine had mainly physiological effects without altering task performance too much. The response to both drugs was different in the two personality types. In the case of phenyltoloxamine, Type A people showed greater hostility and more frequent negative attitudes to the drug situation, possibly because they found the sedating effects of this drug more unpleasant than Type B personalities, who described the drug effect as pleasantly relaxing. Task performance was also different in the two groups, Type A people improving and Type B people getting worse under phenyltoloxamine. The reaction to reserpine also differed in the two personality types. This time it was Type B individuals who expressed greater hostility, presumably because they found the physiological effects of the drug more unpleasant than Type A individuals. The differences in subjective feeling under reserpine were also reflected in the measures of autonomic activity, the physiological changes occurring in the two groups being in opposite directions. Thus the anxious introverted Type B personalities showed an increase in sympathetic predominance of the autonomic nervous system; whereas the more relaxed Type A personalities showed a decrease.

DiMascio and his colleagues have also demonstrated comparable differences in the response of their two personality types to other drugs, such as chlorpromazine and secobarbital. As in the experiment just described, the variations in subjective feeling produced by a drug are often revealed in the kind of physiological change that occurs. Since, as we have seen, this change may be in opposite directions in different people, it becomes important for the psychopharmacologist to identify different reaction-types if he is to avoid oversimplified generalizations about the physiological effects of psychotropic drugs. Some investigators, therefore, have approached the problem of individual differences from the other end, as it were, by selecting a number of 'physiological' types and seeing whether there is a variation in their drug response. In a study of this kind two Continental workers, Servais and Hubin (1964), divided up groups of subjects on the basis of their autonomic nervous systems. Following a traditional classification, they separated their subjects into three types. First, there were those who showed a relative predominance of the sympathetic division of the autonomic nervous system, whom they called sympathicotonics. A second group, named vagotonics, were characterized by relative predominance of the parasympathetic division. A third intermediate group showing stable autonomic balance without predominance of either division were called amphotonics. A comparison was then made of the response of these three types to amphetamine and to the tranquillizer, meprobamate. It was found that the two major types, sympathicotonics and vagotonics, differed considerably in their physiological reaction to both drugs. Whereas sympathicotonics showed a marked rise in pulse rate following the administration of amphetamine or meprobamate, the opposite was true of vagotonics, who reacted with a fall in pulse rate. The result for amphetamine is particularly interesting because it demonstrates that the rise in heart rate which is often said to occur with this drug is only true of certain people.

An important implication of this kind of experiment is that the *average* drug effect observed in a group of people will clearly be as much a function of the individual characteristics of the subjects making up the group as of the pharmacological action of the drug itself. Thus, if a particular personality or physiological type happens to predominate then the overall drug effect may be quite opposite from that observed in a sample made up of people of a quite different type. Sample variations of this sort probably account for the apparently contradictory results sometimes obtained with the same drug in otherwise identical experiments. These individual differences also emphasize how the psychopharmacologist has to look, not just at the overall effect of a drug, but at how particular individuals within his sample react to it. Occasionally, for example, he may find that a drug has apparently had no significant effect on the group as a whole and may be misled into thinking the drug is inactive. However, his measure of average change could well mask a genuine drug effect if different subjects within the group have responded in opposite directions. This is illustrated in another of DiMascio's experiments on personality and drugs (1965). There he studied the effects of three drugs on nonsense syllable learning. The drugs concerned were a sedative, secobarbital, and two tranquillizers, chlorpromazine and trifluoperazine. Compared with a placebo none of these drugs produced very much overall change in the learning scores of the group as a whole. However, when the subjects were divided up into Type A and Type B personalities, some marked drug effects appeared. As shown in Figure 4.3 the two personality types were affected in opposite ways. On all three drugs Type B people (anxious introverts) improved their learning scores, while Type A people (relaxed extraverts) became consistently worse. Clearly these drug effects would not have been isolated if only the average changes in performance had been examined.

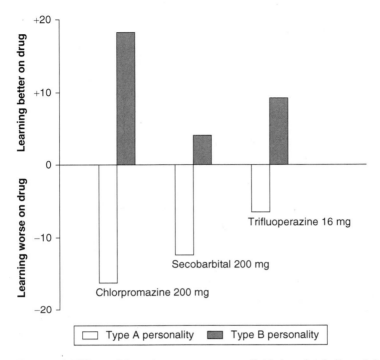

Figure 4.3 Effects of three drugs on nonsense syllable learning in Type A (extravert) and Type B (introvert) personalities. Scores represent differences between drug conditions and an equivalent placebo condition. See text for further description of the two personality types.

Source: From an article by J. D. McPeake and A. DiMascio.

All of the experiments just described have been concerned with individual differences in the response to small single doses of drugs and the evidence suggests that the *way* a person reacts is related to his personality. What, however, about the *amount* of a given drug he can tolerate? To answer this question requires a rather different experimental strategy. Here, instead of giving the same dose of drug to everybody, what we need to do is to administer the drug in a progressive fashion and see whether some people are more rapidly affected by it than others. Put in this way the answer will, of course, almost certainly be 'yes'. What we really want to know is whether variations in susceptibility are a function of personality. The evidence suggests that they are, as is illustrated by the results of an experiment carried out some years ago at the Maudsley Hospital by Rodnight and Gooch (1963).

Rodnight and Gooch were interested in the relationship in normal subjects between personality factors and susceptibility to the effects of nitrous oxide. The procedure adopted was to administer progressively increasing concentrations of nitrous oxide in oxygen to each subject while he performed alternately on two psychological tasks. The gas concentration was raised in a step-wise manner every five minutes. At each stage the subject carried out a simple pegboard test of finger dexterity followed by an arithmetical task in which he was required to double a short list of digits. As expected there were wide individual differences in the rate at which performance of both tasks became impaired. By calculating the slope of performance change on each test it was possible to derive two indices of each subject's susceptibility to nitrous oxide. These indices were then related to scores obtained from the Maudsley Personality Inventory which had previously been administered to the subjects and which gave measures of extraversion and neuroticism. These personality characteristics were chosen because, as discussed briefly already, there were some reasons for believing that extraverts, at least, would be more susceptible than introverts to the depressant effects of nitrous oxide. In fact, the results obtained were rather more complicated than that, though significant relationships with personality did emerge. Overall there was little correlation between drug tolerance and extraversion score, whichever index of gas susceptibility was used. Susceptibility was found, in fact, to depend on the degree of both extraversion *and* neuroticism. Again this was true for both indices of susceptibility. Rodnight and Gooch demonstrated the interaction between extraversion and neuroticism in the following way. First they divided their whole sample of subjects into two halves: those with high and those with low scores on the neuroticism scale. They then separately correlated the indices of gas susceptibility with extraversion in the two halves. Next, correlations with neuroticism were calculated separately for two subgroups divided this time into high and low scorers on the extraversion scale. This analysis uncovered two highly significant relationships between personality and drug tolerance. One was that among subjects having a low neuroticism score it was the introverts who tended to be more susceptible to nitrous oxide. The second was that among the extraverts in the sample it was the more neurotic who were most susceptible. The greatest gas susceptibility was found in subjects who were both highly neurotic and highly extraverted. People of this type tend to be predisposed to hysterical and psychopathic disorders and it is interesting to note that neurotic patients actually diagnosed in that way also show very poor tolerance of depressant drugs, as I shall discuss in more detail later.

The technique used by Rodnight and her colleague has the advantages associated with nitrous oxide that were discussed in an earlier paper. On the other hand, it has the disadvantage that the index of susceptibility it provides is rather cumbersome to compute. Other simpler methods of measuring an individual's drug tolerance have, therefore, been more popular among psychopharmacologists. All of these techniques have been developed and used mainly in a psychiatric setting. Since they will be discussed in detail in the next paper, here I will only describe the principles behind them and the general use to which they have been put in studying variability of drug response among normal subjects. The procedures referred to all involve giving the subject a slow, continuous injection of a drug, usually a depressant, until some predetermined change in his behaviour occurs. The amount of drug injected up to that point, normally corrected for his body weight, then provides an index of his tolerance for the drug. Almost any easily recognizable and measurable alteration in the subject's response can be used as a criterion for assessing when he has reached his drug-tolerance threshold, as it is called. The most commonly used criteria are some change in the subject's brain-waves or autonomic nervous system, or a sudden change in his ability to perform a simple psychological task. An even simpler criterion, if a general depressant drug is being studied, is the point at which the person goes to sleep.

The use of these drug-threshold procedures in normal subjects has generally tended to confirm the findings obtained by Rodnight and Gooch with nitrous oxide. That is to say, the tolerance of other depressant drugs, such as the barbiturates, is related both to how extraverted the person is and to how much anxiety or neuroticism he displays. Thus, the anxious, introverted, obsessional individual will require much more barbiturate to reach a threshold of sedation than the extraverted and rather hysterical personality. The combination of extraversion and neuroticism is seen most clearly in neurotic patients themselves, who simply represent extreme forms of these two personality characteristics. It is not surprising therefore that clear differences have been found in the sedative drug tolerance of chronically anxious or obsessional neurotics and those with hysterical or psychopathic disorders. The variability in tolerance of sedative drugs parallels a broad personality 'dimension' the opposite ends of which are occupied by these two neurotic types. Teasing out the relationships between personality and drug tolerance in normal subjects is rather more difficult because their behaviour is less extreme in all respects. Even so, work that has been carried out so far in this area of psychopharmacology indicates that a substantial part of the individual variability in response to drugs is due to personality factors, particularly those associated with introversion and anxiety. The relative importance of psychological, as distinct from purely physical, variables in determining drug susceptibility is well illustrated in a study recently carried out by a colleague, Dr Herrington, and myself. Over a number of years we have measured sedative drug thresholds in several hundred normal and psychiatric subjects. In calculating our index of drug tolerance we have always applied a correction for body weight to the amount of drug injected up to our chosen criterion of sedation. In this respect we have followed normal pharmacological practice, expressing the drug threshold, in this case for amobarbital, as an index of milligrammes of the drug injected per kilogramme of body weight, mg/kg for short. Quite recently, however, we examined the relationship between weight itself and the absolute, uncorrected amount of drug required to sedate different subjects. Rather surprisingly we found that, although heavier people did tend to take more of the drug, the correlation between weight and absolute amount was actually very small indeed. In fact, in some subgroups of our total sample the relationship was zero or even negative, more drug being required to sedate people who were lighter in weight. On the other hand, drug amount *was* correlated with personality measures and with various physiological measures which are themselves related to personality. Under the particular conditions of our experiments, therefore, a person's tolerance of drugs was much more a function of temperament than of tonnage! Of course, this may not be true in all situations in which drugs are administered. It may not be so, for example, where drugs are given by mouth in small doses or where some other feature of a drug's effect is measured, such as the rate at which an oral dose is absorbed or metabolized. Here, weight or some other physical factor related to it is probably as important. Nevertheless, the result provides a striking example of the major contribution of 'nervous type' to drug susceptibility.

If personality plays such an important role in drug response, how does this arise? To what extent, for example, does heredity determine individual differences in drug tolerance? Like the questions just posed, the answer to them is double-edged. Knowledge of the genetic factors involved in the response to drugs would tell us something about the underlying mechanisms of drug action. At the same time it would also tell us something about the physiological and genetic basis of the personality characteristics that help to determine drug effects. Unfortunately, research on this aspect of human pharmacogenetics – as it is called – has scarcely begun. Most of the work has been concerned with pathological reactions to drugs: for example the abnormal sensitivity to barbiturates found in people suffering from the porphyrias, a group of rare metabolic diseases recently brought to fame as the probable cause of George III's madness.

The few studies of normal human subjects that have been carried out suggest that the individual's reaction to drugs may indeed be determined, to an important degree, by heredity. As in other genetic studies of human characteristics, the evidence is based on the investigation of twin pairs. One such study of a single pair of monozygotic or 'identical' twins, named Albert and Andrew, was described some years ago by Dr Glass in the United States (1954).

Glass was interested to see how similar the twins were in their response to caffeine, which he administered in the form of five cups of strong coffee. The drug effect was measured by getting the twins to carry out a target-aiming task, in which they had to throw a 'dart' – actually a dissecting needle – at a number of small rings drawn on a sheet of paper. Each twin was given a series of trials on the test both with and without the drug. On the first occasion Albert performed under caffeine, while Andrew acted as his no-drug control. On the second occasion their roles were reversed. Figure 4.4 illustrates the twins' performance under each condition. It can be seen that they both responded to caffeine in a remarkably similar fashion, each showing exactly the same kind of performance curve when working under the drug. Dr Glass later confirmed this result in a more controlled experiment in which he used a lactose placebo and administered the drug to the twins, not as coffee, but as capsules of caffeine citrate. The striking similarity in the drug response of the twins contrasts markedly with the great variability found by Glass in a randomly selected group of people whom he also tested under the same conditions. There the performance curves of different subjects varied so widely that he could observe no systematic effect of caffeine. Each person appeared to react to the drug in a manner peculiar to himself.

60 *Gordon Claridge*

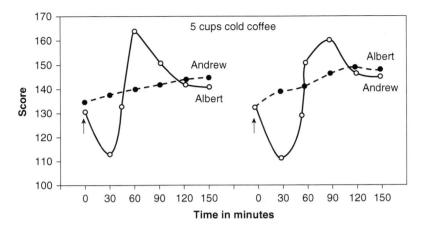

Figure 4.4 Effect of caffeine on the performance of a target-aiming task in a pair of identical twins. Note the very close similarity in the performance curves (solid line) of the two twins after they had drunk five cups of coffee. Dotted lines represent performance on the same task under no-drug conditions.

Source: Reproduced by permission of B. Glass and Association for Research in Nervous and Mental Disease.

Convincing as they are, results from a single pair of twins are hardly conclusive. However, a more complete twin study carried out in our own laboratory by Dr Esther Ross and myself (1973) also supports the idea that the way a person reacts to drugs is determined very much by heredity. We have measured the tolerance of amobarbital in sets of twins, using one of the sedative drug-threshold procedures referred to earlier. Following the normal practice in this kind of work we compared a group of monozygotic, or one-egg, twins with a group of dizygotic, or two-egg, twins. If heredity plays an important part in drug response then monozygotic twins, being genetically identical, should require very similar amounts of drug to become sedated. Dizygotic twins, on the other hand, because they are no more alike than ordinary brothers and sisters, should differ very much more from each other. Figure 4.5 illustrates the results we obtained on eleven monozygotic twin pairs and ten dizygotic pairs. The diagram shows the number of pairs in each group who differed from each other by more than or less than 1 mg/kg, a difference, incidentally, which represents a very small amount of drug indeed. It can be seen that most of the monozygotic twins showed differences of less than 1 mg/kg, some pairs actually having almost exactly the same tolerance thresholds. In contrast, the variation among dizygotic twins was much greater. All but two pairs differed by more than 1 mg/kg, while the average difference was nearly three times that figure.

As a general rule, then, the tolerance of sedative drugs seems to depend very much upon genetic factors. Of course, the results of the experiment just described were not perfect, some monozygotic twins being quite dissimilar in drug tolerance.

Why drug effects vary 61

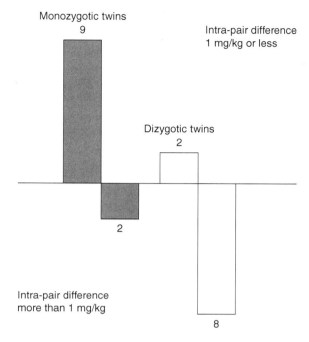

Figure 4.5 Comparison of monozygotic and dizygotic twins on sedative drug tolerance test. Diagram shows the number of pairs in each group who differed by more than or less than 1 mg/kg in the amount of amobarbital required to sedate them.

How did this difference come about if they were genetically identical? It is impossible to say, though it is known that throughout development many influences operate to make monozygotic twins less rather than more alike, so that in research of this kind we are always underestimating the contribution of heredity to a particular characteristic. The fact that some apparently otherwise identical twins can differ does serve to emphasize, however, that all behaviour is the end-product of both heredity and environment, the latter including everything that happens to the individual from conception onwards. All that we can hope to do in twin research is to make a statistical estimate of the *relative* contribution of genetic factors. In the case of drug response heredity does appear to be especially important, despite occasional exceptions due to, as yet, unknown environmental influences.

The variations in drug response described in this paper obviously make life rather difficult for the psychopharmacologist trying to reach some general conclusion about the effects of different psychotropic drugs. All that he can hope to do about such variation is to try and understand how it arises and then control for it in designing his experiments or hope that most of it will be cancelled out when different groups of subjects are being compared. If he is actually interested in variation for its own sake then life is still difficult, though never dull. The dependence of drug response on personality, for example, is an exciting fact, because it opens up an important way of examining the physiological basis of personality, one of the most difficult areas of behaviour to study scientifically. Here we have looked only at normal personality. However, some of the most valuable evidence in this particular branch of psychopharmacology has come from studying how the psychiatric patient reacts to drugs.

Commentary

Despite the uncertainty in the data I felt confident that with the sedation threshold we had demonstrated a strong genetic connection in personality, adding to other evidence using psychophysiological indices. Such measures came to be known as endophenotypes, *viz* biological indices intermediate between the genetic architecture and gross behavioural phenotypes, such as psychiatric diagnosis or personality questionnaire scores. As such, they offered the possibility of establishing a more exact index of the genetic contribution to individual differences. At least that was the hope because, of course, the methodology for exploring the actual genetics of behaviour was many years away in the future. Having now reached that future it has to be said that the reality is still as far removed from the fantasy. The results of the old and the new genetics have scarcely chimed: strong heritabilities for personality traits, established using traditional behavioural genetics methods, have never been replicated in molecular genetics. Plomin, in the new revision of his textbook on the topic, notes that there is no clear consensus about any candidate gene associations for any personality traits – and that where these exist they are very small (Knopik, Neiderhiser, DeFries, & Plomin, 2016). Investigations using endophenotypes – looking at biological susceptibilities for psychological disorders – have fared no better (Flint & Mufano, 2007). So the conundrum remains as to why, using old-fashioned genetics methodology, respectably sized heritabilities can be found for personality and psychological disorder phenotypes and for the biological phenotypes that relate closely to them; yet the connection between the two domains of knowledge remains a mystery. Perhaps the data are so complex that it is too early to tell.

The third sedation threshold paper here is, and was, a bit of a digression. It came about because it had struck me that the question of individual differences in drug tolerance might be of interest to a wider medical community even outside psychiatry: hence the submission to the *British Journal of Anaesthesia*. The message conveyed was straightforward: in judging the dosage required, doctors administering sedative drugs would do better to look not at bodily characteristics but at personality based psychophysiological features. I referred to the latter as 'nervous type'. Looking back I can't imagine why: few readers of the journal would have known what that meant. I can only assume that the editor was sufficiently convinced by the data and arguments presented in the paper that he decided to overlook the eccentric terminology used by the psychologist who had submitted it!

The ideas promoted in the paper had no discernible impact on anaesthetic practice; even where it might have been expected to do so – such as why patients with high sedative tolerance remain awake during their surgical operations. This issue has been of concern for a long time and has been the subject of many publications, including a series of reports from professional bodies. One of these – (NAP5, 2014) – is a multichapter volume covering almost every aspect of what is known in the trade as AAGA (Accidental Awareness during General Anaesthesia). It includes a chapter on individual differences in risk factors, but apart from a brief reference to pharmacogenetics, there is nothing that remotely connects to the personality/drug tolerance research tradition, as represented in sedation threshold studies.

5 The relative influence of weight and of "nervous type" on the tolerance of amylobarbitone sodium

Gordon Claridge

For many years it has been a common clinical observation that personality seems to exert an influence on the tolerance of centrally acting drugs, as reflected, for example, in the larger amounts of barbiturate required to sedate or anaesthetize the very anxious patient. Systematic study of this relationship between drug tolerance and temperamental factors has tended to be carried out, not within conventional pharmacology, but by behavioural scientists interested in exploring the psychophysiological basis of personality. The general theory behind this work is that of nervous typology, namely the view that individual differences in observable personality characteristics arise partly from biologically determined variations in central nervous activity. The notion of nervous typology arose and continues in Russian physiology and psychology (Gray, 1964), but has also been adopted by a number of psychologists in the West who have demonstrated relationships between personality and measures of central nervous arousal (Claridge, 1967; Eysenck, 1967).

The nervous typological analysis of personality has involved the use of many different kinds of experimental procedure, such as the measurement of E.E.G. and autonomic variables as well as performance on psychological tasks that are thought to reflect such central nervous processes as arousal. However, a special place has been occupied by pharmacological techniques since these offer a convenient way of examining nervous typological variation. The most widely studied procedure of this type has been the "sedation threshold" which, as originally devised by Shagass (1954), was a method for determining from changes in the frontal E.E.G. an individual's tolerance of intravenous amylobarbitone sodium. Subsequent modifications to the technique have involved the use of thiopentone as an alternative to amylobarbitone and the adoption of other criteria, either physiological (Perez-Reyes, Shands and Johnson, 1962) or behavioural (Claridge and Herrington, 1960), for assessing the threshold of sedation.

Studies using these different methods of determining the sedation threshold have consistently shown differences between personality types and correlations with other measures of nervous typology. The relevant evidence has been reviewed elsewhere by the present author (Claridge, 1970a) but may be summarized as follows. High sedation thresholds, i.e. high tolerance of barbiturates, have been found to characterize obsessional, anxious, or what have been termed "dysthymic", personalities who, physiologically, show a strong sympathetic reaction to stress and who, on objective psychological tests, perform at a high level of efficiency. Low barbiturate tolerance, on the other hand, is more often associated with personality traits of an hysterical, psychopathic kind, found in individuals who are autonomically less responsive and whose ability for sustained psychological performance is relatively poor.

Although personality, and hence the nervous type, therefore seems to be one of the determinants of barbiturate susceptibility, workers with the sedation threshold have always assumed that the somatic characteristics of the individual are also an important source of variation. Consequently, in calculating the amount of drug required to induce sedation they have always followed conventional pharmacological practice and expressed the sedation threshold as a function of body weight, applying the correction either retrospectively or to the injection rate itself.

The purpose of this paper is to present some data on the relative contribution of weight, on the one hand, and the nervous type, on the other, to individual variation in the tolerance of amylobarbitone sodium as assessed by a sedation threshold technique. The opportunity to carry out the study arose because of the ready availability of appropriate data on a very large number of subjects. The investigation was, in effect, a re-analysis of results collected during a long research programme on the psychophysiological correlates of personality (Claridge, 1967). There, a series of nervous typological measures, including a weight-corrected index of sedation threshold, had been intercorrelated in a group of neurotic and normal individuals covering a wide range of personality. It has therefore been possible to do a comparable analysis, using in this instance an uncorrected measure of drug tolerance.

The sample

The total number of subjects available for study was 192, 34 of whom were normal volunteers and the remainder neurotic in-patients suffering from a range of symptoms which included phobic anxiety, reactive depression, obsessionality, psychopathic behaviour, and hysteria. Most of the subjects were male, only 2 of the normals and 22 of the neurotics being female. The mean age of the total sample was 27.7 (SD 9.99) years, the neurotic subgroup having a mean age of 28.7 (SD 10.53) years and the normal subgroup 23.2 (SD 5.23) years.

The measures

Drug tolerance index

This measure was derived from the sedation threshold data for each subject. It consisted simply of the absolute amount, in milligrammes, of amylobarbitone sodium required to reach threshold. The latter had been assessed using the technique developed by Claridge and Herrington (1960). The procedure involved presenting to the subject a tape-recorded series of random digits played at the rate of one digit every 2 seconds. The subject was required to respond by doubling the digits while receiving a continuous intravenous infusion of amylobarbitone sodium, prepared in a solution of 1 g in 20 ml of water and administered to all subjects at a constant rate of 2 ml/min. The injection was continued until response errors or failures to respond exceeded 50 per cent in two consecutive blocks of five digits. The sedation threshold was taken as the amount of drug administered up to that point, expressed as a function of the subject's body weight in kilogrammes. To distinguish the present, uncorrected, measure it will be referred to here as the "drug tolerance index".

Body weight

Weight in pyjamas or light indoor garments was recorded to the nearest kilogramme immediately before determination of the sedation threshold, which was always measured during the morning after a light breakfast consisting of a cup of tea or coffee and two slices of buttered toast.

Nervous type measures

Five measures from the original investigation were chosen for inclusion here. Full details of the experimental procedures used and the relevant background literature have been described elsewhere (Claridge, 1967). However, it can be stated that all of the measures have been widely studied by behavioural scientists and have a common rationale in that they tap areas of psychophysiological function that can be readily embraced by the nervous typological theory of personality. The original study actually included a much larger number of measures, but the five chosen here were selected because they provided sufficient data to make adequate statistical analysis possible. For, while the drug tolerance index, and of course weight, were available for the total group, particular nervous type measurements were usually taken on only a proportion of subjects. The sample sizes involved for each measure will be given later in the description of results. The particular nervous type measures to be considered here are as follows.

Archimedes spiral after-effect. This refers to the persistence of the visual illusion of after-movement, induced by asking the individual to stare at a rotating disc on which is drawn a four-throw Archimedes spiral. In the present case the subject was required to fixate the rotating spiral for 1 minute and then, after the disc had stopped, to report when the after-effect had disappeared. The length of the after-effect was recorded to the nearest second, the mean of two such trials being taken as the subject's score on the test.

Electroencephalograph alpha index. This measure of "cortical activation" consisted of the per cent time during which alpha rhythm was present in ten randomly selected 10-second samples of the subject's resting (eye-closed) occipital E.E.G., recorded under standard conditions as part of an investigation of the E.E.G. correlates of the spiral after-effect.

Phentolamine response. This was an index of the sympathetic reactivity of the autonomic nervous system, based on the subject's systolic blood pressure response to an intravenous injection of phentolamine. The measure taken was the maximum absolute blood-pressure change (mm Hg) from the pre-injection level, whether an increase or a decrease.

Auditory vigilance. Here a measure was taken of the subject's ability to maintain vigilance on a sustained attention task. He was asked to detect "signals" consisting of sequences of numbers occurring infrequently in an otherwise random series of digits played over a tape-recorder. His score was the total number of "signals" detected in the 30-minute period of the test.

Serial reaction time. Here the subject was required to perform for 10 minutes on a repetitive motor task which involved pressing the key appropriate to one of five lights which were illuminated in random order. The score used was the number of errors made, that is incorrect keys pressed, over the test period.

Result

In the total sample of 192 subjects the correlation between the drug tolerance index and weight was found to be just significantly positive but very low, r being +0.18 ($P < 0.05$). Taking male subjects separately the correlation was again +0.18, this value also being significant at the 0.05 level of confidence ($n = 168$). In females, however, although the correlation was slightly higher (+0.22), it was not significant for the smaller number of 22 subjects involved. When the sample was divided into neurotic and normal subgroups, a slight difference in correlations was found. In the 158 neurotics the value for r was +0.20 ($P < 0.05$), but in normal subjects the correlation fell to zero, r being +0.05 (n.s., $n = 34$).

Turning to the relationship between drug tolerance index and nervous type measures, these results are shown in Table 5.1. For comparative purposes the table also gives the correlations between drug tolerance index and weight for the various samples involved. As can be seen at the extreme right of the table, with one exception the latter were entirely non-significant. The exception was a small, but significant, correlation found in the very large group on whom the spiral after-effect had been measured. In general, then, the results for weight and drug tolerance confirm those for the total sample just considered.

68 Gordon Claridge

Table 5.1 Relationships between drug tolerance index, weight and nervous type measures*

Nervous type measure	n	Correlation with drug tolerance index (mg)	Correlation with weight (kg)
Phentolamine test (max BP change)	34	+0.45 (P<0.01)	+0.21 (n.s.)
Alpha index (per cent time)	54	−0.18 (n.s.) (eta = 0.62, P<0.01)	−0.01 (n.s.)
Spiral after-effect (sec)	168	+0.27 (P<0.001)	+0.18 (P<0.05)
Serial reaction time (errors)	62	−0.33 (P<0.01)	+0.07 (n.s.)
Vigilance (signals detected)	68	+0.25 (P<0.05)	+0.12 (n.s.)

*All correlations are product moment unless indicated.

In the case of nervous type measures, however, all of these showed significant relationships with drug tolerance. For one of the measures—alpha index—a significant departure from linearity reduced the size of r to a non-significant level. However, when this curvilinear regression was taken into account using the correlation ratio (eta) the relationship between alpha index and drug tolerance index became highly significant. Of the other measures the highest correlation was that between drug tolerance and response to phentolamine, where the positive value for r indicated that subjects who were highly tolerant of amylobarbitone sodium also tended to show greater blood pressure rises—i.e. more sympathetic reactivity—on the autonomic drug test. Both performance tests correlated significantly with amylobarbitone tolerance, the signs of the correlations revealing that drug-tolerant individuals made fewer errors on the reaction time task and detected more signals during sustained vigilance.

It is worth noting that all of the correlations with nervous type measures are of the same order and in the same direction as those obtained in the original investigation when the weight-corrected index of sedation threshold was used. This is perhaps not too surprising since there was a very high correlation between sedation threshold itself and the drug tolerance index considered here, the value for r being +0.96. The latter finding, of course, confirms the relatively weak contribution of weight to individual variation on the drug tolerance test.

Discussion and conclusions

The results reported here provide striking evidence that individual differences in the tolerance of intravenous barbiturates are related to variations in nervous type, as measured by a number of quite disparate physiological and behavioural indices. Perhaps what is more important, the pattern of correlations between drug tolerance and nervous type measures is internally consistent. Thus, on all of the nervous typological measures individuals with a strong resistance to amylobarbitone sodium behave as though in a state of high central nervous arousal; while the opposite is true of those with poor resistance to the drug.

Compared with measures of nervous type, the somatic characteristic of weight bore little relationship to barbiturate tolerance and, even though yielding a small but significant correlation with it, provides a poor guide as to the dosage of drug required to sedate the individual. Of course, the writer is aware that this conclusion is confined to the particular conditions of the present investigation, namely the use of an induction procedure to determine the tolerance of one of the barbiturates, amylobarbitone sodium. However, it might be reasonable to expect similar results using other drugs of the same group and a study is in progress to determine the contribution of personality factors to the tolerance of thiopentone.

It could, of course, be argued that the present findings were to some extent dependent on the kind of population studied, namely that it contained a preponderance of neurotic individuals. Two facts would argue against that criticism. First, in the present study the correlation between weight and drug tolerance was, if anything, lower—indeed virtually zero—in the non-patient group compared with the neurotic sample. Secondly, it is generally accepted that the neuroses represent, not qualitative departures from normality, but quantitative deviations along continuously variable dimensions running through the general population. This view is supported, incidentally, by the fact that in our total population the distribution of sedation threshold was entirely normal, the neurotic patients simply defining its extremes. Individuals with dysthymic symptoms occupied the upper and hysterical patients the lower end of the distribution; thus confirming what was said earlier about the observable personality characteristics that parallel nervous type variations.

Finally, it should be noted that even the nervous type measures studied here did not correlate all that highly with barbiturate tolerance, the largest correlation only accounting for about 20 per cent of the variance (compared with about 3 per cent in the case of weight). However, it is probable that further research could increase the predictive value of nervous type measures and provide an accurate guideline to the dosage of barbiturate required by different individuals.

Commentary

There was, however, one positive spin-off to the paper. In the course of writing it I met up with a friendly Glasgow anaesthetist who took an interest in the topic. In the course of our discussion the problem came up of recruiting participants from the general population for sedation threshold experiments.

We agreed that one way round it was to use surgical patients who were destined anyway to be anaesthetised as part of their operation. This led to one more sedation threshold study – the last of a series of experiments on the procedure and the end of any active interest in the biological basis of Eysenck's E and N personality dimensions (Claridge, Donald, & Birchall, 1981).

This point in my commentary signals a marked shift of direction in my research interests: towards the investigation of more serious psychotic disorders, especially schizophrenia. It was not a new preoccupation, going back to when I worked for Eysenck in the military hospital where, stepping out of line from the research programme he had prescribed for me, I conducted parallel experiments with psychotic patients, reported and theorised about in my 1967 book. However it was not until my period in Glasgow (1964–1974) that I returned to the topic, one that in one form or another has defined most of my research ever since. Because of the long timescale several different lines of enquiry have been pursued over the years, and theoretical interpretations changed or modified. It was therefore difficult to decide on a paper as an entry point which represented major themes that have continued to run through my approach to the topic. In the end I decided to start with a paper that continues the drug theme introduced in the previous papers; makes mention of the dimensionality that has always formed part of my thinking about the psychoses; and highlights what I believe to be a useful insight into the biology of those conditions.

The paper makes a case for LSD-25 as a drug model for schizophrenia. It was written long after LSD became a banned substance – so already trumpeting a forlorn message – but part of its content is reporting data from an experiment I myself did with the drug some years before. It was probably the last truly experimental study of LSD carried out in humans in the UK before it was made illegal (given to members of the Glasgow University Department of Psychological Medicine, from a batch of LSD, legitimately sourced from Sandoz the manufacturer, and casually kept by one of my psychiatric colleagues in his unlocked desk drawer!). Although the general argument making the case for LSD should be of interest to the reader, it is the results of that experiment that are the main reason for reproducing the paper at this point. For it presents information about the biological basis of the psychotic state – and possible trait – that I believe to be unique, as explained below.

Comparisons between subject groups or conditions are almost always expressed as a difference in value on some single variable. In the case considered here the metric is different. It consists instead of a comparison of the *covariation* between *pairs* of variables. As will be seen in the paper, this simple shift in data analysis revealed a remarkable phenomenon. The 'psychotic' condition compared with the control condition was always manifest in a *reversal* of the covariation between the two selected variables. There were two other crucial features of the data. First, the variables concerned were measures of, respectively, general arousal and perceptual function. Second, the direction of correlation between them in the 'psychotic' (e.g. LSD) condition was *counter-intuitive*, for example being negative where a positive association would have been expected according to usually accepted psychophysiological principles.

It is fair to point out that, as far as I am aware, no one has ever replicated the results reported in the paper or ever attempted to do so. Indeed for the LSD finding how could they, with the drug being assigned to the wilderness for so many years after our experiment? So whether the results are judged to be an accidental scientific freak, or a valid observation on the biology of schizophrenia, must be considered alongside other evidence – some of which is presented later – and thoughts about the possible mechanisms underlying psychotic disorder.

6 Animal models of schizophrenia
The case for LSD-25

Gordon Claridge

Some difficulties with the animal model

A recent convergence of ideas which I believe is evident in schizophrenia research suggests that it is worth taking a new look at attempts that have been and are being made to establish the biological basis of the disorder through the study of an appropriate animal model. Part of the purpose of this paper is to suggest a new strategy. Before the arguments for adopting the strategy to be proposed are presented, however, it is necessary to consider some of the difficulties inherent in trying to erect an animal model of schizophrenia. These are fourfold.

First, it is conceivable that schizophrenia is an entirely human condition—a view held by those who consider disorders of language, thinking, and social communication to be essential pathognomonic signs of the disease. If this were so, then the search for an equivalent in lower animals, while not completely fruitless, would be extremely difficult. It is true, as Matthysse and Haber (1975) have recently pointed out, that it might be possible to extract certain nonlinguistic characteristics of schizophrenic thinking which could be studied in animals. Indeed, it might ultimately be possible to extend into the area of psychopathology recent work on, for example, social interaction and language acquisition in non-human primates. Unfortunately, while such an approach offers an exciting challenge for the future, its feasibility is at present severely limited by our knowledge, both of schizophrenia and of animal behavior. For the moment our belief that an animal model is viable must rest on the assumption that there are certain essential symptoms of schizophrenia which are mediated through more primitive neurophysiological mechanisms.

In my view there is evidence that this is so. Careful analyses of experiential data obtained from schizophrenics, such as those reported by Chapman (1966) and by Freedman (1974), suggest that thought disorder may be either a secondary elaboration of a more primary physiological disturbance or represent the later stages of an ongoing pathophysiological process which, in the human, inevitably involves the highest cortical functions. Thus, many schizophrenics report that the earliest indication of a change in their mental state, and one which may antedate their hospital admission by weeks, months, or years, is often an initially fleeting alteration in, for example, brightness or size perception or a difficulty in focused attention. As these experiences worsen, the patient may become progressively more anxious and, in an attempt to hold onto reality, develop increasingly bizarre behavioral and thought strategies, such as autism, social withdrawal, and ideas of reference. It seems possible, therefore, that certain core features of schizophrenia reflect a disturbance of brain function that could be accessible to laboratory study in an appropriate animal species. Comparative research might then help to unravel at least part of the total disorder—a part which, in any case, would need to be thoroughly understood before one could go on to study, even in animals, the more complex symbolic and social aspects of schizophrenia.

Nevertheless, narrowing down on the crucial symptomatology of schizophrenia, and doing so in a way which can be plausibly translated across species, is not without difficulty. Here a comparison with depression is instructive. Although the etiology of depression, like that of schizophrenia, is the subject of much controversy, its clinical characteristics can at least be agreed upon. They are easily recognizable, are relatively circumscribed, and are of a form which can be reproduced as a reasonably convincing animal paradigm, as the recent work of Seligman (1975) on "learned helplessness" has demonstrated. In the case of schizophrenia there are, as far as I am aware, no obvious parallel behaviors which occur in animals, either naturally or under experimental conditions. Those that have been studied as possible clinical "markers" seem to be either trivial or very nonspecific. In the first category are the various stereotyped behaviors produced by amphetamine psychosis, which some workers have discussed as a chemical model for schizophrenia (Ellinwood, Sudilovsky, and Nelson 1973, Randrup and Munkvad 1975, and Snyder 1973). Equally unconvincing is the emphasis placed on some general emotional characteristic, as was done in a recent ethological study reported by Chamove, Eysenck, and Harlow (1972). The aim of their experiment was to isolate clusters of monkey behavior corresponding to the Eysenckian dimensions of extraversion, neuroticism, and psychoticism (Eysenck and Eysenck 1975 and 1976). On the basis of factor analysis of their observational data, the authors claimed to have identified a psychoticism component, defined in terms of behavioral units associated with aggressiveness. It is interesting that their alignment of psychotic tendencies with aggressive behavior coincides with Gray's (1973) recent speculation that the activity of the amygdaloid fight/flight mechanism might provide a biological basis for Eysenck's psychoticism dimension. In my view, however, it seems unlikely that aggressiveness, per se, could be regarded as a behavior with sufficient specificity to define schizophrenia, or even one form of it. For one thing, such behavior is not particularly evident in many schizophrenics; on the contrary, passivity is a more commonly observed feature. Furthermore, the trait is found over too wide a range of psychopathological disorders to hold much promise as a criterion behavior for identifying schizophrenia—and nothing else—in an animal species.

The third problem facing animal research into schizophrenia arises from the great heterogeneity observed in the behavior of human psychotic patients. Indeed, many writers would consider it more proper to speak of "the schizophrenias."

74 Gordon Claridge

Variations in the clinical manifestations of schizophrenia have been handled, though not very successfully, in a number of ways. These have included the traditional subdivisions into hebephrenic, catatonic, paranoid, and simple types, as well as the broader dichotomies of paranoid/nonparanoid, process/reactive, and acute/chronic schizophrenia. The existence of such individual variation raises the question whether the different forms of schizophrenia represent quite distinct disorders. If this were the case, comparative research would need to seek, not one, but several animal models of psychosis. An alternative view of the observed heterogeneity is that with the exception of those phenocopies due to definable organic causes such as temporal lobe damage, all forms of schizophrenia arise from a common underlying dysfunction manifesting itself in different ways according to such factors as age, intelligence, preexisting personality, strength of genetic loading for the disorder, and so on. Here a parallel with the effects of lysergic acid on human behavior is worth drawing. Quite apart from the question of whether LSD "psychosis" is an appropriate model for schizophrenia (I will argue later that it is), the response to the drug is certainly known to vary considerably both between individuals and within the same individual on different occasions. Where recognizably "psychotic" symptoms appear, they may take many forms: elated mood, blunted affect, delusional ideation, slowing or poverty of thought, catatonic withdrawal, and so on. These different effects appear to reflect partly situational factors and partly personality variations observable in the normal state, the interaction between them representing the idiosyncratic ways in which individuals handle what presumably is, initially at least, a uniform effect of the drug on the central nervous system. It is quite conceivable that the variations observed between and within individuals in the naturally occurring psychotic states can be explained in a similar way; if this were true, the task for comparative research in the field would, in one respect at least, be somewhat easier since it would involve isolating a single neurophysiological dysfunction which might, in any case, show less heterogeneity because of the fewer sources of individual variation available in animal species.

The final problem about animal research on schizophrenia flows very largely from the previous two just discussed—namely, that because of the great difficulty of defining schizophrenia clinically, experimental studies of human patients have so far failed to identify a *unique* set of parameters which *reproducibly* describe the condition in all its forms. This is a serious lack because even if it is accepted that the gross clinical features of schizophrenia are difficult to translate across species, the demonstration of a narrower set of laboratory phenomena which consistently accompany the disorder in humans would at least offer some safe criteria by which to define an animal model of the condition before looking at its neurophysiological determinants. The failure to find such phenomena is not for want of trying. The staggering literature on schizophrenia attests to the fact that virtually every single biological or psychological characteristic has been explored. Studies have ranged from analyses of the blood, urine, sweat, cerebrospinal fluid, postmortem brains, and fingerprints of schizophrenics to investigations of their vigilance, reaction time, perceptual response, conditionability, drug tolerance, autonomic reactivity, and EEG patterns. The frustrating outcome is not that no abnormalities have been demonstrated (they have many times), but that the range of defects observed has been too great and too variable from study to study to permit much coherent theoretical interpretation. This, of course, has not deterred individual investigators from trying to set up animal paradigms based on their personal evaluation of part of the evidence about human schizophrenia. Apart from work using psychotomimetic drugs, which I will return to later, there are two examples which spring immediately to mind and which will, if nothing else, help to illustrate the problem.

The first has been based on a theory of schizophrenia proposed by Stein and Wise (1971) who argued that the disorder is due to a defect of the "reward system" of Olds and Milner, resulting in an accumulation of 6-hydroxydopamine. Their claim that this substance, injected into the ventricles of experimental animals, reduced self-stimulatory behavior was seen as a parallel to the schizophrenic's postulated inability to appreciate or appropriately perceive reward. Unfortunately, aside from the difficulty of extrapolating these particular data across species, it is by no means obvious that a failure of reward-directed behavior is central to schizophrenia. Certainly, the model proposed by Stein and Wise does not seem to derive from any appreciation of what most workers in human schizophrenia research would regard as the mainstream of evidence or theory about the disorder.

This criticism, at least, cannot be leveled against the second animal model to be quoted, that attempted by Kornetsky (Kornetsky and Markowitz 1975). He has argued that a fundamental deficit in schizophrenia is an impairment of selective attention—a view which, as discussed in the next section, seems to be well supported by the experimental evidence, to which Kornetsky himself has contributed. In his own research on humans, Kornetsky has concentrated on two particular experimental tasks, one of continuous motor performance and the other a more complex digit-symbol substitution test. He considers that behavior on these two tasks reflects the activity of different neural mechanisms—roughly subcortical and cortical in origin—which may be differentially impaired in schizophrenia. Two kinds of evidence are quoted in support of this hypothesis: first, the pattern of scores found in schizophrenics, relative to other individuals, on the two tasks and, second, the differences observed in the way phenothiazines and barbiturates affect test performance. In an attempt to explore the physiological implications of his model, Kornetsky devised a version of his continuous performance task suitable for use with the rat, in which he has investigated the effects of various experimental manipulations, including direct stimulation of the ARAS and administration of chlorpromazine and noradrenaline. Although it is possible to discern some similarity between the results obtained across species, it is not at all clear from the findings reported so far that Kornetsky has succeeded in establishing an animal representation of the true deficit in schizophrenia. On the human side, his choice of parameters for describing schizophrenia seems somewhat idiosyncratic and the theory to which it gives rise is too vaguely stated to convince one that he is not—as he himself admits may be the case—"modeling some unessential correlate of the disease."

It is clear that given our present knowledge of schizophrenia, any decision to pursue the search for an animal model of the disorder must involve a leap into the dark, based on (one hopes) inspired and very much personal guesses about the significance of existing theory and experimental literature. Of course, some constraints can be imposed, and I would suggest three criteria which ought reasonably to be met before any model could be considered potentially viable. First, the general area of behavior studied should be one which experimental psychopathologists agree seems central to schizophrenic disorder. Second, the particular phenomena chosen for investigation should look unusual enough to appear unique to schizophrenia rather than being some nonspecific correlate of disordered behavior in general, or, which is most likely, of the emotional arousal that universally accompanies such behavior. Third, the experimental procedures used for studying the phenomena should be unambiguously reproducible in an appropriate animal species.

The case to be argued here represents an attempt to arrive at a strategy which meets these three criteria. It does so by drawing together certain ideas and experimental data from several different fields bearing on schizophrenia research as they stand at the present time. In constructing the arguments that follow, it was considered useful to let several threads run through the discussion. One is historical and covers the background against which current psychological research on schizophrenia has evolved. Another is theoretical and focuses on the sorts of explanatory model of schizophrenia that psychologists have tried to develop. The third is strategic and concerns methods and data from research in areas allied to, but not specifically directed at, the study of the schizophrenic patient.

Experimental psychopathology of schizophrenia

Perception, attention, and thinking

Until very recently, research by psychologists on schizophrenia has followed an obvious course. It has tried to find laboratory or semi-laboratory parallels of the more prominent clinical symptomatology, usually through comparisons of diagnosed schizophrenic and nonschizophrenic people on tasks derived from general experimental psychology. Among the favorite areas of behavior chosen for investigation have been those of perception, attention, and thinking. No attempt will be made here to give a detailed survey of these studies since they have been thoroughly reviewed by Venables (1964), summarized by McGhie (1969), and are probably familiar by now to most readers. All that will be done here is to draw some general conclusions from this area of schizophrenia research. Before doing so it is perhaps worth inserting a reminder that refers back to the point made earlier, namely that very few studies have demonstrated a difference between schizophrenics and other psychiatric patients (as distinct from normal subjects) that holds up over more than one or two replications of the experiment. This is partly due to the absence of any universally accepted criteria for diagnosing schizophrenia and partly to the heterogeneity of the condition even where the overall diagnosis can be agreed upon. Different investigators have in effect, therefore, been studying dissimilar patient populations. Many workers have further confounded the problem by failing to take account of acute/chronic differences, by using inappropriate control groups, and by ignoring the fact that their patients were on physical treatments which affect the very phenomena they are studying.

For summary purposes it is probably unnecessary to distinguish between the very closely related areas of perception and attention. At the purely perceptual end, an early preoccupation of psychologists was with abnormalities such as those of size constancy that were demonstrable in schizophrenics. Although these experimental results have proved too fragile to withstand repeated replication, they did start off a strand of theorizing which is still relevant. Thus, it was suggested by Silverman (1964a) that the size constancy differences observed in schizophrenics were due to abnormalities in physical scanning of the environment, although early attempts to confirm this by recording eye movements were not particularly successful. A recent study by Holzman et al. (1974) has suggested that schizophrenics (and their healthy relatives) may indeed show abnormal pursuit eye movements though, more recently still, doubts have been thrown on the specificity of their findings (Brězinová and Kendell 1977).

A slightly different, though related, formulation has been used to try to explain the other major defect observed in schizophrenics, namely the abnormality of selective attention. The latter has been a major focus of research by psychologists, who have usually derived their explanatory models from those constructed in general psychology, particularly that developed by Broadbent (1958). Thus, a number of workers have proceeded on the basis that one of the most prominent features of schizophrenia is abnormal filtering of information flowing into the nervous system. Data from the field of attention that have been quoted in support of that theory are varied. Some of it comes from the work of McGhie (1969) using techniques like dichotic listening and reaction time testing with and without distraction. A somewhat different source of evidence, though one worth special mention, is research carried out by Callaway and his colleagues on the auditory evoked response (Callaway and Jones 1975 and Callaway, Jones, and Layne 1965). Their method of correlating successive sets of averaged evoked responses to physically identical auditory stimuli has demonstrated that schizophrenics, possibly due to poor focused attention, show greater variability than normals. Other work on the evoked response has also carried a similar notion through into the very recent literature on schizophrenia. Thus, Rappaport et al. (1975), in a recent study, have shown much greater than normal variability in the visual evoked response of schizophrenics—a result which might be taken to indicate poor filtering of sensory input by such patients. This last study is noteworthy for its careful selection of the patient sample, while the results are particularly interesting because of the extent to which they parallel some effects of LSD to be considered later.

Convergence on a filtering model has also been evident in work on the thinking of schizophrenics. A favorite bridging concept has, of course, been "overinclusion," the most extensive investigations of that notion being carried out by Payne (Payne 1971 and Payne and Hewlett 1960), who postulated that the disorder may be due to a defective cognitive filter which prevents the schizophrenic from screening out irrelevant ideas and maintaining adequately circumscribed conceptual boundaries. Payne's original studies made use of tasks, such as sorting tests, developed within clinical psychology for diagnosing thought disorder. Subsequently, however, in testing out his filter theory, he moved on to examine the performance correlates of overinclusion on dichotic listening, reaction time, and other tasks of attention (e.g., Payne, Hochberg, and Hawks 1970). Thus, although starting from a different point of view, the form and theoretical underpinning of his work eventually merged with that of people like McGhie.

Needless to say, many of the ideas and techniques developed over the past 20 years within this general area of research on schizophrenia have begun to show the frailty of their age. Experimental results have failed to be replicated, clinical tests derived from them have proved diagnostically useless, and abnormal psychologists have been chided for clinging to models of attention that cognitive theorists in general psychology abandoned long ago (Marshall 1973).

Nevertheless, one cannot fail to be impressed by the frequency with which the same theme recurs throughout a now considerable literature: that schizophrenics show, as a fundamental characteristic, some disorder of their ability to respond selectively to stimuli; or, as Venables (1964) in a brave attempt to find a unifying concept named it, some form of "input dysfunction." Although reliable measurement of the disorder has so far eluded experimental psychologists, its importance as a central feature of schizophrenia has, in my view, been established sufficiently for its explanation to be a necessary requirement of any future theories of psychotic behavior. By the same token, any alternative strategy for getting at the biological basis of schizophrenia, such as the use of animal models, would need to demonstrate *some* form of "input dysfunction" as a defining criterion of the psychotic state.

Arousal as a mediating variable

Ever since the 1930s when the notion of "arousal" first became popular in psychology, attempts have been made to use it as an explanatory concept for various psychiatric syndromes. Schizophrenia is no exception. The hope that the condition might reduce to a simple disorder of central nervous system arousal has, over the years, stimulated a great many studies trying to demonstrate that schizophrenics will show abnormalities on physiological indices of EEG and peripheral autonomic activity. Although individual studies have shown differences between schizophrenics and nonpsychotics, the total picture is, to say the least, utterly conflicting. This is partly due to a lack of comparability between different types of measure and to the difficulty of interpreting them as indices of a single global process of "arousal." Another problem has been the usual one of dissimilarity between samples of patients, the finding of great heterogeneity *within* schizophrenic groups, and the tendency (even now!) to ignore the influence of treatment.

Even if these difficulties are set aside, however, the idea that schizophrenia would reduce to a simple upward or downward shift in central nervous system arousal has never, in my view, been a compelling one. Such an explanation could not account for the easily demonstrable fact (Claridge 1967) that similar variations in arousal can be observed in other psychiatric patients, such as neurotics, and that where the latter are used as appropriate controls the differences claimed for schizophrenics disappear. Clearly, if arousal is disturbed in schizophrenia, it can only form one part of a more complex disorder of the central nervous system. Attempts to recognize this fact are contained in those models which have construed arousal as a variable mediating other prominent symptoms of the condition, particularly those discussed in the previous section. Some examples will help to illustrate the point.

The first is the theory of schizophrenia proposed some years ago by Mednick (1958). He argued and provided some evidence that an important feature of schizophrenia is a tendency toward greatly increased stimulus generalization during conditioning, a characteristic thought to be responsible for the schizophrenic's heightened responsivity to remotely associated stimuli in the real-life situation. Thus, Mednick proposed what was, in effect, a learning theory equivalent of overinclusive perception, though he suggested in addition that the high stimulus generalizability of the schizophrenic was coupled to a low threshold for anxiety arousal, the two together combining to make the patient increasingly responsive to remote emotional cues, both internal and external. More recently he has tested out and found some support for this model in his, now classic, high risk study of conditioning and psychophysiological response in the children of schizophrenic mothers (Mednick and Schulsinger 1973).

Other, simpler, examples of the use of arousal as a mediating variable concern the application to schizophrenic behavior of two principles taken over from general psychophysiology, namely the "narrowed attention" and "inverted-U" (or Yerkes-Dodson) principles. The first of these contains the idea that the span of attention broadens and narrows with, respectively, decreases and increases in the arousal level of the organism. Several investigators have used this principle to explain various perceptual and attentional deficits in schizophrenia. Included among these is the altered size constancy referred to earlier which, so the argument goes, is due to an abnormal state of arousal influencing the appreciation of the peripheral cues upon which size judgment depends. Even wider use has been made of the inverted-U principle—that is, the notion that there is an optimum level of arousal for effective performance beyond which behavior "goes into reverse." The principle has appeared in various forms, most notably as the idea of "threshold for transmarginal inhibition" found in Pavlovian physiology (Gray 1964). Applied to schizophrenia a classic example of its use was in the explanation of catatonia, in which extreme behavioral immobility and unresponsiveness may be accompanied by excessively high levels of physiological arousal and where paradoxical alerting effects of barbiturates have been observed (Stevens and Derbyshire 1958).

In general, however, neither of these last two ways of handling arousal as a mediating construct for schizophrenic behavior has achieved much more than very limited explanatory status. The problem is that like the use of arousal alone as an explanatory concept, both principles have found *too wide* an application to other forms of behavior; that is, their operation is not unique to schizophrenia. This is particularly true of the inverted-U or transmarginal inhibition principle which is commonly found to apply in a wide variety of situations; more to the point, it has been fairly successfully used in the general personality field—for example, to explain differences in the "strength of the nervous system" of normal introverts and extraverts (Gray 1967).

Although a disorder of central nervous arousal, on the one hand, and a disorder of perception and attention, on the other, seem to be the two most prominent features of schizophrenia, it is clear that conventional ways of handling their interrelationship have proved of limited value. It was out of an attempt to construe the problem from a different point of view altogether that my own approach to schizophrenia developed (Claridge 1967). The basis of this approach was a series of experiments which, for convenience, can be called the "covariation studies" and which will be discussed in the next section.

Covariation studies of arousal and perception

Since the early 1960s there has been a narrow thread running through schizophrenia research starting from an unusual and fortuitous observation made independently and almost simultaneously by Venables and myself in the course of a series of experiments on the psychophysiology of psychotic patients. The observation was that although schizophrenics did not seem to differ from other individuals on measures of arousal or perception, per se, they did differ markedly if one looked at the *correlation* or covariation between such measures. In my own work this phenomenon was most apparent in the case of two measures which, though rather unusual, were of some theoretical interest at that time, namely the sedation threshold and the Archimedes spiral aftereffect (Herrington and Claridge 1965). The former test, being a measure of the individual's tolerance for injected barbiturates, was considered to provide an index of central nervous arousability while the perceived movement illusion of the spiral aftereffect was thought to reflect, albeit crudely and indirectly, some aspect of sensory input processing. Theory at that time predicted an obvious relationship between them, namely that individuals with high arousal (sedation threshold) would perceive longer movement aftereffects and vice versa. This prediction was fully borne out in neurotic patients (who were the main focus of the study), but a quite different relationship was observed in psychotics. In the latter group the normally expected relationship between the two measures was reversed, schizophrenics with high sedation threshold reporting weak aftereffects and vice versa. Furthermore, psychotics and neurotics did not differ significantly in the range covered on either measure taken individually but only in the correlation between them.

Around the same time Venables (1963) reported a similar finding using two different psychophysiological techniques, namely skin potential (as an index of autonomic arousal) and a measure of the subjectively perceived fusion of brief light flashes (two-flash threshold). Comparing chronic schizophrenics and normal subjects, he showed that apart from a very small group of coherently paranoid patients, schizophrenics differed from normals entirely with respect to the covariation between the two experimental measures.

These two experiments suggested, therefore, that an important charactristic of schizophrenics may be that for any given level of central nervous arousal their degree of perceptual responsivity differs markedly from normal, being either abnormally high or low. Both Venables and myself speculated at the time that this may be due, not so much to a simple shift in either arousal or perceptual function alone, but rather to a failure of homeostatic regulation between the two.

Later attempts to examine this hypothesis further have, with two exceptions, narrowed down on the relationship between two-flash threshold and some index of electrodermal activity, either skin potential or skin conductance. Of the two exceptions one was a study by Krishnamoorti and Shagass (1964) replicating our own findings on sedation threshold and spiral aftereffect. The other is a much more recent investigation by Shagass, Straumanis, and Overton (1975) who compared, in different groups, the correlation between background EEG and certain parameters of the evoked response. Having successfully demonstrated the discriminating power of this technique, the authors concluded that the covariation between different psychophysiological measures may be more significant for understanding psychopathology than the absolute levels of the measures themselves.

Subsequent work on Venables' original measures in psychiatric samples has run a somewhat erratic course, with the phenomenon of altered covariation sometimes appearing, though weakly (Gruzelier, Lykken, and Venables 1972 and Gruzelier and Venables 1975), and in one case (Lykken and Maley 1968) appearing but in the opposite direction to that shown by Venables! One complicating factor that has emerged is the discovery that the relationship between two-flash threshold and electrodermal level is nonlinear. Another difficulty is the neglect of drug effects by investigators of the phenomenon, since the patients studied either currently or very recently had been on large doses of phenothiazines, which almost certainly distort the psychophysiological relationships being sought.

Partly for theoretical reasons and partly in order to escape the *impasse* of working with patients who are either drugged and testable or untreated and possibly uncooperative, we have complemented our patient research with studies of two-flash threshold/electrodermal relationships in normal subjects. The rationale for this strategy was the emerging "dimensional" view of schizophrenia—namely the idea that severe forms of the disorder may only form the end-point of a continuum defining a general personality dimension of "psychoticism" running through the normal population. The arguments for this model have been detailed elsewhere (Claridge 1972 and 1976), but very briefly are as follows.

First, it is being increasingly recognized that the classic schizophrenic syndromes probably represent only severe forms of a broad range of milder conditions, for which the term "spectrum disorders" has been coined (Reich 1975). Second, and in line with this view, the genetic evidence about schizophrenia now makes it at least plausible that the biological characteristics underlying the condition are inherited as a polygenically determined trait or set of traits defining a continuously variable predisposition to psychotic breakdown (Gottesman and Shields 1973 and 1976).

Third, there is acceptable evidence (Reichenstein 1976 and Young 1974) that schizophrenic "symptoms" are widely dispersed and frequently observed in otherwise normal people. Fourth, factor-analytic studies of personality traits in normal individuals have demonstrated the existence of a personality dimension recognizable as "psychoticism" and measurable by self-report inventory, the P-scale of the Eysenck Personality Questionnaire (EPQ) (Eysenck and Eysenck 1975 and 1976). Admittedly the validity of the new Eysenck scale leaves something to be desired when judged against its ability to discriminate schizophrenics from other clinical groups, especially psychopaths. Fortunately, however, other evidence for its validity suggests that the scale may be tapping, if imperfectly, some set of characteristics relevant to schizophrenia. Thus, in her study of the prevalence of schizophrenic symptoms among normal subjects, Reichenstein (1976) found a significant positive correlation between her own inventory and the Eysenck scale. Furthermore, investigations of the cognitive style of individuals with high P scores have demonstrated that they show "loosened" thought processes as measured by divergent thinking tests (Woody and Claridge 1977) and by clinical tests of overinclusion (Walker 1974). Finally, although not throwing direct light on the validity of the Eysenck questionnaire itself, a recent study by Nielsen and Petersen (1976), who constructed a similar scale of what they called "schizophrenism," should be mentioned. The particular interest of Nielsen and Petersen's work is their finding that normal individuals high in the trait showed rapid recovery of the galvanic skin response (GSR), a characteristic which, in longitudinal research, has received considerable attention as a possible psychophysiological indicator for detecting individuals at high risk for schizophrenia (Mednick 1974 and Venables 1977).

These arguments for the dimensionality of psychotic behavior suggest that the study of appropriately selected normal subjects can provide valid data on the biological basis of schizophrenia. With this in mind we have over the past few years been examining two-flash threshold/electrodermal relationships in normal subjects scoring high on the Eysenck psychoticism scale, comparisons being made with individuals equally high in neuroticism, but with low P scale scores. Before those results are considered, some general remarks should be made about the experimental procedure and method of analysis adopted in this and other studies we have done of two-flash threshold and electrodermal activity. Full details can be found in the original publications.

In determining two-flash thresholds we have always used a method of limits procedure to obtain ascending and descending thresholds, the two-flash threshold being taken as the mean of these two estimations. The concomitant measures of electrodermal level used have been those coincident in time with the estimations of the two-flash threshold. A single index of each experimental variable for a given individual has then been arrived at by averaging several measurements taken during a recording session, and it is these data on which any group comparisons of two-flash threshold/electrodermal relationships have been based. The method of analysis has simply involved examining correlations between two-flash threshold and electrodermal level, but here it is necessary to draw attention to one important point which, while slightly anticipating the results, is relevant to their interpretation. Like others working in this area we have consistently found that the regressions of two-flash threshold on measures of electrodermal level are markedly nonlinear. Furthermore the most clear-cut relationships between the two variables have usually been observed in the *low* range of electrodermal level, that is, up to the midpoint of the distribution of skin conductance or skin potential. Beyond that point the relationships with two-flash threshold have been less reliable. For clarity of presentation here the results described initially, therefore, will be for the low range data from the various experiments. I will then come back to consider in more detail, and illustrate, the form the data take when the whole range of electrodermal activity is taken into account.

The result from the first study we carried out in our work on psychoticism in normal subjects (Claridge and Chappa 1973) is shown in Figure 6.1. The groups compared there were selected on the basis of scores on the PEN inventory, an early version of Eysenck's EPQ questionnaire. High P subjects were defined as those with scores of 3 or more, and low P subjects as those with scores of 2 or less, on the psychoticism scale. Matching for neuroticism—necessary because of a correlation between P and N on the PEN inventory—was achieved by selecting from the low P group those subjects with N scores of 12 or above.

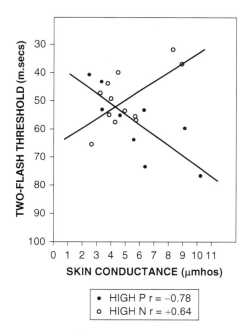

Figure 6.1 High P and high N subjects compared at skin conductance less than 10.25 µmhos.

Note: Correlation and regression lines show the opposite relationships between two-flash threshold and skin conductance in normal subjects with, respectively, high and low scores on Eysenck's P (psychoticism) scale. These results refer to the low range of autonomic arousal (see text). Note that in this and subsequent figures, two-flash threshold is plotted so that changes in an upward direction indicate *improved* perceptual discrimination.

It can be seen from Figure 6.1 that as predicted from the patient research, the difference between the two groups lay, not in either experimental measure by itself, but in the covariation between them, the correlations being highly significant and opposite in sign in high P and low P subjects. A small replication study by Claridge and Birchall (1973) confirmed this result, which continued to hold up with the addition of further subjects to the sample, the correlations between two-flash threshold and skin conductance now obtained by Birchall being −.65 (p < .005) and +.43 (p < .05) in 18 high P and 18 high N subjects, respectively.

Another strategy we have used, and one which actually antedated that just described, was an early investigation of the "covariation phenomenon" in normal subjects given LSD-25 (Claridge 1972). Comparisons were made of two-flash threshold and simultaneously recorded skin potential in subjects receiving, on separate occasions, either a placebo or 100 micrograms of LSD. As shown in Figure 6.2, the main effect of the drug was to cause a marked reversal of perceptual sensitivity as it related to ongoing autonomic arousal, the results exactly paralleling those found using the individual differences strategy of selecting subjects according to their self-rated degree of psychoticism.

Finally, in the previously mentioned recent study (Claridge and Clark, 1982) of untreated schizophrenics tested immediately on admission to the hospital, exactly the same result has emerged; that is, as shown in Figure 6.3, a significantly negative correlation was found between two-flash threshold and, in this case, skin conductance level, the only difference here being that in order to demonstrate the phenomenon it was necessary to apply range correction to the electrodermal measures.

In comparing Figures 6.1, 6.2, and 6.3, it is clear that there is a striking similarity in the results obtained in a variety of situations in which states of psychoticism or psychosis can be inferred: in diagnosed schizophrenic patients, in normal subjects selected by questionnaire, and in individuals under the influence of a psychotomimetic drug. What is especially convincing about this convergence of evidence is the particular direction of the empirical relationships observed in the data. Close examination of Figures 6.1, 6.2, and 6.3 shows that for the "psychotic" condition the covariation of two-flash threshold and electrodermal level is always *negative* over the low range. That is, at low levels of autonomic arousal, perceptual sensitivity is paradoxically excessively high, worsening toward the mid-range. This finding is entirely contrary to the general psychophysiological principle that perceptual sensitivity should improve with increasing arousal, as indeed it does under the "nonpsychotic" conditions of the experiments. Our guess is that the counterintuitive nature of the results found in the psychotic state is not without significance in pointing toward an appropriately unique feature of the central nervous organization as it relates to schizophrenia.

A complication to all of the data described above, however, is the fact, mentioned earlier, that in all three kinds of investigation we have carried out, systematic covariation between autonomic arousal and perceptual sensitivity is most reliably observed in the low range of electrodermal activity. Beyond the mid-range the data always appear to "break away" from linearity of regression. This is most clearly

Animal models of schizophrenia 85

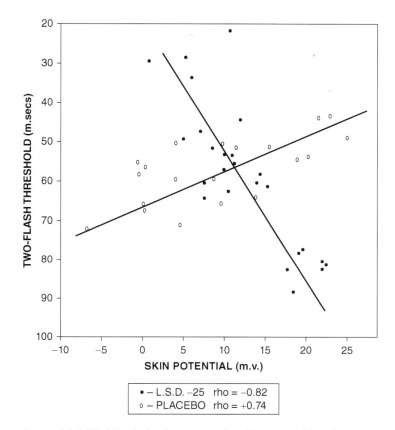

Figure 6.2 LSD-25 and placebo compared at skin potential less than 25 mv.

Note: Correlations and regression lines show the opposite relationship between two-flash threshold and skin potential in normal subjects under LSD-25 and under placebo. These results refer to the low range of autonomic arousal (cf. Figure 6.1 and see text).

illustrated in the results from the LSD experiment, as shown in Figures 6.4 and 6.5. It can be seen that under the placebo condition of that study (Figure 6.4) something approaching a conventional inverted-U relationship was observed. Under LSD (Figure 6.5), on the other hand, the data took on a curious U-shaped appearance, suggesting that beyond the mid-point of electrodermal activity perceptual acuity paradoxically began to improve again. A similar picture was discernible, though less clearly, in the data for acute schizophrenics (Figure 6.6) and in Claridge and Chappa's (1973) data on high P normals (Figure 6.7). It was also found in Claridge and Birchall's (1973) replication of the latter experiment.

It is obvious that compared with the low range data, those for the upper range are much less convincing and only weakly confirm a similarity between the results of the three types of experiment. Such as it is, however, the trend seems to be a reversal of the relationship found in the low to moderate range of electrodermal activity,

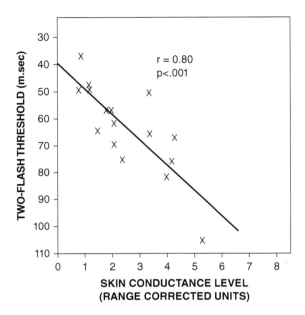

Figure 6.3 Two-flash threshold and skin conductance level (low range) in acute untreated schizophrenics—First testing day.

Note: The scatter plot shows two-flash threshold and skin conductance level (range corrected) in a group of acute, untreated, psychotic patients. These results refer to the low range of autonomic arousal (cf. previous figures and see text).

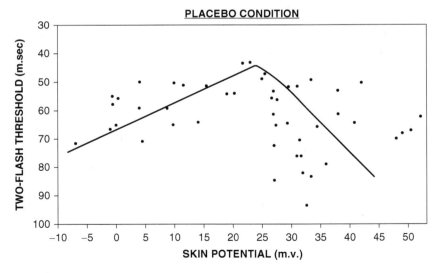

Figure 6.4 Relationship between two-flash threshold and skin potential—Placebo condition.

Note: In the placebo condition of the LSD experiment, the relationship between two-flash threshold and skin potential over the full range of autonomic arousal is shown.

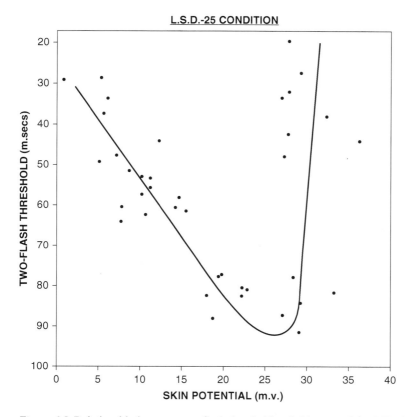

Figure 6.5 Relationship between two-flash threshold and skin potential—LSD-25 condition.

Note: In the LSD-25 condition, the relationship between two-flash threshold and skin potential over the full range of autonomic arousal is shown.

the overall regression being suggestive of a very peculiar U-shaped function—seen most clearly in the LSD study. If one bears in mind the unusual nature of the results found in these experiments, it does at least seem possible to conclude that LSD-25 has psychophysiological effects which can be aligned theoretically with findings obtained using other strategies for investigating the biological basis of schizophrenia. Since it is to be argued here that LSD might therefore provide a useful vehicle for establishing an animal model of schizophrenia, it is appropriate at this point to consider other evidence in support of that thesis.

LSD as a psychotomimetic

During its relatively brief history LSD-25 (lysergide) has been the subject of controversy even greater than that which usually greets new scientific discovery.

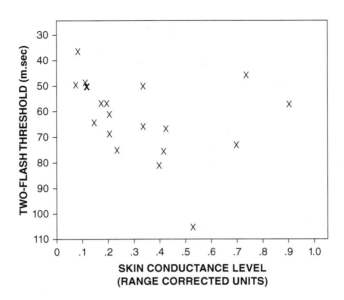

Figure 6.6 Two-flash threshold and skin conductance level (whole range) in acute untreated schizophrenics—First testing day.

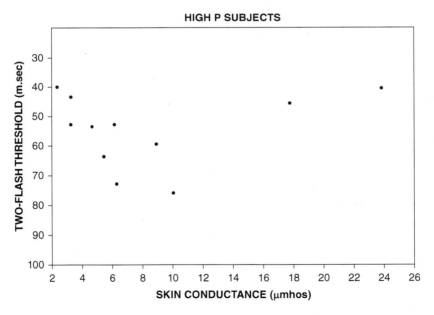

Figure 6.7 Relationship between two-flash threshold and skin conductance level (whole range) in high P subjects.

Note: Subjects are normals with high scores on Eysenck's P (psychoticism) scale.

Synthesis of the drug and observations of its remarkable psychological effects led to an early hope that here at last was the pharmacological agent which would finally unravel the biochemical basis of schizophrenia. The failure to do so, while not surprising—given the limited disease views of the disorder current at that time—led to a period of pessimism about the drug's scientific usefulness. This phase coincided with the "discovery" by drug-cultists of the psychedelic properties of LSD and led eventually, of course, to its proscription by society and to severe limitations of its use in serious research. Actually it was perhaps with some relief that research workers concerned with schizophrenia felt able to dismiss the scientific interest of LSD and to abandon the study of it, though they did so precisely at the time when progress on other fronts of schizophrenia research began to make some, albeit very slow, progress.

An important factor which undoubtedly hastened the decline of interest in LSD was the view, already mentioned, that amphetamine constituted a better pharmacological model of schizophrenia. Work on that drug was linked to, and provided part of the evidence for, the increasingly popular hypothesis that schizophrenia may be due to an excess of dopamine in the central nervous system, especially in the limbic system. Among biochemists searching for the neurotransmitter crucially involved in schizophrenia there was, therefore, a shift of focus away from the "serotonin hypothesis" which the earlier work on LSD had prematurely spawned.

Although the alternative "dopamine hypothesis" has usefully extended our knowledge of the biochemistry of schizophrenia, its current status as an explanation of the disorder is still extremely uncertain (Meltzer and Stahl 1976 and Van Praag 1977). Thus, Meltzer and Stahl (1976), in concluding their recent review of the topic, comment as follows:

> The evidence for a role for DA [dopamine] in the pathophysiology of schizophrenia is compelling but not irrefutable; the "smoking gun" has not yet been discovered. Evidence consistent with the hypothesis still cannot be transformed into basic principles that could conceivably become the theoretical framework into which the majority of clinical as well as biochemical data that concern schizophrenia might be comprehended. [p. 58]

Meltzer and Stahl go on to point out that even if dopaminergic hyperactivity is present in schizophrenia, it may simply be a secondary correlate of transiently increased central nervous system arousal due to some other basic defect. In any case, whether primary or secondary, the involvement of dopamine in schizophrenia does not preclude a pharmacological model based on LSD, since it is known that the latter drug is capable of activating dopamine receptors (Fuxe et al. 1976 and Kelly and Iversen 1975).

Given the still immature state of knowledge about the biochemistry of schizophrenia, there seem on biochemical grounds, therefore, to be no convincing reasons for continuing to reject LSD as a potentially useful drug model. As for its superiority or otherwise to amphetamine on grounds of *clinical* effect, some comments have been made on this point earlier in the paper. It was mentioned there that by comparison with LSD, amphetamine models only part of the schizophrenic spectrum in humans and even then only in chronic dosage, while in animals the "marker" behavior is somewhat trivial. In any case, since the preference for amphetamine has been inextricably linked to the dopamine hypothesis, most of the arguments in favor of the drug fall away given the still uncertain status of that hypothesis. Indeed, since there seems to be a real possibility that schizophrenia will not reduce to a disorder of any *single* neurotransmitter, there is something to be said at present for making one's initial choice of a drug model simply on grounds of "face validity"—that is, which drug looks as though it reliably produces a state akin to, and includes the varieties of, natural psychosis. Were it not for the fierceness with which the amphetamine model has been defended and the LSD model rejected, it would be laboring the point unnecessarily to reiterate the latter's obvious superiority.

Even so it may be, and has been, argued that LSD does not mimic the clinical features of schizophrenia well enough. A particular criticism has been that the disorders of perception observed are mainly auditory in schizophrenia and visual in the LSD-induced state. West (1975), for example, concludes that according to a "rough estimate" only about 5 percent of schizophrenics show visual hallucinations. However, more careful studies suggest a much higher incidence. The most thorough is that carried out some years ago by Chapman (1966) who, on the basis of extensive interviews, examined the subjectively reported symptoms of a group of early schizophrenics. He found that visual perceptual disturbances were very common in such patients, while auditory disturbances, at least in the form of hallucinations, were actually rather rare. More recently a survey by Zarroug (1975) revealed that about 62 percent of schizophrenic patients reported visual hallucinations. That study was carried out in Saudi Arabia and the author emphasizes the possible importance of cultural factors in determining the form psychotic symptoms take, a comment which warns against hard and fast conclusions being reached about the "typical" phenomenology of schizophrenia.

A complicating feature of all of these studies, of course, may be the use of differing criteria for defining hallucinations, as distinct from other perceptual disturbances, such as illusory distortions of the external environment. A proper comparison of schizophrenia and the LSD state requires that similar criteria be applied to both. In such a study Young (1974) recently examined the psychotic symptoms reported by normal subjects, schizophrenics, and regular LSD-takers. Young concluded that LSD-induced and natural psychoses were in most major respects phenomenologically indistinguishable. The main differences related to the greater degree of unpleasant affect, especially anxiety, and the higher frequency of delusions in the schizophrenics. Neither of these, however, argues crucially against LSD psychosis being a good drug model for schizophrenia, if account is taken of the context in which each of these states occurs. Thus, the regular LSD-taker is entering the state voluntarily and with relative control over it; anxiety would therefore be much less than in spontaneously occurring natural psychosis. With regard to delusions, as Chapman (1966) and indeed many writers in the schizophrenia literature have pointed out, these can probably be best understood as attempts by the schizophrenic patient to explain the primary perceptual and attentional disturbances occurring early in the illness. Compared with the schizophrenic the LSD-taker would have less need for such thought strategies though, indeed, as we found in our own study of LSD they can occur, if rarely. Both of the differences between schizophrenia and LSD described by Young could therefore be said to be secondary elaborations on or reactions to a primary psychotic state which is similar in both cases.

In terms of the subjective report, then, the LSD state does not seem to differ from schizophrenia as much as some critics have argued, a view also taken by Davison (1976) who, after reviewing the same question, concludes that although not identical, "individual features of the drug reaction are remarkably similar to some of the experiences of the more acute schizophrenic psychoses" (p. 111). Of course, it could be said that to insist the two be identical is, in any case, to misunderstand the logic of drug research of this kind. Schizophrenia is a complex natural disorder of multiple causation and has many features which are almost certainly not part of the core defect of the disease. Earlier it was argued that the latter was probably some form of "input dysfunction" accounting for the anomalies of perception and attention observed in the early phases of schizophrenia. That defect does seem to be mimicked quite well by LSD, at least as assessed by subjective report.

More objective evidence on this point, from experimental studies of the effects of LSD in humans, is not easy to fit into any coherent picture, partly because many such studies, particularly in the early days of LSD research, were of the empirical "look and see" variety. There was also usually no attempt to make comparisons with schizophrenics on similar tasks, although one study that did do so was an investigation by Wikler et al. (1965). They used a variable foreperiod reaction time procedure to test the hypothesis that LSD-25 would have similar effects on "mental set" to those previously reported as one of the primary deficits in schizophrenia (Rodnick and Shakow 1940 and Shakow 1963). Although their hypothesis was confirmed, similar changes in mental set were also observed under morphine and pentobarbital, suggesting that the effects were nonspecific. Nevertheless, from this and other studies of LSD carried out around the same time (Uhr and Miller 1960) it can at least be said that some of the impairments of performance observed in laboratory investigations of the drug were not inconsistent with those seen in schizophrenics—though admittedly this is a weak conclusion considering the chaotic nature of the evidence there. More recently, however, Silverman (1973) made an exceptional attempt to align LSD reactions and schizophrenia within a theoretical framework which emphasized alterations in sensory responsiveness, or stimulus modulation, as the disorder common to both. His account is interesting in proceeding from a discussion of subjective data of the kind referred to above, to a consideration of experimental studies of sensory sensitivity. In doing so, he pays particular attention to work on the "augmenting-reducing" phenomenon (Buchsbaum and Silverman 1968), the evoked response measurement of which continues to provide a valuable technique for examining sensory nervous system differences in relation to psychopathological states (Buchsbaum, Post, and Bunney 1977 and Landau et al. 1975). Although Silverman's arguments are occasionally somewhat inferential, his conclusion that LSD reactions and schizophrenia are similar psychophysiologically is very convincing and would accord well with the results of our own studies, reported in the previous section, directly comparing the two states on two-flash threshold and electrodermal activity. While the results of the latter studies are rather narrow in thrust and their significance not entirely understood, they do suggest that given the right choice of parameters, a theoretically predictable match can be observed at the psychophysiological level between LSD-induced psychosis and naturally occurring variations.

A third source of support for the LSD state as an appropriate pharmacological model of schizophrenia is work on the drug's effect in animals. Here I shall confine myself to a limited group of studies which, although they are now rarely quoted (indeed never referred to in the schizophrenia literature) are, I believe, of great theoretical interest. The effects observed and the interpretations put on them show a remarkable parallel with some salient features of the work undertaken, albeit quite independently, on schizophrenia.

The studies in question date back, in some cases, almost twenty years and were carried out by Bradley and by Key and his colleagues in the Department of Experimental Neuropharmacology in Birmingham, England. The general theoretical background of the investigations was an early speculation by Bradley (1957) that LSD-25 has its main (alerting) effect on the brain, not through a direct influence on the arousal mechanisms as such, but indirectly by increasing the organism's responsiveness to environmental conditions. He considered that in this respect it differed from amphetamine which had a direct arousing effect on the brain. The evidence for this came from a study comparing the effects of the two drugs on the arousal thresholds (both EEG and behavioral) for direct reticular stimulation and externally applied auditory stimulation. It was demonstrated in cats that while amphetamine globally reduced thresholds for arousal, only that for auditorily applied stimuli was—markedly—affected by LSD, the threshold for direct brain stimulation being uninfluenced. Interestingly, thiopentone and chlorpromazine showed parallel differences, though of course in opposite directions, to those found for amphetamine and LSD-25.

The hypothesis derived from this study—that LSD appears somehow to selectively alter the filtering properties of the brain—was examined in a further experiment by Key (1965), again in the cat. He looked at the effect of the drug on fluctuations in the auditory evoked response recorded from the dorsal cochlear nucleus. Recordings were made under two conditions, while the animal was in a soundproofed box and after transfer to the noisier open laboratory. Key found that compared with a control period, LSD had no effect, as measured by the variability of the evoked response, when the animal was kept under stimulus-attenuated conditions. Under noisier conditions, however, the drug produced marked evoked response variability, indicating greatly increased sensitivity to environmental stimuli. This study is of particular interest in view of some recent reports, referred to in an earlier section, that schizophrenics show excessive variability of the evoked response, an observation interpreted along similar lines to the explanation offered by Key for his finding on LSD.

Finally, a third pair of studies by Key (1961 and 1964) is also relevant. Here he examined the effects of LSD-25 on sensory generalization in cats. In the first experiment the animals were taught a barrier-crossing avoidance response to an auditory stimulus (a pure tone). Generalization effects for tones of differing frequencies were then tested, comparisons being made between three conditions: LSD, chlorpromazine, and a saline control. The two drugs had opposite effects, LSD markedly increasing and chlorpromazine decreasing the amount of sensory generalization that occurred. Similar effects of LSD on generalization for visual stimuli were found in the later study which included a comparison with amphetamine. The latter drug also affected generalization, though only at the highest dose level, and even then the effect seemed to be dependent upon a general increase in responsiveness or arousal not evident under LSD. Key was led to conclude that LSD appears to act primarily by altering the level of significance or meaning that is attached to environmental events, thus causing the animal to respond to stimuli it would usually ignore. Although Key did not draw the parallel, there is clearly a close similarity between these data and their interpretation and those that have emerged out of schizophrenia research itself. That is particularly true of the work of Mednick (1958) who, as will be recalled, has based part of his own approach on a conditioned generalization view of the attention disorder in schizophrenia.

It seems therefore that there are a number of important ways in which LSD and schizophrenia research closely converge, so much so that in my view, LSD-25 still offers the most exact pharmacological equivalent to the natural disorder yet discovered. Its failure to be now recognized as such, apart from the reasons already given, appears to be due to the fact that the kinds of research data and theoretical interpretation—both about LSD and schizophrenia— emphasized here have rarely, if ever, been brought together within the same rubric of discussion. The pharmacological parallels sought in recent years have more often focused on alleged psychotomimetic effects of other drugs, notably amphetamine, and usually starting from a biochemical standpoint. To anyone familiar with the material presented here, that focus is actually somewhat surprising since amphetamine, by comparison with LSD, produces only a crude analogue of schizophrenia and even then only in very high doses in the human subject. It seems logical, on the other hand, if one is to pursue a pharmacological route into an animal model of schizophrenia, to choose a drug which produces the closest available parallel to the natural state. That drug, I believe, is still the remarkable, if sometimes cursed, psychedelic—LSD-25.

An animal research strategy using LSD-25

From the discussion so far two main conclusions can be reached. First, certain core features of schizophrenia appear to reflect disorder at a sufficiently "low level" in the central nervous system to be potentially reproducible in a non-human species. Secondly, LSD-25 has a number of effects which parallel those characteristics thought to be central to schizophrenia. The arguments for reviving the use of LSD as a method of inducing a "psychotic state" in an animal therefore seem very strong. The next problem to be considered is the selection of the optimum "marker behavior" for defining such a state objectively, before carrying out further analysis of its underlying physiological determinants. If one sets aside changes in gross behavior, which are difficult to define and measure reliably, the experimental literature already reviewed points to a number of possibilities. Thus, the changes in conditioned generalization and evoked response variability reported by Key might provide the basis for developing an appropriate index of the effects of LSD. Or changes in performance on attentional tasks might be considered. Another possibility would be derived from the "covariation" strategy outlined earlier. This would involve trying to map out the effect of LSD by examining changes in the interrelationship between some measure of ongoing tonic arousal and an index of perceptual sensitivity, say an evoked response correlate of two-flash threshold. That approach would have several advantages.

First, as we have seen, it has already worked in human subjects given LSD and the extrapolation to animals would be minimal.

Second, results obtained using the strategy in humans under LSD are empirically consistent with those found elsewhere in schizophrenia research.

Third, the particular phenomenon of altered covariation of function seems to occur only in the context of studies focusing on psychotic behavior, whether drug-induced or observed naturally in normal humans or schizophrenic patients. It therefore seems unique enough to warrant further neurophysiological investigation.

Fourth, the method is relatively "passive" and, unlike a paradigm based on conditioned generalization, for example, it would involve little prior training of an animal. This would be particularly true if an evoked response measure were substituted for the two-flash threshold index used so far in the human studies. The possibility of doing so is strongly supported by evidence that there are detectable visual evoked response correlates of two-flash discrimination in the cat (Lindsley 1957) and in the human subject (Andreassi et al. 1971 and Vaughan 1966).

Whatever the "marker behavior" chosen to define an LSD-induced state, the purpose of doing so in an animal subject would, of course, be to investigate its underlying mechanisms through further physiological manipulations. The possible focus for such manipulations raises many difficult questions and is perhaps the weakest link in the chain of arguments presented here. However, it is worth considering briefly some of the ways in which psychologists have recently been led to speculate about the neurophysiological basis of "input dysfunction" in schizophrenia. These ideas will be discussed in the final section.

Some physiological speculations

As indicated in a previous section, the early theorizing about schizophrenia indulged in by psychophysiologists was based on a very molar view of the nervous system—indeed it was scarcely physiological at all—and was descriptive rather than explanatory of the empirical data. The main conclusion that could be reached was that in schizophrenia there seems to be *something* wrong with both tonic and phasic aspects of arousal, perhaps due to a failure in the homeostatic regulatory mechanisms of the central nervous system and perhaps involving reticulocortical loops. Since that time speculation has become, if not less vague, at least more physiological; interest has converged on the hippocampus and, to a lesser extent, the amygdala as possible neural mediators of the attentional and arousal dysfunctions observed in schizophrenia. The definitive discussion of this hypothesis is a recent paper by Venables (1973) in which he attempts to bring up to date his earlier theorizing about schizophrenic "input dysfunction" (Venables 1964). In his later paper Venables draws a parallel between work on attention in schizophrenia and animal research on the hippocampus. In linking the two he quotes evidence that the hippocampus seems to be critically involved in attention, particularly through its role in "gating" or filtering sensory input (Douglas 1967, Douglas and Pribram 1966, and Kimble 1968). Venables further supports his argument with several other lines of evidence. The most convincing of these are the supposed selective action on the hippocampus of certain tranquilizing drugs (Killam, Killam, and Shaw 1957), the clinical similarity between schizophrenia and temporal lobe epilepsy (Flor-Henry 1969 and Slater and Beard 1963) and the appearance of schizophrenic-like symptoms in patients with hippocampal tumors (Malamud 1967).

Another psychophysiologist who has narrowed down on the hippocampus is Mednick (Mednick and Schulsinger 1973). He has done so on the basis of results emerging from his 20-year followup of the children of schizophrenic mothers, arguing for a similarity between the peculiarities of conditioning, extinction, and orientation found in his "sick group" and those observed in hippocampectomized animals. Admittedly his findings have not been replicated by more recent research (Mirdal et al. 1977), and in any case, as Kessler and Neale (1974) have recently pointed out, there are a number of flaws in Mednick's argument relating these abnormalities to birth trauma. However, failure of Mednick's anoxia hypothesis would not preclude the possibility that the hippocampus, through some subtle variation in its normal functioning, is critically involved in the attentional deficits observed in schizophrenia.

One particular feature of the hippocampus that may be of special interest in the present context concerns its supposed reciprocal relationship with the brainstem reticular formation (Redding 1967 and Vinogradova 1975). Variations in the feedback loop between these two structures have already been proposed as a possible physiological basis for certain normal personality characteristics (Gray 1970). In applying this model Gray has placed emphasis on variations arising from differences in the level of reticular arousal, the normal feedback properties of the loop being maintained. An entirely speculative, though not inconceivable, extension of the model is that alterations in the nature of reticulo-hippocampal feedback itself might give a physiological explanation of the failure of homeostasis postulated by Venables and myself to account for our findings of altered covariation between perceptual response and arousal in schizophrenia. Thus, it is perhaps not without interest that in theorizing some years ago about schizophrenia (Claridge 1967) I argued for the existence of two hypothetical systems whose functions were not dissimilar to those assigned to the hippocampus and ARAS. These were named at that time the "tonic arousal system" and the "arousal modulating system," the latter having a role in selective attention and also exerting an inhibitory influence over tonic arousal. It was hypothesized that schizophrenia was accompanied by a relative dissociation of these two mechanisms resulting from a partial failure or reversal of feedback between them. There is clearly some alignment between this molar theory and the more physiological model, developed with different emphasis and from a quite different point of view, by Gray. Taken in conjunction with evidence (Adey, Bell, and Dennis 1962) that LSD-25 disrupts hippocampal activity, abolishing its theta rhythm, these ideas might suggest a starting point for reexamining the underlying mechanisms of an LSD-induced psychotic state in animals and might eventually lead to a greater understanding of the neurophysiological basis of the natural disease in humans.

Postscript

The purpose of this paper has been to argue the case for reexamining LSD-25 as the basis for an animal model of schizophrenia. I think it is evident from the preceding discussion, however, that the conclusions reached emerged from an interdisciplinary view of research on schizophrenia and from a belief that continued progress in the area will only be possible if several different strategies, linked by a common conceptual thread, are used—simultaneously or by successively testing out on animals ideas generated in human research and vice versa. Of course, even if an animal model of schizophrenia is possible, it will be necessary to return, for our ultimate insight, to the schizophrenic patient; it is unlikely that animal research could provide a complete account of what, in some ways, *is* a peculiarly human disorder. If the arguments presented here are vindicated by the appropriate animal experimentation, it could well be that an important intermediate stage in understanding natural psychosis in man would be the revival of human research on LSD. As the example quoted earlier illustrates, particularly valuable might be further work on its psychophysiological effects, since psychophysiology occupies a crucial position as a bridging discipline within which to examine, in the intact human subject, the implications of direct studies of the brain. Such research could be—indeed may be preferably—done using extremely small doses of LSD sufficient to produce detectable physiological change but without the disruption of psychological control sometimes associated with the drug. Even so, in the present climate of opinion such a suggestion is undoubtedly controversial and raises many ethical questions. Although the present paper has provided no answers to those questions it has perhaps drawn attention to some of the scientific evidence which bears on their debate.

Summary

Some of the difficulties of trying to establish an animal model of schizophrenia are first considered. Then, after a review of the evidence on the experimental psychopathology of schizophrenia, particularly that concerned with attention and arousal, it is concluded that the core feature which needs to be modeled in animals is some aspect of "input dysfunction." It is argued that, of the pharmacological strategies, LSD-25 comes nearest to meeting that requirement, for two reasons. First, the phenomenology of an LSD "model psychosis" closely parallels that of the natural disease. Secondly, the experimental effects of the drug, both in animals and man, are very similar to or can be closely aligned theoretically with those of schizophrenia. An example is quoted from work in the author's laboratory where LSD was found to produce psychophysiological effects virtually identical to those observed occurring naturally in acute psychotic patients and in normal subjects high in "psychotic" personality traits. It is suggested that the rejection of LSD as a drug model was premature, especially as the currently popular preference for amphetamine has not been vindicated, either by the latter's ability to mimic an important central feature of the psychotic state or by work on dopamine as a specific common mediator of amphetamine psychosis and of schizophrenia.

Commentary

The argument that the covariation studies of two-flash threshold and electrodermal activity described truly tell us something interesting about the biology of psychosis would be considerably strengthened if a similar effect could be observed in psychotic patients. The next paper describes an investigation that tried to address that issue. The study protocol required that we test only patients who were not currently receiving and had not previously received any major (antipsychotic) tranquilisers. The problem of doing this has to be borne in mind. Testing unmedicated clinically psychotic patients on laboratory measures of the kind we were using was rarely done at that time, on both feasibility and ethical grounds. (I recall – digressing slightly – that this caused me to rant and rage at the hundreds of studies carried out by scientists on medicated schizophrenics that mostly generated, in my view, scientifically worthless results.)

As it turned out, from a practical viewpoint testing schizophrenics free of drugs proved to be not as difficult as we had thought it might be, or as the nurses and psychiatrists had gloomily predicted; so much so that one of the consultants on his ward round managed to forget that he had agreed to keeping one of his patients off medication for the several days required by our research! Although day-to-day management of the study was straightforward, the results it generated were quite messy with considerable intra- and inter-individual variability in the experimental measures. Some selection and statistical manipulation of data were necessary to demonstrate the sought-after covariation effect. Readers must judge for themselves whether we achieved our objective. In that regard it is fair to point out that many years ago Herrington and I had demonstrated a similar effect in a comparable group of young drug-naïve schizophrenics, on two quite different psychophysiological measures (Herrington and Claridge, 1965). We showed an unexpected *negative* correlation between the sedation threshold and the Archimedes spiral after-effect. The latter of course is an antique, arcane measure now scarcely mentioned; but the important point is that the comparison was between two particular things that seem crucial to demonstrating the covariation effect: one perceptual (spiral after-effect) and the other to do with general arousal (sedation threshold).

My own conclusion therefore is that the effect is a genuine phenomenon showing us something unusual about the 'psychotic' nervous system and, although the patient experiment reproduced here signalled the end of my study of it in human subjects, I have often mused about the interpretation of the effect. In doing so I have sometimes wondered whether the nature of the particular variables that seem to covary in such a peculiar way in psychosis is significant. Perhaps the form of the data and the kind of measures in which it is observed reflect psychophysiologically what Bleuler (1911/1950) regarded as a key feature of schizophrenia: the splitting or dissociation of cognition and affect.

7 Covariation between two-flash threshold and skin conductance level in first-breakdown schizophrenics

Relationships in drug-free patients and effects of treatment

Gordon Claridge and Kenneth Clark

In efforts to establish differences between psychopathological groups, it has sometimes been more informative to examine, not variations in a single experimental measure, but rather the way in which pairs of measures covary when they are plotted against, and correlated with, each other. This method of analysis has now been successfully applied to several disparate kinds of psychophysiological data: sedation threshold and Archimedes' spiral aftereffect (Krishnamoorti and Shagass, 1964; Herrington and Claridge, 1965), two-flash threshold and electrodermal activity (e.g., Venables, 1963), background electroencephalogram and evoked potential (Shagass et al., 1975), and, most recently, visual evoked potential augmenting-reducing in relation to both level of platelet monoamine oxidase activity (Haier et al., 1980) and tonic skin conductance (Birchall and Claridge, 1979).

To date, most research using this "covariation" method has focused on two-flash threshold and some index of electrodermal activity, following Venables' (1963) early finding that two-flash discrimination and skin potential level were correlated in opposite directions in normals and chronic nonparanoid schizophrenics. Subsequent attempts to replicate that observation were only partially successful, leading to equivocal, and sometimes contradictory, results (Lykken and Maley, 1968; Gruzelier et al., 1972; Gruzelier and Venables, 1975). However, in no case was a drug-free group of patients used—a surprising fact in view of the known effects of major tranquilizers on the two measures being studied (Gruzelier and Corballis, 1970; Spohn et al., 1970).

In addition to the complicating effects of drugs, there has also been disagreement about how to interpret those differences that have been found in schizophrenics. The controversy has concerned the exact form of the underlying relationship between two-flash threshold and electrodermal activity. The patient research carried out both by Venables and Gruzelier and by Lykken and his co-workers proceeded from the assumption that, in both schizophrenics and nonschizophrenics, the two measures are related in a curvilinear fashion, forming a conventional inverted-U; that is, perceptual discrimination is poor at low levels of skin potential (or conductance), it then rises to an optimum, and thereafter deteriorates again. Any differences observed between schizophrenics and others could then be explained by the fact that the groups being compared were, when tested, operating over different ranges of "arousal"; the extent and sign of correlations found between two-flash threshold and electrodermal level would thus merely reflect the section of the inverted-U curve being sampled in a particular group.

Starting from a slightly different empirical base, we have reached another conclusion. In an early attempt to establish a pharmacological model of Venables' (1963) original study of schizophrenic patients, we examined, in normal subjects, the effect of LSD-25 on the covariation between two-flash threshold and skin potential. The experiment clearly demonstrated (Claridge, 1972) that, while under placebo the basic form of the relationship between the two measures *was* an inverted-U, this was not so under LSD. There, although curvilinearity was maintained, the direction of the relationship was totally reversed and now formed a U-shaped function; that is, perceptual discrimination was worst in the mid-range of skin potential, being extremely good at either very low or very high levels.

Further evidence for this paradoxical U function was later found in a series of studies using a different strategy (Claridge and Chappa, 1973; Claridge and Birchall, 1973, 1978). In these studies, subjects were selected for high or low scores on the psychoticism (P) scale of an early version of the Eysenck Personality Questionnaire (EPQ), developed by Eysenck and Eysenck (1975) as a measure of psychotic traits in normal people. In subjects with high P scores, the relationship between two-flash threshold and, in this case, skin conductance followed the same U function as that found previously under LSD; the data for low P scorers formed a conventional inverted-U.

The present study was designed to test two related hypotheses arising from the previous work. The first concerned the form of the covariation between two-flash threshold and electrodermal level, when examined in schizophrenic patients who were drug free and who had not previously had major medication for a psychiatric illness. We predicted that the data in such patients would follow a U rather than, as surmised by others, an inverted-U function. The second hypothesis concerned the effects of subsequent medication on that relationship. Our expectation was that a U function would no longer be observed, though the exact form of the relationship could not be predicted with certainty; we therefore tested the null hypothesis that there would be no association between two-flash threshold and skin conductance in patients under medication. It should be emphasized that this second part of the study was not intended as an investigation of any specific form of drug treatment, no attempt being made to interfere with dose schedules or drug type. Our aim was merely to try to assess what effects the use of medicated patients might have had in previous studies of two-flash threshold and electrodermal activity in schizophrenics.

Method

Design. The overall design of the study involved the repeated testing of patients both before and during their treatment. Before treatment, the patients were tested daily, the first session being either the day of admission or the day afterwards. Our aim, to carry out at least three consecutive pretreatment test sessions, was achieved in all but two patients. During treatment, the testing days were not consecutive but occurred at intervals up to the patient's discharge from hospital or until continued testing was considered unlikely to add any further useful information. The length of time varied from 2 to 81 days. The number of times patients were tested during the first 3 weeks of treatment ranged from 1 to 6, averaging 3.9; all but one patient was seen at least twice.

Subjects. The total number of patients on whom some data were collected was 21, though only 20 patients were tested in the treatment phase. The patients represented, over the 2-year period of the project, the consecutive admissions for first-breakdown schizophrenia, with two restrictions. One was that patients be testable on the experimental procedures used. The other was that they meet our criteria for drug status on admission. In order to ensure the latter, every effort was made, through careful inquiry and close collaboration with the admitting agencies, to ascertain the recent history of patients selected. In this regard we were satisfied that no patient had previously received major tranquilizers, though the possible use of minor tranquilizers in some cases could not be ruled out. All of the patients had been given an unequivocal diagnosis of schizophrenia, agreed upon by at least two psychiatrists, one of whom was always the consultant in charge of the case; diagnosis was based on the narrow criteria for schizophrenia conventionally used in Scottish psychiatry, requiring the presence of first-rank symptoms. Eight of the 21 patients were male and 13 female; the mean age of the sample was 25.35 years, with a range from 16 to 42 years.

Of the 20 patients tested during treatment, all received some form of phenothiazine medication, in doses dictated by their clinical needs. In addition one patient was taking a mild tranquilizer, another haloperidol, and nine received a course of electroconvulsive therapy (ECT). In the last cases testing was avoided on the day of and the day after ECT. Nine patients were receiving some form of night sedation and eight an antiparkinson drug. The treatment regimes were therefore typical of those encountered by research workers in the United Kingdom.

Two-flash threshold. A Ferranti type CL-64 cathode tube, reduced in intensity with a Kodak neutral density filter and situated at eye-level 2.2 m from the subject, was used to determine the two-flash threshold. Paired light flashes, 5 msec in length, were presented every 6 seconds, the interflash interval being gradually altered in 2 msec steps. For each determination both an ascending and a descending series were used, the two-flash threshold on a particular occasion being the mean of an upper and a lower threshold. In the ascending series, starting from a point below the subject's approximate threshold, the interflash interval was increased until the subject changed his judgment from "one" to "flicker" on four consecutive presentations. The reverse procedure was used for the descending series.

Skin conductance. Throughout determinations of the two-flash threshold, skin resistance was continuously monitored on a Grass polygraph, using silver/silver chloride electrodes with a KCl electrolytic jelly, made up according to the formula recommended by Venables and Martin (1967). Electrodes were attached to the distal phalanx of the left index finger (active site) and to the ventral surface of the left forearm, approximately 10 cm above the wrist. During each estimation of the two-flash threshold, a resistance reading coinciding with both the upper and lower thresholds was read from the polygraph chart. The mean of the two readings was taken as the skin resistance level corresponding to that particular determination of the two-flash threshold. For presentation and analysis of results, resistance readings were converted to conductance units. All measurements were recorded in a sound-proofed, air-conditioned room maintained at a temperature of 20°C ± 1°C and a humidity of 40% ± 5%; the recording equipment itself was in an adjoining room.

Other measures. Shortly after a patient's admission the psychiatrist in charge was asked to complete a rating scale (Canter, 1972) covering three main characteristics: looseness of thinking, delusional thinking, and retardation of thought. The psychiatrist was also asked to list any other salient features of the patient's clinical state. Then, just before discharge from hospital, the patient was asked to complete two personality questionnaires, the Cattell 16 PF and the PEN inventory, the earlier version of Eysenck's new EPQ referred to above. For these two questionnaires, completed forms were obtained from 19 and 17 patients, respectively.

Experimental procedure. At the beginning of the first test session, a great deal of care was taken to reassure the patient and accustom him to the laboratory environment. After attachment of the electrodes, the two-flash threshold task was explained and a trial run attempted. In most cases this was sufficient, and once it was clear that the patient had grasped the procedure the first determination proper was made. Our aim was to obtain four such determinations in all, separated by a rest of 5 minutes. It was not always possible to do so; nor was it always possible to adhere to a strict interval between determinations. However, even in the exceptional cases, at least two estimations of the two-flash threshold were made. On subsequent occasions, when the same experimental procedure was followed, these difficulties did not arise because of the patients' greater familiarity with the laboratory. Throughout testing, however, one of the experimenters usually remained with the patient in order to continue reassurance and to ensure his cooperation with the two-flash threshold task.

Results

Pretreatment phase. For each session on which a patient had been tested, a single value for the two-flash threshold and its corresponding skin conductance level was calculated, by averaging the several readings obtained on that occasion. Since the electrodermal data were to be considered in both raw and range-corrected form, the latter transformation was additionally applied to all of the skin conductance values, following the method described by Lykken (1975); the minimum and maximum readings on which this range-correction was based were those reached by the patient at any time during the pretreatment phase. With the exception of the two patients who were tested only once, there were therefore up to four sets of two-flash threshold data and four sets of skin conductance readings, both raw and range-corrected. However, since only three patients went on to a fourth day of testing, those data were not included in the final analysis. The results to be presented concern the covariation between two-flash threshold and skin conductance level for data collected over 3 successive days of testing, the sample sizes for sessions 1, 2, and 3 being 21, 19, and 14, respectively.

Examination of the data in plotted form for each of the sessions taken separately revealed a bunching of two-flash threshold readings over restricted ranges of skin conductance, first in the lower and later in the upper range. This phenomenon meant that on any particular session there were too few readings covering the full range of electrodermal activity to test the covariation hypothesis adequately. It was therefore decided to pool the data for all three sessions, giving a total n of 54 two-flash threshold and skin conductance readings.

Calculating product moment correlations for the data in this form revealed a small negative association between two-flash threshold and raw skin conductance, r being -0.28 ($p < 0.05$); the corresponding value using range-corrected skin conductance was 0.07 (NS). A correlation ratio calculated on the latter data was, however, significant, eta being 0.52 ($p < 0.01$); using raw skin conductance readings eta was not significant, its value being 0.18. This initial analysis suggested therefore that, for range-corrected skin conductance at least, there was a significant departure from linearity. In order to examine its exact form, these data were then subjected to quadratic regression analysis (Table 7.1).

The analysis was carried out, not only for the total sample of subjects, but also for two subsets of patients called the "long delay" and "short delay" groups. Before examining the results in detail, it is necessary to comment briefly on the reasons for this further breakdown of the data. It had been observed during the course of the analysis that the patients fell naturally into two subgroups: those who were treated very quickly after admission (7 patients) and those in whom treatment was delayed much longer (14 patients). The intervals before treatment for these short delay and long delay patients differed markedly, and significantly; the mean times were, respectively, 2.4 days (range 1–3 days) and 5.3 days (range 3–9 days), t being 3.70 ($p < 0.005$). Subsequently, it was also found that the two groups differed in a number of clinical and personality characteristics. Although short delay and long delay patients did not differ on the thought disorder ratings given by psychiatrists,

Table 7.1 Pretreatment quadratic regression analysis: Two flash threshold (y) against range-corrected skin conductance level (x)

Subjects	Correlation (y against x^2)	Regression equation
Total group	$r = -0.22$ $n = 54$ NS	$y = 54.9 + 81x - 81x^2$
Long delay group	$r = -0.42$ $n = 42$ $p < 0.01$	$y = 39.5 + 156x - 156x^2$
Short delay group	$r = +0.24$ $n = 12$ NS	$y = 51.5 - 78x + 78x^2$

the psychiatrists' spontaneous comments more often referred to the short delay as being overactive, of labile mood, aggressive, and so on. Only 1 of the 14 long delay patients was described in that way. Furthermore, inspection of the personality data—collected at the end of the project—revealed that, when the appropriate scales from the Eysenck and Cattell questionnaires were combined, long delay patients were significantly more introverted (joint probability less than 5%). Subdivision of the sample in this way therefore seemed to have some, albeit *post hoc*, validity and, as eventually turned out to be the case, appeared to be worth preserving in analyzing the psychophysiological data.

Returning to Table 7.1, it can be seen that for the total group the linear correlation (y against x^2) derived from the quadratic regression analysis was negative in sign—indicating a U-shaped parabola—but it was not significant. However, inspection of the separate analyses for the long and short delay subgroups indicates why this was so: in the former the data did conform significantly to a parabolic U, whereas in the latter the trend was, if anything, in the opposite direction, though not significant.[1]

In summary, then, the pretreatment covariation between two-flash threshold and range-corrected skin conductance level in this sample of schizophrenics was, as expected, significantly curvilinear. However, its exact form, considered over the group as a whole, was complex—the predicted U-shaped function appearing only in patients from the long delay group. In the latter, our hypothesis was

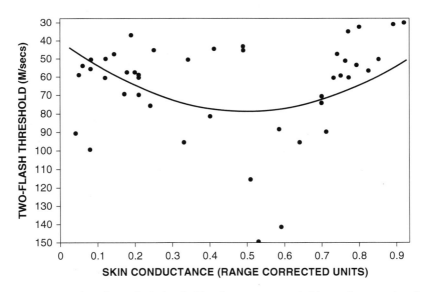

Figure 7.1 Plotted two-flash threshold and range-corrected skin conductance data for long delay patients, combining 3 days of testing.

Note: Drawn curve is derived from equation shown in Table 7.1 and illustrates the U form of the function (two-flash readings are plotted so that changes in an upward direction indicate *low* threshold, i.e., improved discrimination).

confirmed, the data following a parabola in which improved perceptual discrimination appeared to be associated with both low and high levels of electrodermal activity (Figure 7.1).

Treatment phase. In a comparable analysis of the treatment phase of the experiment, pooling of the data was again considered advisable; range-correction of the skin conductance readings was not undertaken, however, since the transformation seemed inappropriate. Because the number of testing sessions and their timing varied considerably in different patients during this phase, it was felt necessary, in selecting data for pooling, to choose roughly equivalent points after treatment had begun. This was done by taking a 6-day interval and, beyond the first session, considering only data collected on, or as near as possible to, the 6th, 12th, and 18th days after the start of each patient's treatment. This gave a total of 62 two-flash threshold and (raw) skin conductance readings on which covariation analysis could be based. Initial statistical tests with product moment correlations and correlation ratios indicated that, with one exception, there was no systematic relationship— either linear or curvilinear— between the two variables during the treatment phase. The exception was a significant value for *eta* (0.67, $p < 0.05$, $n = 23$) in the short delay patients. However, quadratic regression analysis of the data for this group was nonsignificant, indicating, as did visual inspection of the plotted scores, that whatever curvilinear relationship existed was clearly complex and different from the inverted-U function seen in the pretreatment phase.

When the psychophysiological measures were considered individually, they showed considerable and rather complex changes over the course of the experiment, especially in the treatment phase. Trends in the data across time are shown in Tables 7.2 and 7.3. One interesting feature (Table 7.2) was the unexpected *rise* in average skin conductance level before treatment; unexpected because a fall in this measure of "autonomic arousal" might have been anticipated in patients who appeared to become habituated to the experimental setting and to become clinically more accessible.[2] During treatment, this upward trend in skin conductance was sharply reversed, especially in the short delay group. As seen in Table 7.3, two-flash threshold also showed marked changes, though somewhat different in the short and long delay groups: in the former, discrimination worsened considerably just before treatment and remained relatively unchanged thereafter; in the latter, it progressively deteriorated over the course of the experiment. Finally, it can be seen that, reflecting the variability in the data, there were great fluctuations in the variance of both measures at different points before and during treatment.

Discussion

It is evident from the results of this investigation that the failure in previous similar studies to control for the effects of treatment on their schizophrenic samples was indeed a serious methodological error. That must partly account for the conflicting results obtained and the misleading conclusions drawn from earlier attempts to establish the exact form of the relationship between two-flash threshold and electrodermal level in schizophrenia. Even in drug-free patients, the underlying function

Table 7.2 Means and variances of skin conductance (micromhos) before and during treatment in total sample and in short and long delay groups

Subjects	Pretreatment			Treatment days			
	1	2	3	1	6	12	18
Total sample							
n	21	19	14	20	20	18	18
Mean	6.30	7.05	8.75	7.27	6.73	6.60	6.20
Variance	6.31	10.23	29.47	15.68	6.94	10.94	5.62
Short delay group							
n	7	5	—	7	7	7	7
Mean	6.34	7.38	—	8.50	7.07	5.78	5.90
Variance	7.30	10.00	—	25.50	9.61	15.20	6.80
Long delay group							
n	14	14	14	13	13	11	11
Mean	6.57	6.90	8.75	6.60	6.54	7.20	6.31
Variance	7.30	10.90	29.47	10.70	5.10	8.60	5.32

Table 7.3 Means and variances of two-flash threshold (msec) before and during treatment in total sample and in short and long delay groups

Subjects	Pretreatment days			Treatment days			
	1	2	3	1	6	12	18
Total sample							
n	21	19	14	20	20	18	18
Mean	63.9	71.9	67.6	79.8	81.5	91.2	99.0
Variance	269	634	1117	1302	1446	1721	3754
Short delay group							
n	7	5	—	7	7	7	7
Mean	74.3	103.0	—	84.3	84.2	85.5	89.9
Variance	233	2567	—	1474	1474	876	1289
Long delay group							
n	14	14	14	13	13	11	11
Mean	61.4	65.2	67.5	77.4	79.9	94.9	103.9
Variance	325	356	1117	1300	1176	2440	5270

relating the two measures together was not easy to discover, partly, we believe, because of the inherent instability of the psychotic state, reflected here in the large individual shifts and group variances for both psychophysiological indices. Adding the heterogeneous effects of treatment must inevitably confound the relationship even further. Our findings confirm that where a systematic association can be observed, it is certainly curvilinear and follows the U-shaped function predicted from our earlier research. That conclusion requires the proviso that the U function was evident only in the larger group of patients whom we designated "long delay" and who were clinically less emotionally responsive and more introverted in basic personality. The different pattern observed in the data for short delay patients is open to at least two interpretations. One is that they represented a psychophysiologically distinct subset of psychotics. Another is that their psychophysiological response reflected the residual effects of drugs administered, unknown to us, before admission. Three facts argue in favor of the former rather than the latter explanation. First, we in fact have no evidence that the drug status of short delay patients on admission was any more or less doubtful than that of long delay patients. Secondly, when the patients were actually known to be under the influence of drugs, the experimental measures behaved in a markedly different way from that seen in the short delay patients during the pretreatment phase. Thirdly, the fact that a U-shaped relationship between skin conductance and perceptual response was confined to the more introverted long delay patients is consistent with other recent evidence pointing in the same direction. Thus, reexamination of our own earlier data on two-flash threshold and skin conductance in normal subjects who had high scores on the Eysenck psychoticism scale revealed that a U-shaped relationship between the two measures is evident only in the more introverted members of the sample (Claridge, in press). The same observation has been made by Robinson (personal communication) who, at our suggestion, reanalyzed data from a similar study by Robinson and Zahn (1979); while we (Claridge, in press) also obtained a result consistent with both of those findings using augmenting-reducing of the visual evoked potential, instead of a two-flash threshold, as a measure of perceptual responsiveness. There are several indicators therefore that the psychoses may be heterogeneous with respect to the phenomenon researched here, its appearance being especially associated with the simultaneous presence of introverted personality traits; that may be another reason for previously conflicting results.

Finally, the relevance of these results for explanatory models of psychosis deserves brief comment. Studies using the covariation strategy in either clinical or normal samples all seem to agree in two respects. First, the measures successfully covaried are always indices, on the one hand, of perceptual or sensory response and, on the other, of tonic arousal. Secondly, where psychosis or some degree of "psychoticism" is implicated, the direction of covariation always takes an unusual form, similar to that observed here. This consensus confirms a suggestion made some years ago (Claridge, 1967, 1972) that what the covariation strategy may be tapping are different "styles" of central nervous system (CNS) organization, predisposed to different kinds of disorder, and that schizophrenia represents, in pathological form, a relative failure of CNS homeostasis associated especially with altered regulation over sensory input. It is of particular interest, therefore, that one of the most recent attempts (Haier et al., 1980) to apply the covariation strategy—to augmenting-reducing and level of platelet monoamine oxidase activity—gave rise to the similar notion of an "unbalanced" nervous type, describing individuals who show certain psychophysiologically unstable combinations of the two measures and who look as though they may be at greater risk for psychiatric breakdown.

Acknowledgments

The study described was carried out while the authors were staff members of the University of Glasgow, Department of Psychological Medicine, Southern General Hospital, Glasgow, Scotland. Grateful thanks are due to the patients and to the psychiatric and nursing staff who cooperated in the project.

Notes

1 This trend toward an inverted-U relationship in short delay patients was significant when their skin conductance data were considered in their raw form. However, further regression analysis using raw skin conductance revealed no other significant relationships and is therefore not presented here.
2 It was this progressive rise in skin conductance over days which, as observed earlier, prevented a proper test of our pretreatment hypothesis for the full electrodermal range; patients almost all tended to fall in the low range on the first day and to shift mainly into the high range by the third day. However, it is worth noting, as reported elsewhere (Claridge, 1978), that when considered separately, the first-day data for low range patients very strongly and at a very high level of significance defined the lower arm of a U function, thus providing additional support for our hypothesis.

Commentary

Although my interest in what I called the covariation effect waned after the patient study, I continued to be fascinated by LSD, fuelled mainly by annoyance that such a powerful drug model for psychosis had been ignored for so long by the scientific Establishment. I therefore felt it was worth reproducing here a paper I wrote expressing this view. The paper is somewhat out of sequence, being published nearly twenty years after my original excursion into LSD research. But the story it tells is, I believe, still valid and chronicles a wasted era in neuroscience pursuing flawed biological and animal models of schizophrenia, for purely sociocultural reasons.

8 LSD
A missed opportunity?

Gordon Claridge

Introduction

The textbook history of LSD will be familiar to most readers of this journal [*Human Psychopharmacology*]: its synthesis, as d-Lysergic acid diethylamide, in 1938 in the Sandoz Laboratories; Hofmann's stumbling, five years later, on the weird mental effects of the substance; the excitement in psychiatry at the fortuitous discovery of what promised to be a powerful chemical key to human psychosis; the expressed disillusionment with that; the relatively short life of LSD as a legal drug; and finally its banishment to the dubious margins of society, where it has remained ever since—joined, indeed overtaken, by other newer 'psychedelics' (as they were once called). Beneath that account, however, there is another story—one which the Editor asked me to try to piece together, following some remarks I made about LSD during an interview that he published in a previous issue (Claridge and Healy, 1994). My comments concerned the failure of LSD to catch on as a drug model for psychosis, despite its manifest superiority to the more favoured amphetamine (dopamine) paradigm. I should add that in discussing the question here the emphasis will not be so much on arguing the case for LSD: this was done in an early paper of my own (Claridge, 1978) and later by Fischman (1983) in a more comprehensive review of phenomenological and pharmacological evidence. Although occasionally drawing on those discussions and some later evidence, the present paper will concentrate rather more on the reasons for the neglect of LSD.

The gist of the story can be summed up in a single question: How could it possibly have come about that a drug which even commonsense tells us can turn us temporarily crazy—and which pharmacologists actually labelled 'psychotomimetic' and 'hallucinogenic'—failed at a certain point to continue to have at least *some* scientific interest for those seeking to understand naturally occurring forms of madness? (Here for 'drug' we could of course substitute 'drugs' and include other psychotomimetics such as mescaline, but it is LSD that spearheaded the downfall of the line of enquiry to which I am referring.) The ostensible scientific reasons, to be discussed later, are well-rehearsed and, taken individually and without much further thought, might appear to be convincing; they have certainly been happily accepted and reiterated by several generations of clinicians and basic researchers. Then there have been the practical constraints imposed on research by criminalization of LSD: this was bound to stifle the opportunity and motivation to work on the drug.

Nevertheless, the ignoring of LSD might still seem remarkable to an external, but informed, observer. The legal restrictions were always less problematical for animal research; while, on the human side, even before the official proscription of LSD a not inconsiderable amount of information on its effects had accumulated. Here I am referring not to experiential and clinical data—which of course have been profusely documented—but to laboratory studies covering a wide range of physiological and behavioural phenomena, including sensation, perception, psychomotor performance, and EEG and autonomic functioning. As early as 1960 such evidence—alongside reference to the pharmacodynamics of LSD—figured prominently in, for example, Uhr and Miller's edited book, *Drugs and Behaviour*, and the same themes were elaborated by Leavitt (1974) in his later volume of the same name. So, even with the possibility of further human research ruled out, there was already a body of knowledge about LSD available for interested scientists to draw upon, had they wished to try to sketch out an albeit rudimentary model for psychosis. But the majority chose not to do so and that particular line of thought, together with the studies that might have supported it, sank out of sight and are rarely, if ever, referred to in the contemporary literature.

As a background to understanding why this happened, we first need to examine briefly the clinical concept of psychosis and how differences and changes in viewpoint about it have influenced basic research in the area. The debate has been mostly conducted, as it will be here, with reference to schizophrenia. However, one issue, itself contentious but relevant to the LSD story, should be mentioned (it will occasionally be returned to): according to some opinion there is only an arbitrary distinction to be made between schizophrenia and other, affective, forms of psychotic disorder and a common theory might account for both.

The psychiatric background

The history of schizophrenia research is a history of controversy. The most enduring point at issue—and the one at the nub of many of the other disputes—concerns the relative emphasis to be placed on the psychology, as compared with the biology, of the disorder. This question has been formulated in a number of different ways and discussed with varying degrees of polarized opinion; but it still continues (for a contemporary version of the debate see *Journal of Mental Health* 1993). The argument reached its most furious in the 1960s and early 1970s, with the presence of the school of so-called 'radical psychiatry', represented in Britain in the writings of R. D. Laing (1960) and his followers. Laing's (and others') exclusively sociopsychological account of schizophrenia, as a disorder originating in family dynamics, was revolutionary in two respects. First, it was political in a general sense, challenging the existing social order on behalf of individuals whom others had previously labelled as ill but who, by now having their odd experiences legitimized, felt themselves to be liberated in their deviance. Secondly, it threatened an Establishment psychiatry which at that point was, paradoxically, broadminded in its approach to mental illness, but thereby weak in alternatives: although neuroleptics and other physical treatments were in routine use and biological (including genetic) investigations of schizophrenia already had a long history, there was no sense that a systematic nervous system theory of psychosis existed.

LSD (and other hallucinogens) formed, of course, a seamlessly joined part of that era. Thanks to Laing, the existentialist preoccupations of the schizophrenic and of the LSD-tripper were alike since, after all, their mental states were sometimes indistinguishable; at least they were similar enough often enough for some psychiatrists and clinical psychologists to take LSD (as I did) in order to try to get some feel for the inner world of their psychotic patients. It is true that psychiatry, in the interests of a neat nosology, tried and still tries to make a formal distinction between LSD psychosis and acute schizophrenia; but this has never seemed very convincing and has little factual basis (Vardy and Kay, 1983). In the same vein, but for another purpose—arguing against LSD as a suitable drug model in research—it has been persistently stated that there are crucial differences in phenomenology; *viz.* that LSD produces largely visual, and acute schizophrenia largely auditory, effects. As both Fischman (1983) and I myself (Claridge, 1978) pointed out, this too is flatly contradicted by the evidence. Taken in isolation the mistake is relatively trivial, but it nevertheless assumed considerable force as a piece of received wisdom in subsequent attempts by psychiatry to distance itself from LSD and other hallucinogens.

When it came, the backlash against the radical movement was brutal, as psychiatry entered its present thoroughly organic phase and strong biological theories of the psychotic states were reasserted. Considering the implications for the progress of LSD (which by the late 1960s had been banned in Britain), it is scarcely possible after several decades to determine the precise motivations and directions of causation in the events that occurred. But it is also difficult to believe that the sidelining of LSD did not cause some sighs of relief in certain quarters of conventional psychiatry. With emphasis constantly being placed on the drug's mind-altering qualities LSD had always raised awkward questions about what should be regarded as the valid data for study in schizophrenia and the other psychoses. In this respect it is instructive to note that Fischman's defence of LSD ranged widely, attempting an integration of material as far apart as neuropharmacology and ego-psychology. Yet when it appeared in 1983 his remarkable article would already have seemed time-warped to the unsympathetic: such conceptualizations did not sit easily in a discipline which by then was well on the way to defining its subject matter in objective medical terms and, in the case of the psychoses, as diseases of a neurological type. (This retreat from the psychological should not be underrated and has recently led to some realization that psychiatry's neglect of the schizophrenic's subjective experience has gone too far (*Schizophrenia Bulletin*, 1989).)

Another consequence of the more forceful organic style that developed in psychiatry, and which is relevant here, concerns the narrowing of the boundaries used to delineate different psychotic disorders. This was particularly true in the United States where—reflecting the strong influence of psychological formulations of the disorder—a very broad definition of schizophrenia had held sway; it was considerably pared down when revising the *Diagnostic and Statistical Manual (DSM)* into its third edition (American Psychiatric Association, 1980). In Britain the definition had always been more circumscribed, but this was now emphasized more, in keeping with the strict formulation of schizophrenia as a discrete disease entity which, it was hoped, might prove to have a single identifiable cause. As it has turned out, this has not so far been the case; furthermore even the differentiation of schizophrenia from affective psychosis has again recently been challenged on several fronts (Kendell, 1991; Taylor, 1992). But, at the time, the idea that was emerging—of a more restrictive, organically based view of schizophrenia—was an appropriate antidote to the open, wishy-washy psychiatric thinking with which LSD was inevitably associated. The suggestion in basic research that there might be an appropriately matching, straightforward drug model for schizophrenia, without the embarrassing complications of LSD, was a godsend to this new psychiatry.

Choosing a drug model: amphetamine versus LSD

The events related above form only one theme in the story of the abandonment of LSD. On the scientific front the search for a cause of schizophrenia in some form of brain dysfunction has gone on for most of this century and the use of LSD as a vehicle for conducting such enquiry forms the serious side of the history of the drug. Such research was carried out much in the spirit already outlined, *viz.* with hope of discovering a single neurophysiological or neurochemical aberration that could account for the symptoms of schizophrenia. Indeed, very early on the answer seemed to be signalled, in Woolley and Shaw's (1954) proposal— leading to the 'serotonin hypothesis'—that LSD blocked 5HT receptors in the brain. But it was the alternative 'dopamine hypothesis' that won the day, to become the standard biochemical explanation of the aetiology of schizophrenia. The timing of the appearance of this model, compared with the 5HT theory, is probably significant. Developed more than a decade later, it did not get into its full stride for some time, making the *Schizophrenia Bulletin*—the serialised guidebook for workers in the area—by 1976 (Meltzer and Stahl, 1976); in other words, at the optimum point to feed into psychiatry's new organic phase. Since the latter coincided with increased efforts to discover improved antipsychotic medications, it was also natural that the dopamine theory should be extensively examined—and substantially developed— within a pharmacological context, utilizing a drug-based animal model of schizophrenia. The choice of amphetamine for this purpose henceforth defined a major research strategy for workers in the field.

On the face of it, the arguments for the amphetamine/dopamine model are logically watertight, being based on several apparently mutually supportive assumptions about the reciprocal dopaminergic and behavioural effects of amphetamine and of the neuroleptic drugs. The neurochemical link here is beyond dispute; but close inspection shows the rationale elsewhere to be quite flawed. The most obvious point is a simple one about 'ecological validity'—a concept from psychology which, roughly translated, denotes the extent to which a laboratory phenomenon has a convincing reference point in the real world. Judged by this criterion, amphetamine has poor ecological validity: the drug is not a natural psychotomimetic and, although capable of producing some limited features of schizophrenia in human subjects, it generally does so only in large doses and/or chronic usage and perhaps even then only in the predisposed. (As David Healy pointed out in our interview, women took it for years as a slimming aid, without it apparently causing any great problems.) Finding behavioural equivalents of schizophrenia in amphetamine-treated animals is therefore bound to be strained. By comparison, the excellent ecological validity of LSD can even be discovered in the spontaneous comments made by animal researchers on the behaviour of their subjects administered the drug. Here are two examples. The first is taken from Jacobs and Trulson (1979) who, discussing the possible consequences of LSD on serotonergic neurons, note: '... [that it] consistently produces an animal that is hypersensitive to virtually all environmental stimuli and hyperactive in virtually all situations. Through a general inhibitory function, serotonin neurons may serve to modulate an organisms's behavior and *maintain it within narrowly specified limits*' [my italics].

The second example is a remark made by Key (1961) in one of a number of early papers emanating from the Birmingham University neuropharmacology group, which in the late 1950s and early 1960s conducted a series of unique LSD experiments with cats. In the study in question Key examined the effect on discrimination and sensory generalization; he concluded that unlike amphetamine (examined elsewhere (Key, 1964)): '... LSD 25 is able to alter the level of significance or meaningfulness of stimuli, thereby producing an increased amount of generalization.... the level of significance of sensory information is altered [and] ... distortions of perception may occur, for the animal now responds, pays attention or arouses to stimuli which normally would not produce such an effect.'

What is remarkable about these observations is the extent to which they chime with the theoretical and clinical focus of schizophrenia research at the time (Venables, 1964; McGhie, 1969). Yet they appear to have been made in ignorance of that work; at least the authors include no reference to the relevant human literature—or even, in the case of Key, to schizophrenia!

Another, rarely voiced, criticism of the amphetamine/dopamine model concerns the assumed unequivocal therapeutic action of the neuroleptic drugs in schizophrenia. This crucially underpins the model; yet it can be challenged on two grounds. First is the well-documented failure of a proportion (up to 25 per cent) of schizophrenics to respond to conventional neuroleptics, coupled to carefully researched data that in some cases non-neuroleptic treatment might actually signify better long-term outcome (Matthews *et al.*, 1979). Secondly there is the evidence, discussed for example by Healy (1990) and confirmed in the introspective reports of patients themselves, that the so-called antipsychotics do not actually have much of their primary influence on the central 'positive' symptoms of schizophrenia (e.g. those reliably induced by LSD); where these are mitigated it appears to be through secondary effects on more general mood and motoric symptoms.

There is the impression, then, that the amphetamine/dopamine model has always had an illusory precision and that the preference for amphetamine over truer psychotomimetics was always an uneasy compromise between social acceptability and intellectual rigour. On the scientific side, the choice seems to have been partly dictated by the simultaneous existence of the dopamine hypothesis, leading to some circularity of reasoning when combining the various assumptions into an integrated theory. It should be added that such criticisms are now being preempted by the emergence of a more broadly based approach to the neurochemistry of psychotic disorder; this has brought with it the virtual demise of the simplistic version of the dopamine hypothesis, which is now coming under fire as an exclusive biochemical account of schizophrenia (Lieberman and Koreen, 1993). Part of the impetus for the change has come from work on the atypical antipsychotic drugs, covering a range of new compounds (Gerlach, 1991). The therapeutic effectiveness of some of these substances (e.g. clozapine) cannot be solely attributed to their blockade of dopamine (D2) receptors in the meso-limbic system—the traditionally proposed mechanism for antipsychotic drug action and one which, as Meltzer (1991) points out, has been 'a basic tenet of neuropsychopharmacology for more than three decades.' The search for alternative routes to clinical efficacy therefore now includes the study of other neurotransmitter systems, among them 5HT; indeed, ironically for the ageing advocates of LSD, serotonin is assuming a revived importance in schizophrenia and other mental health research (Bleich *et al.*, 1988; Leonard, 1994).

Given the limitations of the original amphetamine/dopamine model, it might be asked why it survived for as long as it did. Perhaps the main scientific reason is that an inexact theory is better than none, and work inspired by the paradigm did help to establish beyond doubt that a disturbance of brain dopamine is implicated in psychotic disorder. This in itself was a major achievement, even though the success might not be attributable to any unique specificity of the model, as a theory either of psychosis or of drug treatment: such a 'hit' might have been inevitable anyway, given the rôle of dopamine in those (limbic) brain areas which mediate general emotional and attentional processes known to be disturbed in most mental illnesses, including schizophrenia. It is also possible that, once the model was formulated, it was necessary to pursue a single-minded track in schizophrenia research, as a necessary precursor to developing more elaborate theories. Scientists were no doubt helped in this endeavour by the narrow disease mentality that, as noted earlier, increasingly pervaded psychiatry and didactically influenced the style and aims of basic research on serious mental disorder. Thus, the notion of schizophrenia as a single cause organic disease did not encourage looking beyond the predefined boundaries of possible aetiology. Nor did it indicate a need to bring to bear on laboratory data any insight into the clinical features of the disorder being studied: few experimental neuroscientists will ever have talked to a schizophrenic. Had they done so, they might have been struck sooner by the limitations of the models they were using, including, in drug research, their pharmacological strategies.

As it was, it took others outside the main axis of influence in schizophrenia research to challenge some preconceptions in the field and establish an alternative line of thinking about the nature of psychosis. Originating in a convergence of clinical, personality, and experimental psychology it has within it only a very narrow thread concerned with drugs, and an even narrower one relating to the present topic. Nevertheless it needs to be considered, as part of the LSD story.

An alternative construction of psychosis

Simultaneously with the Laingian revisionism of the 1960s, another, less advertised, challenge to orthodox psychiatric thinking began to emerge. Also opposed to the medical model and to constructions of psychological disorders as simple neurological diseases, in other respects it differed entirely from the radical psychiatry movement. Contrary to the latter's emphasis on sociopsychological causes, explanations of disorder were thoroughly biological. However, unlike organic psychiatry, accounts of mental illness were formulated, not as discrete pathophysiology, but as extreme aberrations of central nervous system processes considered responsible for normal temperament or personality: the dimensionality between normal and abnormal, at both behavioural and biological levels, was therefore a central feature. Eysenck (1967), as a pioneer in this approach, applied it initially to the less serious psychological disorders and only later, and on a broader theoretical front, was it used to encompass the psychoses, including schizophrenia. Now, as a perspective on the latter it comprises a significant body of knowledge coming under the heading of 'schizotypy (or, more generally, psychosis-proneness) research.' Here schizotypy refers to a set of biological, cognitive, and personality traits, capable of being present in healthy individuals, but otherwise predisposing to psychosis; it has been and is currently being extensively investigated from many points of view, including the genetic, the psychometric, and the experimental (for reviews see Claridge, 1987, 1994a; Meehl, 1990; Raine et al., 1995).

Several other features of this theoretical approach need to be stated, in order to underscore the differences between the medical and experimental psychological positions. First, it is important to emphasize the latter's essentially *psychobiological* view of psychiatric illness (Claridge, 1994b). This means that, in psychotic disorder for example, the subjective state assumes as much importance as the biology for constructing theoretical models or choosing research strategies; hence the significance placed earlier on ecological validity in comparing LSD and amphetamine as drug models. Secondly, unlike discrete disease theories, there is no commitment to the idea of single causes leading to discontinuous illness states. On the contrary, a necessary precondition for understanding the biology of psychosis would be an understanding of the biology of 'psychosis-proneness' as a confluence of individually normal personality traits. These, it is accepted, are likely to be multiply determined; so that, with respect to the neurochemistry, the idea of anything other than a complexly interacting system would be quite foreign. In the same vein, drug manipulations are mostly seen as serving to test out macroscopic theories, the detailed biochemistry of which is, for the moment, necessarily somewhat sketchy; more important is the perceived 'match' between the drug used and the individual differences (normal and abnormal) under investigation. Here drugs offer a complementary way of exploring otherwise naturalistically occurring biological variations.

For obvious reasons, testing out such ideas with respect to psychosis, by administering LSD to human subjects, is rare. But in my 1978 article, arguing the case for LSD as an animal model, I quoted an example that formed part of my own early work on the psychophysiology of schizophrenia. Details are contained in the original paper and the references cited there, but the basic observations were as follows. From a series of laboratory experiments utilizing measures of perceptual sensitivity and of general arousal we had concluded that an unusual, and perhaps unique, feature of the psychotic nervous system is a degree of 'dissociation' of function, possibly stemming from relatively weak homeostatic regulation. The empirical evidence for this proposal was a peculiar profile observed on the psychophysiological measures we were using; such that, different from control comparisons, the degree of sensory responsiveness was out of keeping with the subject's prevailing level of physiological activation; e.g. a very high sensitivity to visual stimuli could occur in conjunction with very low tonic arousal. The effect was demonstrated in acute untreated schizophrenic patients, normal subjects high in psychotic traits, and, subsequently, schizophrenics' relatives (Claridge *et al.*, 1985). It was also exactly reproducible in human volunteers under LSD (but not dexamphetamine).

At the end of the 1978 article I concluded that the 'arguments for reviving the use of LSD as a method of inducing a "psychotic state" in an animal therefore seems strong.' However, it was some years before the opportunity arose to pursue that idea—in the monkey, using as a 'marker' behaviour a measure of the 'dissociation' between arousal and sensory sensitivity previously observed in our human subjects. The eventual paper reporting the substantive part of that work remained in the drawer (Claridge *et al.*, unpublished), after several failed attempts at publication—not, I hasten to add, in this journal! The present Editor has agreed to indulge my vanity by agreeing to the inclusion here of a 'paper-within-a-paper' summary of that report, as a logical sequel to and illustrative example of the earlier case I made for LSD as an animal model.

An LSD effect in the monkey

The subject was a male cynomolgus monkey in whom two psychophysiological indices were recorded. Sensory responsiveness was assessed with an EEG visual evoked potential (VEP) procedure once widely used in schizophrenia research and successfully employed in one of our human experiments referred to above (Claridge *et al.*, 1985). It consists of examining stable individual differences and state variations in the relationship between VEP amplitude and the intensity of the evoking flash stimuli. In the present instance EEG was recorded between electrodes implanted on the dura and positioned at sites corresponding to the human C_z (vertex reference) and O_z placements. VEPs (P_1–N_1 amplitudes) were obtained by averaging over 32 stimulus presentations at each of five flash intensities, *viz.*

6.3, 8.7, 13.5, 18.4, and 37.0 foot-lamberts. In order to sustain attention during VEP measurement the animal was taught to pull a handle in response to each flash onset and concomitantly, as a measure of general tonic arousal, skin conductance (SCL) (initially registered as resistance) was recorded throughout from the animal's left foot.

The experiment proper consisted of a series of testing periods, conducted on separate days and interspersing 17 saline control sessions with 17 sessions of intramuscular administration of 1.0 µg/kg LSD-25. The latter was deliberately (and successfully) chosen as a low dose in order to avoid disrupting the monkey's lever-pressing performance and hence introducing unwanted non-specific effects into the results. Even so, statistical analysis was confined to VEP data associated with performance levels exceeding 75 per cent correct responses to the flashes.

Interest centred on the pattern of covariation between SCL and VEP amplitude/intensity slope, especially over the low range of skin conductance, where it was expected, for LSD, that there would be relatively greater response to the brighter flashes. To examine this, VEPs were arranged according to flash intensity and then further sorted according to whether the simultaneously recorded SCL fell into a low or high range, respectively defined as < 6.0 µmhos and > 8.0 µmhos. The data in this form are shown in Figure 8.1, where it can be seen that LSD selectively and progressively—as a function of stimulus intensity—enhanced VEP amplitude in those cases where, paradoxically, general arousal was low. Statistical analysis by three-way ANOVA showed significant effects for the two important main factors (flash intensity and treatment) and for the SCL range × treatment interaction.

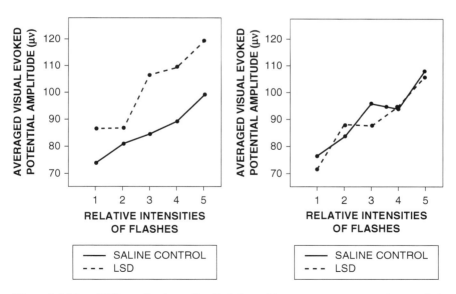

Figure 8.1 Mean VEP amplitudes at five flash intensities over two concurrently recorded ranges of SCL: low range (left) and high range (right).

Other unusual effects of LSD, reported more fully elsewhere (Wingate, 1982), were also noted in this and other experiments conducted then. For example, over time the drug caused a gradual increase in muscle tonus. On the other hand it had a marked *depressant* effect on SCL, both within and between sessions—observable as an immediate effect, even with a smaller dose of 0.5 μg/kg. These changes, together with those already described, closely parallel features we have observed in and in relation to human psychosis. They suggest that the LSD-induced and naturally occurring state are highly similar psychophysiologically; being characterized, not by a simple shift in, but by a complex 'dissociation' of, sensory, autonomic, and somatic arousal systems.

Conclusions

Seen in isolation and now considerably removed in time from the human research that inspired it, the experiment just described looks, even to me, like a bit of curiosity; for the physiological 'dissociation' that we found in both natural and drug-induced psychosis still defies a full explanation. The relevance here, however, is in illustrating how the study of LSD helped to validate an existing—and, I would argue, already empirically well-established—model for certain features of schizophrenia; at the same time, the experiment further strengthened the case for LSD as a drug model for the disorder. There might be a lesson here for current animal research in the area. Thus, it might be appropriate to use LSD (rather than amphetamine) to establish a bench-mark for the viability of theories of psychosis, whether these are neurochemical, neurophysiological, psychophysiological, or behavioural. The failure of LSD to have a 'psychotic' effect in the animal, as predicted by the model in question, could be seen as weakening that model and a possible reason for rejecting it. Two contrasting contemporary examples from near to my own field will help to illustrate the point.

The first concerns 'latent inhibition', an animal learning paradigm for schizophrenia that has enjoyed some popularity in certain quarters in recent years (e.g. Gray *et al.*, 1991). The neurobiological case for this model rests very heavily on simple amphetamine/dopamine theory, including observations that amphetamine abolishes latent inhibition, in both animals and humans. However, I suggest that its specificity in modelling human psychosis is seriously undermined by the failure of LSD to have a comparable effect (reported in Cassaday *et al.*, 1993; and Cassaday, personal communication). A more optimistic conclusion can be reached with respect to the second example to be quoted. There the phenomenon of interest has been startle habituation, investigated within a general theory about failures in sensorimotor gating in schizophrenia (Geyer and Braff, 1987). In that case, LSD *has* been shown to have predictable effects in animals, consistent with observations in schizophrenic patient and other human subjects; thus indicating, I would argue, that the paradigm is along the right lines in trying to identify unique characteristics of the psychotic nervous system.

Complementing this use of LSD as a 'checking strategy' in animal modelling of schizophrenia, the study of the drug could have other applications, similar in aim but along different lines. Although further experimental research on humans is precluded, as noted in the Introduction, a considerable amount of information has already accumulated on the effects of LSD. This constitutes an invaluable data base which schizophrenia researchers could do worse than consult from time to time. Given the crab-wise fashion in which science proceeds, there are undoubtedly old findings in the LSD literature that at the time were relatively uninterpretable, but which might fall into place in the light of modern theory. As someone with a psycho-biological view of psychotic disorder, I personally would wish to include here introspective data, in addition to laboratory findings. Finally, there is the possibility to re-examine the human effects of LSD among those who still take it, albeit illegally; a good example is Strassman's (1992) recent exploiting of that fact to provide further evidence of the serotonergic mediation of hallucinogenic drug action. Much might be learned about naturally occurring psychosis if such work were brought more into the centre stage of schizophrenia research.

The arguments in favour of LSD (or some equivalent hallucinogen) as a drug model for psychosis should hardly need labouring further; but its past neglect remains a fascinating piece of social history. Looked at now, from a distance and in the light of some retreat from simplistic accounts of the biology of schizophrenia, the rejection of LSD might just seem like a remarkably crass piece of scientific misjudgement. But as I have intimated earlier, it is unlikely that that was all it was. Science always has to operate within the sociopolitical constraints of its time and, to a degree, is only permitted or encouraged to pursue ideas with which the prevailing Establishment is comfortable. In the worst, and fortunately rare, instance—as in pre-war Germany—it can amount to deliberate collusion between science and political ideology (Müller-Hill, 1988). Mostly—to mix the analogies—it is a two-way osmosis, only subliminally perceivable. Such was the case, I believe, with LSD. Whether in the long run it mattered, as far as our understanding of serious mental illness is concerned, will perhaps only be known when the combination lock—as it is proving to be—on schizophrenia is finally opened.

Commentary

I was not, it seems, alone in my despair at the neglect of LSD as a drug having genuine scientific and human interest. A prominent and outspoken enthusiast for many years has been Amanda Neidpath, director of the Oxfordshire-based Beckley Foundation. After lengthy campaigning and in collaboration with Professor David Nutt of Imperial College London, Amanda has very recently obtained ethical permission to carry out experiments using LSD in human volunteers. Their team of investigators has now reported a comprehensive neuro-imaging study of the drug showing remarkable changes in brain connectivity that could account for the dramatic psychological effects of LSD (Carhart-Harris et al., 2016). In the conclusions to their paper the authors speculate on various future implications of their work. Among their suggestions is the therapeutic use of LSD, where they quote a previous study of theirs on the treatment of depression using the closely related drug, psilocybin. Successful though that experiment was – dare one say it in a group of highly selected intellectually sophisticated clients – I personally am unconvinced by the idea of treatment applications being the main focus of future LSD research. Better is its use in the exploration of fundamental brain processes, including the neurobiology of psychosis and schizophrenia risk; thus getting back to the original logistics that inspired work on the drug many years ago. As it happens, this more basic research aim has found expression – albeit differently – in a longstanding interest in the use of LSD to investigate creativity (divergent thinking), articulated by Amanda Neidpath (personal communication; see also the Beckley Foundation website). Although not always acknowledged, this converges closely with the psychosis risk issue, via the notion that a potential for original thinking represents a positive facet of vulnerability for psychotic illness (the madness/creativity debate). That topic is eventually addressed as part of the final research theme discussed here, presented as a series of papers about the 'dimensional' phase of my work on psychosis.

It might seem that the origin of my research on dimensions of psychosis needs no explanation, grounded as it surely must be in the Eysenck dogma. However, the truth is more complicated. Its origin can be traced to my first meetings with people diagnosed as 'schizophrenic', while I was a student working as a nurse in a hospital for the mentally ill. What puzzled me about these patients was that they did not seem to fit the account given by the psychiatrist in my undergraduate lectures, as neurologically impaired dementing individuals. On the contrary, behind their insane ramblings and delusional thoughts they seemed to have perfectly healthy, intact psyches. I was of course to learn eventually that this was not some brilliantly original insight on my part: many people had noticed it. It was to be brought home to me in the most satisfyingly coincidental way while working in the military hospital. This turned to be the same institution where R. D. Laing – the eventually famous radical psychiatrist – had communed with psychotic patients and formulated his existential ideas about schizophrenia that led to his classic book *The Divided Self* (Laing, 1965). By another chance turn of events Laing, as a junior psychiatrist, had also passed through the Glasgow department where I later worked. I never met him there, but his presence hung over the place – *cui bono*? LSD!

As a result of this early clinical experience I developed a broad view of the dimensionality of psychosis. I realised that Laing was also proposing a continuity model: understanding schizophrenia was inescapably rooted in understanding healthy psychology, and the medical model was flawed. But for Laing the explanation was sociocultural, diametrically opposite to Eysenck's thoroughly biological theory. Intriguingly, over a short distance therefore Eysenck and Laing (unwittingly) agreed with each other, before diverging along paths of mutual dislike. Clinical psychology reflected this division quite sharply – and was very anti-Eysenck – at one point, during the period in the 20th century when the psychedelic movement was most feverish and Laing's popularity was at its height. Personally, I found myself on both sides of the fence, probably more sympathetic to Laing's rather than Eysenck's version of anti-Establishmentarianism!

Notwithstanding the above, my first venture into publishing on the topic (see below) was classic Eysenck, even including the phrase 'nervous types' in the title. Published in the *British Journal of Psychiatry* it was an attempt to convince a psychiatric audience of a psychophysiological, personality-based view of schizophrenia. It drew heavily on our LSD data as a way of trying to argue for schizophrenia being, not a qualitatively distinct disease, but an aberration of dynamic brain processes as conceived of in nervous typological theory.

9 The schizophrenias as nervous types

Gordon Claridge

Introduction

Despite over half a century of intensive research the essential nature of the schizophrenias still remains an enigma. Attempts to account for the disordered behaviour of the schizophrenic have ranged over the full spectrum of the biosocial sciences, explanations being sought both in the biochemistry of the organism and in the interpersonal relationships of the whole individual. Sitting somewhere between these two extremes is the psychophysiological view. As a conceptual and methodological approach to behaviour in general, psychophysiology concerns itself with the problem of integrating neurophysiological and psychological data, attempting to bridge the gap between these two disciplines. Of course, the potential value of describing behaviour at a different level of explanation, either more molecular or more molar, is not denied. However, the peculiar contribution of psychophysiology is its concentration on data gathered at the interface between the brain and behaviour. As such its techniques are chosen so as to allow guesses to be made about the functional systems in the brain that underly behaviour. They naturally include the study of E.E.G. and autonomic response but also extend to the measurement of various phenomena derived from conventional experimental psychology, such as perceptual thresholds and vigilance (Claridge, 1970b). The theoretical concepts of psychophysiology reflect its mongrel background and include such terms as 'arousal', a notion originating in academic psychology, but made respectable by neurophysiologists.

For the psychophysiologist the problem of understanding the psychiatric disorders can be formulated as the special problem of understanding individual differences in the activity of those neural mechanisms that underly behaviour in general. Thus, individual differences in anxiety-proneness may be viewed and measured as variations in central nervous activation or arousability (Duffy, 1962; Malmo, 1957). Furthermore, it is usually assumed that the pathological states found among psychiatric patients are simple extensions of those processes responsible for the biological basis of normal personality. The latter view owes a great deal to the dimensional theory of personality developed by Eysenck (1947; 1957b), particularly his attempt to anchor the major personality dimensions to their physiological substrate. Eysenck's theory was, in its turn, originally derived from the Russian notion of 'nervous typology', an approach to temperamental variation pioneered by Pavlov, and in recent Soviet research applied to human personality differences by Teplov and his followers (Gray, 1964). The Russian version of nervous type theory has traditionally been couched in language unfamiliar to the Western reader, using such terms as 'strength of nervous system' and 'stimulus in dynamism'. However, Gray (*op. cit.*, 1967) has argued convincingly for the equivalence of Russian and Western ideas, an integration of the two also being evident in recent translations of Eysenck's original excitation-inhibition theory into the terminology of an arousal model of individual differences (Claridge, 1967; Eysenck, 1967).

Whether or not particular research has been carried out within the Eysenckian framework, the most successful application of psychophysiology to abnormal personality has occurred with respect to the neurotic disorders. Thus, a number of writers have provided evidence of greater autonomic arousal in neurotic patients with anxiety (Lader and Wing, 1964; Kelly, 1966), a finding according well with the predictions of early activation theorists like Duffy (1934). Similarly, the present author, working more from a neo-Eysenckian viewpoint, has shown clear differences between defined groups of dysthymics and hysterico-psychopaths on a variety of measures, both physiological and experimental psychological (Claridge, 1967).

To date less progress has been made in attempts to understand the functional psychoses as psychophysiological disorders having a dimensional basis comparable to the neuroses. There are perhaps two main reasons. The first is that 'disease' views of these conditions still prevail, despite the continued failure to establish a discrete organic basis for their aetiology. The second is that even those adopting a dimensional position have found it difficult to devise adequate theoretical models to account for psychotic disorders, which, compared with the neuroses, must be psychophysiologically much more complex. Nevertheless, despite the immature nature of existing theorizing in the field, a psychophysiological/dimensional explanation of the functional psychoses seems to hold promise. In any event, it is the main purpose of this paper to argue for the value of such an approach.

In doing so some reference will be made to the contribution of work on drug-induced model psychoses. This is partly because of its obvious relevance to the problem under discussion, but mainly to illustrate, in a climate of disillusionment about psychotomimetic drug research, how it may still further our understanding of the natural psychoses if carried out from a well-defined theoretical viewpoint.

Drug techniques have an important place in psychophysiological research because they allow the experimenter to test out hypotheses about the neural mechanisms underlying behaviour by manipulating them pharmacologically (Claridge, 1970a). As far as individual variations are concerned, Russian workers have traditionally used drugs to establish nervous typological differences in animals and men; a research strategy formally recognized in the West by Eysenck, whose original theory contained an explicit postulate linking personality to psychotropic drug effects (Eysenck, 1957a). In the abnormal field, it is again the neuroses that have yielded the most promising results so far. Indeed, arousal models of neurotic personality differences have rested very heavily on the psychopharmacological approach; as witnessed, for example, by work on the 'sedation threshold' and similar drug techniques (Shagass and Jones, 1958; Claridge and Herrington, 1960). Comparable research on the psychoses has been less successful. The main reason is similar to that which explains the general lack of progress in understanding the psychoses: namely a greater difficulty in conceptualizing the psychophysiological effects of those drugs—the psychotomimetics—which come closest to simulating the natural state. Thus, it is relatively easy in the case of, say, ordinary sedative/hypnotics to provide a conceptual model which can explain both their general effects on behaviour and the nervous typological differences observed in response to such drugs. The psychotomimetics, on the other hand, clearly have a much more intricate action on the central nervous system, making them complicated psychopharmacological tools with which to work. It is therefore particularly difficult to think of a theoretical model in which the drug-induced and naturally occurring states can be matched together.

Past attempts to do so have, like studies of the schizophrenias themselves, been concentrated at two extremes. On the one hand, drugs like LSD-25 were investigated, at the peak of interest in them, from a purely chemical viewpoint in the hope, so far unsubstantiated, that the 'cause' of schizophrenia could be chased down to the biochemistry of the brain. On the other hand, attention was focussed on the subjective, experiential effects of the psychedelics, a fascinating exercise but one limited in the scientific data it can yield. Few systematic studies have been carried out within the kind of psychophysiological framework argued for here. In the meantime the hallucinogens have become a social problem, and behavioural scientists have become wary of giving them experimentally to human subjects. It is hoped that this paper will help the reader to re-evaluate their place in research on the nature of the schizophrenias.

As implied earlier, the approach to schizophrenic behaviour adopted here contains two assumptions. One is that the functional psychoses are not qualitatively distinct illnesses but represent the end-points of personality characteristics running through the general population. In this respect they are considered to be entirely similar to the neuroses. The second assumption is that, like other personality characteristics, the tendency to schizophrenic breakdown has, underlying it, certain definable psychophysiological processes; or, put another way, it represents a particular kind of nervous typological organization. Each of these two points will be considered further in more detail.

Illness or dimension?

While it is not difficult to understand how, in the early days of their description, the schizophrenias came to be regarded as qualitatively distinct diseases, what is surprising is that such a view continues to be so widely held. Indeed, to some not schooled to think in terms of the medical model, the most striking fact is the intellectual contortion required to maintain the disease position in the fact of mounting evidence to the contrary. The evidence itself comes from various sources. The first is of a clinical, diagnostic kind. For example, the major British textbook of psychiatry (Slater and Roth, 1969) opens its long account of the schizophrenias by pointing to the difficulties of actually defining the boundaries of these disorders. The problem was recognized by early observers, such as Bleuler (1911) and Kretschmer (1927) and is a still familiar one to most clinicians. Depending on the criteria adopted in a particular clinic, a proportion of patients can always be found whose symptoms are either not numerous or severe enough for them to be placed in anything other than an indeterminate category. In other words, they show all the signs of falling on a continuum somewhere between 'normality' and severe disorder. Such patients have been variously described as 'atypical', 'schizophreniform', 'latent', 'schizoaffective', 'pre-psychotic', 'schizoid', 'pseudoneurotic schizophrenic', 'borderline' . . . The list is endless, and while presumably aimed at preserving the disease model actually does much to undermine it.

The problem of defining the schizophrenias is not one that is solely confined to the appraisal of patients referred for psychiatric diagnosis. It may actually be difficult, if not impossible, to decide where the normal merges into the pathological. Individually, all of the behaviours found in the psychotic patient may occur in the so-called 'normal' person—and can do so to a varying degree. Thinking and language perhaps provide the best examples. Weird ideas that may be regarded as schizophrenic delusions in one context may be considered mere irrational beliefs in another, even though both may be equally bizarre and be held with equal tenacity. By the same token, the styles of expression said to characterize schizophrenic communication, both written and spoken, are frequently and increasingly found in socially acceptable art forms. Furthermore, the borders between the eccentric and the psychotic become harder to define as society adopts more flexible standards of conventional behaviour. Indeed, in some subcultures the previously conventional has already become the eccentric.

This view of the schizophrenias is also firmly supported by a wide range of evidence from scientific studies of these conditions. Over the years many hundreds of measurements of different kinds—biochemical, physiological, and psychological—have been taken on schizophrenic patients. To the writer's knowledge in no case has the distribution of scores indicated a clear qualitative difference between schizophrenics and other groups. Instead, schizophrenics fall on a graded continuum with normals, occupying an extreme position, either at one pole of the continuum or spanning a general population average. The latter finding, of greater heterogeneity or variance, is, as Kety (1960) has pointed out, one of the few consistent facts about schizophrenia.

Eysenck (1960) in particular has argued forcibly in favour of the dimensional hypothesis, and in a series of studies with his colleagues has made a direct statistical attack on the problem. The earliest studies, based on the factor analysis of psychiatric ratings (Trouton and Maxwell, 1956) and the canonical variate analysis of objective test data (Eysenck, 1955b; S. B. G. Eysenck, 1956) provided evidence for the existence of a personality dimension of psychoticism. More recent work has been aimed at developing a questionnaire, the PEN inventory, for measuring psychoticism in addition to the well-established dimensions of extraversion and neuroticism (Eysenck and Eysenck, 1968).

Another important source of evidence comes from the field of genetics, an area well-trodden by those searching for a biological solution to the psychoses. Although many genetic models have been proposed these have required considerable straining of classical Mendelian principles in order to maintain the assumption that what is to be explained is the transmission of a qualitatively distinct disease or group of diseases. In fact, it is becoming increasingly obvious that a limited gene hypothesis is inadequate to explain all of the facts about the schizophrenias. A much more plausible one is a polygenic theory which assumes that individuals inherit varying degrees of predisposition to schizophrenic breakdown, in much the same way as they inherit the tendency to neurotic reactions. Two eminent workers in the field, Gottesman and Shields (1968), have put forward convincing arguments, based on schizophrenic twin research, in favour of this point of view. They quote two kinds of evidence. One is the tendency for the concordance rates of schizophrenia in monozygotic twins to increase significantly as a function of severity of the psychotic reaction, a finding predictable from the polygenic model since the greater the genetic loading the less environmental factors would lead to discordance and vice versa. The second kind of evidence is derived from psychometric studies of twins concordant and discordant for the diagnosis of schizophrenia. Using the MMPI, Gottesman and Shields demonstrated similarities in the personality profiles of MZ probands and their co-twins. Where the latter were not themselves psychiatrically ill the individual scale scores were less abnormal, but the similarity in profile *shape* was retained, with a high point on Schizophrenia (Sc). The authors concluded, somewhat optimistically it is felt, that scores derived from the MMPI might be used to delineate the personality structure of individuals with a strong genetic predisposition to react to stress with a schizophrenic breakdown.

A further line of reasoning, also from the field of genetics, is contained in arguments that have been put forward to account for certain paradoxical facts about the manifestation rate of schizophrenia in the population. Given the reduced fertility of the schizophrenic patient, and without accepting an excessively high mutation rate, which is extremely unlikely, it is difficult to explain why the condition remains so common. One explanation is that proposed by Huxley et al. (1964), who suggested that the schizophrenic genotype may carry with it certain biological advantages, perhaps reflected in an increased immunity among schizophrenics and their relatives. Support for this theory has recently been obtained by Carter and Watts (1971), who demonstrated a significantly reduced incidence of accidents and viral infections in schizophrenics' relatives.

The picture that begins to emerge, therefore, is of schizophrenic predisposition as a continuously variable personality dimension inherited as a set of polygenically determined characteristics which are maintained at an adequate level in the population through selective genetic control. This notion is not incompatible with the fact that extreme loading on such a dimension may lead to the severely disturbed behaviour that is currently identified as schizophrenic 'illness'. A similar situation exists in the case of other psychiatric disorders. Neurotic anxiety is a good example. Very high (or very low) degrees of anxiety can result in grossly maladaptive behaviour, sometimes as mentally crippling or socially undesirable as that found among psychotic patients. Yet variations in anxiety-proneness are an accepted part of normal personality differences. Furthermore, despite its ability to disrupt behaviour, anxiety serves a useful biological purpose; for as the Yerkes-Dodson principle illustrates, it is only at optimally moderate levels of anxiety that efficient psychological performance can occur (Yerkes and Dodson, 1908).

Given that schizophrenic predisposition can be viewed in a similar way, the question that remains is: What psychological characteristics have the biological utility to form a major parameter of personality yet show continuity between normal adaptive behaviour and disruptive mental disorder? The most commonly held opinion, and the one for which the strongest arguments can be advanced, is that the characteristics in question have something to do with the cognitive and selective attentional aspects of behaviour, seen at the psychological level as styles of thinking in the normal individual and as thought disorder in the schizophrenic patient. Like anxiety, such behaviour clearly had important survival value during the evolution of man, though, again like anxiety, perhaps only at certain optimum levels.

The notion of an alliance between great wits and madness, to paraphrase Dryden, is not a new one, and observations of schizophrenic thinking and life styles in the writings and personalities of famous creators in the arts and sciences are too familiar and well-documented for the point to be laboured further here. More recent formal studies of the problem are of interest, however. For present purposes these can be considered as falling into two main groups.

The first kind of study has been concerned with the relationship between creativity and personality traits in psychiatrically normal individuals. Before considering this evidence, it is first necessary to comment briefly on the status of creativity as a topic in general psychology. The psychometric analysis of creativity has given rise to a vast literature, and, while opinions differ on whether it can be considered entirely independent of general intelligence as normally defined, a valid distinction can be made between the divergent modes of thinking required to solve problems of an 'open-ended' kind and the convergent thinking style tapped by conventional intelligence tests (Butcher, 1968). As a recognizable feature of cognitive functioning, creativity can be variously described as the ability to take conceptual leaps in the face of minimal information, the ability to see remote connections between apparently unrelated items, and the ability to retain a flexible approach to problem-solving in order to seek a solution whether one is possible or not. A number of studies have examined the personality profiles of individuals judged to be high in creative talent, both in the arts and sciences. Most of these investigations agree that such people do differ in certain important respects from the general population. McKinnon (1962), using the MMPI with a group of architects, found that scores on all of the scales of that test were elevated to a varying degree, with a small but positive correlation between rated creativity and Schizophrenia (Sc). He concluded that the results were indicative of greater unusualness of thought processes and a freer expression of impulse and imagery in his subjects. Several other similar studies have made use of the Cattell 16 Personality Factor questionnaire. Cattell and Butcher (1968), and Cattell and Drevdahl (1955), reporting on a group of eminent research scientists, described them as significantly sizothymic (withdrawn), emotionally unstable, self-sufficient, and bohemian. Some of these traits were also found by Drevdahl (1956) to differentiate creative and non-creative students. In a more recent investigation, Cross *et al.* (1967), also using the 16PF, clearly differentiated artists from a matched control group on a number of traits. Artists were found to be low in emotional stability and super-ego strength and especially high in autistic or bohemian tendency.

In some respects the personality traits found by 16PF users to characterize the creative thinker are very similar to those shown to be abnormal in psychotic patients. Thus, McAllister (1968), using Foulds' system of classifying psychiatric illness, reported that non-integrated psychotics, and to a lesser degree integrated psychotics, deviated markedly from average in sizothymia and autistic tendency. In other respects, however, the profiles of creative thinkers and diagnosed schizophrenics differ noticeably from each other. That is particularly true of Cattell's second factor, Intelligence, on which schizophrenics score very poorly but on which creative thinkers are universally high. This finding accords well with the conclusion reached by most workers who have examined the trait characteristics of creative thinkers; namely, that while such people emerge as unusual individuals they almost always show the strong intellectual and emotional controls indicative of the integrated personality. Nevertheless, it is of interest that the traits on which the creative thinker does appear to deviate from average are precisely those which, within the range of normal variation, may reflect an increased loading on an underlying personality factor associated with schizophrenia.

The second group of studies providing evidence for a continuity between normal and pathological thinking has focussed on thought disorder itself. The rationale for their inclusion here is the apparent resemblance between the cognitive style that characterizes the creative process and schizophrenic loosening of ideational boundaries, a disorder most commonly investigated recently under the heading of 'over-inclusion' (Payne and Hewlett, 1960), but a classically described feature of schizophrenia (Bleuler, *op. cit.*). It scarcely requires a conceptual leap to see the schizophrenic's tendency to follow irrelevant themes in his stream of thought as an extreme example of divergent thinking, the main difference being that in one case it is an uncontrolled activity and in the other a rationally directed one.

Experimental support for this hypothesis comes from a series of studies that have examined psychiatrically well individuals for evidence of deviant performance on tests specifically designed to measure thought disorder in psychotic patients. Most studies in this area have used the research strategy of looking at thought disorder test performance in individuals who are considered genetically predisposed to schizophrenia. Thus, in an early investigation Rapaport (1945) demonstrated that loosened thinking, as measured by an object sorting test, was characteristic of pre-schizophrenic patients and non-psychiatric subjects judged to be of schizoid personality. Subsequent investigators have narrowed down on those individuals whose predisposition to psychosis can be presumed from the fact that they have a schizophrenic relative. The first study of this type was carried out by McConaghy (1959), who instead of 'overinclusion' has preferred the term 'allusive thinking' as a description of the same characteristic of conceptual loosening (McConaghy, 1960). Using Lovibond's (1954) version of the Goldstein-Scheerer Object Sorting Test, McConaghy demonstrated a significant degree of allusive thinking in the parents of schizophrenics, a finding later replicated by Lidz and his colleagues (Lidz et al., 1963; Rosman et al., 1964). Phillips et al. (1965) reported that the siblings as well as the parents of schizophrenics scored abnormally on tests of thought disorder, Romney (1969) obtaining similar results, which while not quite statistically significant on a small sample were in the predicted direction. Some further confirmatory evidence comes from Mednick's ongoing follow-up study in Denmark of children of schizophrenic mothers (Mednick and Schulsinger, 1968). Compared with matched control subjects these 'high-risk' children have already proved to have loosened thinking and a high frequency of idiosyncratic responses on continuous association tests.

Other work of a slightly different kind has shown that it is not necessary deliberately to select individuals according to their genetic predisposition in order to demonstrate unusual thinking styles on thought disorder tests. Thus, a colleague of the present author, using the Object Classification Test (Payne, 1962), showed that creative artists tended to produce a high number of unusual sortings, indicative of over-inclusion, and as a group fell midway between schizophrenic patients and unselected control subjects (Canter, unpublished study). Finally, McConaghy and Clancy (1968) examined allusive thinking with the Object Sorting Test in a group of normal university students and their parents. They found a significant tendency for students with high scores on the test to have a high-scoring parent. In their paper McConaghy and his colleagues made similar points to those being argued here, namely that modes of abstraction seen in psychosis are also found generally in the population, that these may be characteristic of creative thinking, and that, as such, they may reflect part of the biological advantage of the schizophrenic genotype.

In arguing here for a dimensional view of the schizophrenias many gaps have clearly been left unfilled. Lack of space, of available evidence, and of creativity on the part of the writer preclude detailed analysis of the questions that remain. However, some of the main points arising from the above discussion merit brief comment. The most important questions concern the heterogeneity observed within the clinically diagnosable schizophrenias. Thus, in arguing for a similarity between overinclusion and certain aspects of the creative process, no account has been taken of the fact that not all schizophrenics show thought disorder of an overinclusive kind. Some demonstrate the opposite—overexclusion. In fact, if a dimensional view of the problem is taken some of these difficulties can be resolved, at least in principle. Thus, simultaneous variations along other personality and cognitive dimensions could adequately account for differences in the way schizophrenic reactions manifest themselves. In this respect there is already some evidence (Claridge, 1967) that introversion-extraversion may be an important dimension differentiating individuals prone to particular kinds of schizophrenic reaction. At a cognitive level it is feasible that the predisposition to schizophrenia actually reflects a dimension ranging from overexclusion to overinclusion, its biological advantage lying in genetic selection for some optimal intermediate value.

Other more difficult problems arise from the possibility that the dimensions making up the personality may have an interacting effect on behaviour. One consequence of such an interaction is that it may itself determine an individual's predisposition to schizophrenic breakdown. Quite apart from exogenous factors, such as environmental stress or upbringing, it seems likely that, even given a high predisposition to schizophrenia, actual breakdown may occur only if the loading on some other dimension, or dimensions, has a critical value. The point is well-illustrated by the evidence already reviewed on the differences in intelligence that are found when schizophrenic patients and creative individuals are compared. Thus, it may be that the very creative person, though highly predisposed to schizophrenia, does not become clinically psychotic because high general intelligence confers some immunity in the form of adequate intellectual and personality reserves. Or, put the other way round, the absence of such reserves may make the psychotically predisposed individual more vulnerable to stress. In the event of breakdown the same kind of interaction may also determine its severity, nature, and course. For example, two equally predisposed individuals may react in different ways depending on their intellectual level. This may be particularly true of the kind of thought disorder they show, since the latter is almost certainly determined, not only by the specific cognitive styles thought to be associated with the schizophrenias, but also by general intelligence. In this respect it is worth noting that there is evidence for differences in the intellectual levels of various subtypes of schizophrenia even before breakdown (Mason, 1956).

The above considerations clearly illustrate how, even assuming a view of the schizophrenias taken here, the problem is an extremely difficult one to disentangle. However, the present discussion has served to outline the broad principles of the dimensional approach prior to a consideration of its nervous typological aspects, a question taken up in the next section.

The nervous typological model

Given a 'normal variant' view of schizophrenia, its behavioural analysis can, of course, be undertaken at any level of description—biochemical, psychophysiological, or social/psychological. However, the psychophysiological approach has certain advantages, already outlined, and the remainder of this paper will discuss the schizophrenias and schizophrenic predisposition within the framework of the nervous typological theory of personality. As already stated previously, the general assumption of this theory is that, at a biological level, differences in personality depend upon variations in the organization of central nervous processes.

The germ of a nervous typological description of the schizophrenias was contained in some of Pavlov's own speculations about their pathogenesis, his suggestion being that different kinds of psychotic reaction depend upon abnormal weakening or strengthening of the cortical inhibitory processes (Ivanov-Smolensky, 1954). More recently, Eysenck (1961), in a short-lived attempt to account for the genotypic basis of psychotic behaviour, also made use of inhibition as an explanatory concept, hypothesizing that the main characteristic of schizophrenia was the abnormally slow rate at which reactive inhibition is dissipated. However, this hypothesis has proved to have little generality beyond the particular empirical data upon which it was formulated, namely pursuit-rotor reminiscence scores (Claridge, 1960; Broadhurst and Broadhurst, 1964).

Other contemporary theorists seeking a single psychophysiological concept to explain the schizophrenias have chosen that of arousal. It can be stated at the outset that in their most basic form—that schizophrenia is a state of heightened (Fish, 1961) or diminished (Weckowicz, 1958) arousal—such models have, like Eysenck's reactive inhibition hypothesis, proved far too simplistic. Apart from contradicting one another, they fail to give any account either of the heterogeneity of the schizophrenias or of the obviously extensive involvement of all aspects of psychological function in psychotic disorder. Put more concretely, they do not even get beyond the first stage of explaining why it is that neurotics, also in varying states of arousal, are not psychotic!

More sophisticated theorizing and methodology, however, have helped to sustain models of schizophrenia that incorporate the notion of arousal, two developments in the field being of particular interest. One has been the careful examination of arousal variations *within* groups of schizophrenic patients. Thus, Venables and his colleagues have shown relationships between arousal level and narrowly defined characteristics of schizophrenia, such as behavioural withdrawal and paranoid-non-paranoid symptomatology (Venables and Wing, 1962; Venables, 1967). Similarly Herrington and Claridge (1965), finding a wide range of arousability in early psychosis, were able to demonstrate that differences in psychophysiological status were associated with such clinical features as thought disorder and mood disturbance.

The second and perhaps more interesting development has been the demonstration that schizophrenic patients differ from others, not so much in their absolute levels on given psychophysiological measures, but rather in the way in which different measures co-vary together; suggesting that it is the organization, not the deviation, of central nervous activity that is critically important in the schizophrenias. Empirically this difference in central organization is reflected in the correlations between measures that are considered to tap important aspects of psychophysiological function. Thus, some years ago Herrington and Claridge (*op. cit.*) reported that the correlation between two such measures—the sedation threshold and the Archimedes spiral after-effect—was significantly *negative* in early psychotics but significantly *positive* in neurotic patients; yet the range of scores on each measure taken individually was identical in both groups. Around the same time Venables (1963) described a similar reversal of correlation using two quite different measures, skin potential and the fusion threshold for paired light flashes (two-flash threshold). Comparing normal subjects and chronic schizophrenics, he found correlations of opposite sign in the two groups, the direction of the relationships indicating that high autonomic activity was associated with poor perceptual discrimination in the former and heightened discrimination in the latter. Again both schizophrenics and normals spanned similar ranges on both measures.

The result for the sedation threshold and spiral after-effect was later confirmed by Krishnamoorti and Shagass (1964), though Venables' finding has proved more difficult to replicate exactly. Lykken and Maley (1968) compared schizophrenic and non-psychotic patients on two perceptual measures, two-flash threshold and critical flicker fusion, and two autonomic indices, skin potential and skin conductance. They found that the perceptual and autonomic measures were certainly associated differently in the two groups, but that the pattern of correlations was diametrically opposite to that reported by Venables. The Lykken and Maley result in non-psychotics confirmed those obtained in an earlier series of studies by the same group of authors (Lykken *et al.*, 1966) and that reported by Hume and Claridge (1965) for normal subjects. To complicate matters further, Hume (1970) recently replicated Venables' original findings in schizophrenics but found zero correlations between two-flash threshold and skin potential in normal and neurotic subjects.

Some recent results from our own work, however, help to explain some of the differences between these various sets of data, as well as providing further clues about the possible nature of central nervous organization in the schizophrenias. The results in question come from a study of LSD response in normal volunteers carried out in our laboratory some years ago and reported briefly elsewhere (Claridge and Hume, 1966). The aim of the experiment was to set up a drug model of Venables' comparison of schizophrenic and normal subjects. It was predicted that the overall effect of LSD would be not so much to produce a change in arousal *per se* but rather to alter the co-variation between autonomic and perceptual function, as reflected in the correlation between skin potential and two-flash threshold. A recent re-analysis of the data from this experiment has unearthed some interesting relationships, shown in the accompanying figures, which bear out this prediction. It can be seen that when the placebo and LSD conditions are compared there is indeed a systematic association between two-flash threshold and skin potential, the relationships being curvilinear but of opposite direction under the two conditions. That for placebo (Figure 9.1) is of the more usual inverted-U type, perceptual discrimination improving up to an optimum level of autonomic arousal and then deteriorating. Under LSD (Figure 9.2), on the other hand, heightened perceptual sensitivity appears to occur when the concurrent level of arousal is either very high or very low, being poorest at a moderate arousal level.

These results clearly help to account for the contradictory findings obtained in the group comparison studies described a moment ago. Thus, whether positive, negative, or zero correlations appear in particular groups may depend critically on the range of arousal over which subjects are tested. The point is well illustrated in Figure 9.3, where the placebo and LSD data from Figures 9.1 and 9.2, up to a skin potential level of 25 mv., have been superimposed. It can be seen that the correlation between two-flash threshold and skin potential is significantly negative under LSD (−0.82, $p < .01$), but significantly positive under placebo (+0.74, $p < .01$). In the *upper* range of skin potential, however, the correlations, while much lower, are reversed in sign, now being positive for LSD (+0.11) and negative for placebo (−0.32).

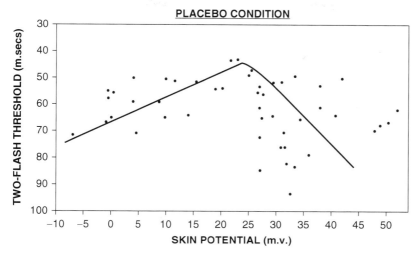

Figure 9.1 Measures of two-flash threshold and skin potential taken from ten subjects during the first hour under a placebo condition. Note that for convenience the signs of skin potential readings have been reversed. The scale for two-flash threshold is arranged so that changes in the upper direction indicate improved perceptual discrimination.

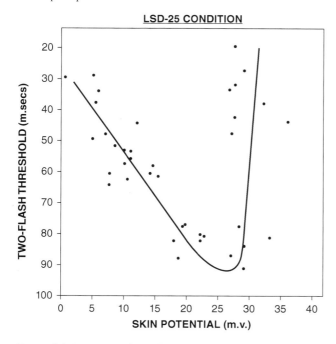

Figure 9.2 Measures of two-flash threshold and skin potential taken from ten subjects during the first hour under 100 μg. LSD-25. Interpretation of the scales is as for Figure 9.1.

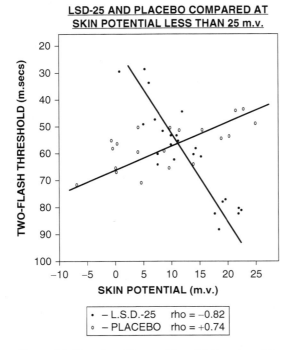

Figure 9.3 Data from Figures 9.1 and 9.2, up to a skin potential value of 25 mv., demonstrating how two-flash threshold and skin potential co-vary in opposite directions under LSD-25 and under placebo conditions.

This curious effect of LSD provides a remarkable pharmacological parallel of the naturally occurring state. It is also of great interest because of the light it may throw on the psychophysiological basis of the drug's action and therefore perhaps of the naturally-occurring psychoses. A commonly held view of the latter is that they are characterized by a weakening of central nervous homeostasis, an explanation that could also account for the LSD effects just described. Thus, according to Russian nervous typological theory (Gray, 1964), the deterioration in perceptual sensitivity found in our experiment at very high arousal levels in the placebo condition would be ascribed to the fact that homeostatic or 'protective' inhibitory mechanisms begin to intervene once arousal reaches a critical level. Applying the same argument to the opposite function obtaining under LSD, it could be concluded that such mechanisms operate there in reverse leading, at high arousal levels, to inappropriately heightened sensitivity to the environment. If, as Venables (1963) indeed argued, there is a similar weakening or failure of feedback mechanisms in natural psychosis, then physiologically this would represent a highly unstable state of affairs since marked changes in arousal in *either* direction could result in disproportionate alterations in perceptual sensitivity which would be very disruptive of mental function. Such a model might be ideally placed to account for many of the symptoms of the schizophrenic patient.

The notion of altered feedback was, in fact, implicitly incorporated in the present author's 'dissociation' theory of schizophrenia proposed a few years ago (Claridge, 1967) and considered to account for the inverted relationships between sedation threshold and spiral after-effect observed in schizophrenic patients. The theory itself was actually based on a long series of psychophysiological studies of neurotic, normal, and psychotic subjects. This research, which included two factor analyses of some of the more important measures, demonstrated two recognizable components of psychophysiological activity. One, clearly identifiable as a classic factor of arousal, as conventionally defined, accounted particularly for variations in autonomic responsiveness and sedation threshold. The second was mainly associated with EEG., particularly alpha rhythm, variables which, in turn, were related to the spiral after-effect. This latter component was therefore regarded as having a partly inhibitory feedback function, being concerned with the modulation of sensory input into the nervous system and with the selectivity aspect of attention. The model proposed that these two mechanisms are functionally related in the sense that variations in one are linked to variations in the other. The direction of this co-variation was considered to provide the nervous typological basis of the major neurotic and psychotic syndromes. One mode of co-variation was that postulated in neurotics and reflected empirically in the positive correlation between sedation threshold and spiral effect. There it was considered that the high levels of arousal (sedation threshold) found in dysthymic neurotics are associated with extreme selectivity or narrowing of attention, leading to prolonged spiral after-effects. The opposite would be true of hysterico-psychopathic individuals. The model further proposed that the reverse situation could occur, namely that high levels of arousal could co-exist with *poor* modulation of sensory input and vice versa; thus leading to negative correlations between sedation threshold and spiral after-effect. It was this dissociation of psychophysiological function—dissociation, at least, as judged against the neuroses—that was considered characteristic of schizophrenic patients.

A further feature of this model was the proposal that the dissociation of function found in the schizophrenias could occur in one of two directions, leading to different clinical syndromes. That conclusion was based on experimental evidence concerning the clinical and behavioural correlates of sedation threshold/spiral after-effect variation. Thus, it was found that schizophrenics showing evidence of high arousal and poor selective attention—high sedation threshold/low spiral after-effect—were more often paranoid, behaviourally active, emotionally reactive and, consistent with their weak attentional control, more overinclusive in their thought disorder. Those in the opposite psychophysiological state—poorly aroused (low sedation threshold) and with highly narrowed attention (high spiral after-effect)—tended to be retarded, affectively flattened, socially withdrawn and, if thought-disordered, more often concrete and overexclusive.

There seems, therefore, to be mounting evidence which enables us to reach three minimum conclusions about the psychophysiological basis of the schizophrenias. First, the differences between the latter and other psychiatric disorders, as well as the reason for variations within the schizophrenic syndromes themselves, seem to lie in the way the central nervous system is organized rather than in any single disturbance of function. Secondly, two important processes involved seem to be those of arousal and attention. Thirdly, the organization of central nervous function in the schizophrenias—as well as in other states—can be usefully examined by looking at the functional relationships between carefully chosen measures of psychophysiological activity. This emphasis on organization, rather than deviation, has actually been neglected by most psychophysiologists working on the problem of individual differences; or, if recognized, it has been done so only implicitly. Such neglect is the more surprising in view of the fact that psychophysiology has itself nurtured at least two examples of such an approach to behavioural analysis. One is the well-studied inverted-U function relating arousal to psychological performance (Hebb, 1955). The other is the 'narrowed attention' principle, namely the hypothesis put forward by a number of workers that the range of cues to which the individual responds diminishes as arousal rises and vice versa (Callaway and Dembo, 1958; Easterbrook, 1959). It should not surprise us too much if we need to seek other functions to account for other forms of central nervous organization. Indeed, it is perhaps not coincidental that the two principles just quoted seem, if anything, to work in reverse in schizophrenia.

Given the value of the psychophysiological approach, a question that remains is whether the disturbances of function seen in schizophrenic patients represent the nervous typological basis of a continuous personality dimension. Or, put another way, to what extent do the arguments presented in the previous section for a dimensional model of schizophrenia, find support in the psychophysiological evidence? At a purely theoretical level it is not difficult to visualize the cognitive styles, seen in the normal as creativity and in the schizophrenic as thought disorder, as having a common psychophysiological basis in the attentional control mechanisms of the central nervous system. Indeed, a number of workers concerned with trying to explain such phenomena as over-inclusion have argued some of the links in this chain of reasoning (Payne, 1960; McGhie, 1969; Silverman, 1964b, 1967; McConaghy, 1961). Furthermore, in formulating the dissociation theory of schizophrenia described above it was certainly our view that differences in the relative balance between the two mechanisms of arousal and input modulation accounted not only for the extreme reactions seen in psychiatric patients but also for normal personality variations. Thus, the kind of co-variation observed in the neuroses was considered to define a neuroticism dimension of dysthymia-hysteria, for which there was strong experimental evidence. It was also postulated, however, that cutting across this was a second dimension of 'psychoticism' characterized by relative imbalance between arousal and input modulation. The view that we were dealing with characteristics running through the general population was supported by the fact that only by selecting out psychiatrically defined criterion groups of psychotics and neurotics was it possible to demonstrate the reversals of correlation between sedation threshold and spiral after-effect discussed earlier. In an unselected group of normal subjects the correlation between these measures was zero, suggesting that both kinds of co-variation between arousal and input modulation were represented. Furthermore, in those normal subjects whose sedation threshold/spiral after-effect performance resembled that of diagnosed schizophrenics evidence was found for unusual response patterns on thought disorder tests, even though such individuals were not overtly ill.

More recent work from our laboratory has extended these findings and provided further evidence for the dimensional/nervous typological model of schizophrenia. Thus, in one study, just completed, normal subjects were categorized according to their scores on Eysenck's new PEN personality questionnaire (Claridge and Chappa, 1973). It has been found that certain individuals, including, significantly, those obtaining high scores on the P (psychoticism) scale of that inventory, show a pattern of psychophysiological response identical to that previously observed in schizophrenic patients.

Other evidence has come from several studies in which, using the author's personality theory as a starting-point, comparisons have been made of normal individuals, classified this time not on the basis of their personality inventory scores but on nervous typological grounds according to whether or not they showed a psychophysiological resemblance to schizophrenic patients. A particularly convincing example of this strategy has been its application to the analysis of individual differences in the response of subjects taking part in the LSD experiment described earlier. There the subjects were divided according to whether the psychophysiological change they showed under LSD was or was not like that previously found in schizophrenics; the assumption, of course, being that the drug would exaggerate, or throw into relief, nervous typological differences in the predisposition to schizophrenia. The actual measures used to classify the subjects were chosen on the basis of our previous work as representative of the two psychophysiological systems discussed earlier, namely tonic arousal and input modulation. These were the rates of change (regression slopes) for heart rate and spiral after-effect, the former being chosen as a suitable equivalent of the sedation threshold.

The subjects were divided into two groups. The first consisted of those who showed a schizophrenic-like reaction to LSD, that is either an increase in heart rate accompanied by a decrease in spiral after-effect or a decrease in heart rate and an increase in after-effect; the second group consisted of those subjects showing the opposite combinations of change. Classified in this way the ten subjects available divided equally into two groups of five individuals, referred to here as P-responders and NP-responders, respectively.

Comparison of these two groups revealed a number of important differences between them, both clinical and psychophysiological. After taking LSD each individual had been rated on a three-point scale for severity of reaction to the drug, this being done by an independent observer, a psychiatric colleague of the author. It was found subsequently that all five P-responders had ratings of 3 (severe), while only one of the NP-responders was rated as having had a severe reaction; of the remaining four NP subjects two were given a rating of 2 (moderate) and two a rating of 1 (mild). The difference between these two distributions proved to be statistically significant (Fisher exact probability test, $p < .05$). Consistent with the above result was the further finding that two of the ten subjects were unusually affected by LSD, one having a marked paranoid episode with loss of insight that lasted for several hours and the other subsequently requiring phenothiazine medication for a few days after the LSD experience; both of these individuals had been classified on nervous typological grounds as P-responders.

Psychophysiological differences between the two types were also found on a number of parameters. Thus, under LSD P-responders showed a significantly greater fall in two-flash threshold, i.e. improvement in perceptual discrimination, than did NP-responders (Mann-Whitney U Test, $p < .02$); suggesting that the former were particularly sensitive to what in general is a marked effect of LSD (Claridge and Hume, *op. cit.*). However, some of the most striking differences between the groups occurred in their response, not to LSD, but to dexamphetamine which had been administered on a separate occasion as part of the design of the original experiment. Under dexamphetamine P-responders showed a significantly greater rise in skin potential—or increase in autonomic arousal—than NP-responders (Mann-Whitney U Test, $p < .07$); while the groups also differed quite clearly in their change in spiral after-effect. As shown in Figure 9.4, the predominant tendency among P-responders was for the spiral after-effect to show a progressive increase under dexamphetamine, only one subject showing a fall. All of the NP-responders, on the other hand, reacted to the drug with a gradual drop in spiral after-effect. The difference between these two distributions was highly significant (Mann-Whitney U Test, $p < .008$).

The results just described provide striking confirmation of the fact that if the problem is approached from a well-defined theoretical viewpoint it is possible to demonstrate a continuity between the clinically observed psychoses and normal personality; thus adding evidence, at the nervous typological level, to that reviewed in the previous section. The difference in response, particularly clinical response, to LSD observed in our P and NP-responders suggests that the method of classifying our subjects was a valid one and that we were indeed selecting out individuals who were, respectively, high and low on a personality dimension concerned with the predisposition to schizophrenia. From a psychophysiological point of view it is also of some interest that the response to dexamphetamine was also capable of bringing out differences between the groups, so offering further evidence of quite fundamental variations in the nervous typological organization underlying the personality dimension. Some implications of this latter finding will be discussed further below.

Discussion and conclusions

The purpose of this paper has been to present the arguments in favour of a particular view of the schizophrenic disorders, namely one that tries to steer a path between conceptualizing them as either purely biochemical diseases or as entirely psychologically determined reactions. In arguing the case for a dimensional/nervous typological approach it has been necessary to range wide over a number of research areas which, directly or indirectly, can contribute to our understanding of the schizophrenias. Thus the dimensional view of these conditions rests heavily on facts both from genetics and from clinical and psychological studies of

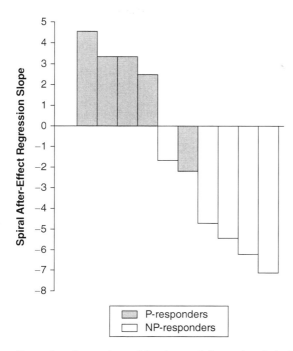

Figure 9.4 Comparison of the slopes of change in spiral after-effect under 10 mg. dexamphetamine in 'psychotic' and 'non-psychotic' responders to LSD-25. Note that P-responders tend to show a predominant rise, and NP-responders a predominant fall, in spiral after-effect with dexamphetamine.

psychotic and normal behaviour. Furthermore, as befits the probable nature of schizophrenic nervous function, the psychophysiological evidence is complicated. However, some consistent trends are beginning to emerge and point to the schizophrenias as being intricate disorders of central nervous organization. As such their explanation will demand the search for new principles of psychophysiological function, more complex than those that have sufficed so far in the field. Illustrating this point very well are the two examples quoted earlier, namely the inverted-U and narrowed attention principles often used as explanatory concepts in behavioural research. Neither of these principles seems capable of accounting for the psychophysiological relationships observed in the schizophrenic disorders and their pharmacological equivalent. Indeed, it begins to look as though it is their very failure to work, or even their tendency to work in reverse, that may explain the unusual central nervous organization associated with the schizophrenias and with the personality characteristics predisposing to them.

Some emphasis has been placed here on the use of drug research strategies for exploring nervous typological variations. Past experience has suggested that such techniques are uniquely valuable for throwing into relief the psychophysiological concomitants of personality. If it is also a viable notion that the predisposition to schizophrenia represents a major dimension of personality, then it too should benefit from a combined nervous typological and psychopharmacological attack. Of course, it could be, and is often, argued that the effects of the psychotomimetics do not resemble the natural psychoses sufficiently for their continued study to be worthwhile. However, this view is based on a misunderstanding of the logic of drug research in behavioural analysis. It is not to be expected that the model psychoses will exactly mimic the naturally occurring states (though actually they sometimes do so to a remarkable degree!); for the latter are complex disorders of the total personality, involving long-term psychological and behavioural adjustments and having central nervous factors only as their physiological substrate. It would be just as fallacious to argue that, because conventional sedatives and stimulants do not produce exact behavioural analogues of the psychoneuroses, such drugs are of little value in examining the psychophysiological basis of these conditions. As far as the psychotomimetics are concerned, there is considerable evidence, reviewed elsewhere (Claridge, 1970a), that drugs like LSD are of unique interest precisely because their curious effects on important processes like arousal and attention are so similar to those observed in schizophrenic patients. It is considered that the reason there have so far been few successful attempts to integrate facts about both within a single theoretical framework arises from the failure to recognize psychotomimetic drug research as an exercise in nervous typological analysis, of the kind illustrated in this paper.

A more powerful argument against the continued use of psychomimetics is an ethical one. Thus, it is unfortunate that those drugs which come closest to matching the naturally occurring psychoses are currently proscribed by society, leaving the genuine research worker in considerable doubt as to the ethics of administering substances like LSD even to volunteers under close supervision. However, it is possible that other, more acceptable, drugs could prove equally useful pharmacological tools for examining the nervous typological basis of the schizophrenias. The results reported here would suggest that dexamphetamine merits further investigation from this point of view.

A practical and not too fanciful consequence of such research might be the development of a pharmacological procedure for detecting individuals highly predisposed to schizophrenic breakdown. The need for, and feasibility of, such a development is supported by the view of Gottesman and Shields (*op. cit.*), who, concluding their discussion of the probable polygenic basis of schizophrenic inheritance and noting its close similarity to diabetes millitus as a threshold characteristic, make a plea for a diagnostic instrument with the power of the glucose tolerance test. Sedman and Kenna (1965), who found that sensitive, schizoid personalities showed a more pathological response to LSD, considered that that drug might serve such a purpose. In view of what has been said, it is possible that dexamphetamine could prove to be a more acceptable and practical alternative.

If a single conclusion had to be reached from the evidence reviewed here it would be that a sudden breakthrough in establishing the 'causes' of the schizophrenias now seems unlikely. Instead it looks as though the understanding of them will come slowly through careful dissection of those aspects of normal behaviour which in exaggerated form present as the schizophrenic disorders. In this paper we have emphasized the value of analysing such disorders at the nervous typological level of behaviour. This is because it is considered that the methods and concepts of psychophysiology are ideally placed for integrating the available facts. However, psychophysiology as a methodology or as a theoretical approach has no prerogative in the field. Indeed, its contribution may ultimately prove to be an intermediate one—that of providing a more objective system of classification, so enabling a more complete understanding to be gained of a group of personality disorders which are, at one and the same time, both biological and psychological.

Summary

Arguing from genetic, clinical and statistical evidence it is concluded that there is little support for the traditional view of the schizophrenias as qualitatively distinct diseases. A view more consistent with available facts is that they represent, in an exaggerated form, cognitive and personality characteristics found distributed among the general population. Starting from this dimensional view it is further argued that the predisposition to schizophrenia, like other personality dimensions, has a discoverable psychophysiological basis, in the form of a particular kind of nervous typological organization. The two most important processes involved seem to be those of arousal and attention, and evidence is reviewed in support of the author's theory that it is the manner in which these two processes co-vary that is uniquely different in schizophrenics and in normal individuals highly predisposed to schizophrenia. The special importance of drug techniques as nervous typological tools is emphasized and illustrated with some recent experimental findings on LSD-25. It is concluded that research such as that described may eventually lead to the development of pharmacological procedures which can identify individuals who are psychophysiologically predisposed to schizophrenic breakdown under stress.

Acknowledgements

The author wishes to thank the Mental Health Research Fund for the provision of certain apparatus used in the studies described in this paper. Thanks are also due to several colleagues, particularly Dr. H. J. Chappa, for the many hours spent in discussing the ideas presented here.

Commentary

If there appears to be a long time gap up until the next paper there are good reasons for this. It was a period when we were pursuing several lines of enquiry and, given the limitations on space here, it was difficult to find representative individual papers for all of them. The work is therefore divided according to three main topics that enclose the various research areas I was working on. The first topic covers theoretical issues and the question of how to conceptualise the dimensionality of schizophrenia. The second is the questionnaire measurement of psychotic traits. And the third has to do with experimental paradigms for investigating schizotypy. The coverage of these topics starts with the opening, theoretical chapter of my 1997 edited book on schizotypy, which can also act as a source of other information on our research (Claridge, 1997c).

Long before the book was even planned I had come across the concept of schizotypy (Rado, 1953; Meehl, 1962) and decided that the idea offered a better way of conceptualising the dimensionality of schizophrenia than Eysenck's psychoticism construct, which I had frequently criticised over the years. However, I was also unhappy with the way schizotypy had been interpreted by some writers, including Meehl himself. The subject has already been mentioned in the overview paper reprinted at the beginning of this book and will arise again later in several contexts; but it is worth recapping at this point because it is crucial to my arguments about the dimensionality of psychosis which have often been misunderstood or misinterpreted.

Some of the confusion about psychoticism lies in Eysenck's hijacking of the term and his using it in two distinctly different ways, both controversial. The later revised version of his theory – psychoticism equates to antisocial behaviour – would be judged unacceptable by most observers as a sole or even part explanation of psychosis. The original version – psychoticism as a broad generic personality dimension equivalent to neuroticism – might seem more congenial; but in fact has only been judged as such by dedicated followers of Eysenck. It is the later theory, and its implications, that more sharply expose the controversies in the topic. In practice the debate reduces to a disagreement mostly between American and European writers on schizotypy. There are two strands in the dispute. One is whether the schizotypy/schizophrenia domain is now too restrictive and would be better expanded to include other forms of psychosis – on the back, that is, of convincing evidence for what has been called the unitary view: that schizophrenia and bipolar disorder are overlapping illnesses. 'Psychoticism' might suitably capture the dimensionality aspect. The other point of disagreement concerns the interpretation of dimensionality in schizophrenia/psychosis: whether it is narrowly confined to a spectrum of *illness* (the American view) or whether it can also encompass healthy *personality* traits. That issue forms the focus of the accompanying paper.

10 Theoretical background and issues

Gordon Claridge

It should be noted at the outset that there is something of a mismatch between the leading title of the book from which this paper is extracted and the book's actual content. 'Implications for health' of schizotypy—as stated in the book's subtitle—sits uneasily with the latter's presumed basis in disease. 'Schizotypy' is a narrow term unambiguously connected to schizophrenia: historically, conceptually, clinically, and of course etymologically. No one even half familiar with the field could therefore be blamed for believing that, in so far as the book refers to mental illness, it will do so mostly with regard to schizophrenia. Yet there are other forms of madness, and even those who set out to study 'schizophrenia' soon find themselves straying beyond its boundaries, however defined. Furthermore, they do so—and this is the point—unavoidably. So, although in starting this paper as I have, I might appear to be prejudging one of its conclusions and so biasing the reader, this is not the case. It is merely a matter of fact—and part of the background we need to discuss here—that the ideas presented in the book have originated from a number of different sources; and that, where these origins have been psychiatric, they are not always strictly to be found in the schizophrenia literature *per se*. It is simply that schizophrenia has become the dominant idea, the shorthand term, the everyday metaphor for madness—whichever way one wishes to look at it—in the field of study that we are concerned with.

Attempts to extrapolate from the abnormal to the normal have naturally been shaped by the clinical *Zeitgeist*. Consequently, 'schizotypy', as the less deviant bedfellow of 'schizophrenia', has come into common usage among professionals as a way of expressing, for those who believe in it, the apparent dimensionality of psychosis. As we shall see, there are other labels but, for one reason or another, none is an ideal substitute: either a label is as restricted in meaning as 'schizotypy', but less well-known; or it sounds clumsy and is awkward to use grammatically; or it is already in use with a different meaning. To anticipate, I am referring here to, respectively, 'schizoidness', 'psychosis-proneness', and 'psychoticism'. For the moment, for want of a neat alternative, we are stuck with 'schizotypy' as the best generic descriptor we can find. I will certainly mostly use it here, though, like the authors of later chapters, sometimes in a rather loose or extended sense, and occasionally, where the context demands it, I shall resort to other terminology.

The above preamble serves to introduce the two main strands of the discussion in this paper. One concerns the question of continuity in serious mental illness: whether it exists and, if so, how far it can be generalized—into other, lesser forms of psychological disorder or even the healthy personality; and, if the latter, how that can be reconciled with the notion of a pathology for the abnormal state. The other strand is contained in the point we started from, viz. the overall scope of the subject matter with which we are dealing. This can be translated into the question taken up first, concerning the heterogeneity of psychosis.

Varieties of psychosis

Although not a formal psychiatric criterion for the distinction between 'mad' and 'not mad' (or 'psychotic' and 'not psychotic'), there is a good working agreement about what roughly distinguishes these two classes of mental illness. The 'not mad' (or 'not psychotic') refers to forms of distress or departure from the norm—for example neurotic anxiety, mild depression, antisocial attitudes, excessive narcissistic preoccupation—for which the average person can summon up some sympathy; he or she may already have been there or have become aware of the possibility, or they might have enough insight into their own personalities to know that they are not too far removed from the deviant characters they read about in novels, newspaper reports, or psychiatric glossaries.

The 'mad' (or 'psychotic'), on the other hand, evoke puzzlement, fear, a feeling of alienation, and a sense that the sufferer's behaviour and experience are strange and beyond the reach of empathy and ordinary rationality. As it happens, this is a false comparison. On closer inspection and with more careful thought, the sense of 'there but for fortune' attends, for many people at least, *both* the more serious, mad, psychotic aberrations *and* those of a lesser quality. Nevertheless, there *is* some distinction—the degree of insight into the state of the self when most disturbed is probably as good a rule of thumb as any for drawing it—and the notion survives of madness (psychosis) as somehow being recognizably different from other forms of psychopathology.

From the earliest times it has been observed that these serious disorders of mind can manifest themselves in various forms. Indeed, despite differences in terminology and explanation, there is a surprising continuity over the ages in the described phenomenology (see Cutting (1985) for a useful chronological listing). Distinctions encountered frequently refer to groupings according to such features as: deranged emotions or 'affections' (from melancholia to manic excitement); disturbed volition, deteriorating into apathy or 'dementia'; and disordered thinking, sometimes amounting to 'possession' by delusional beliefs that fly in the face of reality. The credit for first moving to shape these observations into the beginnings of a modern psychiatric nosology is commonly ascribed, jointly, to Emil Kraepelin (1919) and Eugen Bleuler (1911). As Berrios (1995) has recently pointed out, the account is an oversimplification of the historical progression which, not unusually, proceeded more unevenly than is usually portrayed. Nevertheless, as influential figures, Kraepelin and

Bleuler certainly represent landmarks in the attempt, throughout the nineteenth and early twentieth centuries, to provide a classification of serious mental illness that acknowledged both its unity and its variety. Kraepelin's contribution was the distinguishing of an affective, manic-depressive form from *dementia praecox*. The latter term gathered together several conditions—hebephrenic, catatonic, and some forms of paranoid illness—into what were perceived to be deteriorating mental diseases. It was the third group that Bleuler subsequently wrote about as 'the schizophrenias', a term that soon became singularized; misleadingly so, and for reasons which seem only to do with the awkwardness of linguistic usage. For even in the modern psychiatric glossaries, ICD-10 (World Health Organization 1992) and DSM-IV (American Psychiatric Association 1994), the criteria for an overall diagnosis of 'schizophrenia' can be made on the basis of widely differing sorts of criteria: the classic ones of delusions and hallucinations, certainly, but also disorganized or derailed speech, or flattened emotional expression.

Several issues that we now need to consider lie in the background to these attempts to describe and classify the psychotic disorders. The first is the stance, taken currently and in the past, on the question of there being a discoverable neuropathology for such conditions. Although later appearing to have some doubts, Kraepelin certainly considered initially that the composite illness, *dementia praecox*, was an organic disease. Bleuler, however, was less sure from the beginning and his explanation of schizophrenia was more of a compromise between the biological and the psychological. This reflected his view that among the primary features of schizophrenia—and perhaps constituting its biological substrate—is a loosening of associative thought. According to Bleuler, this then led—through a 'splitting' of psychological functions—to hallucinatory and delusional experiences. Yet it is the very presence of the latter, more bizarre features—the so-called 'first-rank symptoms' of Schneider (1959)—that has persuaded others to have a more straightforward medical view: that these are the direct signs of an underlying neurological disease process.

The failure, as yet, to find a unique pathology for schizophrenia—or most of its forms—means that the debate about its nature rumbles on, with organic, psychological, and psychobiological accounts still in play (see *Journal of Mental Health* 1993). For the moment, the most we can probably conclude is that, given the very strange nature of psychotic experiences, it is intuitively unlikely that there will be *no* associated aberrant brain function. On the other hand, it is equally unlikely that any pathology that is discovered will be as unsubtle as it is in most genuine neurological diseases, such as Alzheimer's disease, which is often used as a paradigm by some schizophrenia researchers. Of the three options considered above, a psychobiological perspective on schizophrenia seems the most promising, leaving open for consideration the full range of theoretical and empirical approaches. This means, as far as the ideas presented in this book are concerned, that although of interest—and certainly referred to—such biological evidence as presently exists is not crucial one way or the other to the central thesis about schizotypy, or any broader equivalent, as they relate to psychosis.

There are, incidentally, other reasons for drawing attention here to Alzheimer's and other neurological diseases as poor models for understanding schizophrenia. Despite the early use of the term 'dementia' in connection with it, there is no evidence that schizophrenia leads to any cognitive impairment (in the dementing sense), or indeed to any impairment that cannot be explained as a secondary consequence of other factors. On the contrary, as any perceptive clinician can vouch, individuals with the diagnosis can retain remarkable powers of intellect and creativity despite years of illness, social neglect, hospitalization, and damaging drug regimes. This is unlike neurological diseases proper which—to paraphrase Jaspers (1913), who drew a similar comparison—merely 'smash' the brain and generally, in the end, kill the person.

Turning to a second point at issue that runs through the classification of the psychoses, a persisting question has been whether Kraepelin was right to separate off manic-depressive insanity (bipolar affective disorder) from *dementia praecox* (schizophrenia). The attraction of doing so was that it helped to sustain a sound medical model that relied on being able to identify distinct diseases, definable according to their clinical course, treatment response, prognosis, and hopefully, eventually, a knowledge of their aetiology. The argument has been a persuasive one for psychiatrists right up until the present day, and schizophrenia and bipolar disorder remain officially listed as different illnesses in both ICD-10 and DSM-IV. However, this tradition has not gone unchallenged. Indeed the notion of there being only a *single* form of insanity goes back well into the early history of psychiatry, long antedating Kraepelin, and expressed as several versions of an *Eintheitpsychose* (or unitary psychosis) theory (see Berrios 1995).

In recent years there has been something of a revival of the unitary psychosis theory, centering partly on observations that bipolar affective psychosis and schizophrenia do not appear to be as distinguishable as was once thought, and partly on the failure to establish what McGuffin *et al.* (1987), writing from a genetics viewpoint, call 'lines of cleavage' among the schizophrenias as a group.

The overlap between bipolar and schizophrenic psychoses is evident in a number of ways (Taylor 1992). Most obviously, at the symptom level statistical analyses trying to find a clear point of rarity between these two forms of psychosis have generally failed to do so (Brockington *et al.* 1979; Kendell and Brockington 1980). Writing about the evidence elsewhere, Kendell (1991) comments that '... it is time we questioned Kraepelin's paradigm of distinct disease entities and of two discrete types of functional psychosis'. To an extent, of course, this is already acknowledged in the inclusion in the psychiatric glossaries—both ICD and DSM—of a 'schizoaffective' form of psychosis; though, interestingly, the condition is listed as a variant of schizophrenia, rather than being recognized as genuinely intermediate.

Other evidence for the *Eintheitpsychose* theory comes from the effective interchangeability of treatments between the two forms of psychosis (Klein and Fink 1963; Overall *et al.* 1964; Delva and Letemendia 1982; Abraham and Kulhara 1987). Then, on a more scientific front, there are observations that many experimentally established differences claimed for schizophrenia can often be found in affective disorder. Kendell (1991) comments, too, on this phenomenon, as follows:

> Time after time research workers have compared groups of schizophrenics and normal controls and found some difference between the two which they assumed to be a clue to the aetiology of schizophrenia, only for someone else, years later, to find the same abnormality in patients with affective disorders. Of all the dozens of biological abnormalities reported in schizophrenics in the last 50 years, none has yet proved to be specific to that syndrome. All have been found, although often less frequently, in patients with affective psychoses, and none has been demonstrated in more than a minority of schizophrenics.
>
> (pp. 14–15)

Examples of this overlap in experimental data range from pursuit eye movement aberrations (Iacono *et al.* 1982) and enlarged ventricles (Dolan *et al.* 1985) to the demonstration that 'overinclusive thinking'—a classically described feature of *schizophrenic* cognition (Cameron 1938; Payne *et al.* 1959)—also occurs in mania (Andreasen and Powers 1974).

Genetic findings (for example, Baron and Gruen 1991) on the intermingling of familial liabilities to schizophrenia and affective disorders can also be used to support the *Eintheitpsychose* model. The most explicitly stated psychiatric interpretation of such evidence is that offered by Crow (1986, 1991). He has argued forcefully for a continuum of psychosis, running from normal, through affective disorder, to schizophrenia, and biologically mediated by genetic influences on the neurodevelopment of brain asymmetry (Crow 1990). It remains to be seen whether such a sweeping generalization about aetiology proves fruitful; the theory has difficulties, for example, explaining the differences in clinical presentation between the schizophrenias or between the latter and affective psychosis. Nevertheless, together with Kendell's opinions, it puts down a strong marker that even psychiatry is having new (or at least renewed) thoughts about the viability of its earlier, more discrete disease modelling of psychosis to which it has been wedded for most of this century.

The blurring of the edges between the major forms of functional psychosis is not, however, the only point at issue in defining their status as psychiatric illnesses. An additional question about continuity concerns the extent to which they themselves merge into other, less serious, disorders. This is taken up in the next section.

Borderlands of psychosis

For reasons similar to those already outlined, post-Kraepelinian, organic psychiatry has also been slow to acknowledge that the outer boundaries of psychotic disorder are not as clearly demarcated as it would like. As discussed elsewhere (Claridge 1987), this 'fuzziness' does not in any way threaten the idea of psychological disorders as diseases, though it does open up further issues about psychiatric classification and its relation to the medical model. With a long-standing awareness of such questions, and despite its inherent conservatism, psychiatry has actually generated a considerable amount of interest in the topic of 'the borderline'. (I should mention that for the moment I am using this term in a very general sense, simply to refer to any psychological disorder that could represent a mild variety of, or be phenomenologically continuous with, one of the major forms of psychosis. As becomes clear later, 'borderline' also has a more technical meaning.)

The history this century of the general notion of 'the borderline' can be traced to several quite different clinical and theoretical perspectives. In an early guise it emerged as the notion of 'schizoidness', which from the very beginning formed an intrinsic part of the concept of schizophrenia. Manfred Bleuler (1978), who inherited his father's psychiatric mantle, makes this very clear. The term 'schizoid personality', he points out, took 'shape in conversations among the doctors of Burghölzi [the Zurich hospital where he and his father worked] in connection with the expression of "schizophrenia" around 1910'. The description was partly intended to capture the mental state of individuals who were strange or eccentric, but not showing the full-blown symptoms of schizophrenia. Since then it has established itself as part of the psychiatric nomenclature, finding its way into the psychiatric glossaries as 'schizoid personality disorder'. The defining features (as an Axis II disorder in DSM-IV (American Psychiatric Association 1994) include such signs as indifference to social relationships, constricted affect (cold, aloof), and a preference for solitary activities.

'Schizotypy' emerged much later. It was first used by Rado (1953), an American psychoanalyst, who coined it—in the form 'schizotype'—as an abbreviation for 'schizophrenic genotype.' As the derivation of the term indicates, it was meant to signify the hereditary disposition to schizophrenia, being roughly equivalent to 'schizoid personality' and to another descriptor used by E. Bleuler (1911), viz. 'latent schizophrenia'. Rado considered that schizotypy stemmed from psychodynamic personality traits concerned with the self-regulation of hedonic tone and expressed as 'an integrative pleasure deficiency' (anhedonia). According to him, adaptations that cope more or less effectively with this deficiency—preventing breakdown into open schizophrenia—nevertheless leave the individual with a personality structure identical to what would now be called 'schizoid personality disorder'.

The most vigorous immediate proponent of Rado's ideas was Paul Meehl (1962). He sharpened up the genetic formulation of schizotypy by coining the term 'schizotaxia' to denote what, in the genotype, is supposedly inherited in schizophrenia. For Meehl 'schizotypy' defined the phenotype, according to four behavioural traits: cognitive slippage (a mild form of thought disorder), interpersonal aversiveness, anhedonia, and ambivalence. At that stage, like Rado, he regarded anhedonia as the primary expression of schizotaxia, but in a later revision (Meehl 1990) he placed greater emphasis on the cognitive slippage component of schizotypy.

Meehl's change of opinion on this last point might partly reflect the general widening that has occurred in the definition of 'schizotypy' since Rado first introduced it. For two meanings have emerged, brought out by Kendler (1985) in a review of some ideas in the area. Kendler notes two different ways in which observers have attempted to characterize the 'schizophrenia spectrum'. One—signified by 'schizoid' (though Kendler does not note this) and closer to the original usage of 'schizotypy—stresses *personality* features. The other includes the latter, but also places emphasis on expression of the schizophrenia spectrum as attenuated forms of psychotic *symptoms*. It is a bias towards the latter that has crept into some recent usage. This is revealed by the kinds of psychometric instrument developed to measure schizotypy. It is also evident in the clinical indicators chosen to define Schizotypal Personality Disorder (SPD), another of the Axis II disorders related to schizophrenia, included in the DSM. As well as personality traits, such as social anxiety and eccentricity, the criteria also cover manifestly symptom-like features, for example transient illusory experiences and odd speech.

Most of the current research on the dimensionality of schizophrenia (the schizophrenia spectrum) is done under the umbrella of this broadened schizotypy concept (see Raine *et al.* (1995) for recent 'collected works'). This, in turn, is underpinned by the theory—for which there is reasonably good evidence (Ingraham 1995)—that schizotypy describes some aspect of the genetic basis for the predisposition to the schizophrenias. Twin questions that remain uncertain concern the precise definition of the schizophrenia spectrum itself (Levinson and Mowry 1991) and the exact components of schizotypy that relate to it. Regarding the latter point it has been argued (Torgersen 1994) that, from a genetics perspective at least, it is just a few of the specifically personality-based (schizoid) elements that are critical. On the other hand, there is evidence that narrowly schizoid and broader schizotypal subtypings overlap considerably (Coid 1992), as do the so-called Cluster A personality disorders in DSM-IV (viz. schizotypal, schizoid, and paranoid) in their relation to schizophrenia (Varma and Sharma 1993). For the moment there would seem to be an advantage in continuing to work within a wide, rather than a narrow, construction of schizotypy/schizoidness. (For an excellent recent discussion of this issue from a developmental perspective see Wolff (1995).)

It could be argued that the remit for schizotypy research should be—indeed already is—even broader, given the discussion in the previous section about the arbitrary division between schizophrenic and affective psychosis. Attempts to pursue 'the borderline' in the case of the latter have been less successful than for schizophrenia—strangely perhaps, though it might simply reflect comparatively less, or a different kind of, research effort. Nevertheless, there is a large, albeit somewhat chaotic, background literature on aspects of 'the borderline' that lie outside that referred to so far with respect to schizotypy (see Stone (1980) and, for a summary account, Claridge (1995)).

The work in question started from a similar point as that now subsumed under schizotypy research; also influenced by attempts—mostly by psychoanalysts—to define the outer boundaries of schizophrenia. Coining the term 'schizoaffective' formed part of this, as did the appearance of labels such as 'borderline schizophrenia' and 'pseudoneurotic schizophrenia'. Eventually the focus of attention shifted towards examining some of these intermediate conditions more from a view of their being personality disorders and the descriptor, 'borderline', in its more technical sense, was born. The main landmark here occurred through the revision that produced the DSM-III (American Psychiatric Association 1980)—specifically the recognition of two forms of 'borderline' disorder: one schizotypal (SPD), already referred to, and the other BPD. Unlike SPD, BPD is defined much more explicitly in terms of personality-based features of an aberrant kind, such as impulsivity, affective instability, and self-damaging patterns of behaviour.

Given the strong mood element in its definition, it would be a neat solution if BPD bore a relation to affective psychosis which mirrored that connecting schizotypy to schizophrenia. The evidence being equivocal, opinions on the issue are strongly polarized. Some (For example Paris 1994) dismiss the idea of a primary association to any Axis I psychosis; others (Stone 1977; Marziali et al. 1994) have argued that there is evidence connecting some forms of BPD to major mood disorder. A third view is that BPD is so ill-defined that, given nevertheless that it describes some fairly disturbed psychological functioning, it is bound almost by default to show a degree of relationship to psychosis (Tyrer 1994). If this were true then presumably it would be expected that the association would be to the affective (or schizoaffective), rather than to the narrowly schizophrenic, form of psychotic disorder.

Two other points are relevant here. One is evidence, some dating back to the DSM revision (Spitzer et al. 1979), that there is a considerable overlap between the schizotypal and borderline forms of personality disorder (see also George and Soloff 1986). This in itself, together with the co-morbidity of both BPD and SPD with several other types of Axis II personality disorder, would argue for a broad interpretation of continuity in this clinical domain, in the form of a '*psychosis* spectrum'. The second point, however, is that the existing psychiatric nosology already contains a clinical entity—in DSM-IV 'cyclothymic mood disorder'—which could provide an alternative or additional way of pursuing the 'borderline' variant in affective psychosis. Interestingly, with one small exception, this possibility has been entirely ignored by schizotypy researchers.

Although by no means a fully delineated framework for research or clinical practice, it is beyond reasonable doubt that in the illness domain there is strong dimensionality, connecting the psychoses to lesser variants of abnormal behaviour, particularly the personality disorders. A further, more radical question is how far this continuity can be extended back into the normal, healthy population.

Dimensions of psychosis

Except for an oversimplistic, all-or-none, theory of disease, the ideas presented in the previous section are perfectly compatible with a medical model of psychiatric disorder. Dimensionality within the clinical sphere is easily explicable in terms of a *forme fruste* concept of disease, viz. that the symptoms of illnesses can manifest themselves with varying severity, dependent upon the degree of expression of the relevant underlying cause. This, in turn, will be influenced by the presence or absence, or strength or weakness, of other modifying factors in the aetiology.

In personality psychology the concept of dimensionality is somewhat different, if only because it refers to continua that describe smoothly varying individual differences in healthy functioning that have no necessary reference point in abnormality (except in a purely statistical sense). Yet the two constructions of continuity do often come close together—and can do so unproblematically. Anxiety is a case in point. The notion of anxiety as a healthy personality trait (or transient adaptive state) is perfectly reconcilable with its expression as anxiety *disorder*. One is seen as merely flowing from the other, only a slight twist being needed to transform healthy into less-healthy functioning. Even the measured signs give us little clue as to where the transition occurs: scales of anxiety traits do not look all that different from scales of anxiety symptoms.

Viewing psychosis—especially schizophrenia—in a similar way has, predictably, proved more difficult. But not impossible. Here I am *not* referring to the ideas of the existentialist radical psychiatry of the 1960s. Long before that, 'dimensionality' formed part of a more received psychiatric (and psychological) wisdom about psychosis. The coining of 'schizoid', in connection with schizophrenia, is an example. As mentioned earlier, Eugen Bleuler was always somewhat uncertain about the status of schizophrenia as organic disease: there was a hint from the outset that the idea of disordered personality within schizophrenia could not be fully separated from the concept of schizophrenia itself and that something in the condition, while puzzling, was understandable, perhaps even continuous with normality. Jung (1960), a colleague of E. Bleuler's at the Burghölzi, with a deep interest in schizophrenia at that time, contributed to the debate.

Taking up this historical theme, Manfred Bleuler (1978) comments on why the 'discovery' of schizoid personality seemed so important to the appreciation of the quality of psychosis. He writes:

> To anyone who had accepted the concept, much of what constitutes the essence of schizophrenia was bound to appear to him as not quite so 'crazy' psychologically. The magic touch of the concept lay in the fact that it brought the mental patient closer to the heart and to the understanding of his doctor. It helped to establish a clear pathway to a 'psychodynamic' schizophrenia theory and to a sympathetic meeting with the mentally ill patient that was unencumbered by the hard, cold dogmas depicting the mental patient as something different, inaccessible, and beyond the reach of human empathy.
>
> (p. 434)

As M. Bleuler further notes, all of this resulted in schizoidness (or 'schizoidia') being seen sometimes as personality deviation and sometimes as an incipient sign, or mild form, of disease.

One person who combined both usages of 'schizoid' was Kretschmer (1925). He considered schizoid qualities as both clinical manifestations and traits of normal temperament, and established the first important dimensional model of psychosis in the modern period. His theory is also significant because it brought schizophrenia and affective psychosis (as manic depression) into the same domain:

152   *Gordon Claridge*

these two disorders defined the end-points of a dimension of normal personality, 'schizothymia – cyclothymia', which had 'schizoid' and 'cycloid' temperaments as intermediate aberrant forms. Kretschmer considered that variations along this dimension were constitutional, related to somatotype. His biological perspective accorded well with an emerging organic (genetic) view of psychosis that prevailed in the 1930s. But in other respects Kretschmer's theory was out of line and before its time. For example, it failed to identify a mechanism whereby temperamentally normal or mildly aberrant personality disorder could be seen to translate into manifest psychotic illness. Dimensional theories of psychosis remained, and to an extent still remain, only half-formed, the inherent ambiguities in them not fully articulated.

Figure 10.1 summarizes some of the above discussion by highlighting one source of confusion—the way in which dimensionality in psychosis has been variously construed. It draws a distinction between what, on the right of the diagram, I have labelled 'quasi-dimensional' and 'fully dimensional' interpretations, respectively. Quasi-dimensional corresponds to the *forme fruste* view of illness referred to earlier: continuity in psychosis certainly exists, but only in so far as it

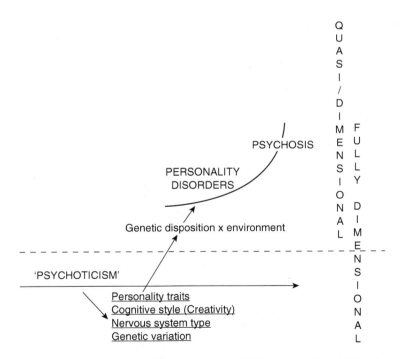

Figure 10.1 Comparison of quasi-dimensional (disease-based) and fully dimensional (personality-based) continuity modes of psychosis. Note that, in the fully dimensional part of the model, the term 'psychoticism' has a more comprehensive meaning than Eysenck's usage (see note in, and later part of, main text for further elaboration).

represents a variation in an underlying disease process. The aetiological questions for this type of theory concern the nature and cause of the neurological 'lesion' or functional incapacity. Regarding diagnosis and nosology, typical issues for debate include those discussed in the previous section about the relationship between full-blown psychosis and personality disorders, such as SPD, and the nature of the schizophrenia spectrum.[1]

The fully dimensional version is very different: it *encloses* the quasi-dimensional component but is otherwise more personality-based. Crucially, it adds another level of continuity, in the form of psychotic traits that constitute part of normal individual differences. These traits describe *both* sources of healthy variation *and* predisposition to disorder (psychosis-proneness). In other words, the fully dimensional model pursues the similarity to trait anxiety and anxiety disorder discussed above. The only difference from that example would seem to lie in the sharper discontinuity that might accompany the shift from the healthy state to disorder (represented in the figure as crossing the dotted line into the zone of functioning to which quasi-dimensional theorists confine themselves). It will be recalled that it was this bigger leap—and perhaps only that—which seemed to make the difference between extrapolating the fully dimensional view from the lesser (neurotic) illnesses to psychosis.

A radical feature of the fully dimensional construction of psychosis—distinguishing it from the quasi-dimensional alternative—concerns its approach to the study of 'aetiology'. Instead of taking the pathological as its only possible reference point, it also pays attention to a full range of data about normal individual differences: cognitive, personality, social, genetic, and so on. As predisposing influences, all of these are intrinsically part of the antecedent causes of psychotic illness, as well as of the intermediate disorders of personality associated with it. By the same token, a variable expression of these same predispositions also allows for the possibility of other, more healthy or adaptive outcomes, in favourable circumstances or enriching environments.

The two versions of dimensionality shown in Figure 10.1 roughly align to the psychiatric and the psychological; not surprisingly, the quasi-dimensional view finds more favour among medical observers. However, there is not a perfect correspondence in that respect. Among psychologists, at least, there is a marked Transatlantic difference in usage. Most North American workers on schizotypy, for example, are very committed to a quasi-dimensional explanation of the schizophrenia spectrum. Their theoretical position on this is largely due to the influence of Meehl, for whom schizotypy, as noted earlier, lies firmly in the domain of disease—as partially expressed 'schizotaxia'. Furthermore, the latter is considered by Meehl to be mediated by a single major gene. If true, this is certainly compatible with a continuum theory of the *quasi-dimensional* type (Roberts and Claridge 1991); but it probably rules out a *fully* dimensional interpretation, of the kind presented in Figure 10.1.

The notion of psychotic traits having healthy qualities seems quite foreign, then, to North American schizotypy researchers. Here, by way of illustration, I might mention one strong adherent of Meehl's theory who recently looked at me in complete incomprehension when I tried to explain to him the notion of the 'happy schizotype', a term which Charles McCreery has coined to designate individuals who seem perfectly content in their 'psychotic' personalities.

A diametrically opposite point of view to Meehl's—on the continuity question—and illustrating the Transatlantic divide is Eysenck's. He proposes a fully dimensional model close to that shown in Figure 10.1—indeed his theory partly inspired it. If there is a difference, it lies in the fact that Eysenck's version is even more 'fully' dimensional than that suggested here. This is because Eysenck appears to take little or no account of the discontinuities between traits and symptoms implied in the transition from adaptive personality to illness. For him all psychiatric disorders, including the psychoses, do seem merely to represent the end-points of continuously variable dimensions (Eysenck 1960).

This last feature of Eysenck's theory is, in my view, a weakness. As the late Graham Foulds (1965) pointed out many years ago, there is a logical distinction to be made between personality traits and the symptoms of illness, as two different universes of discourse. Admittedly, in some instances—for example anxiety, referred to previously—the differentiation can in practice be difficult to make, but it is nevertheless necessary to preserve it, in order to accommodate the fact that functional shifts do occur on entry into ill (or other unusual) states to which the relevant traits predispose the person. It is particularly important to recognize this in the case of psychosis, where such discontinuities may be very marked. However persuasive the personality-based dimensional view is in accounting for certain features, it is not an *alternative* to a medical paradigm for psychological disorders, as Eysenck has sometimes argued. It can, in fact, provide only a partial explanation, needing also to incorporate—as the fully dimensional model proposed here does—the element of discontinuity contained in disease theory.

Eysenck's theoretical position is also notable in two other respects. One is for his having formulated his views of psychosis largely outside the mainstream of schizotypy research; he has been driven more by attempts to develop his own ideas on personality structure, extending them into the sphere of 'psychoticism' and psychosis. The other is for his embracing *Eintheitpsychose* theory. He did so very early on (Eysenck 1952b), in the face, it has to be said, of considerable derision from some members of the psychiatric Establishment and long before some of them rediscovered the concept for themselves!

Taken together, the above two qualities of Eysenck's theory have caused it to emerge as a distinct alternative to all other contemporary views on the dimensionality of psychosis. His individual-differences approach is historically more in line with the personality, than with the now more prevalent clinical, constructions of psychosis-proneness, Eysenck being particularly influenced by Kretschmer's early schizothymia—cyclothymia theory of temperament (Eysenck 1952a). But Eysenck even departs drastically from that, with his proposal of 'psychoticism' (P) as a general personality factor common to *all* psychosis and introversion-extraversion (I-E) as the dimension differentiating the schizophrenic and manic-depressive forms (Eysenck and Eysenck 1976). This suggested arrangement certainly deals, in principle at least, with the questions raised earlier, arising from the apparent overlap between the two types of psychosis and the probable need to try to bring them within the same domain.

Yet Eysenck's further development of his ideas about psychoticism over the years has had other consequences that have caused his theory to appear to stand even more alone. The most significant is the adoption of what many would regard as an idiosyncratic approach to the questionnaire measurement of 'psychoticism'. In evaluating this latest view of psychotic traits I believe it is necessary to bear in mind an important distinction, crucial to understanding Eysenck's theory-building. I am referring to the different contributions Eysenck has made to the topic, as reflected in (1) his original very general theoretical statements about the dimensional structure of personality; and (2) his later, more current, interpretations of 'psychoticism' within that structure. The former, *qua* pure theory, could be claimed to be a quite viable, if unusual, alternative to more conventional approaches currently in vogue in schizotypy research: locating individuals in a dimensional framework of E, P (and N) might well be as informative a guide to their 'psychoticism', 'schizotypy', or 'psychosis-proneness' as more symptom-based evaluations, or accounts in terms of traditional personality descriptors, like 'schizoid' or 'cycloid'. However, Eysenck has gone further than that and, in doing so, has somewhat foreclosed the debate on the meaning of 'psychoticism' as an individual-differences construct. He has chosen to interpret psychoticism as a general dimension of antisocial behaviour and to formulate a theory of clinical psychosis based on the notion of a continuum of what is, effectively, aggressiveness; this runs from altruism at one end, through normal hostility, psychopathic personality disorder, and affective psychosis, to schizophrenia at the other (Eysenck 1992b). The scheme Eysenck proposes certainly offers a partial solution to some of the questions raised here about the nature of the 'psychosis spectrum' and its relation to psychosis itself; for example the possible merging of some forms of personality and psychotic disorder. But, as brought out in later papers here, his theory seems to fall short of what a *comprehensive* account of 'psychoticism'—in the broader sense in which we would like to use it here—should look like.

Conclusions

Several issues have been brought out in this paper: the breadth of the concept of madness; the relationship to less serious, but apparently associated, personality disorders; the defining role of biological or organic factors; and the terminology that can best capture the continuity within psychosis. But the main issue was the comparison drawn between the two models of dimensionality that have implicitly shaped research on the subject matter with which this book is concerned. Indeed, as the title indicates, that theme lies at the centre of the book. For, among other implications that later papers deal with, probably one of the most important questions that currently needs to be answered is about schizophrenia: whether it is a neurological disease or a personality deviation.

To anticipate an obvious retort to that statement, 'it' is probably neither, in two senses. First, some individuals who can be labelled 'schizophrenic' undoubtedly do have a diagnosable organic brain disease. But for the majority of cases—those that fall within the purview of this book—the evidence suggests that is not the case, and a more subtle explanation has to prevail. Even so—and this is the second reply to the expected objections to my earlier remark—neither simple biological aberrations nor understandable psychological reactions are likely to suffice as an explanation. Both Bleulers, and many other authors, have taught us that. Subsequent papers do not answer the questions that still persist, but perhaps they will give pause for thought to those readers who feel that they already 'know' what schizophrenia is.

Note

1 In Figure 10.1 I have borrowed the term 'psychoticism' from Eysenck. However, it is important to note that I have used it in a much broader, and in several other respects different, sense from that in which he uses it (Eysenck 1992b; and see later in this text). For the purposes of the figure I have preferred this to 'schizotypy' because it illustrates the general case better. In practice it would be expected that different expressions of 'psychoticism' might generate their own versions of the model, e.g. 'SPD' would substitute for 'personality disorders' along a 'schizophrenia spectrum' (Claridge 1994a).

Commentary

During the period now under review, and somewhat beyond, we put a good deal of effort into the questionnaire measurement of psychotic traits, having become disillusioned with the later versions of the Eysenck psychoticism scale. There were already instruments available in the American literature but these were too tainted, I felt, with the Meehl symptom-based, narrow view of schizotypy. We chose instead to model our first scales on 'borderline' features recognised by psychiatry as in the group of personality disorders that formed mild variants of psychosis. Two scales were produced – known simply as STA and STB and jointly as the STQ – first published by Claridge and Broks (1984). The STQ was subsequently used in many experimental and clinical studies (see my 1997 book for examples and references). Almost all of that work involved the STA, the strictly schizotypy scale; little was done with the STB which tapped more emotional traits reminiscent of the clinical diagnosis of Borderline Personality Disorder. However, the fact that the STB existed at all within the STQ – and, crucially, correlated highly with the STA – was a further sign that my thinking at that time was already moving away from the narrowly defined limits for psychotic traits preferred by many schizotypy researchers. My revisionist alternative was made more explicit in the next phase of our questionnaire construction, as the next paper explains.

The paper reports a large scale study, conducted jointly with Liverpool University, of the factor structure of psychotic traits in the general population. Setting aside, as investigators, preconceptions about the possible outcome, we administered a collection of questionnaires – bigger than any previously used in one study – that purported to measure psychotic personality features: not just schizotypy labelled scales, but also others of, for example, mania – and even the Eysenck psychoticism scale. Factor analyses of the data produced a clear result. They confirmed a unitary psychosis interpretation, schizotypy and non-schizotypy scales being interlinked in an inextricably connected factor structure.

Immediately following on from this paper, and completing the questionnaire story, is an account of the working questionnaire that came out of the joint Liverpool study. Its development formed part of the postgraduate work of Oliver Mason who has gone on to become a leading light in the field and an ally of mine in pushing forward the European view of 'schizotypy'. Notably the four-scale questionnaire he devised – the *Oxford-Liverpool Inventory of Feelings and Experiences* (or *O-LIFE*) – was deliberately named to emphasise its origins in personality rather than pathology. (Also, I can wickedly reveal, to take advantage of the coincidence of the Liverpool connection and the abbreviation of his name – Oli – by which he is always known!) Since its introduction, the *O-LIFE* has become one of the most respected and widely used questionnaires in experimental and clinical studies.

11 The factor structure of 'schizotypal' traits
A large replication study

Gordon Claridge, Charles McCreery, Oliver Mason, Richard Bentall, Gregory Boyle, Peter Slade and David Popplewell

The past decade has witnessed a rapidly growing interest in the construction of questionnaires for measuring psychotic traits among general population samples. A good deal of this effort has been inspired by 'schizotypy', a concept formulated by Rado (1953), and later elaborated by Meehl (1962, 1990), to denote the genetically determined disposition to schizophrenia. Attempts to measure schizotypy by questionnaire go back some years (Golden & Meehl, 1979) but have recently been given extra impetus by the need, established elsewhere in schizophrenia research, for measures that might help to define risk for the disorder. Research on the latter has relied substantially in the past upon longitudinal studies of vulnerable children (Watt, Anthony, Wynne & Rolf, 1984); but this is an expensive and time-consuming procedure, a fact that has encouraged the use of alternative, cross-sectional strategies to complement the classic high-risk designs (Claridge, 1994a; Lenzenweger, 1994). A logical part of this development has been the construction of self-rating questionnaires which can act as easily administered screening instruments, used to select (mostly adult) individuals for further examination in genetic, clinical and laboratory studies that bear on the causes, antecedents and mechanisms of schizophrenia (see Raine, Lencz & Mednick, 1995, for reviews of different activities in schizotypy research and for detailed evidence concerning the validity of the schizotypy construct).

The psychotic traits questionnaires that have appeared have had varying theoretical and empirical origins. Not all have been constructed explicitly from a 'schizotypy' viewpoint, some being only marginally, if at all, influenced by that idea. The most notable of these exceptions is Eysenck's P scale, which belongs with a more general individual differences research tradition, representing an attempt by Eysenck to extend his previously two-dimensional personality theory into three dimensions, to include psychoticism (Eysenck & Eysenck, 1976). Eysenck's construction of the latter as a *general* dimension encompassing *all* forms of psychosis reflects his *Einheitpsychose* view of psychotic disorder, and contrasts markedly with the narrower, schizophrenia, focus of traditional schizotypy research inspired by Meehl. Recently, however, there have been signs that these two approaches are beginning to converge, with the realization, even among some followers of Meehl, that 'schizotypy' may be too restrictive a term for the broad range of psychotic traits covered by current questionnaires.

Thus, the Chapmans, who have contributed the greatest number and variety of scales to the area, regularly refer to their instruments as 'psychosis-proneness' scales (e.g. Chapman, Chapman & Miller, 1982).

Indication of this need to broaden the schizotypy concept—or, if nothing else, evidence of its multidimensional structure—has come from a series of factor-analytic studies reported by different workers, utilizing both scale and item data. The results naturally vary, depending partly on the range and type of measures included in particular studies. Nevertheless, a consistent pattern emerges. Thus, all of the scale analyses reported so far confirm the existence of more than one component; apart, that is, from Kelley & Coursey (1992a) who described a single factor—of general schizotypy though one which they admit was based on data from an unusually homogeneous sample of subjects. Even the relatively smaller study by Raine & Allbutt (1989) revealed two factors: one was something like Kelley & Coursey's, the other an asocial form of anhedonia. In all of the other analyses 'general schizotypy' has been more precisely defined, the most consistent observation being the emergence of a factor that corresponds to the 'positive symptomatology' of schizophrenia, as represented in cognitive and perceptual aspects of schizotypy. As in the Raine & Allbutt (1989) analysis, some anhedonic component—relating to 'negative symptom' schizophrenia—is also regularly found, as well as another, nonconformity or antisociality factor (Kendler & Hewitt, 1992; Muntaner, Garcia-Sevilla, Fernandez & Torrubia, 1988). In studies where *items* rather than scales have been analysed a similar separation of 'positive' and 'negative' components has been observed (Gruzelier, Burgess, Stygall, Irving & Raine, 1995; Raine, Reynolds, Lencz, Scerbo, Triphon & Kim, 1994; Venables, Wilkins, Mitchell, Raine & Bailes, 1990).

The most comprehensive published analysis, in terms of the number of scales included, was an early investigation of the structure of schizotypy by Bentall, Claridge & Slade (1989). Their study, which forms the background to the present report, made use of a multi-scale questionnaire (CSTQ) described in detail in the next section, consisting of 18 existing scales: the Eysenck Personality Questionnaire (EPQ), 10 of the most prominent schizotypy scales in use at the time, and four clinical scales for assessing delusional beliefs. Bentall *et al.* carried out two separate principal component analyses, one with and one without the four delusional scales. In the latter case three factors emerged, two corresponding to the positive and negative components referred to earlier and a third representing a mixture of cognitive disorganization and social anxiety; this appeared to represent a further subdivision of the positive/negative distinction of schizophrenia. Bentall *et al.* noted that their three factors showed a striking resemblance to a similar three obtained by Liddle (1987) in his study, in patients, of schizophrenic symptoms; Liddle referred to his factors as reality distortion, disorganization and psychomotor poverty. Bentall *et al.*'s second principal component solution, with the delusional scales included, produced four factors. Three were similar to those found in their first analysis; the fourth was labelled 'disinhibited or asocial schizotypy', corresponding to the 'non-conformity' component found by some other workers, and originally by Muntaner *et al.* (1988). Subsequently, in an unpublished study of the CSTQ using another, somewhat bigger sample, McCreery (1993) closely replicated the Bentall *et al.* finding, with one difference: he demonstrated their four-component solution even with the delusional scales removed.

Updating the smaller Bentall *et al.* and the unpublished McCreery analyses, this paper presents the results for what is now a large accumulated data set on the CSTQ. It also reports on a subsidiary aim of the study: to investigate the relationship between the Eysenck dimensions and the factor structures that have emerged from previous analyses of strictly schizotypy scales. We were led to do this by two contrasting comments that have appeared in the recent literature. The first is Kelley & Coursey's (1992a), who have suggested that both the Bentall *et al.* and the Muntaner *et al.* (1988) studies failed to define the structure of schizotypy unambiguously due to the inclusion of the EPQ scales, which were not specifically designed to measure such traits. The second is from Eysenck & Barrett (1993) who, drawing upon their reanalysis of the Kendler & Hewitt (1992) correlation matrix, claim to find three factors that map directly onto the Eysenckian three-dimensional framework—with, as they put it, 'little trace of schizotypy left, and no evidence of any single factor corresponding to such a factor'. Here we aimed to test this claim by analysing our data with and without the Eysenck scales.

Method

The scales

As noted earlier, the data came from the CSTQ, consisting of the following scales:

(a) the Extraversion, Neuroticism, Psychoticism and Lie scales of the EPQ (Eysenck & Eysenck, 1975).
(b) Claridge & Rawlings' STQ, consisting of the Schizotypal Personality and Borderline Personality scales (Claridge & Broks, 1984).
(c) Chapman and Chapman's scales measuring Physical Anhedonia; and Social Anhedonia (Chapman, Chapman & Raulin, 1976); Perceptual Aberration (Chapman, Edell & Chapman, 1980); Magical Ideation (Eckblad & Chapman, 1983); and Hypomanic Personality (Eckblad & Chapman, 1986).
(d) Launay & Slade's (1981) Hallucination scale.
(e) Nielsen & Petersen's (1976) Schizophrenism scale.
(f) Golden & Meehl's (1979) seven-item Schizoidia scale from the MMPI.
(g) Four symptom scales from the Delusions Symptoms States Inventory (Foulds & Bedford, 1975), named Delusions of Contrition, Delusions of Persecution, Delusions of Grandeur and Delusions of Disintegration.

The questionnaire was administered in two parts. The first part, consisting of 145 'Yes/No' items, included the four Eysenck and the two Claridge scales; the remaining scales, 275 items, formed the second part and required a 'True/False' response.

Sample

The sample available for analysis consisted of 1095 subjects. The bulk of it was obtained by combining the samples of the Bentall *et al.* (1989) and McCreery (1993) studies, 180 and 695 subjects, respectively. This set was supplemented with individuals who had completed the CSTQ as part of the procedure in a variety of experimental and other investigations of schizotypy. Subjects were recruited from various sources, including the Oxford Subject Panel, as student or health professional volunteers or, in the case of the largest subset (408 subjects), through a media appeal by McCreery in connection with a study of out-of-the-body experience. Of the total sample, 715 were female and 378 were male, sex being unrecorded in two cases. The mean age was 39.97 years (SD = 16.86).

Results

Description of data

Table 11.1 shows the mean scores, standard deviations and measures of skew for all of the CSTQ scales administered. Also included are correlations with age and *t* tests for sex difference comparisons. It can be seen that all of the scales correlated significantly with age—to at least the .05 level—though numerically the values were rather small; the exceptions where there was a sizable correlation with age included P, STB and HoP (all negative) and L (positive). Similarly, many of the sex differences were statistically significant. In general these were again numerically rather small, though there were more substantial sex differences for P, SoA and PhA (males > females) and Mgl and STA (females > males). These age and gender effects accord with the known properties of the various scales concerned.

Statistical analyses

General considerations. The correlation matrix for the full set of 18 CSTQ scales is shown in Table 11.2. For the purposes of further analysis it was decided to omit the four Foulds delusional scales, for two reasons. The first was practical. As noted in the Introduction, the unpublished analysis by McCreery (1993) of a subsample of the present data had already demonstrated virtually similar four-factor solutions, whether or not the Foulds scales were removed; indeed, their inclusion actually had the effect of reducing the total variance accounted for from 70.9 per cent to 65.4 per cent. The second, more theoretical reason for omitting the Foulds scales stemmed from their psychometric properties. The scales were originally devised as symptom assessment procedures to aid in the diagnosis of clinical psychosis. Consequently they contain many 'strong' items which few ostensibly normal subjects endorse and which result in markedly skewed distributions (see Table 11.1). Such extreme skew is difficult to normalize by any of the standard transformations; so there is some question as to the statistical propriety of including them in a factor analysis, with its underlying assumption of bivariate normal distribution.

Table 11.1 Means, SDs, indices of skew and effects of sex and age for the 18 scales

	E	N	P	L	STA	STB	SoA	PhA	MgI	PAb	HoP	LSHS	NP	MMPI	dC	dG	dP	dD
Means	12.77	12.24	3.56	7.45	16.50	6.21	12.77	13.46	7.93	5.90	16.10	3.67	6.59	2.43	0.67	1.3	0.33	0.78
SD	5.20	5.44	2.65	4.14	7.53	3.84	6.03	7.38	5.98	5.87	9.31	2.79	3.34	1.52	1.24	1.59	.89	1.22
Skew	−.44	−.074	.95	.55	.15	.51	.80	.77	.86	1.86	.47	.56	.02	.54	2.60	1.36	4.14	1.98
Sex (t)	4.56	4.62	6.07	5.43	6.16	.35	5.01	6.96	4.92	2.38	1.38	4.55	2.67	.93	2.05	3.33	1.49	2.06
Sex (p)	.00	.00	.00	.00	.00	.73	.00	.00	.00	.02	.17	.00	.01	.35	.04	.00	.14	.04
Age (r)	−.13*	−.16*	−.37*	.43*	−.22*	−.40*	.12*	.12*	−.12*	−.18*	−.33*	−.16*	−.06	−.09*	−.10*	.23*	.10*	−.06

*Significant at .01 level.
Key. E, N, P, L = Extraversion, Neuroticism, Psychoticism, Lie scales of EPQ.
STA = Schizotypal Personality; STB = Borderline Personality.
SoA = Social Anhedonia.
PhA = Physical Anhedonia.
MgI = Magical Ideation.
PAb = Perceptual Aberration.
HoP = Hypomanic Personality.
LSHS = Hallucination Scale.
NP = Schizophrenism Scale.
MMPI = Schizoidia Scale from MMPI.
dC = Delusions of Contrition; dG = Delusions of Grandeur; dP = Delusions of Persecution; dD = Delusions of Disintegration.

Table 11.2 Correlation matrix for 18 scales

	E	N	P	L	STA	STB	SoA	PhA	MgI	PAb	HoP	LSHS	NP	MMPI	dC	dG	dP	dD
E	1.00																	
N	-.14	1.00																
P	.07	.15	1.00															
L	-.11	-.15	-.33	1.00														
STA	.05	.63	.27	-.14	1.00													
STB	.08	.64	.44	-.34	.68	1.00												
SoA	-.42	.18	.15	.11	.23	.14	1.00											
PhA	-.30	.04	.11	.21	-.13	.02	.40	1.00										
MgI	.20	.30	.25	-.03	.70	.44	.18	-.12	1.00									
PAb	.07	.33	.31	-.09	.66	.47	.19	-.08	.69	1.00								
HoP	.40	.38	.43	-.17	.61	.61	.12	-.11	.64	.55	1.00							
LSHS	.15	.40	.21	-.08	.73	.52	.15	-.12	.70	.65	.63	1.00						
NP	-.32	.69	.13	-.09	.55	.49	.35	.13	.28	.30	.26	.38	1.00					
MMPI	-.14	.45	.24	-.05	.41	.46	.25	.17	.34	.27	.34	.30	.41	1.00				
dC	-.06	.38	.28	-.10	.40	.49	.265	.15	.38	.44	.37	.36	.35	.41	1.00			
dG	.14	.24	.34	-.10	.43	.38	.21	-.02	.55	.45	.62	.45	.23	.30	.39	1.00		
dP	.07	.18	.24	-.02	.30	.31	.17	.07	.38	.38	.33	.32	.20	.23	.45	.39	1.00	
dD	.10	.22	.23	-.01	.54	.35	.19	-.02	.67	.65	.49	.64	.21	.28	.40	.45	.46	1.00

Key. See Table 11.1

Out of interest, both principal component analysis (as used in our previous tests of the data) and maximum-likelihood factor analysis were undertaken. In fact the results using these two procedures were virtually identical and only the maximum-likelihood findings are presented here. Two such analyses were carried out—one with and one without inclusion of the EPQ E, N and L scales. (There seemed no theoretical reason for excluding P since it purports to tap the domain of psychosis-proneness.)

Analysis with Eysenck scales. The full correlation matrix shown in Table 11.1 was subjected to maximum-likelihood factor analysis with oblique rotation using the direct oblimin procedure, applying the scree test to estimate the appropriate number of factors. The scree plot is shown in Figure 11.1, from which it was decided that a fourth factor solution was the best representation of the data. Table 11.3 shows the pattern matrix after oblique rotation of these first four factors. The factors bear a very close resemblance to those found previously in the Bentall *et al.* study. Factor 1, accounting for the greatest part of the variance, is reminiscent of the positive symptom features of schizophrenia. It appears as 'aberrant perceptions and beliefs', with high loadings on the hallucinatory scale (LSHS), the Chapmans' PAb and MgI scales and Claridge's STA. Interestingly, the tendency to cyclothymic mood (HoP) also has a high loading, indicating that this major factor is not confined to schizophrenia-related features. Factor 2 is characterized by high loadings on the Nielsen-Petersen Schizophrenism scales, Eysenck's N, and, to a lesser extent, the two Claridge scales. All of these instruments contain items covering social anxiety and/or cognitive signs such as attentional difficulties and distractibility. It could be labelled 'cognitive disorganization with anxiety'. The third factor appears to define a component of 'asocial behaviour' with associated impulsiveness and mood-related disinhibition, revealed in high positive loadings on Eysenck's P scale, Claridge's STB and the Hypomania Scale. The high (negative) loading on L suggests that the latter acts, in this instance, as a social conformity scale. Finally, Factor 4, which we would label ' introvertive anhedonia', comes close to a description of the schizoid personality features in schizotypy, namely solitariness and lack of feeling. In the full clinical domain it would correspond to the negative symptom aspects of schizophrenia. Correlations between these four factors were low to moderate and much as expected. They ranged from zero (Factors 3 and 4) to 0.36 between Factor 1 and the other cognitive factor, 'cognitive disorganization'.

Analysis without E, N and L. Figure 11.2 shows the scree plot for the comparable analysis omitting three of the scales from the EPQ; also shown is the scree plot for the complete analysis reported in the previous section. A four-factor solution is again suggested, though it should be noted that in order to accept that it is necessary to relax the Kaiser criterion of an eigenvalue greater than unity; the fourth factor in the smaller analysis had an eigenvalue of only 0.87. However, accepting a fourth factor seems justifiable given the virtually identical scree plot profiles (as compared in Figure 11.2) with and without the Eysenck scales, as well as the firm indication, in the former case, of an interpretable fourth factor.

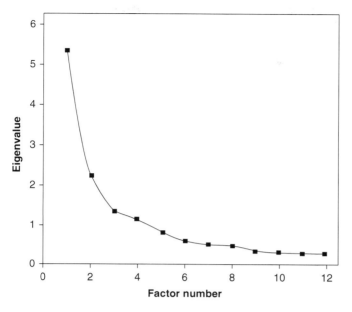

Figure 11.1 Eigenplot for maximum-likelihood analysis.

Table 11.3 Rotated (oblimin) pattern matrix for the maximum-likelihood analysis

	Factor 1	Factor 2	Factor 3	Factor 4
E	.25	−.33*	.30*	−.53*
N	.05	.84*	.09	−.06
P	.17	−.11	.61*	.27
L	.11	−.14	−.44*	.13
STA	.65*	.44*	.00	−.07
STB	.24	.48*	.48*	−.02
SoA	.22	.05	−.07	.68*
PhA	−.15	−.02	.11	.58*
MgI	.91*	−.04	−.06	.00
PAb	.76*	.03	.01	.06
HoP	.63*	.01	.39*	−.09
LSHS	.78*	.15	−.05	−.08
NP	.10	.73*	−.06	.17
MMPI	.19	.33*	.17	.21

*Factor loadings > .3.
Key. See Table 11.1

Factor loadings for the smaller analysis are shown in Table 11.4, where it can be seen that, as far as factor content is concerned, the results were exactly the same as when the three Eysenck scales were included. Factor 1 is again very

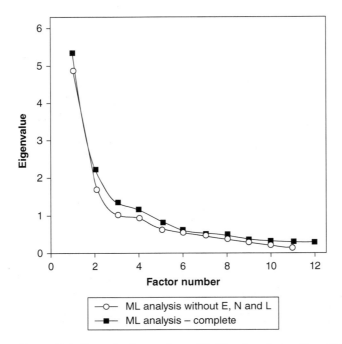

Figure 11.2 Eigenplot for maximum-likelihood analysis without E, N and L scales.

Table 11.4 Rotated (oblimin) pattern matrix for the maximum-likelihood analysis excluding E, N and L scales

	Factor 1	Factor 2	Factor 3	Factor 4
P	.10	−.03	.10	.57*
STA	.57*	.48*	−.10	.01
STB	.03	.58*	−.17	.55*
SoA	.19	.12	.64*	−.09
PhA	−.19	−.01	.64*	.14
MgI	.92*	−.09	.04	.00
PAb	.75*	.01	.04	.06
HoP	.56*	.01	−.09	.40*
LSHS	.75*	.15	−.06	−.01
NP	.02	.75*	.14	−.09
MMPI	.11	.33*	.18	.20

*Factor loadings > .3.
Key. See Table 11.1

strongly defined by the scales measuring psychotic-like perception and belief and Factor 2 by the cognitive disorganization tapped in the Nielsen–Petersen and STA scales. The only departure from the other analysis was that, as revealed in comparing Tables 11.3 and 11.4, the third and fourth factors were transposed. Factor 3 is now 'introvertive anhedonia' and 'asocial behaviour' now becomes the fourth, slightly marginal, factor, defined by P and Hypomanic Personality.

Discussion

The study reported here—the largest to date in this area—leaves little room for doubt that four factors are necessary to account for the variations described. Furthermore, the factors that emerge appear to have ecological validity in mapping on to recognizable clinical features of the syndromes to which they purport to relate. What, then, are the implications of the results for defining the boundaries of the schizotypy concept?

One way to address the question is relatively narrowly, with respect to those scales that belong in the 'classic' schizotypy tradition and which were specifically designed to measure features extrapolated from schizophrenia. If we do so it becomes clear that schizotypy is *not* a unidimensional construct—any more than schizophrenia is a homogeneous condition—and even the traditional schizotypy scales break into three components. The more critical question is whether there is evidence that other psychotic or psychotic-like characteristics overlap with or, alternatively, clearly separate off from strictly schizotypal features. Notable here is the observation that scales deliberately designed *not* to measure schizotypy had high (sometimes extremely high) loadings on the main 'schizotypy' factors. A good example is the consistently high loadings of the Chapmans' Hypomanic Personality Scale on the leading 'positive schizotypy' factor that appeared throughout the data. Another instance is the similar showing of the STB scale, again designed to measure traits derived from borderline, not schizotypal, personality disorder and therefore arguably closer to affective than to schizophrenic psychosis (Stone, 1980). There would therefore appear to be a good case for redefining the domain sampled in a more general way, as psychosis-proneness or psychoticism, rather than schizotypy. This would certainly be in keeping with the trend in certain quarters of clinical psychiatry to revert to the notion of *Einheitpsychose*, arguing against discrete disease entities and in favour of arbitrary boundaries between schizophrenic and manic-depressive forms of psychosis (Kendell, 1991).

An *Einheitpsychose* theory is of course the position adopted by Eysenck, though applied in his case to normal individual differences, and even then based on a very particular construction of 'psychoticism' that is only interpretable when used alongside his other personality dimensions. Comparing the two perspectives on the data described here—the Eysenckian and the non-Eysenckian—the results reported are unambiguous. Our factor analysis omitting three of the EPQ scales does not support either the argument that some previous accounts of the structure of 'schizotypy' have been distorted by the inclusion of the Eysenck scales, or Eysenck's even stronger contention that the structure can actually be explained in terms of E, N and P. On the contrary, our findings—obtained on a more representative set of data—indicate that the four-factor structure of psychosis-proneness can stand alone without two of Eysenck's major dimensions (E and N); and that if the structure had to be reduced to three it would, ironically, mean discarding the very component that is mostly defined by Eysenck's own psychoticism scale, which scarcely figures elsewhere in the factor matrix.

These observations mirror the flawed nature of Eysenck's interpretation of psychosis-proneness. Ever since its inception the P scale has come under fire for its poor validity as a measure of psychotic traits and its failure to capture the essential qualities of psychosis (Claridge, 1981, 1983); most commonly it has been regarded as a scale, rather, of *psychopathic* characteristics (Zuckerman, 1989). However, far from taking this as a criticism Eysenck has actually made it the centrepiece of his explanation of psychosis: according to him 'psychoticism' represents a dimension of aggressiveness defined at its far end by schizophrenia (Eysenck, 1992b). The idea of aggressiveness as a core aetiological feature of schizophrenia is both counter-intuitive to the impression of the majority of schizophrenic patients and contrary to the clinical evidence (Buckley, Walshe, Colohan & O'Callaghan, 1990). It is also flatly contradicted by the results reported here, and in other similar factor-analytic studies of psychotic traits. The strongest component of psychosis-proneness that invariably emerges in all of these studies (except those reported by Eysenck himself) is not aggressive affect but what we have designated here 'aberrant perceptions and beliefs'. It is this cognitive trait characteristic that looks as though it might represent the unique, necessary element in the disposition to psychosis. The role of the other slightly less specific components—including the asocial traits used to define Eysenckian psychoticism—might then be to combine and interact with that primary cognitive feature to define the vulnerability to particular forms of psychotic illness.

As noted at the beginning of this paper, definition of the traits predisposing to schizophrenia and other functional psychosis serves a number of purposes. One is that it represents the first stage in an effort to develop more objective, laboratory based indices of risk by helping to select individuals for further, experimental, studies of the correlates of psychosis-proneness. So far work along those lines has proceeded in a somewhat haphazard fashion, mostly confined to studies of single empirically derived scales. With greater theoretical sophistication and an understanding of the structure of psychosis-proneness now beginning to emerge, a new generation of experimental studies is promised that tries to isolate the, probably different, correlates of its various components.

Acknowledgement

For their contributions to the data set analysed here the authors wish to thank Janie Brod, Julie Evans, Michael Jackson, Emmanuelle Peters and Alex Richardson.

12 The Oxford-Liverpool Inventory of Feelings and Experiences (O-LIFE)

Further description and extended norms

Oliver Mason and Gordon Claridge

1. Introduction

Over the past several decades many self-report scales have been developed for measuring, in non-clinical individuals, what has variously been termed schizotypy, psychosis-proneness, or psychoticism (for reviews see Chapman et al., 1995; Mason et al., 1997b).[1] Of the three descriptors mentioned the most commonly used has been 'schizotypy', reflecting a major research focus on schizophrenia and the schizophrenia spectrum. Even so, the scales themselves have differed in coverage and item content. Some, such as Raine's (1991) Schizotypal Personality Questionnaire, have a broad remit, designed to represent the DSM symptoms of Schizotypal Personality Disorder; others, like the Perceptual Aberration Scale (Chapman et al., 1978) and the Hallucination Scale of Launay and Slade (1981), have been of more limited scope.

In response to the evident heterogeneity of the construct there has been a series of attempts to establish the underlying structure of schizotypy, usually by factor analysis. The number of components emerging from these studies has varied from two to four, depending on the range and item content of scales included in the analyses (Mason et al., 1997b; Vollema and van den Bosch, 1995). However, a consensus now seems to have been established that schizotypy reduces to three components which correspond well to the three-factor model of schizophrenic symptoms (Vollema and Hoijtinkm, 2000). As for the identity of these components, the majority opinion is that they consist of factors of 'positive schizotypy', 'cognitive disorganisation', and 'negative schizotypy', though Venables and Rector (2000) differ in describing the latter as 'social impairment'.

It was against this background that the Oxford-Liverpool Inventory of Feelings and Experiences (O-LIFE) was developed and first published (Mason et al., 1995). Compared with other instruments in the field, the questionnaire is unusual in several important respects, empirical and theoretical. Uniquely, the questionnaire's items are based on what, to date, is the most extensive study of 'schizotypal' traits undertaken: viz. factor analysis of some fifteen existing psychosis-proneness scales in over 1000 subjects (Claridge et al., 1996). The latter study was an expansion of an earlier investigation of the same scales in a smaller sample reported by Bentall et al. (1989). Both sets of analysis produced similar results. In addition to the three schizotypy components referred to earlier as being found by most other workers, we also identified a fourth factor which we labelled 'asocial behaviour': this loaded on three scales not included by other workers in their analyses, viz. the Eysenck P-scale (Eysenck and Eysenck, 1975), the Hypomania scale (Eckblad and Chapman, 1986), and the Borderline Personality (STB) scale published by Claridge and Broks (1984). Working with the larger of our two data sets referred to above, the O-LIFE was constructed, initially through exploratory factor analysis, and then by confirmatory factor analysis (Mason, 1995). Mirroring our original analyses of psychosis-proneness questionnaires the O-LIFE was designed to have four scales. As described in more detail later, these are: Unusual Experiences (UnEx), Cognitive Disorganisation (CogDis), Introvertive Anhedonia (IntAn), and Impulsive Nonconformity (ImpNon).

The existence of a fourth scale in the O-LIFE – unlike comparable questionnaires – needs further comment. It could be suggested that the discovery of this additional component in 'schizotypy' merely reflected the wide range of scales included in our original data set: confirmation of the cynical adage that you get out of factor analysis what you put in! However, we would claim something more substantive. Elsewhere (Claridge, 1997c) we have argued that, as presently envisaged, the schizotypy construct is too restrictive and that a broader concept of psychosis-proneness might more accurately reflect the clinical reality. We are referring here to the unitary view of psychosis and the possibility that schizophrenias and bipolar disorder have common features. Quoting evidence about symptom and therapeutic overlap, several prominent psychiatric writers (e.g. Kendell, 1991) have championed this *Einheitpsychose* theory, a model that is now receiving increasing support from studies demonstrating that schizophrenia and affective disorders may share a common biological susceptibility (Berrettini, 2003; Freedman et al., 2000; Perry et al., 2001).

Work with psychosis-proneness scales is in keeping with that evidence. For example, Heron et al. (2003) recently reported that their questionnaire measure of 'schizotypy' lacked specificity in distinguishing schizophrenia from bipolar disorder. And, notably, inclusion in our own analyses of the Chapman's Hypomania scale and our Borderline Personality scale did not just help to define the fourth, Impulsive Nonconformity, factor; they also had substantial loadings on other 'regular' schizotypy components, such as susceptibility to aberrant experiences and magical ideation. In other words, if such scales are allowed into analyses of 'schizotypy', a broader domain of psychosis-proneness is indeed revealed. At the very least the four-scale structure of the O-LIFE allows for this possibility to be investigated.

O-LIFE is also unique in being predicated on a different view of the dimensionality of psychotic traits, compared with most other scales of its type. Elsewhere (Claridge, 1997c) we have made the distinction between what we have termed 'quasi-dimensional' and 'fully dimensional' models of schizotypy. The former is based on the notion of schizotypy as a *forme fruste* of schizophrenic disease, thus limiting its dimensionality to the clinical schizophrenia spectrum. In the psychometric domain quasi-dimensionality finds expression as the taxonomic, mild illness model of schizotypy adopted by Meehl and his followers (Meehl, 1990;

Lenzenweger and Korfine, 1995). The fully dimensional model, on the other hand, emerged out of personality theory and regards psychotic characteristics as no different from other individual differences traits – such as anxiety – that potentially have either healthy or unhealthy outcomes.

Space does not permit elaboration of the debate surrounding these two models of psychosis (for a detailed discussion see Claridge, 2006). Suffice it to say that the evidence is strongly weighted in favour of the fully dimensional model and the design of the O-LIFE reflects this. Thus in constructing the questionnaire we deliberately focussed on trait, rather then symptom features, avoiding as far as possible 'stronger' clinically worded items. This, we believed, would make the instrument particularly useable in non-clinical populations, ideally suited for addressing such issues as risk for psychosis.

Since its introduction, the O-LIFE has enjoyed wide currency. Early work by Mason et al. (1995) established its high internal consistency: for Unusual Experiences $\alpha = 0.89$; for Cognitive Disorganisation $\alpha = 0.87$; for Introvertive Anhedonia $\alpha = 0.82$; and for Impulsive Nonconformity $\alpha = 0.77$. These results have since been confirmed by Rawlings and Freeman (1997: 0.77, 0.81, 0.85 and 0.72). Test–retest reliability is similarly high, across all four scales being greater than 0.70 (Burch et al., 1988). Confirmatory factor analysis has identified a very acceptable degree of goodness of fit of the four factor solution in the absence of any other acceptable models (Mason, 1995b). It has been translated into several languages, including Spanish (Barrantes-Vidal, 1997), Hebrew (Kravetz et al., 1998), Swedish (Goulding, 2004), Hungarian (Magos, personal communication) and Japanese (Bando, personal communication). It has also been used in a variety of studies across many research domains, firmly establishing its construct validity as a genuine measure of schizotypal traits. Laboratory investigations have demonstrated predictable effects in relation to neuropsychological function (Rawlings and Goldberg, 2001; Avons et al., 2003); on several perceptual and attentional paradigms (Tsakanikos and Reed, 2003; Mason et al., 2004; Steel et al., 2002; Jolley et al., 1999); in psychophysiological responding (Mason et al. 1997a); on reasoning tasks (Sellen et al., 2005) and in learning, notably on measures of 'latent inhibition' (Gray et al., 2000; Tsakanikos et al., 2003; Moran et al., 2003). Differences have also been found in hemispheric function: for language task performance (Nunn and Peters, 2001; Kravetz et al., 1998), face processing (Mason and Claridge, 1994), and handedness (Shaw et al., 1999). On a more clinical front the O-LIFE has been used successfully to investigate schizotypy in relation to such topics as dissociative experience and childhood abuse (Startup, 1999), membership of new religious movements (Day and Peters, 1999), and paranormal beliefs and experiences as a function of mental health (Goulding, 2004). Finally, a recent large quantitative genetic analysis has established convincing heritability for the O-LIFE scales, along the lines predicted for schizotypal traits (Linney et al., 2003).

The main purpose of the present paper is to present more extended normative data for the O-LIFE. Currently the only published, rather limited norms for the questionnaire are those contained in Mason et al. (1995). Here we report on a much larger data set.

2. Methods

2.1. Sample

O-LIFE scores were collected from a total of 1926 participants (521 males and 1405 females, age range 17–85) who completed the questionnaire in conventional paper-and-pencil form as part of one or other of several experimental studies. The remainder were recruited across a range of sites in the United Kingdom: 1226 participants were obtained from a twin study (Linney et al., 2003; one from each twin pair); 201 were obtained from two unpublished studies (Corr, two unpublished laboratory studies; personal communication); and 499 participants were recruited from a range of other smaller published and unpublished experiments, with between 40 and 70 participants. Due to the differing styles of studies, the method of recruitment varied. Those from the twin study were obtained from a national UK register established for research purposes. The majority of participants in the experimental studies were recruited by advertisement, by word of mouth, or by a search strategy aimed at recruiting matched controls (in the case of a clinical study). Though we cannot formally ascertain its representativeness, to our knowledge the total sample includes both the employed and the unemployed, students and medical workers, in addition to the great majority found through both the twin register and through advertisements that may be presumed to attract a wide cross-section of the population. Essentially participants were included where the aim of original recruitment was to obtain an ostensibly normal sample and where the minimum requirement was met that age and gender were known for each subject. The majority of studies attempted to rule out psychiatric illness, usually by a single question requesting details of any psychiatric history, though formal screening for psychiatric disorder was carried out only for those participants acting as controls in patient studies.

2.2. Questionnaire

As noted earlier, the Oxford-Liverpool Inventory of Feelings and Experiences (O-LIFE) has four scales (items are listed later). The Unusual Experiences (UnEx) scale contains items describing perceptual aberrations, magical thinking, and hallucinations. It is phenomenologically related to positive symptoms of psychosis, and measures a trait often termed positive schizotypy. The Cognitive Disorganisation (CogDis) scale taps aspects of poor attention and concentration as well as poor decision-making and social anxiety. It can be seen to reflect thought disorder and other disorganised aspects of psychosis. The Introvertive Anhedonia (IntAn) scale contains items that describe a lack of enjoyment from social and physical sources of pleasure, as well as avoidance of intimacy. It can be seen to reflect weakened forms of 'negative symptoms', so-called negative schizotypy, or alternatively the schizoid temperament. The Impulsive Nonconformity (ImpNon) scale contains items describing impulsive, anti-social, and eccentric forms of behaviour, often suggesting a lack of self-control.

3. Results

Mean score and other data for the four scales are shown in Table 12.1. For the purpose of presenting the normative data the sample has been further classified according to age and gender. Because schizotypal personality differences are most often studied, and are arguably of greatest relevance, during late adolescence and early adulthood, the first reference cut-off point for age was under 22 years. This was also chosen as it broadly approximates to the age of an undergraduate population – one frequently accessed in studies in psychology. Subsequent divisions were placed at, respectively, 30, 40, 50, and 60 years of age to produce clearly defined age groups for the construction of norms, as it has frequently been observed that scores change (mostly decline) with age.

Several percentiles were calculated for both males and females in the different age groups (see Table 12.2). These are reported for common criterion points for participant selection – the median, upper and lower quartiles, and the upper decile. It is not suggested that these are in any sense clinical cut-offs, and clinical norms have not been established. However, they do help to define, for the purposes of experimentation, those people scoring above a given psychometric point in the distribution.

Gender differences were examined by ANCOVAs for each of the four sub-scales with age entered as a covariate (see Table 12.3). Significant results were obtained for Cognitive Disorganisation ($F = 5.08$, $p = 0.024$), Introvertive Anhedonia ($F = 17.56$, $p < 0.001$) and Impulsive Nonconformity ($F = 43.70$, $p < 0.001$). Estimated means and effect sizes are given in Table 12.3. UnEx, CogDis and ImpNon all correlated negatively with age ($r = -.18$, $-.22$ and $-.38$, respectively), while IntAn correlated positively with age ($r = .19$), with no significant differences between the relative size of correlations in males and females on any scales (calculated according to Howell, 1992: p. 251). Mean scores across the sub-scales for all age groups are illustrated in Figure 12.1. Partial correlations were conducted between the sub-scales controlling for sex and age (see Table 12.4): CogDis correlated to a considerable degree with UnEx and mildly with both ImpNon and IntAn; ImpNon was moderately correlated with UnEx.

Regression equations were calculated so as to allow an estimated score to be computed from age and sex information (male = 0, female = 1). Beta coefficients and associated standard errors of estimates are provided in Table 12.5.

4. Discussion

The more extensive norms published here should improve the usefulness of the O-LIFE for anyone employing the questionnaire in clinical and experimental research; though in that regard it is encouraging that the psychometric properties of the questionnaire, as reported here, are largely unaltered compared with previous investigations. Thus, the gender differences seen for the sub-scales Introvertive Anhedonia and Impulsive Nonconformity, and the relationships with age are consistent with other reports in the literature (Mason et al., 1995; Burch et al., 1988).

Table 12.1 Norms for males and females by age group

Age group	N size Female/Male	Unusual Experiences Female	Male	Cognitive Disorganisation Female	Male	Introvertive Anhedonia Female	Male	Impulsive Nonconformity Female	Male
Under 22	237/159	10.21 (6.40)	10.08 (6.16)	12.68 (5.71)	11.96 (5.66)	5.03 (4.02)	6.06 (3.97)	9.27 (3.90)	9.80 (4.41)
21–30	250/152	9.72 (6.55)	9.83 (6.36)	11.74 (5.70)	11.05 (5.73)	5.15 (3.85)	6.26 (4.97)	8.86 (3.86)	10.26 (3.84)
31–40	233/53	8.67 (6.22)	8.11 (5.94)	10.55 (5.56)	9.68 (6.73)	5.96 (4.00)	6.68 (5.25)	7.62 (3.86)	8.58 (3.91)
41–50	226/65	9.03 (6.29)	7.72 (5.88)	11.32 (6.01)	9.66 (6.16)	7.41 (4.84)	7.48 (4.73)	6.72 (3.51)	7.94 (4.11)
51–60	225/41	7.69 (5.60)	7.76 (5.71)	9.16 (5.64)	9.17 (5.63)	6.74 (4.38)	8.32 (5.67)	5.51 (3.48)	7.73 (3.20)
Over 60	234/51	6.74 (5.03)	6.90 (5.64)	8.65 (5.23)	8.59 (5.83)	7.23 (4.54)	8.59 (4.77)	4.64 (2.92)	6.67 (4.44)
Combined	1926	8.82 (6.16)		10.73 (5.87)		6.38 (4.49)		7.69 (4.12)	

Table 12.2 First quartile, median, third quartile and 90th percentile for males and females by age group

Age group	N size Female/Male	Unusual Experiences Female	Unusual Experiences Male	Cognitive Disorganisation Female	Cognitive Disorganisation Male	Introvertive Anhedonia Female	Introvertive Anhedonia Male	Impulsive Nonconformity Female	Impulsive Nonconformity Male
<22	237/159	4, 9, 15, 19.2[a]	4, 9, 15, 19	8, 13, 17, 21	8, 12, 16, 20	2, 4, 7, 10	2, 5, 8, 11	6, 9, 12, 14	6, 10, 13, 15
22–30	250/152	4, 9, 14, 20	4, 9, 14, 19	7, 12, 17, 19	11.5, 15, 15, 19	2, 4, 8, 10	2, 5, 9, 13.7	6, 9, 12, 14	6, 10, 13, 15.7
31–40	233/53	4, 7, 12, 18	4, 7, 10, 18.4	6, 10, 14.5, 19	6, 8, 15, 21	3, 5, 8, 12	3, 5, 11, 15.8	5, 7, 10, 13	6, 9, 11, 14
41–50	226/65	4, 8, 12, 19	4, 6, 10, 17	6, 11, 16, 20	6, 9, 15, 19.4	4, 6, 11, 15	4, 7, 11, 13.4	4, 6, 9, 11	5, 7, 11, 14
51–60	225/41	3, 6, 10, 15	3, 6, 12, 17.8	4, 8, 13, 18	5, 9, 14, 17.8	4, 6, 9, 12	4, 7, 11, 17.6	3, 5, 8, 10	4, 7, 10, 12.8
>60	234/51	3, 5.5, 10, 14	3, 5, 5, 9, 15.8	4, 8, 13, 16	4, 7, 13, 17.8	4, 6.5, 10, 14	4, 8, 11, 15.8	3, 4, 6, 9	3, 7, 10, 13

a 25th/50th/75th/90th percentiles.

Table 12.3 Effect sizes and estimated means for UK males (*n* = 521) and females (*n* = 1405)

Scale	Estimated means		F	Effect size (r)
	Female	Male		
UnEx	8.71	8.84	0.17^{ns}	(0.011)
CogDis	10.14	10.81	5.08*	0.057
IntAn	7.07	6.11	17.56**	0.107
ImpNon	8.55	7.27	43.7**	0.154

ns non-significant, *p < .05, **p < .01.

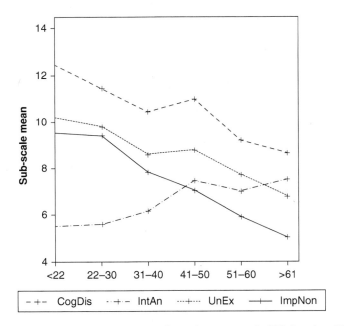

Figure 12.1 Sub-scale means for each age group in UK data (*n* = 1926).

Table 12.4 Partial correlations between sub-scales (controlling for sex and age) (UK sample, *n* = 1926)

	Unusual Experiences	Cognitive Disorganisation	Introvertive Anhedonia	Impulsive Nonconformity
CogDis	0.48**	–	0.32**	0.39**
IntAn	0.09**	0.32**	–	0.28**
ImpNon	0.39**	0.28**	–0.07**	–

ns non-significant, *p < .05, **p < .01.

Table 12.5 Regression equations based on sex and age (UK sample, $n = 1926$)

Scale	Beta coefficients			R	Standard error of the estimate
	Constant	Age	Sex		
UnEx	11.11	−0.065	0.131	0.182	6.082
CogDis	12.51	−0.077	0.667	0.228	5.695
IntAn	6.049	0.050	−0.958	0.202	4.398
ImpNon	13.38	−0.090	0.94	0.431	3.740

In particular, participants over fifty on average scored lower on all but the Introvertive Anhedonia scale which showed modest increases with age.

Two points about the practical use of the O-LIFE need to be made. The first concerns the summing of scores from two or more of the O-LIFE scales to produce a single measure. We are aware that some workers using the questionnaire have done this, occasionally revealing significant effects in their experimental data. However, we would caution against the practice, on both theoretical and empirical grounds. There is much evidence that psychosis proneness/schizotypy is a construct with separable and well-identified components and what it means to combine these is largely unknown and the effects difficult to interpret. In our view it would be better to retain the multidimensional approach to measurement and research in the area; in the case of the O-LIFE by considering its four scales separately. For that reason we have not provided composite norm figures here; though of course anyone wishing to use the O-LIFE in that way could easily calculate their own from the data contained in the appropriate tables.

The second (and related) practical point arises from the inclusion in the O-LIFE of the fourth scale, Impulsive Nonconformity. The reasons for the latter's presence in the questionnaire were explained in the Introduction, when discussing the scope of the psychosis proneness construct and our choice of four scales for the O-LIFE. As noted there, the decision was partly empirical – the data dictated a four component solution to the factor analyses – and partly theoretical, based on a sympathy for a unitary theory of psychosis. All of that is immaterial to whether the O-LIFE is chosen and how it is used as a research tool. UnEx, CogDis, and IntAn can stand alone as scales for measuring the three agreed components of schizotypy, in the narrow sense. Indeed some researchers, to our knowledge, use the O-LIFE in this way, paying no attention to their ImpNon data. By the same token, the availability of the ImpNon scale in the O-LIFE does offer, compared with other questionnaires, a more comprehensive instrument for those wishing to leave their thinking open to the unitary theory of psychosis and psychosis proneness.

Several limitations should be acknowledged alongside the obvious observation that these are UK-based norms so do not necessarily describe other populations. More detailed demographic breakdown, by ethnic and social background for example, would clearly have been desirable. The range of sources tapped for participants led to an over-representation of females relative to males. This has the undesirable consequence that a slightly lower degree of statistical confidence is present for male norms though these are still based on an adequate sample size.

Acknowledgements

The authors would like to thank Philip Corr, Julia Hay, Yvonne Linney, Emmanuelle Peters, Craig Steel, and Eliane Young for contributing data to the analyses reported here.

Note

1 'Psychoticism' is used here in a generic sense, not to be confused with the meaning associated with the Eysenck P-scale, which most would agree measures antisocial aspects of personality and psychological disorder.

Appendix A

Unusual experiences

Do you believe in telepathy?
Do you ever feel sure that something is about to happen, even though there does not seem to be any reason for you thinking that?
Do you ever suddenly feel distracted by distant sounds that you are not normally aware of?
Do you often have days when indoor lights seem so bright that they bother your eyes?
Does your sense of smell sometimes become unusually strong?
Have you felt as though your head or limbs were somehow not your own?
Have you sometimes sensed an evil presence around you, even though you could not see it?
Have you wondered whether the spirits of the dead can influence the living?
On occasions, have you seen a person's face in front of you when no one was in fact there?
When in the dark do you often see shapes and forms even though there's nothing there?
When you look in the mirror does your face sometimes seem quite different from usual?
Are your thoughts sometimes so strong that you can almost hear them?
Can some people make you aware of them just by thinking about you?
Do ideas and insights sometimes come to you so fast that you cannot express them all?
Do the people in your daydreams seem so true to life that you sometimes think they are real?

The Oxford-Liverpool Inventory of Feelings and Experiences 179

Do you sometimes feel that your accidents are caused by mysterious forces?
Do you think you could learn to read other's minds if you wanted to?
Does it often happen that nearly every thought immediately and automatically suggests an enormous number of ideas?
Does a passing thought ever seem so real it frightens you?
Does your voice ever seem distant or faraway?
Have you ever felt that you have special, almost magical powers?
Is your hearing sometimes so sensitive that ordinary sounds become uncomfortable?
Do you ever have a sense of vague danger or sudden dread for reasons that you do not understand?
Do you feel so good at controlling others that it sometimes scares you?
Have you ever thought you heard people talking only to discover that it was in fact some nondescript noise?
Have you felt that you might cause something to happen just by thinking too much about it?
Have you occasionally felt as though your body did not exist?
Have you sometimes had the feeling of gaining or losing energy when certain people look at you or touch you?
Are the sounds you hear in your daydreams really clear and distinct?
Do your thoughts sometimes seem as real as actual events in your life?

Cognitive disorganisation

Are you easily distracted when you read or talk to someone?
Do you ever feel that your speech is difficult to understand because the words are all mixed up and don't make sense?
Do you often experience an overwhelming sense of emptiness?
Do you often feel lonely?
Is it hard for you to make decisions?
Are you a person whose mood goes up and down easily?
Are you easily hurt when people find fault with you or the work you do?
Are you sometimes so nervous that you are 'blocked'?
Do you dread going into a room by yourself where other people have already gathered and are talking?
Do you easily lose your courage when criticised or failing in something?
Do you find it difficult to keep interested in the same thing for a long time?
Do you frequently have difficulty in starting to do things?
Do you often feel that there is no purpose to life?
Do you often have difficulties in controlling your thoughts?
Do you often worry about things you should not have done or said?
Do you worry about awful things that might happen?
No matter how hard you try to concentrate do unrelated thoughts creep into your mind?

When in a crowded room, do you often have difficulty in following a conversation?
Are you easily confused if too much happens at the same time?
Are you easily distracted from work by daydreams?
Do you often feel 'fed up'?
Do you worry too long after an embarrassing experience?
Would you call yourself a nervous person?
Do you often hesitate when you are going to say something in a group of people whom you more or less know?

Introvertive anhedonia

Can you usually let yourself go and enjoy yourself at a lively party? *negative*
Do people who try to get to know you better usually give up after a while?
Do you feel that making new friends isn't worth the energy it takes?
Do you find the bright lights of a city exciting to look at? *negative*
Do you like going out a lot? *negative*
Do you prefer watching television to going out with other people?
Do you usually have very little desire to buy new kinds of food?
Is it fun to sing with other people? *negative*
Are people usually better off if they stay aloof from emotional involvements with people?
Are there very few things that you have ever really enjoyed doing?
Are you much too independent to really get involved with other people?
Are you rather lively? *negative*
Can just being with friends make you feel really good? *negative*
Do you have many friends? *negative*
Do you like mixing with people? *negative*
Do you think having close friends is not as important as some people say?
Does it often feel good to massage your muscles when they are tired or sore? *negative*
Has dancing or the idea of it always seemed dull to you?
Have you often felt uncomfortable when your friends touch you?
Is trying new foods something you have always enjoyed? *negative*
On seeing a soft thick carpet have you sometimes had the impulse to take off your shoes and walk barefoot on it? *negative*
When things are bothering you do you like to talk to other people about it? *negative*
Do you feel very close to your friends? *negative*
Do you love having your back massaged? *negative*
Have you had very little fun from physical activities like walking, swimming, or sports?
Do you enjoy many different kinds of play and recreation? *negative*
Is it true that your relationships with other people never get very intense?

Impulsive nonconformity

Do people who drive carefully annoy you?
Do you often feel like doing the opposite of what other people suggest, even though you know they are right?
Do you often feel the impulse to spend money which you know you can't afford?
Do you often have an urge to hit someone?
Do you sometimes talk about things you know nothing about?
Are you usually in an average sort of mood, not too high and not too low? *negative*
Do you at times have an urge to do something harmful or shocking?
Do you ever have the urge to break or smash things?
Do you often change between intense liking and disliking of the same person?
Do you stop to think things over before doing anything? *negative*
Do you think people spend too much time safeguarding their future with savings and insurance?
Have you ever blamed someone for doing something you know was really your fault?
Have you ever cheated at a game?
Have you ever felt the urge to injure yourself?
When in a group of people do you usually prefer to let someone else be the centre of attention? *negative*
When you catch a train do you often arrive at the last minute?
Would being in debt worry you? *negative*
Would you take drugs which may have strange or dangerous effects?
Do you consider yourself to be pretty much an average kind of person? *negative*
Have you ever taken advantage of someone?
Would you like other people to be afraid of you?
Do you often overindulge in alcohol or food?
Would it make you nervous to play the clown in front of other people? *negative*
All items scored +1 for 'yes', 0 for 'no' except *negative* items for which +1 for 'no', 0 for 'yes'.

Commentary

The third major area of interest brought together in my 1997 book (and beyond) was research on experimental paradigms for investigating and explaining schizotypy (the question was almost always formulated under the heading, 'schizotypy'). For obvious reasons, given the nature of schizophrenia, the approach has been strongly cognitive or neurocognitive: examples from my own work referred to in the 1997 book are negative priming, subliminal priming, latent inhibition, local-global processing, and hemisphere asymmetry, including handedness. I have chosen the last of these as an illustration, for several reasons. First, as an entirely intuitive, unscientific observation it has always struck me that a clue to understanding psychosis probably might lie in variations in brain lateralisation. Second, handedness offers a convenient way of assessing this – in the large samples that are a vital prerequisite for research into any aspect of individual differences. The third reason for choosing this particular paper relates to the measure of handedness used in the study: Annett's questionnaire (Annett, 1985). Although reasonably well celebrated in handedness research circles, Annett's work has been rather controversial because of the multi-category nature of her scale and the genetic theorising behind it. This appealed to the maverick in me, especially as the questionnaire had not previously been used in a study of schizotypy.

13 Schizophrenia risk and handedness
A mixed picture

*Gordon Claridge, Kenneth Clark,
Caroline Davis and Oliver Mason*

Introduction

A dysfunction of cerebral lateralisation has frequently been invoked to explain both schizophrenic symptomatology (Crow, 1990; Flor-Henry, 1969; Gruzelier, 1994), and schizophrenia risk (Claridge & Broks, 1984; Gruzelier & Richardson, 1994). One prediction from such hypotheses has been that the disorder should be associated with a variation in handedness. The form of this variation has generally been expected to show as a shift away from right hand dominance—as either increased left or mixed handedness, or both. This has been extensively examined in diagnosed schizophrenics, as well as in subjects showing the features of "schizotypy". The latter is an extensively studied and now well validated descriptor of the traits predisposing to schizophrenia (Claridge, 1997b; Raine, Lencz, & Mednick, 1995). One feature of research on schizotypy, of relevance here, is the development over the past decade or so of many self-report scales for assessing the characteristic in non-clinical individuals. This has included attempts to establish, through factor analysis of such scales, its dimensional structure (Claridge et al., 1996; see also Mason, Claridge, & Williams, 1997, for a review). On that point, there is good agreement that a clear distinction can be made between components of schizotypy that correspond, on the one hand, to the positive symptoms of schizophrenia—the tendency to report unusual perceptual and cognitive experiences—and, on the other, to the negative symptomatology of social withdrawal and emotional unresponsiveness.

Studies of handedness using patient samples have yielded variable results. Some have demonstrated more sinistrality among schizophrenics (Chaugule & Master, 1981; Clementz, Iacono, & Beiser, 1994; Gur, 1977; Nasrallah, McCalley, & Kuperman, 1982). Others have found, in varying degrees, a raised prevalence of mixed handedness, but without an increase in pure left handedness (Cannon et al., 1995; Green, Satz, Smith, & Nelson, 1989; Malesu et al., 1996; Nelson, Satz, Green, & Cicchetti, 1993). There have, however, been null findings (Lishman & McMeekan, 1976) and indeed even reports of increased dextrality among schizophrenics (Fleminger, Dalton, & Standage, 1977; Taylor, Dalton, & Fleminger, 1980). A further point to note is that results sometimes appear to depend on diagnostic grouping of patients. For example, Taylor, Dalton, and Fleminger (1982), although reporting no overall effects in schizophrenics, did find some excess of left-handers in deluded males; while Taylor and Amir (1995) recently found that an observed shift away from dextrality in a schizophrenic sample was accounted for by a raised incidence of mixed handedness among patients with combined schizophrenic and affective features (schizoaffective psychosis).

More consistent results have emerged from studies of handedness in relation to schizotypy, or so-called "psychosis-proneness", among normal subjects. With the exception of Overby (1993), who found no difference, all investigators have reported a shift away from dextrality in high, compared with low, schizotypes. This was revealed as increased mixed handedness in studies by Chapman and Chapman (1987), Kim, Raine, Triphon, and Green (1992), and Richardson (1994), and in one of two investigations by Poreh (1994); in Poreh's second experiment it appeared as greater sinistrality alone. Elsewhere, Poreh, Levin, Teves, and States (1997) found that high schizotypy was associated with greater rates of both left and mixed handedness, as did Kelley and Coursey (1992b). Notably, where significant effects have been reported in these investigations they have always referred to differences on scales assessing the "positive symptom" aspects of schizotypy.

The studies reviewed—both in clinical and normal populations—have based their classification of handedness on measuring devices of varying sophistication. For example, Overby (1993), the only worker to report negative findings in relation to schizotypy, relied on self-assessment according to a single question, a method resulting in an extremely low incidence of mixed handedness. Even investigators using more elaborate assessment procedures have generally been content with a simple three-way classification of handedness. This might be justified: a crucial question about handedness is indeed whether it should be regarded as a categorical or a quantitative variable (see Bishop, 1990). The fact that a categorical view has so far prevailed in the research considered here suggested to us that the alternative, quantitative, approach would be worth testing.

The aim of the present study, therefore, was to undertake a more fine-grained analysis of hand preference than hitherto, in a large sample of general population subjects assessed for schizotypy. Of necessity this required an instrument that yielded a measure of handedness along a quantitative scale. The questionnaire chosen was that developed by Annett (1970) whose hand preference scale has been widely researched and is claimed by its author to be well grounded, both empirically and theoretically (Annett, 1995).

Method

Subjects

Subjects consisted of 681 volunteers (349 male 332 female), recruited from university, hospital, school, and general community sources in England and Canada. The mean age for the total sample was 30.78 yrs (range 14–80). Mean age for males was 32.94 yrs (range 14–76) and for females 28.52 yrs (range 14–80).

Measures

Schizotypy. This was measured with the Oxford schizotypal personality scale (STA) (Claridge & Broks, 1984), a 37-item self-report questionnaire based on the DSM-III diagnostic criteria for Schizotypal Personality Disorder (American Psychiatric Association, 1980). The item content of the scale is strongly weighted towards the positive symptom aspects of schizotypy, as defined earlier. It has been successfully employed, and is currently in use, in a wide range of schizophrenia-related projects (Claridge, 1997b) and is generally regarded as a valid test of schizotypal characteristics.

Handedness. As noted earlier, this was assessed on the Annett (1970) hand preference questionnaire. Here subjects are asked to indicate whether they use the right, left, or either hand for twelve common actions (six primary and six non-primary). Individual records were scored in two ways. It was first done according to Annett's seven-category classification. This depends on criteria being applied in sequence, as for a decision tree, with "writing" as the first criterion. The scoring is a revision by Annett (1985) of her original procedure, which yielded *eight* handedness subgroups. [To be consistent with Annett's current practice we have retained her labelling of categories as "1" (fully right) to "8" (fully left), with "5" deleted.]

A second, simplified and more conventional, scoring of the handedness data was also used, in which subjects were assigned to one of three categories, of left, mixed, and right. For this purpose, following Annett (1985), "either" responses were scored as for the writing hand, giving three classes:

> Right-handers who used the left hand for none of the actions.
> Left-handers who used the right hand for none of the actions.
> Mixed-handers who used the right or the left hand for different actions.

Results

Three-class analysis

Considering, first, the data subdivided into just three categories of handedness, the mean STA scores for each of these are shown in Table 13.1, in the total group, and also subdivided according to sex. It can be seen that overall there was a progressive increase in schizotypy from right, through mixed, to left, the effect being somewhat more marked in females. A two-way ANOVA (Hand Class × Sex) performed on the data demonstrated an overall significant difference for Hand Class, $F(2, 675) = 4.88$, $P < .01$. There was also a significant sex difference, with women, as routinely found, showing generally higher STA scores, $F(1, 675) = 4.37$, $P < .04$. However, there was no Sex × Hand interaction. Post-hoc t-tests showed STA scores to be higher in the mixed-handers than in the right-handers, $t(644) = 2.94$, $P < .003$. Left- and mixed-handers did not differ significantly from each other, while the comparison between left- and right-handers just failed to reach significance, $t(432) = 1.78$, $P < .08$.

186 Gordon Claridge et al.

Table 13.1 Mean schizotypy (STA) scores for three hand-preference classes

		Hand-preference class		
		Right	Mixed	Left
Total	Mean	14.91	16.64	17.14
	SD	7.14	7.43	7.10
	N	399	247	35
Males	Mean	14.67	15.81	14.75
	SD	7.30	7.73	6.12
	N	205	132	12
Females	Mean	15.16	17.58	18.39
	SD	6.98	7.00	7.38
	N	194	115	23

Seven-class analysis

Schizotypy data for the seven hand-preference classes are shown in Table 13.2. These were subjected to a two-way ANOVA (Hand Class × Sex), which showed a highly significant difference between hand categories, $F(6/667) = 3.43$, $P < .002$. As before, there was a significant sex difference in STA, but no Sex × Hand Class interaction.

As illustrated in Figure 13.1, the pattern of STA across hand class was highly unusual. Average score increased from fully right (Class 1) through Class 2 to Class 3, but then showed a marked dip in Class 4—defined as right-handed writers with an otherwise strong leftward bias. Mean STA then rose again in the fully left (Class 8) and mixed left subjects (Classes 6 and 7). Post-hoc *t*-tests used to examine these data further pointed to several significant differences involving Class 4 (see Table 13.3). Class 4 individuals had significantly lower STA scores than full left-handers (Class 8), and compared with all of the other mixed groups,

Table 13.2 Mean schizotypy (STA) scores for seven hand-preference classes

		Hand-preference class						
		1	2	3	4	6	7	8
Total	Mean	14.91	16.74	18.05	13.56	17.20	15.80	17.14
	SD	7.14	7.84	7.08	6.84	7.76	6.37	7.10
	N	399	72	75	39	41	20	35
Males	Mean	14.67	15.09	17.32	14.12	16.52	14.22	14.75
	SD	7.30	8.22	7.30	7.21	8.93	6.36	6.12
	N	205	32	44	26	21	9	12
Females	Mean	15.16	18.05	19.10	12.46	17.90	17.09	18.39
	SD	6.99	7.36	6.73	6.16	6.45	6.38	7.38
	N	194	40	31	13	20	11	23

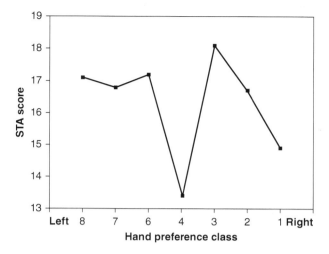

Figure 13.1 The significant dip in mean STA score (ordinate) at Class 4 on handedness scale from fully right to fully left (8 at left and 1 at right of abscissa, respectively).

Table 13.3 Significant STA differences among seven hand classes

	8	7	6	4	3	2
7						
6						
4	*		*			
3				*		
2				*		
1					*	*

*= $P < .05$

apart from Class 7. They were in fact more like full right-handers, from whom they did not differ significantly and who also had lower STA scores than two (Classes 2 and 3) of the mixed groups. It is also worth noting that the Class 4 mean was significantly lower when compared against the combined mean for the remainder of the sample, $t(679) = 2.06$, $P < .04$, and against the general population norms for the STA, $t(2034) = 2.16$, $P < .05$.

Finally, although the Hand Class × Sex interaction demonstrated that there were no significant gender differences, visual inspection of the data did suggest that the observed effect was more marked in females. This was probably brought about by the higher overall schizotypy of women, allowing for more variability on that measure. However, the crucial point—and this may be more important than absolute STA score differences—is that the *profile* of schizotypy change across hand classes was identical in men and women. This was easily demonstrable by calculating Strahan's (1966) d-coefficient, allowing us to compare the directional change of STA scores in males and females, irrespective of absolute values. The value of d was +1.0, indicating perfect profile concordance.

Discussion

The results described here both partly support and partly contradict previous findings in the area investigated. On the one hand, we confirmed that high schizotypy is associated with a significant shift away from dextrality, mostly towards increased mixed handedness. On the other hand, unexpectedly, subjects with the *greatest* degree of mixed handedness—seen in Annett's Class 4—showed the *lowest* average schizotypy level. Interestingly, this effect would not have been discovered had we confined ourselves to the simpler three-category classification of hand preference. Where that simple three-way grouping was used, we found increased mixed and left handedness in high schizotypes, fitting most of the results reviewed in the Introduction.[1]

According to our observations, the putative relationship between mixed handedness and schizotypy (and presumably schizophrenia) reflects an association with the mild ambidextrousness primarily seen in Annett's Classes 2 and 3. By contrast, the fact that the most mixed (Class 4) subjects were the *least* schizotypal of the mixed groups—being more like full right-handers—indicates that some forms of mixed handedness might actually be incompatible with schizotypy.

One explanation of the results that has to be considered is that they reflect some trivial test-taking response set common to both the schizotypy and handedness questionnaires. It is possible that individuals who are very hesitant about their self-report of hand preference ("mixed" handed) are also unwilling to commit themselves to affirmative replies on the relatively "strong" items found in our schizotypy questionnaire, such as "Have you ever felt when you looked in a mirror that your face seemed different?". It was suggested to us that this explanation could be tested by examining the frequency with which low STA scorers gave "either" responses on the Annett questionnaire. "Either" responses are not usually counted on the Annett scale, but they did occur sufficiently often in our data to make such an analysis possible. It turned out that there was a small correlation between the two measures, significant at least in women, $r(194) = 0.17$, $P < .01$. However, the sign of the correlation was *positive*, opposite to that predicted from the response bias hypothesis. The result, such as it was, therefore simply provided some further support for the general association between ambiguous handedness and schizotypy, indicated by the three-class analysis.

Another possible interpretation of the results is suggested by Annett's own observations about the special nature of Class 4 individuals. She has commented on their unusually superior spatial ability, when compared with other mixed-handedness groups (Annett, 1992). Indeed, a comparison of our own STA data with spatial test scores supplied by Dr Annett shows a striking similarity in the profiles relating to handedness (see Figure 13.2). As presented there, the results are of course only correlational in form, but they strongly suggest a real association between spatial ability and absence of schizotypal traits. A further point is also worth noting. By Annett's definition, Class 4 individuals fall at the centre of the continuum of right minus left hand skill on the peg-moving task she has used to validate her hand-preference questionnaire. Significantly, subjects selected as having little asymmetry in peg-moving performance—the most mixed handed—also manifest a general intellectual superiority (Annett, 1991, 1993; Annett & Manning, 1989, 1990).

There therefore appears to be a group of mixed-handed people (including a high proportion of Annett's Class 4 subjects) who have some cognitive advantages and who, if our data are representative, have few schizotypal characteristics, indicating low vulnerability for schizophrenia. How is it possible to reconcile this conclusion with the opposite, currently more popular, theory that a shift from dextrality *increases* schizophrenia risk? The question can be usefully addressed in the light of Annett's theory of handedness; that the latter partly reflects the action of a "right shift" (rs) gene for cerebral dominance and cognitive processing, operating within

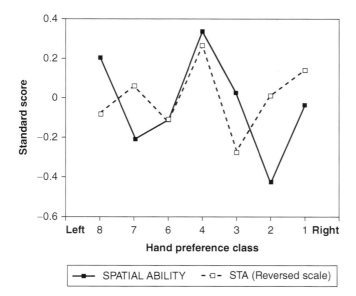

Figure 13.2 Mean schizotypy and spatial ability scores in standardised form (ordinate) across handedness classes, from fully right to fully left (8 at left and 1 at right of abscissa, respectively). The spatial ability measure represents the average of two samples—undergraduates and young teenagers—Dr Annett (1992) originally reported on separately, but whose data she combined and kindly supplied to us for the purpose of this paper. [Note: In a personal communication Dr Annett confirms our own inspection that the overall spatial score profiles across hand classes—with a peak in Class 4—are remarkably similar in her two samples, the only ambiguity being as to whether Classes 6 and 7 subjects are poor in spatial ability.]

a balanced polymorphism mode of inheritance (see Annett, 1995, for a recent comprehensive update of her ideas). According to Annett, Class 4 individuals are presumed to be less likely to have the rs gene than other right handers, or to be heterozygous, a status that carries with it some intellectual advantages. It is possible that an accompanying feature is a relative freedom from the aberrant cognitive functioning found in schizotypy—and responsible, where there is a clinical outcome, for the positive symptoms of schizophrenia.

However, the routes to mixed and left handedness are diverse (Perelle & Ehrman, 1982) and the shift from dextrality associated with *raised* schizotypy might have a quite different origin. Of particular interest here is the observed influence of birth stress on handedness (Coren, 1995), an effect that chimes well with extensively documented evidence on the role of pregnancy and birth complications in the aetiology of schizophrenia (McNeil, 1988; Mednick, 1970; Parnas et al., 1982). It is possible that the mild mixed handedness observed in some schizophrenic and highly schizotypal people is one indicator of an exogenous neurodevelopmental influence on brain laterality (Yeo, Gangestad, & Daniel, 1993); as distinct, that is, from the more purely genetic origin postulated for Annett's Class 4 individuals.

This interpretation of our data is of course entirely speculative. Among other criticisms, it could be said that it rests too heavily on Annett's genetic theory of handedness, which is by no means universally accepted (McManus, Shergill, & Bryden, 1993; Previc, 1996). There are also too many unknowns in our understanding of schizophrenia and schizotypy, on the one hand, and handedness (or brain laterality in general), on the other, to warrant adding even further to the over-exotic theorising that already exists on how the two domains might be connected. A further note of caution stems from the fact that most mentally disordered people are right handed—as, by the same token, are most healthy individuals low in schizotypy. If handedness were ultimately shown to code for some CNS feature relating to risk for, or protection from, schizophrenia, this could only be true in a limited sense, in some cases, or as one part of a complex of predisposing factors. Nevertheless, we believe that the findings reported here give an intriguing twist to the literature on handedness and schizophrenia and, if replicated, could cause us to rethink the current tendency to interpret such data in wholly pathological terms.

Commentary

Despite the interesting findings that emerged from the above study, it cannot be claimed that the data, or our theoretical speculations about them, added substantially to our knowledge of psychosis proneness, which was our aim. Inclusion of the paper is more for completion, marking the end of a distinct phase of research effort. It coincided with what I believe has been a disillusionment generally with findings in research that seeks laboratory-based correlates of, and indices of risk for, psychosis. No smoking gun has yet been found. Work continues of course but in my own research I have preferred to pursue other lines of enquiry.

It will be obvious by now that my personal stance on schizotypal and other psychotic traits is that they serve a dual function: (a) as predispositions to (sometimes devastating) mental illnesses and (b) as healthy adaptive personality characteristics. The question is: how are the latter expressed, behaviourally and psychologically? One line of enquiry is into the correlation with enhanced religious and spiritual beliefs, a topic to which two of my former graduate students – Mike Jackson and Miguel Farias – have made major contributions (Jackson, 1997; Farias, Claridge, & Lalljee, 2005). Another is the connection to creativity, a topic in which I have taken a particular interest in the later stages of my career. Inspired by the age-old 'great wits and madness' debate, the subject has generated a huge amount of literature, and continues to do so. My own fascination with it, I now realise, goes back – as do several things that critically shaped my thinking – to the military hospital days. For in the last chapter of my 1967 book I see there is a paragraph discussing the implication for creativity research of the results I had reported on psychotics' performance. This was also seen to be consistent with a theory I had constructed to explain my findings based, that is, on others' writings about the similarity between styles of schizophrenic and original ('allusive') thinking. It was many years later, deep into the schizotypy days, before I took up the subject again: with a jointly authored book, *Sounds from the Bell Jar* (Claridge, Pryor, & Watkins, 1990), reporting biographical analyses of some psychotic authors; followed by an edited collection of papers written by my undergraduates that included individual biographies and experimental studies (Claridge, 2009b).

I have chosen to represent this phase of my work with two pieces. One is a short essay, written with Dr Barrantes-Vidal, my colleague in Barcelona, focusing on the uneasy boundary between mad thought and sane creativity. The other is a very recent paper reporting a study of comedians, using the *O-LIFE* to assess the level of psychotic traits. There are several reasons for including the comedians paper. Although generating humour is a perfect example of original thinking, research on comedians themselves within the context of the madness/creativity debate has been much neglected compared with more traditional examples in the arts and sciences. We were also able to recruit a substantial sample of participants. And, finally, the study is a good example of using the *O-LIFE* as a profiling instrument: examining scores not on single scales taken alone, but in combination. Analysing the data in this way produced an interesting result: admittedly one which most comedians I corresponded with thought was rather obvious! But such is psychological science and what better test of validity can there be than that!

14 Creativity

A healthy side of madness

Gordon Claridge and Neus Barrantes-Vidal

Madness – or psychosis as it is more technically known – is still one of the most mysterious mental disorders of humankind. It refers to an altered state of mind where the individual loses contact with reality by having distortions in the perception of the outer and/or inner world (hallucinations, altered sense of self and the environment) and odd, false ideas that are held with strong conviction despite contrary evidence (delusions). These alterations of thought and perception are defining features of madness, but the psychotic state spans almost all psychological functions, such as mood, energy, motivation, volition, cognition, and psychomotor and physical functioning.

Descriptions of madness stretch back to antiquity, but its scientific study started in the late 19th century, with the emergence of an experimental psychopathology that was a meeting point between psychiatry and a newly born psychology. However, the former's influence was much greater as psychiatry took over the care of the mentally ill and – in keeping with its medical tradition – sought a cause for their ailments in the brain. This hope for an organic explanation of psychosis was inspired by a significant early breakthrough in psychiatric research: the discovery that one 'mental syndrome', General Paralysis of the Insane (GPI), was actually due to syphilis infection affecting the central nervous system. The promise, then, was that psychiatry would progressively uncover the neuropathological bases of all mental disorders, including psychoses such as schizophrenia – or *dementia praecox* as, significantly, that illness was earlier known.

This 'broken brain' view of madness has dominated the thinking of professional psychiatrists ever since. Apart, that is, from pockets of resistance from some radical thinkers; notably, in Europe, writers such as R.D. Laing (1960), whose book, *The Divided Self*, challenged the whole medical orthodoxy in psychiatry with the argument that madness is more about existential crisis than brain disease. However, Laing's rejection of *any* involvement of biology in psychosis – seen by some as itself a sign of insanity! – eventually led to the movement he started imploding. Ever since, Establishment Psychiatry has continued true to its faith in the neuropathological model. In this it has been encouraged by impressive advances in recent decades in neuroscience and molecular genetics.

The reality is, however, that despite an awesome research effort over several decades, no single neurobiological abnormality has been found that is really specific to psychosis or any of its varied manifestations. We are therefore driven to the conclusion that it is the conceptualization of the nature of psychosis that needs to be revised. Indeed there are very interesting signs of debate about this; even maybe of the onset of what some have called a paradigm shift in psychiatry (e.g., Kendler, 2005, 2012; Read, Bentall, & Fosse, 2009). While not all authors make the same points, we would suggest that there are three issues that signal some change in the way psychosis is coming to be viewed.

One is the realisation, based on considerable evidence, that environmental social adversity is a risk factor for the development of psychosis (Bendall, Jackson, Hulbert, & McGorry, 2008; Read, Fink, Rudegair, Felitti, & Whitfield, 2008). This is significant when put together with more general evidence about the critical rôle that the wide social and interpersonal environment has in the development and functionality of the brain across the lifespan (e.g., Roth & Sweatt, 2011; Teicher, Samson, Sheu, Polcari, & McGreenery, 2010). Such observations seriously challenge the orthodox medical view that psychosis is straightforwardly a genetically conditioned brain disease, as it indicates that the environment and individual variation not only merely colour the expression and adaptation to the malfunction, but also causally contribute to the development of the disorder. Evolutionary science (cf. Brune, 2011) has also shown that wide individual variation in terms of genetic, biological, and behavioural features is the norm rather than the exception and that there are not univocally 'good' and 'bad' traits for adapting to the environment. In other words, the evolutionary machinery selects in favour of wide variety, which enables the species to have a varied selection of individuals who are more apt to fit into very different circumstances and demands.

Another sign of change about how psychosis is viewed is the shift away from the idea that its different expressions constitute discrete diseases, each with a distinct ('broken brain') aetiology. This has mostly been discussed with respect to schizophrenia and manic-depression (bipolar affective disorder), where there is now convincing evidence for the so-called unitary model, supported by observations of a significant clinical and genetic overlap between the two disorders (Marneros & Akiskal, 2007; Lichtenstein, Bjork, Pawitan, Cannon, Sullivan, & Hultman, 2009).

Thirdly, the adoption of a dimensional view has broadened the scope of what can be considered legitimate material for discussion within the rubric of psychosis. The idea of a continuum between madness and sanity has been largely developed by psychologists; but in recent years the model has also been adopted by some psychiatrists wishing to recognise that psychotic symptoms can occur along a spectrum of severity, frequently observable in the general population (Johns & van Os, 2001; Stip & Letourneau, 2009). Admittedly, that usage of the continuum idea is not in itself particularly novel since it merely recognises that all illnesses – physical as well as mental – can indeed manifest their signs and symptoms to a varying degree. In principle it could be consistent with a modified version of the broken brain theory of psychosis. But at least it suggests a move in the right direction among some clinical psychiatrists.

Elsewhere (Claridge, 1997c), in contrast to that nuanced version of the broken brain theory, we have suggested a more radical alternative; what we have labelled a 'fully dimensional' model. This has its historical origins, not in psychiatry, but in personality psychology, specifically trait theories which see dimensions of personality as having a dual function: describing *both* healthy individual differences *and* predispositions to psychological disorders. Trait anxiety and anxiety disorders are the least controversial examples; but the same principle can be applied, we would argue, to more serious mental illnesses.

The arch-exponent of this fully dimensional interpretation was the late Hans Eysenck who, in his early theorising, introduced the concept of 'psychoticism' to capture the idea of a healthy personality dimension connecting normality to psychosis in the clinical sphere (Eysenck, 1952b).[1] However, most of the research on the topic has been carried out under the heading of 'schizotypy', with a primary focus on schizophrenia and the schizophrenia spectrum, including the development of questionnaires for measuring specifically schizotypal traits within the general population. But, notably, when a more open stance has been adopted to such work 'schizotypy' has begun to look like a too restrictive concept and Eysenck's term 'psychoticism' – in its original sense – a more appropriate label for capturing the range of variations within this personality sphere. Illustrating the point is the *Oxford-Liverpool Inventory of Feelings and Experiences (O-LIFE)*, the only questionnaire developed within the fully dimensional model and, equally to the point, based on a more comprehensive data set of items than those used hitherto (Mason, Claridge, & Jackson, 1995; Mason & Claridge, 2006).

The *O-LIFE* contains four partly correlated subfactors: '*Unusual Experiences*', '*Cognitive Disorganisation*', '*Introvertive Anhedonia*', and '*Impulsive Nonconformity*'. Interestingly, this pattern copies that expected from the unitary model of psychosis referred to earlier; *viz Impulsive Nonconformity* is weighted heavily on bipolar (cyclothymic) traits and overlaps considerably with the more 'schizophrenic' features represented in the other scales. Furthermore, another finding with the *O-LIFE* suggests that the 'unitary' view of psychosis and psychoticism can actually be extended beyond the schizophrenia/bipolar connection. Thus, another of the *O-LIFE*'s scales – *Introvertive Anhedonia* – has been shown to correlate strongly with Asperger/autism traits (Rawlings, 2008; Claridge & McDonald, 2009). It would therefore seem that within the broad rubric of 'psychoticism' there are several personality trait profiles each having a different adaptive and risk potential.

As we have emphasised, a cardinal feature of the fully dimensional model is that psychotic traits, like other personality features, are essentially healthy forms of individual variation, even though carrying their own risks for psychological disorder. The point is well illustrated from a practical standpoint by results obtained with the *O-LIFE*. Some of the items on that questionnaire, and others like it are occasionally (and not unexpectedly) slightly odd, including asking about such things as 'hallucinations and belief in magic', 'the paranormal', and so on. Many people in the general population endorse such items, and scores on the questionnaires can be very high, in the absence of any concurrent signs of serious mental illness. Indeed it is precisely this fact that leads to the conclusion that the traits being tapped are essentially healthy, their translation or not (and usually not), into psychiatric symptoms depending on other modulating factors. In favourable circumstances or in individuals with moderate weighting on psychotic traits or with other protective or facilitative personality and cognitive characteristics there will be favourable outcomes: these can include enriching religious or spiritual experiences (Clarke, 2010, Lukoff's chapter in this book), or, as discussed here, signs of enhanced creativity.

The link between madness and creativity has been the subject of an age old and controversial debate which, even in the relatively recent literature, has stimulated numerous books, review papers, and scientific articles (Richards, 1981; Jamison, 1993; Sass & Schuldberg, 2000; Nettle, 2001; Barrantes-Vidal, 2004; Claridge, 2009b; Silvia & Kaufan, 2010; Carson, 2011). It would be impossible here even to summarise their conclusions, but one message is clear. Trying to reconcile the idea that devastating mental illnesses can be associated with the proficiency of creativity thought has perplexed some writers on the topic. But the dilemma can be easily resolved. For it follows from the fully dimensional model we have described here that it is potentially adaptive psychotic *personality traits*, not psychotic *clinical symptom*s, that explain the link between the two domains. While clinical psychosis can indeed destroy creativity, psychoticism *may* enhance it. The late Janie Brod (1997), in her own review of the topic, put it as graphically as any:

> Is there a causal relationship between states of 'madness' and concurrent acts of creativity? Do you have to be mad to be creative? Could you be more creative if you were able, somehow, to hurl yourself into the depths of 'madness'? Of course not! The answer is 'no' to all three questions. States of 'madness', or, to use a less folksy term. psychosis, involve a number of severely debilitating symptoms which tend to disable many of the cognitive, affective, and behavioural processes required for intelligently adaptive functions in general. This includes creative functioning ... the relationship is not between psychosis and creativity, but, rather, between 'schizotypy' or 'psychoticism' and creativity. In other words, the positive link is with non-clinical expressions of schizotypal temperament and information processing style ...

She adds:

> The point is made again here, because it seems, as yet, not to have permeated the comprehension of many researchers, both within the field of creativity research and outside it.

In judging Brod's comments it should be borne mind that even those who have passed the threshold into clinical insanity are not mad all the time; indeed the psychotic state is frequently intermittent, with periods of relative normality; such is the nature of the spectrum. By the same token, so-called healthy psychoticism is not always strictly neutral with respect to psychopathology; even people whose psychotic traits operate within a normal range, free of the clinical symptoms of insanity, may show some degree of psychic distress. Evidence for this is to be found in the raised anxiety/neuroticism seen in people with high ratings on the features of psychoticism concerned with its 'positive' features; i.e. hallucinations and unusual experiences.[2] It is also neatly illustrated by the findings from a recent study carried out by one of us (GC) of imaginary friends in childhood (Isard & Claridge, unpublished study). Adult participants were asked if, as children, they had had one or more imaginary companions. As predicted, those who reported that they had were higher in psychotic traits than control subjects, and were more creative. However, more of them had also been referred at some point in their lives to the mental health services: not, it should be added, for problems related to psychosis – but mostly for anxiety and depression.

There are several possible, no doubt interacting, causes for this. One – biological – explanation could be that there is simply some natural association between the disposition to experience positive psychotic-like experiences and the tendency to be anxious – a sort of shared sensibility or what has sometimes been called 'skinlessness'. In the imaginary companion case just mentioned some anecdotal observation suggests that that might be so, though systematic studies do not strongly bear it out (Taylor, 1999). However, it might be true more generally, across a broader range of expressions of psychoticism.

Another reason for the anxiety found in some individuals high in psychoticism might be that becoming preoccupied with mystical things serves to derail, or distract from, the mundane mental functioning demanded in day-to-day life, causing discomfort. Consequently there might be a drift into eccentricity, giving an appearance of 'living too much inside their own heads', disregarding convention, and avoiding 'normal' social intercourse. Disapproval from others around them is then likely to make them even less adapted, exacerbating their sense of isolation, diminishing their self-esteem, and increasing their anxiety or depressiveness.

Thirdly, there is the possibility that high ratings on psychotic traits are themselves actually caused in part by early adversity or abuse, with an inevitable common element of negative affect (anxiety/neuroticism and depression). It is certainly true that, in addition to the strong genetic influence on the temperamental make-up, child abuse will add to the load of liability for psychotic breakdown; the association between early adversity and high psychoticism ratings probably reflect this (Steele, Marzillier, Fearon, & Ruddle, 2009). It also points to a causal connection. In one illustrative study adults with a history of child physical abuse reported a greater interest in psi and a belief in spiritualism and witchcraft (Perkins & Allen, 2006). The authors concluded that these cognitions act as powerful strategies that abused individuals use in taking refuge from the painful reality of the real world.

A flight into fantasy as an escape from a horrible reality can, in the presence of talent, be expressed as creativity. A case in point was Hans Christian Andersen, considered at some length by Anthony (1987) in his account of vulnerable and invulnerable children. As Anthony discusses, Andersen had both a grandfather and a father – to whom he was very close – who was or was to become clinical insane. He therefore both (presumably) inherited the same vulnerability and, because of his relatives' mental condition, was reared in less than ideal circumstances. He dealt with this by withdrawing at an early age into fantasy play and then into his writing, through which he was able to transform his cruel world into fairy tales. He himself apparently never succumbed to serious mental illness – only temporary depressions in between his bouts of writing – the working of his imagination keeping the worst of his evident psychoticism mostly at bay.

What we learn from the discussion so far – and considering the theme of this book – is that how individuals 'manage' their psychoticism/psychosis, and what sorts of people need to do it, is a question that can be posed right along the trait/symptom spectrum described. In other words, it is not narrowly about someone having to deal with acute, full-blown bouts of insanity; it is as much to do with people channelling the unstable energies of borderline psychotic states, or, in the case of healthy (albeit sensitive) individuals, finding ways to express their creative talents.

Someone who understood very well many of the distinctions we have made here was the late Anthony Storr whose book *The Dynamics of Creation* (1972) is remarkably contemporary in its theoretical and clinical orientation. This is so in several respects. For one thing Storr recognised the essentially dimensional nature of psychopathology and, relating it to creativity, drew upon examples over a wide spectrum; stressing the blurred boundary between frank illness and personality variation. He also emphasised the wide variability in manifestations of psychosis and psychoticism and the different ways in which these might relate to creativity. While not using the term 'psychoticism', he implicitly relied on a similar assumption as that here; *viz* that variations within states of insanity are strongly reflected in personality and temperament. Here he made particular use of the older, well-established distinction between, on the one hand, the schizoid, schizothymic, introverted 'type' and that more associated with the manic-depressive, cycloid, cyclothymic, extraverted temperament.

Storr's open, broadly based view of psychopathology stemmed from his Jungian background. In his writings Jung had ranged over many topics including schizophrenia, the psychology of introversion-extraversion, and the philosophy of religion. Much of this naturally rubbed off on Storr though we can only speculate whether Storr was also influenced by knowledge of Jung's own mental breakdown. In many accounts of Jung's life the latter is euphemistically referred to as a 'mid-life crisis', but Jung himself leaves us in doubt as to its true nature:

> It is, of course, ironical that I, a psychiatrist, should at almost every step of my experiment have run into the same psychic material which is the stuff of psychosis and is found in the insane. This is the fund of unconscious images which fatally confuse the mental patient.
>
> (C.G. Jung, 1963)

It was through the process of dealing with this turbulent period of his life that Jung moved into his more mystical phase of thinking and writing, while retaining his sanity. He was indeed a true archetype *(sic!)* of the creative psychotic.

Storr's own insights into creativity equally emphasised using it to help or restore self-esteem or gain insights. How this is achieved is different, he argued, in those of cyclothymic, manic-depressive temperament as compared with schizoid persons. The latter are typically aloof, detached from and have little need of other people: indeed may find them unreliable and not a good reference point for life. Creative outlets will reflect this preoccupation with objects, the inner world, and the lack of need to conform to a shared emotional matrix. Scientists are typically described in this way (Storr cites Einstein); another good example is Outsider Art ('*Art Brut*') where the individuals in question – sometimes referred to as on the Asperger spectrum, closely related to schizoidness – paint or sculpt according to their own rules (Cardinal, 2009). By comparison, according to Storr those of extraverted, manic-depressive temperament will have a different reason to boost self-esteem through creativity. Highly dependent on others for approval, and subject to mood swings, they seek to keep depression at bay through creative work. Many artists, musicians, and writers have been considered to fall into this category (Hershman & Lieb, 1998).

An additional important theme running through Storr's writings on creativity concerns the rôle of solitude, a topic to which he returned in two later books (1988a, 1988b). The wish to be alone, the deliberate separating of oneself from others, and the personality trait of introversion have commonly been regarded as abnormal, even as signs of neurosis. The view is especially prevalent in societies, such as North America, where popularity and sociability are considered indices of psychological health. Most self-help books promote the dogma, usually under the mistaken non-Latinate spelling of the desired trait as 'extroversion'! Storr was one writer who challenged the idea. He argued that, while human beings are of course social animals, powerfully driven by affiliative needs, they also by nature have a strong impersonal motive, evolved to deal with matters outside the interpersonal domain, where a degree of solitude may be beneficial or even essential. This is true of most creative activity – discovery, invention, artistic production – or working through to personal insights, away from others.

Of course, in judging this theory one must take account of the ever present factor of individual personality differences which at the extremes distort the average picture. As we have seen, in some highly schizoid or autistic individuals the need for others is entirely abandoned; the opposite is true at the other end of the spectrum. But this does not, in our view, take away from the general principle, proposed by Storr, that solitude and social intercourse are equally valid natural needs that complement each other in contributing to mental health. The special significance of solitude in creativity is that it opens up space in which to solve problems, develop theories, resolve issues, or convey feelings in artistic expression. All of these may have therapeutic value.

A genre that represents some of the above is the autobiographical novel. While most fiction contains an element of autobiography, autobiographical novels go beyond this, to give virtually complete accounts of the author's life experience. But they may do so in quite different ways, as two contrasting examples will illustrate. Both, in their day, were quite prominent English authors, though are now long since forgotten.

Dorothy Richardson (1873–1957) is now mostly discussed as the literary figure who first used the writing method of 'stream of consciousness' – or, as it is sometimes known, 'interior monologue'. The method avoids straightforward concrete narrative *about* a character or characters, in favour of telling the story as if from within, in terms thoughts, memories, perceptions, and feelings, written in a continuous free associative flow. According to Wallace (1989) Richardson 'discovered' the method in a sudden insight, after years of struggling to write a novel, but dissatisfied with the conventional form. The circumstances of her discovery are interesting. Wallace describes it thus:

> Richardson, 39 years old, was alone in a cottage in Cornwall, beginning her major life task, when she had a great insight, a turning point in her work ... Her solitude there was almost total ... she saw no one except a cleaning woman who came once a week to bring provisions. She had written copiously, a 'mass of material', making repeated attempts over a period of about four years ...

Having found a new style of working Richardson set about writing *Pilgrimage*, a mammoth sequence of thirteen books, the central character of which was Miriam Henderson. Miriam was, of course, herself and the work autobiographical – which no one realised.

Dorothy Richardson's choice of and ease with the stream of consciousness writing mode probably tells us something about her psychology and her motivation for spending the whole of the second half of her life exploring herself in the depth and manner in which she did. As a grammatical form the method is discursive and lacks an obvious structure; the links between ideas and phrases are often loosely connected, making the underlying meaning often difficult to fathom. In short, it looks like what a clinician would label psychotic thought *disorder*. Seen in this way stream of consciousness writing could be construed as a literary version of psychotic thinking. This is by no means a trivial observation. Some writing that passes as 'stream of consciousness' prose, if it lacks literary merit, certainly *is* the product of a disorganised cognitive style – a difficulty in focused attention and thought – that is a characteristic part of psychoticism (and indeed reflected in the *O-LIFE* as a scale in its own right). We believe that this has genuine significance on the literary front. It is no coincidence that one of the most prominent stream of consciousness writers – Virginia Woolf – suffered serious psychotic episodes that finally resulted in her suicide. Elsewhere, in a special literary and psychological study of some psychotic authors – including Woolf – we noted how, in unedited form, their writings often appeared unfocussed, chaotic, even clinically thought disordered (Claridge, Pryor, & Watkins, 1990). This was true of Woolf, so we could conclude that in adopting the stream of consciousness mode of writing she was simply putting her natural psychotic cognitive propensity to stylistic literary use.

Returning to Richardson, she did not, as far as we know, suffer any psychiatric breakdown, or show signs of serious psychopathology. However, her upbringing and early life were far from healthy: a rigid father who insisted on treating her as a boy and a depressive mother who eventually committed suicide, virtually in the presence of Richardson herself, creating considerable guilt and remorse. It would be surprising if she did not both inherit and acquire some traits that placed her on the psychoticism spectrum, as we have defined it here. We might then begin to understand how and why Richardson, having discovered her natural style of expression, turned it from being a risk factor for mental illness into a means for confronting the conflicts in 'Miriam's' life.

Our other example of an autobiographical novelist is a quite different case. Like Dorothy Richardson, Antonia White (1899–1980) also wrote only about herself, but in an entirely different sense. White – another of the authors studied by Claridge et al. (1990) – was a highly unstable woman who hovered on the edge of psychosis throughout her life. In personality she was impulsive, reckless with money, socially and sexually promiscuous, and, as her two daughters attested to in their own writings, an erratic and neglectful mother. As a counterpoint to her need for constant attention and stimulation White would often withdraw from company in order to try to write (sometimes unsuccessfully) her mostly narcissistic prose; the solitude probably helped – just about – to ward off the threat of insanity that constantly plagued her. The first major breakdown she did suffer – in her early twenties – was almost maniacal in quality and led to her admission to the Bethlem Royal Hospital ('Bedlam'). Years later she gave an account of that experience in her autobiographical novel, *Beyond the Glass*, a book written at uncharacteristic speed, as though exorcising some demons.

We noted in discussing White's work that she was not a great writer. Unlike Richardson, her style was noveletish and the content of her work at its best when simply narrating events in her own life. How closely she did that in *Beyond the Glass* is startling if we examine what happened to 'Clara', the heroine, before and after she entered the asylum, and compare that with the real-life events. Uniquely, we had the chance to do so after getting permission to study Antonia White's hospital case-notes covering her stay in the Bethlem Hospital in the 1920's. The match was almost perfect: she had not been writing fiction at all!

Whether autobiography, semi-autobiography, autobiography masquerading as fiction, or fiction concealing from the reader some personal experience, there is a vast literature writing about one's own mental illness, stretching back centuries (see Sommer & Osmond, 1960, 1961 for comprehensive listings up to that time). One of the earliest, mediaeval, accounts is the extraordinary *The Book of Margery Kempe*; ironically not written by her since she was illiterate, but by a scribe. Starting with Kempe, Dale Peterson, in his *A Mad People's History of Madness* (1982), collected together other notable examples, or extracts from them, including: *The Life of the Reverend Mr George Trosse Written by Himself, and Published Posthumously According to his Order in 1714; A Narrative of the Treatment Experienced by a Gentleman, During a State of Mental Derangement; Designed to Explain the Causes and the Nature of Insanity, and to Expose the Injudicious Conduct Pursued Towards Many Unfortunate Sufferers Under That Calamity* (John Percival, 1838 and 1840); *Memoirs of My Nervous Illness*

(Daniel Paul Schreber, 1903); *The Maniac: A Realistic Study of Madness from the Maniac's Point of View* (E. Thelmar, 1909); *Brainstorm* (Carton Brown, 1944); *I Never Promised You a Rose Garden* (Joanne Greenberg, 1964).

And such books continue to appear. To name but a few: *Portrait of a Schizophrenic Nurse* (Clare Wallace, 1965); *Operators and Things* (Barbara O'Brien, 1976); *The Trick is to Keep Breathing* (Janice Galloway, 1989); *The Loony Bin Trip* (Kate Millett, 1990); *Girl Interrupted* (Susanna Kaysen, 1993).

In addition to these published works there is a never-ending stream of unpublished accounts by people wanting to describe and make sense of their psychotic experiences. Over the years the first author has accumulated several boxes full of such self-reports (some cited below). These range from quite lengthy typewritten documents to mere handwritten scraps, or letters. The phenomenon seems to be confined to serious mental illness. Granted, sufferers from other psychological disorders – like OCD or anorexia – are often prompted to write about their illnesses. But they are far outnumbered by patients and ex-patients who feel the urge to share their experience of psychosis.[3] Why is this?

One reason is the sheer number of ways that mental life can alter in the psychotic state. The mind can go astray in all modalities – hearing, vision, touch, smell – and in all domains – emotion, thinking, language. And it can also do so to great extremes; for example, emotion that can swing wildly between ecstasy and despair; or, as if to defy this, the absence of all feeling:

> Experiences I do not have are good, evil, love, hate, existential death, ecstasy, mystical experience, etc, all experiences belonging to the mind, soul or personality of man. I cannot describe how I 'feel' because there is no feeling or experience to describe.

Over and above the sheer variety and intensity of change there is, most strikingly, the incongruity: the distortion and loss of reality that comes about through the misperception of imagined events, or the misinterpretation of real but, for most people, unfamiliar events, such as hallucinations, spiralling in the psychotic mind into false beliefs. Typically:

> I have dealt with a totally delusional world in which I was God – the Creator and the Sufferer – and that trees held magical power while a great wall and glass dome cut me off from the rest of humanity . . .

There is already here the raw material for stirring the imagination to try to explain the experience to the self; most psychotics – however inchoately – attempt to do so and that in itself, we believe, provides its own evidence for the link between creativity and madness.

The ideas dreamed up may be simple reactions to immediately felt symptoms – but sometimes they are remarkably close to the theories proposed by professional psychologists. A notable example is the following:

> So the mind must have a filter which functions without our conscious thought, sorting stimuli and allowing only those which are relevant to the situation in hand to disturb consciousness. And this filter must be working at maximum efficiency at all times, particularly when we require a high degree of concentration. What had happened to me in Toronto was a breakdown in the filter, and a hodgepodge of unrelated stimuli was distracting me from things which should have had my undivided attention.
>
> (Norma MacDonald, 1960)

This often quoted passage, from the self-report of one schizophrenic woman, precisely articulates an experimental paradigm that dominated laboratory research on attention in schizophrenia for more than two decades (McGhie & Chapman, 1961; Venables, 1973). A more uncanny – because introspectively less obvious – illustration of the same point relates to the explanation of psychosis (and psychoticism) that variation along the spectrum has something to do with cerebral asymmetry, perhaps incomplete lateralisation of the brain (Satz & Green, 1999; Richardson, Mason, & Claridge, 1997). This 'discovery' has been made, even to our own knowledge, by more than one schizophrenic patient! In one case it was formulated as the belief that his mind was, literally, unbalanced and could only be corrected by specially constructed shoes. Another person put it as follows:

> All of a sudden I've just done a switch. The left side of me wants to do the right thing and the right side of me wants to do the right thing.

Often the chaotic states of mind engendered by psychosis 'solidify' into more elaborate narratives (clinicians call them systematic delusions). These take the form of obsessively constructed and often tightly argued theories of almost anything: the human psyche, the cosmos, history, the fundamentals of life. The scope of the thinking here can be outside a box of almost endless proportions.

Taken out of the context of their place in illness, the symptoms of psychosis can appear to be so bizarre as to be hilariously funny. To the sufferer, for obvious reasons, they are only occasionally so. Often it is in novels that the humor mostly shows through (Kesey's (1962) *One Flew Over the Cuckoo's Nest* comes to mind). Or it is implied, for example by one ex-sufferer in a recollection of his own psychotic symptoms:

> Thank you, Dr – for listening to me, and reading my letter with a straight face. I know it's your job but you must surely have felt like having a laugh sometimes . . .

Occasionally, even in the state of, or on the verge of madness, comedy and laughter can be used as a protective shield to prevent succumbing to the absurdity of the experience. Peter Chadwick (2001) discusses this in relation to Des, a long standing 'schizotypal' friend who, he notes, 'has made sure that he mixes with people who share his sense of humor and who can share his desire to lighten his load by laughing at it'. Chadwick later counsels on the use of humour as part of his prescription for combating the unwanted intrusions into consciousness that can so easily slip into the psychotically prone mind and get distorted into paranoid and other dysfunctional beliefs.

We see here, then, the tragicomedy of madness: the facility to produce ideas that are so outside the normal frame of references, so bizarre that they can be personally destructive, extraordinarily amusing, or sometimes both at the same time. It is therefore not surprising to discover, as we did in a recent study of a large group of performing comedians, that they score very highly in psychotic traits (Ando, Claridge, & Clark, 2014). Illustrating the point more dramatically are the autobiographies of some well-known comedians. One of the most striking examples is the English comedian, the late Spike Milligan, erstwhile 'Goon' and lifelong manic-depressive (Milligan & Clare, 1993). At times so depressed he was scarcely able to speak, in his more manic phases Milligan used his freely associating thought processes to generate zany humor and wildly ridiculous ideas that were indeed the stuff of 'madness'. Milligan's illness *was* his comedy.

In this paper we have traced a number of interlacing themes connecting creativity to psychosis. Part of our argument has been based on scientific evidence, part on biographical material. We believe that, taken together, these sources lift the topic out of the realms of speculation; that indeed – to quote Dr Johnson – 'all power of fancy over reason is a degree of madness'. As important, however, is the more general conclusion to be reached about the nature of psychosis. With notable exceptions, disorders like schizophrenia have traditionally been regarded as neurological diseases, as an example of the 'broken brain' phenomenon, deficit states in which the possibility of return to normal functioning is, by definition, lost. Admittedly in recent years psychiatry has started to move away from the simplistic all-or-none version of that idea, adopting a more dimensional view of symptoms. The fully dimensional, personality based version of that model described here goes further, retaining a greater connection to health and normality than in previous conceptualisation of psychosis. As such, the model is more able to incorporate the idea that, behind (or beneath) the appearance of dysfunctionality in madness, there is a retained sense of the self, of the traits that define *both* the person when well *and*, ironically (and tragically), the disposition to illness.

To illustrate the point, it is fitting to close with one further piece of autobiography, the thoughts of a woman, diagnosed schizophrenic, and sculptor. Here she describes the agonies of her illness, yet also her joy at occasionally being able to see beyond the madness of it:

> The reflection in the store window – it's me, isn't it? I know it is, but it's hard to tell. Glassy shadows, polished pastels, a jigsaw puzzle of my body, face, and clothes, with pieces disappearing whenever I move . . . Schizophrenia is painful, and it is craziness when I hear voices, when I believe that people are following me, wanting to snatch my very soul. I am frightened too when every whisper, every laugh is about me . . . Schizophrenia is frustrating when I can't hold onto thoughts; when conversation is projected on my mind but

won't come out of my mouth ... But I know I'm still me in the experience. And I'm creative, sensitive. I believe in mysteries, magic, rainbows, and full moons ... Should I let anyone know that there are moments, just moments, in the schizophrenia that are 'special'? When I feel that I'm travelling to someplace I can't go to 'normally'. Where there's an awareness, a different sort of vision allowed me? Moments which I can't make myself believe are just symptoms of craziness and nothing more ... These 'special' moments of mine – there are so few, but I look for them and use them to help me pass through the schizophrenic episodes. And I can't even predict when or if these moments will come. But I won't deny their existence; I won't tell myself it's all craziness.

(McGrath, 1984)

Notes

1 Unfortunately in his later writings Eysenck (Eysenck, 1992b) seriously distorted and narrowed the interpretation of psychoticism, to mean antisocial behaviour. The reader should bear in mind that when we use the term here it is in its original, more general sense.
2 Interestingly, this is not true of the 'negative' component of psychoticism representing inherently more introverted, anhedonic personality features: there anxiety/neuroticism is actually rather low and seems, as noted earlier, to reflect more autistic traits.
3 The same is true of course in the visual arts, as witness, among others, the large permanent exhibition of paintings at the Bethlem Royal Hospital and the famous Art Brut collection in Lausanne.

15 Psychotic traits in comedians

Victoria Ando, Gordon Claridge and Ken Clark

> 'There is always some frivolity in excellent minds; they have wings to rise, but also stray.'
>
> (Joseph Joubert in Auster, 2006)

The age-old belief that creativity is associated with madness captures the public imagination and in recent years has increasingly become the focus of research for many professional psychologists and psychiatrists, who have provided substantial evidence to support the idea (Silvia & Kaufman, 2010). A convincing interpretation of these findings suggests that the connection is mediated through an association with personality and cognitive traits that underlie and predispose to psychosis (Brod, 1997). This idea has been most commonly studied under the heading of 'schizotypy', denoting schizophrenia-like characteristics that can be observed widely in the general population, in the absence of symptoms of overt psychotic illness. It is now clear that the same formulation can be expanded to include the other major form of psychosis, bipolar disorder, with a corresponding broadening of terminology in the personality sphere to refer to psychotic traits in general (Claridge & Barrantes-Vidal, 2013). Almost all the work within the above theoretical framework has been concerned with conventional creative forms within the arts and sciences. In contrast, despite being prime examples of creative thinking, comedy and humour have been largely neglected. There has been the occasional clinical observation that the rate of psychiatric disturbance in comedians seems high (McBride, 2004); but, with rare exceptions (Rawlings, 2008) – and then more concerned with humour appreciation – there has been little systematic research on the topic. Where personality in comedians has been studied, this has involved questionnaires such as the 'Big Five' (Greengross & Miller, 2009), which does not cover psychotic traits. Outside this specifically 'madness/creativity' literature – in more general writings about humour – the issue of humour as creativeness has been addressed, in both systematic review (O'Quin & Derks, 1999) and elsewhere. Having a good sense of humour is thought to be a healthy and desirable trait, and refers to the readiness to respond positively to potentially funny stimuli, to the ability to use comedy as a coping strategy (Chapman & Foot, 1976), and to the tendency to laugh and make others laugh (Forabosco, 1998). Incongruity theories describe humour as a creative process in which two normally disparate concepts or situations need to be brought together in an unexpected or incongruous manner. That is, humour arises when an idea or concept is suddenly viewed from an unusual perspective. Koestler (1964) coined the term 'bisociation' to describe the juxtaposition of two typically incongruous frames of references, which are placed together to create humour. These theories suggest that humour involves 'sudden, surprising shifts in the processing of information' (Lefcourt & Martin, 1986). The creative elements needed to produce humour are strikingly similar to those characterising the cognitive style of people with psychosis (both schizophrenia and bipolar disorder).

Cognition in full-blown schizophrenia is associated with confusion, disorganisation, fragmentation, and thought and speech containing illogically connected ideas – the form of thought disorder known as 'overinclusive thinking' (Cameron, 1944). It is unsurprising, therefore, that people in an acute schizophrenic state have difficulty generating and understanding humour (Marjoram et al., 2005). However, in a more muted form overinclusive thinking is conceptually similar to divergent thinking, a term often applied in general psychology to explain creative thinking. This helps to resolve the apparent paradox that, although schizophrenic psychosis itself may be detrimental to humour, in its lesser form – as schizotypal personality – it might reflect a heightened disposition to promote humour, through a greater ability to associate odd or unusual things: in popular parlance to 'think outside the box'.

The picture for bipolar disorder is somewhat more straightforward, at least with respect to its mania side. Manic thinking is manifestly overinclusive (divergent); or what in this context has been described as combinatorial – defined as the ability to 'combine ideas or categories of thought in order to form new and original connections' (Jamison, 1993). Such thinking is much more pronounced among individuals with bipolar disorder than in those with schizophrenia, or in controls (Solovay et al., 1987). It is easy to see how this can account for the relationship between the manic side of bipolar disorder and comic performance, facilitated through a synergism of very high mood and rapidly changing ideation. A notable example here is the English comedian Spike Milligan, who experienced manic-depressive episodes throughout his life (Milligan & Clare, 1993). Milligan certainly used the freely associating thought processes of his manic states to generate the zany humour and the wildly ridiculous ideas that were the hallmark of his comedy. Depression, however, with its slower thinking and anhedonia seems incompatible with creativity. Nevertheless, in the talented it might motivate the person to find ways of alleviating the low mood – in other words, to act as a form of self-medication. Pursuing this theme, Hugelshofer et al. (2006) suggested that humour actually provides protection against the development of hopelessness and consequent depression. Being creative – writing, composing, painting and being humorous – might therefore be an outlet, an escape from the pain of depression. The poet and writer Antonin Artaud, who himself experienced serious mental illness, wrote, 'No one has ever written, painted or sculpted, modelled, built or invented except literally to get out of hell' (1992). Against this background we set out to test the hypothesis that comedians would resemble other creative individuals in showing a higher level of psychotic characteristics, both schizophrenic and manic depressive. For reasons intimated earlier, these effects should best be revealed by examining differences on measures of personality traits relating to psychosis, rather than in the clinical characteristics of psychosis itself. To this end we examined a large group of comedians on the short version of the Oxford-Liverpool Inventory of Feelings and Experiences (O-LIFE), a four-scale self-report inventory covering both schizophrenic and bipolar features (Mason et al., 2005). This instrument has been widely used in previous research on creativity (Nettle, 2006; Claridge, 2009). As controls we used another group of performing artists, namely actors. To establish their personality status relative to the general population, both of these groups were compared with the normative data for the O-LIFE questionnaire.

Method

Participants were recruited online and asked to fill in an online questionnaire. Recruitment of comedians was carried out by emails to online comedian agencies, comedy clubs, comedian associations and comedian societies mainly in the UK, USA and Australia; these were found by a Google search or on recommendation from other comedian or comedy societies. Comedy societies affiliated with UK universities were also contacted, as were comedy societies found on the social network Facebook. In a similar way the questionnaire was also sent to online acting societies, clubs and associations in the UK, USA and Australia, and to actors affiliated with UK universities, by email or Facebook. As part of the questionnaire, participants were asked to supply other basic information: age and gender, type of comedian (or actor), amateur or professional status, and length of time they had been performing. Participants were given the opportunity to receive their individual O-LIFE scores once the questionnaire was completed, as an encouragement to take part. Otherwise, it was emphasised that the survey was strictly anonymous.

Questionnaire

The questionnaire administered included all the items from the short version of the O-LIFE (Mason et al., 2005). This consists of four scales measuring different aspects of schizotypy/psychoticism, as follows:

(a) Unusual Experiences (UnEx), measuring magical thinking, belief in telepathy and other paranormal events, and a tendency to experience perceptual aberrations;
(b) Cognitive Disorganisation (CogDis), measuring distractibility and difficulty in focusing thoughts;
(c) Introvertive Anhedonia (IntAn), measuring a reduced ability to feel social and physical pleasure, including an avoidance of intimacy;
(d) Impulsive Non-conformity (ImpNon), measuring a tendency towards impulsive, antisocial behaviour, often suggesting a lack of mood-related self-control.

General population O-LIFE scores used for comparison formed part of the normative data for the short O-LIFE, obtained from a variety of studies of the questionnaire, and supplied by Oliver Mason (personal communication, 2012).

Results

The target sample of comedians consisted of 523 individuals (404 men and 119 women) with a mean age of 31.31 years (s.d. = 9.77). The control sample comprised 364 actors (153 men and 211 women) whose mean age was 30.45 years (s.d. = 13.32). These samples were designated the 'performance groups'. The norms group consisted of 831 people (246 men and 585 women), with a mean age of 30.70 years (s.d. = 6.10). Although there was an imbalance for gender across the three groups, there was no significant overall difference in age: one-way analysis of variance (ANOVA) $F = 1.13$, NS. Comparing the two performance groups on other variables, 57% of the comedians and 73% of the actors were amateurs, and time in their respective professions fell into similar bands: comedians 1–3 years 54%, 4–7 years 46%; actors 1–3 years 70%, 4–7 years 30%. As for type of comedian (or actor), both groups were offered several (not mutually exclusive) options to choose from, but in each case one form predominated. Thus, among comedians 85% described themselves as 'stand-up', with only a small degree of overlap with the other categories offered, of 'writer', 'sketch' and 'musical'. Similarly for actors: 94% named 'theatre' as their preferred genre, with relatively few choosing 'musical', 'pantomime' or 'circus'. The exception there was that most also indicated that they worked in film.

Table 15.1 shows the mean scores for the three groups on the four O-LIFE scales. These data were analysed by multivariate analysis of variance (Table 15.2). There was a highly significant difference across the norms group and the two performance groups. Consistent with the norms for the O-LIFE there was also a significant gender difference, but no gender × group interaction. Gender was therefore not considered further at this stage of the analysis. Considering pairwise comparisons between groups (Tukey test), both comedians and actors had significantly higher O-LIFE scores than the test norms on all scales ($P < 0.001$), with the exception that actors did not differ from the norms on IntAn ($P < 0.35$). Actors also scored significantly lower than comedians on that scale ($P < 0.001$), as well as on CogDis ($P < 0.026$) and ImpNon ($P < 0.02$). However, the performance groups scored equally highly on UnEx.

O-LIFE scores

The pattern of O-LIFE scores observed in the two performance groups prompted us to look more closely at their respective profiles across the four questionnaire scales. To conduct this comparison the O-LIFE scores for participants in those two groups were converted into z-scores. The two groups showed markedly different profiles (Figure 15.1), particularly defined by the high IntAn and ImpNon scores observed in comedians compared with actors. Further inspection of these profile data revealed some gender differences (Figure 15.2). Two things stand out: one is that the overall profile for the comedians group is even more exaggerated in women, and the second is the striking gender difference among the actors group, women scoring notably low on IntAn yet high on ImpNon, mirroring and accounting for the overall trend in that group. Male participants, in comparison, had a flat, unremarkable profile across all four scales.

Table 15.1 Scores on the Oxford-Liverpool Inventory of Feelings and Experiences for the two performance groups and normative data

	Score, mean (s.d.)			
	IntAn	UnEx	CogDis	ImpNon
Comedians				
Men ($n = 404$)	3.09 (2.10)	4.55 (2.89)	5.75 (2.77)	4.57 (2.22)
Women ($n = 119$)	2.75 (2.26)	5.18 (2.65)	6.22 (2.68)	5.08 (2.11)
Total ($n = 523$)	3.01 (2.14)	4.70 (2.85)	5.86 (2.75)	4.68 (2.21)
Actors				
Men ($n = 153$)	2.62 (1.95)	4.35 (2.98)	5.37 (2.94)	4.04 (2.46)
Women ($n = 211$)	2.10 (1.85)	4.97 (2.82)	5.67 (2.64)	4.60 (2.30)
Total ($n = 364$)	2.32 (1.91)	4.71 (2.90)	5.54 (2.77)	4.37 (2.38)
Norms				
Men ($n = 246$)	2.39 (2.10)	3.20 (2.77)	4.32 (2.86)	3.37 (2.11)
Women ($n = 585$)	2.08 (1.89)	3.84 (3.12)	5.14 (2.89)	3.61 (2.08)
Total ($n = 831$)	2.17 (1.96)	3.65 (3.03)	4.89 (2.91)	3.54 (2.09)

CogDis, Cognitive Disorganisation; ImpNon, Impulsive Non-conformity; IntAn, Introvertive Anhedonia; UnEx, Unusual Experiences

Table 15.2 Multivariate analysis of variance of data from the Oxford-Liverpool Inventory of Feelings and Experiences

	Sum of squares	d.f.	Mean square	F	Significance
Group					
IntAn	115.05	2	57.53	14.40	$P < 0.0001$
UnEx	559.05	2	279.53	32.43	$P < 0.0001$
CogDis	414.17	2	207.09	26.09	$P < 0.0001$
ImpNon	465.38	2	232.69	48.82	$P < 0.0001$
Gender					
IntAn	49.63	1	49.63	12.42	$P < 0.0001$
UnEx	127.79	1	127.79	14.83	$P < 0.0001$
CogDis	88.61	1	88.61	11.17	$P = 0.001$
ImpNon	61.45	1	61.45	12.89	$P < 0.0001$
Group × gender					
IntAn	2.67	2	1.34	0.33	$P = 0.72$
UnEx	0.03	2	0.01	0.00	$P = 0.10$
CogDis	17.83	2	8.92	1.12	$P = 0.33$
ImpNon	7.73	2	3.87	0.81	$P = 0.44$

CogDis, Cognitive Disorganisation; ImpNon, Impulsive Non-conformity; IntAn, Introvertive Anhedonia; UnEx, Unusual Experiences

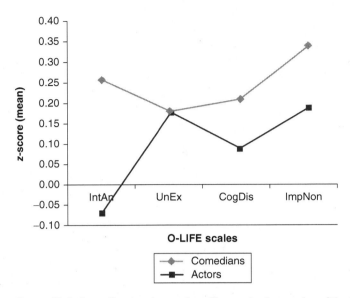

Figure 15.1 Comedians' and actors' profiles on the four scales of the Oxford-Liverpool Inventory of Feelings and Experiences (O-LIFE). CogDis, Cognitive Disorganisation; IntAn, Introvertive Anhedonia; ImpNon, Impulsive Non-conformity; UnEx, Unusual Experiences.

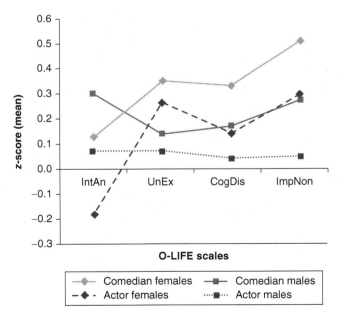

Figure 15.2 Gender differences in comedians' and actors' profiles on the four scales of the Oxford-Liverpool Inventory of Feelings and Experiences (O-LIFE). CogDis, Cognitive Disorganisation; IntAn, Introvertive Anhedonia; ImpNon, Impulsive Non-conformity; UnEx, Unusual Experiences.

Discussion

The results of this study substantially confirmed our expectation that comedians would behave like other creative groups in showing a high level of psychotic personality traits. They did so across all the domains sampled by the questionnaire we used, from schizoid and schizophrenic-like characteristics through to manic-depressive features. The most striking result, however, was the comedians' unusual personality profile observed across the four O-LIFE scales, scoring highly on both IntAn and ImpNon. This is of interest because the scales in question tap seemingly opposite personality characteristics: unsociable, depressive traits in the case of IntAn and more extraverted, manic-like traits in the case of ImpNon. We believe that the profile represents the personality equivalent of bipolar disorder, corresponding to what in an older personality literature would have been termed 'cyclothymic temperament'. This is illustrated in the self-description given by one of our (male) comedian respondents:

> I can say about myself that I don't think I'm one specific way. Sometimes I'm extremely introverted or uncomfortable socially and other times I'm the life of the party type of person. I believe though that if I'm in a situation where I might feel judgement for my inability to be/act 'normal', either founded by paranoia or legitimacy, I'm more likely to act out/overcompensate in the 'not afraid what anyone thinks' department.

Existing alongside high ratings on the two cognitive scales of the O-LIFE – UnEx and CogDis, both of which measure out-of-the-ordinary ways of thinking – it is possible to see how these various features combine synergistically to facilitate comedic performance. Or, as another of our respondents put it:

> Comedians train their brains to think in wide associative patterns. This relates to joke writing, where the word 'bicycle' brings up a picture of a bicycle in the mind of a non-comedian, but for the comedian it's like running a search on the internet – everything related pops up, from images of fat people riding bicycles naked and getting chafed to the fact that Lance Armstrong only has one testicle . . . I agree that some disorders have the helpful attribute of removing filters. Bipolar is usually hyperverbal, and means that focus keeps shifting, the way it must to absorb everything at once.

The O-LIFE factors are regarded conceptually as trait dimensions, intended as descriptors of predispositions to disorder – in the case of manic-depressive traits the tendency to experience consecutive changes in mood. Yet it is also helpful to take a slightly different, state, perspective on the matter, to see whether this gives any further insight into the psychology of the comedian; in other words to ask how (especially) the affective traits, shown to be important here, play out in the actual comedic situation. As it happens, when we were writing this paper a news item addressing the issue appeared across the British media about and by the celebrated English comedian Stephen Fry (Sherwin, 2013). Fry, who has a diagnosis of bipolar disorder (by his own reckoning 'bipolar lite') and is currently president of the mental health charity Mind, recently confessed to a suicide bid he had made and, in the course of talking about it, elaborated further on a typical mental state he had while performing. In the following, Fry is referring to this in the context of his role as the jokey compere of BBC television's highbrow quiz show, *QI*:

> There are times when I'm doing *QI* and I'm going 'ha ha, yeah, yeah', and inside I'm going 'I want to fucking die. I . . . want. . . . to . . . fucking . . . die'.

Fry's comment (expressed in characteristically robust fashion) serves to illustrate how two conflicting emotional traits typically found in comedians might be evoked simultaneously to shape their behaviour, one being used to cope with the other. There is something reminiscent here of the psychoanalytic notion of the 'manic defence' (Klein, 1940).

Using actors as controls for our comedian sample proved informative in several ways. It showed that although both groups had performing in front of an audience in common, they had distinctly different personality profiles. Most notably, the actors were low in the introversion traits measured by the IntAn scale, while sharing with comedians the more extraverted traits measured by the ImpNon scale. These personality profiles could explain how each relates to their respective audiences, and what motivates them to do so. The high IntAn rating in the comedians group suggests that, at one level, such individuals are indifferent to the audience; only their simultaneous disposition to the extraversion that forms part of ImpNon perhaps allows engagement to occur in public performance. Actors, on the other hand, being more congruent in their introvert/extravert tendencies, might be motivated towards a more straightforward, 'genuine' engagement with an audience, as acting seems to demand.

The results presented here convincingly demonstrate that, as creative people, comedians rate highly on the same personality traits as those regularly observed in other creative individuals. The traits in question are rightly labelled 'psychotic' because they represent healthy equivalents of cognitive and temperamental variations which, in pathological form, predispose to and mediate the symptoms of psychotic illness: features such as moodiness, social introversion and the tendency to lateral thinking. Humour and the conditions for it are particularly good examples of this 'madness/creativity' connection and deserve more attention than they have received hitherto. Of particular interest would be to supplement psychometric studies of the kind reported here with more detailed, biographical investigations such as those undertaken in other parts of the creativity literature.

Limitations

Although the use of an online methodology allowed us to collect a substantial sample of participants, a limitation of the study was that it did not enable us to assess the response rate of those surveyed, or to judge the representativeness of the samples. In addition, refinement of the method would have made it possible to examine differences between subtypes of comedians (and actors), most of whom reported themselves as falling into one type. A particular consequence of this was that we were unable to assess the importance of the fact that comedians (mostly) write their own material and actors (mostly) do not.

Acknowledgements

We thank Oliver Mason for supplying updated normative data for the Oxford-Liverpool Inventory of Feelings and Experiences and Stephen Thompson and Christian Ancliffe for their invaluable help with the recruitment of many of the comedians who participated in the study.

Commentary

The collection concludes with a paper from a very recent book jointly edited with Oliver Mason, featuring contributors updating evidence on major themes in psychosis proneness research. The book is entitled *Schizotypy: New Dimensions*. I wanted to call it '*Psychoticism*', but as the junior partner in the enterprise I was overruled, on the grounds that the shadow of Eysenck's usage still hangs too heavily over the term and the subject matter of the book would be misunderstood. I was therefore wryly amused that I somehow managed to wangle myself into writing the final paper (reproduced here), ensuring that I had the last word and that the full story would be told!

16 Old thoughts: new ideas: future directions

Gordon Claridge

The previous papers of this book have assembled considerable evidence for how, as a dimensional construct, schizotypy can inform our understanding of schizophrenia. The exact nature of that dimensionality was not addressed in detail by any of the contributors: that was not their brief. But when, as in several cases, authors did have cause to raise the issue, it was satisfying to see that they invariably phrased the prevailing opinions in the debate in a form similar to that stated in my 1997 book on schizotypy. Two different perspectives on dimensionality were mentioned. One, named 'quasi-dimensional', refers to schizotypal features (clinical or subclinical) as literally forming part of the schizophrenia spectrum, manifest as mild disease. The other view, called 'fully dimensional', sees schizotypy as a set of adaptive healthy personality traits that can (but need not) transform into disease at their extreme. That idea seems to have survived the ravenous appetite of some wolfish critics: if only among the present editors' selection of (eminent) researchers in the field.

When I originally proposed the fully dimensional model, I also raised another question about schizotypy, asking whether the term was too narrowly focused on schizophrenia and whether a broader term, taking in all forms of psychosis, might be better. That issue has been less well publicised and, when it has been discussed, has generally been misinterpreted or received a lukewarm response. It therefore seemed appropriate in the final paper of this book to revisit the question and offer the suggestion again as a thought for future theorising and research. Doing so will clear up some misunderstandings that have bedevilled the topic, and also help to elucidate some further aspects of dimensionality, as it relates to psychological disorder.

Given the focus of this book, and since Meehl was the first psychologist to use the term 'schizotypy', it is appropriate to start by examining where his (quasi-dimensional) theory lies in the historical landscape of attempts to dimensionalise serious mental illness (see Figure 16.1). As shown in the figure, two main themes can be recognised. On the right is what can broadly be designated a *medical* tradition of thought, represented here by Eugen Bleuler whose redefinition of Kraepelin's *dementia praecox* as schizophrenia marked the beginning of an era of systematic clinical description. At the time, under the influence of Kraepelin, a firmly stated categorical classification of mental illness was in place. Even so, some sense of 'dimensionality' was evident in the thinking of both men. Bleuler (1911/1950) – and even Kraepelin (1913/1919) himself – noted that some individuals could show schizophrenic-like characteristics that did not amount to the symptoms of the full-blown illness. This was often true of the relatives of clinically diagnosed schizophrenics. Bleuler used the term 'schizoid' to describe such people. The eventual emergence of the notion of a 'schizophrenia spectrum' was an obvious development and Meehl's adoption of schizotypy offered a scientific approach to measurement and definition, based on statistical analysis. His main innovation was the development of taxonometric methods that claim to identify individuals within a population who are schizotypes – as distinct from non-schizotypes. Logically, this opens up a methodology for comparing people who fall within and outwith the schizotypy taxon for evidence – biological, behavioural, cognitive – of the features responsible for schizophrenia.

Chronologically in parallel with this medical movement, there was another research tradition that also sought to dimensionalise psychopathology, but more radically (see left side of Figure 16.1). Here the starting point was not mental illness, but individual differences in personality. According to that view, psychological disorders could be seen as extreme expressions of personality and temperamental dimensions underlying health. As an ideology it was also more broadly based – not narrowly focused on schizophrenia. Here the significant historical figure was Ernst Kretschmer (1925) who was a near contemporary of Bleuler. As a psychiatrist himself, he formed a bridge between the medical and personality traditions depicted

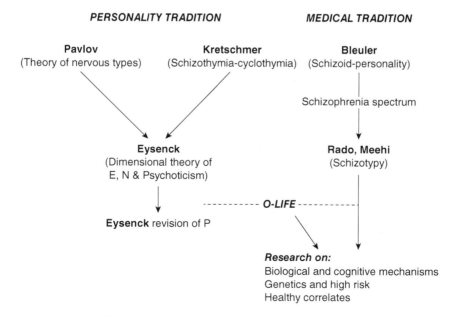

Figure 16.1 Two historical traditions in proposals to dimensionalise psychosis.

in Figure 16.1. Indeed, his work can be seen as more a contribution to the field of personality psychology than to psychiatry. Especially relevant was his proposal for connecting types of psychosis to normal temperaments through a dimension of 'schizothymia–cyclothymia'. The endpoints of this dimension were defined by, respectively, schizophrenia and manic depression ('bipolar disorder' as it is now called), but its continuous nature allowed for corresponding differences in normal temperament, as well as, towards the two extremes, clinically 'borderline' variants of schizoid and cycloid.

Kretschmer's writings greatly influenced Hans Eysenck who, in the modern period, was the person who did most to pioneer the idea of psychological disorders as extensions of normal personality. Eysenck is best known for his attempt to explain milder, neurotic, disorders – considered to reflect different combinations of his two major personality dimensions of neuroticism (N) and introversion-extraversion (I-E) (Eysenck, 1957b). However, from the very beginning of his career, Eysenck (1952b) had postulated a third dimension of 'psychoticism', or (P). At that stage P was considered to be comparable to N, as a descriptor of general traits that all forms of psychosis have in common. Types of psychosis – schizophrenia and manic depression – could be accounted for by reference to variations along the I-E dimension; in a manner *exactly* comparable to the explanation of neurosis as combinations of N and I-E. Eysenck arrived at this theory by rejigging, through factor analysis, Kretschmer's schizothymia–cyclothymia dimension (1952a). It is worth noting that in proposing this general psychoticism construct Eysenck was not stating anything new: he was merely adopting the unitary (or *Einheitpsychose*) construction of psychosis, which, until Kraepelin came along, was a commonly held view of madness during the nineteenth century (Berrios, 1995).

Despite the very different conclusions to be drawn from their work, as contemporaries, Eysenck and Meehl had curiously similar research aims and methodologies, at least up to a point. Both used statistical techniques to establish a subject matter of interest within psychopathology; and then they applied laboratory techniques to examine the biological and behavioural origins of the variations they had identified. Here the parallel ends, however. On the statistical front, Eysenck sought to establish fundamental, orthogonal and fully continuous dimensions of personality that could define all forms of serious mental illness; Meehl to develop measurement techniques that could identify qualitatively distinct types of people whose nature was uniquely 'schizophrenic'. Matching this distinction, their explanations of biological causation were also entirely different in form. Consistent with the medical model of schizophrenia, Meehl proposed an explanation of schizotypy that drew upon a similar *broken brain* view of its neurobiology and genetics. In contrast, Eysenck – finding inspiration in Pavlov's theory of 'nervous types' (see Figure 16.1) – believed that the biology of both normal and abnormal personality lay in *naturally occurring variations* in brain function: personalities simply have different kinds of brain.

There is a final point to be noted in Figure 16.1. The diagram portrays the later convergence of the medical and personality traditions as an eventual confluence of research effort on the dimensionality of psychosis. This is misleading in one respect. The *unitary psychosis/psychoticism* theme on the left side of the diagram — and, in particular, concern with the dimensionality of bipolar disorder — has largely disappeared from view: attention has shifted almost entirely to the schizotypy–schizophrenia connection. Insofar as this gap in research effort was accounted for by Eysenck's influence, it can easily be explained. On returning after several decades to his third major dimension, Eysenck set out to specify psychoticism (P) more precisely (Eysenck & Eysenck, 1976). He did so in the most unexpected way, defining it in terms of antisocial traits, most commonly found in psychopaths — far removed from the cognitive and affective characteristics that most writers, irrespective of their stance on other issues, would consider central to psychosis, especially the schizophrenias. Psychoticism and the P-scale, Eysenck's questionnaire measure of his supposedly broader dimension, actually became narrower in scope and more idiosyncratic in content. Over several versions its items gradually moved away from those typically found in the schizotypy questionnaires of the time and became more slanted towards impulsivity, aggressiveness and non-conformist behaviour. This formulation of psychoticism was heavily criticised (Claridge, 1981, 1983) but it remained Eysenck's theoretical position to the end of his life. So, in his latest statement (Eysenck, 1992b), he presented a model of psychosis consisting of a continuum ranging from criminality, through affective disorder, to schizophrenia. True, a unitary dimensional theory linking schizophrenia and bipolar disorder, but deeply flawed as a comprehensive account of psychotic traits and states. And far removed from 'Version 1' of Eysenck's theory in which psychoticism supposedly collected together elements that the two major psychoses had in common, while preserving the differences between them.

This ill-considered revision of his theory left Eysenck and his P-scale isolated from mainstream research in the area. Scientific enquiry was consolidated around clinical schizophrenia as the reference point, with schizotypy questionnaires as measures of its dimensional features. There were increasingly few studies using the P-scale that could seriously expect to reveal insight into schizophrenia, or even psychosis in a broader sense.[1] The side-lining of the P-scale by serious schizotypy researchers had its impact on questionnaire development and interpretation. Illustrative here is the research leading up to and including the development of the Oxford-Liverpool Inventory of Feelings and Experiences (*O-LIFE*) (Claridge et al., 1996; Mason, Claridge, & Williams, 1997), an inventory that was intended to bridge the gap between the personality and medical traditions. Work on the questionnaire was unique in including the most comprehensive set of scales hitherto subjected to statistical analysis, in order to try and establish, definitively, the factorial structure of psychotic traits. The items and scales that were included covered not just regular schizotypy measures but others to do with hypomania and borderline personality (and Eysenck's P-scale). As well-recorded elsewhere, these analyses identified the three main factors now named in the O-LIFE as Unusual Experiences (UnEx), Cognitive Disorganisation (CogDis), and Introvertive Anhedonia (IntAn) – scales generally accepted as comprehensively defining schizotypy.

However, the O-LIFE data set also contained a fourth factor – eventually labelled Impulsive Non-conformity (ImpNon). This additional factor is mostly ignored by workers using the O-LIFE – presumably being regarded by them as a statistical aberration, a best ignored distraction from retaining the neat schizotypy structure traditionally supplied by the other three factors. Yet it has become increasingly obvious that the presence of ImpNon in the so-called 'schizotypy' domain seriously questions whether the schizotypy–schizophrenia spectrum can be studied in isolation from other psychotic features. In other words, should we not be considering a more inclusive formulation of psychosis and psychotic traits, closer to Kretschmer's? And, dare I say it, closer to Eysenck's (Version 1) theory?

One reason for stating this comes from the pattern of factor loadings found in the analysis of scales used in the construction of the O-LIFE (Claridge et al., 1996). The ImpNon factor was, not unexpectedly, partly defined by Eysenck's P-scale. But, more interestingly, other scales also had high loadings, notably a hypomania scale included in the study. Furthermore, this same fourth factor contributed strongly to the main positive symptoms factor (Perceptual Aberration Scale) that is used, as we know, to describe a major feature of schizotypy. In other words, ImpNon was *not* some isolated artefact of the analysis: instead, having connection to manic-depressive traits, it intermingled with and contributed in a real sense to the domain we have been accustomed to label 'schizotypy'. Of further interest here is the behaviour in the factor solution of another scale: the Borderline Personality Scale (STB) (Claridge & Broks, 1984). Like hypomania, the STB also cross-correlated with the other factors, particularly CogDis, again suggesting shared variance with 'schizotypy'. This result chimes with earlier reports that the STB correlates highly with the Schizotypal Personality Scale (STA), the better known schizotypy scale, developed at the same time by Claridge and Broks. In their paper they refer to STA/STB correlations as high as 0.59 (Rawlings, 1983) and +0.71 (Claridge, Robinson, & Birchall, 1983), putting beyond reasonable doubt the extendability of schizotypy beyond its usually accepted boundaries.

Why are these results for borderline personality of interest here? Two reasons. One is that some authors have argued that some types of borderline personality – although not necessarily all (it is a notoriously difficult concept to define) – might represent attenuated forms of bipolar disorder, forming part of its spectrum (Akiskal, 1996; Perugi, Fornaro, & Akiskal, 2011). Second (more a mystery than a reason), in its early history the attempt to characterise psychiatric states that fell on the edges of full-blown psychosis was an inchoate mixture of features found in schizophrenia, manic depression and everything in between – and generating many different labels that captured a mixture of schizophrenic, affective, neurotic and personality disorder characteristics (see Claridge [1995] for a discussion of this topic). Subsequent attempts to bring order to the field revealed the existence of two clusters: 'schizotypal borderline' and 'borderline borderline' (Spitzer, Endicott, J, & Gibbon, 1979). These were separate yet overlapping, exactly like the pattern of correlations for STA and STB described earlier. Oddly – and this is where the mystery lies – when using those data to set up new diagnostic guidelines for personality disorders in *DSM-III*, the committee of the American Psychiatric Association assigned one form (schizotypal) to the 'Mad' (A) cluster and the other (borderline) to the 'Bad' (B) cluster. What this effectively did was to take out of the arena for debate – or, put more crudely, deliberately cause to be ignored – the question of whether the two forms of borderline might share common descriptive and aetiological features across psychosis. In short, despite the evidence, 'borderline borderline' was no longer seen to be part of a psychosis spectrum.

Returning to ImpNon, this has recently been shown to correlate significantly with independently assessed bipolar symptoms (Alminhana et al., submitted; Nettle, 2006); its place as a measure of psychotic traits in the affective sphere is therefore well established. However, Nettle goes further than that in addressing the overall structure of psychotic traits. Writing in the context of creativity research, he proposes 'thymotypy' and schizotypy as forming two related subdimensions, of equivalent status, that relate to creativity (Nettle, 2001). It is an interesting suggestion, given that creativity is an expression of psychotic traits where the influence of both schizophrenic and bipolar features – often overlapping or intermingling – is particularly evident. Two recent examples illustrate the point. Both used the O-LIFE to assess psychotic traits, in one case in comedians (Ando, Claridge, & Clark, 2014) and in the other case in poets (Mason, Mort, & Woo, 2015). In the former study, the comedians were found to have very high scores on all the O-LIFE scales. But most notable was their performance across the scales: very high on both IntAn and ImpNon, a combination that was interpreted to signify in comedians a predominantly manic-depressive (bipolar) personality profile. The Mason et al. study extended these results by showing with Hirschfeld's (2000) Mood Disorder Questionnaire that the poets had a very high incidence of bipolar symptoms. On the O-LIFE, although unlike the comedians not differing from controls on IntAn, the poets did have significantly high scores on the other three scales.

This evidence from questionnaire data exists against a background of increasing support for a unitary view of clinical psychosis, an old idea that was strongly resisted for much of the twentieth century but which has seen a revival in recent years (Marneros & Akiskal, 2007). That, together with a general loosening of categorical boundaries supposedly defining distinct psychiatric diseases without overlap, and a greater acceptance in psychiatry of dimensional models, further strengthens the case for subsuming the schizophrenia and bipolar spectra under the same heading. Whether 'psychoticism' is a suitable overarching label for that spectrum is a moot point. Eysenck's idiosyncratic use of the term still lingers and continues to cause confusion whenever the matter is discussed by psychologists. However, this will hopefully fade with time and 'psychoticism' does seem the most obvious term to use. It is also significant that 'psychoticism' has found its way into *DSM-5* as one of five dimensions in the so-called PID-5 for assessing personality disorder traits (American Psychiatric Association, 2013). There it appears to describe a dimension of lucidity versus poor reality testing. This may not precisely coincide with the usage intended here, but it does at least draw away from Eysenck's later definition of P.

Another quandary is how best to designate and measure the subdimension that sits alongside schizotypy in the broader spectrum of psychoticism (or whatever we might decide to call it). As we have seen, there are several possibilities. One is ImpNon from our own O-LIFE, but that seems to be too psychometrically grounded to be suitable. The same is true, to a lesser extent, of borderline personality and anyway, conceptually, it is a very amorphous construct; features that overlap with psychosis would need specifying more precisely. Historically, 'cyclothymia' is the obvious choice but nowadays that seems to have morphed into a description of a clinical subsyndrome of bipolar illness, rather than a personality trait or dimension as it was traditionally used. Cyclothymia's only appearance in the broadly personality literature seems to be as a subscale in the TEMPS-A temperament scale described by Akiskal and his colleagues (Akiskal et al., 2005): opportunities otherwise for measuring affective traits it might tap are through hypomania or mood rating scales, such as the Mood Disorder Questionnaire (Hirschfeld, 2000) used by Mason in his study of poets described earlier. One research task for the future, therefore, is to consolidate measurement, terminology and theory around a concept that sits alongside schizotypy, symmetrically and of equal status as a second subdimension of the psychosis spectrum. My own best guess for a likely candidate is Nettle's use of 'thymotypy', referred to earlier.

A final word on the quasi- versus fully dimensional issue. This has continued to be a bone of contention, often eliciting strong statements, especially from critics in the US who through their loyalty to Meehl are fierce adherents to the 'quasi' model. An illustration was a recent exchange in the journal *Personality and Individual Differences*. The trigger was a paper published by Rawlings, Williams, Haslam, and Claridge (2008a) throwing doubt on the idea of schizotypy as a universally observed distinct taxon. A reply from members of the Meehl school was brutally dismissive (Beauchaine, Lenzenweger, & Waller, 2008). Yet – and here I naturally write from a partisan position as originator of the fully dimensional approach – much of the argumentation in that exchange was based on two misunderstandings by Beauchaine and his colleagues (see Rawlings, Williams, Haslam, & Claridge, 2008b). The first arose through their conflation of the pure dimensional issue with that pertaining to the influence of Eysenck's theorising about (P) – a confusion I hope I have cleared up here for good. The second was their failure to understand that the quasi- and fully dimensional models are not mutually exclusive. If the two models are judged as rivals, it is only true insofar as the fully dimensional model is the more comprehensive: it includes the features focused upon by quasi-dimensionalists, but adds to them. Thus, full dimensionality refers to *healthy traits* when describing variations in the personality domain and shifts to specifying *unhealthy symptoms* at the illness end of the spectrum. What this means statistically is whether a dimensional or a taxonomic picture is revealed in data will depend on the kind of individuals sampled: fully dimensional and trait-like in the mid-range of the population; dichotomous and quasi-dimensional in people further up the spectrum who are pre-psychotic, or in the zone of risk. Traits and symptoms certainly have different properties: the former are more continuous, follow normal distributions and are ego-syntonic; the latter are ego-dystonic and more often dichotomous and skewed in their distribution. But this does not mean that they cannot lie on a continuum with one another – or a pseudo-continuum if one wants to be pedantic about it. (See a recent position paper by Mason [2014] for a detailed analysis of the implications of these points for measurement and theory in schizotypy research.) There are many instances when this is true, where personality and illness connect (Claridge and Davis, 2003): trait anxiety and anxiety disorder are a case in point. There is good evidence that schizotypy and schizophrenia (or psychoticism and psychosis) merely form another example.[2]

The central question therefore is *not* whether trait-like features and symptom-like features can exist in adjacent related domains of variation, one describing healthy and the other a failure in function (and one defining risk for the other). The more interesting question is how trait becomes symptom: under what conditions healthy adaptation becomes illness. It is a universal question, not confined to psychopathology. Thus, analogous to the quasi/fully dimensional distinction made here for normal and abnormal personality we may note the case of blood pressure and essential hypertension: how the former can exist as a healthy trait, yet also constitute a risk for the pathologically high blood pressure that can issue in a serious failure of function, such as heart failure or stroke. Anticipating much of what in a different context I have tried to convey here – and in a passage that I have had occasion to quote on a number of occasions – W.B. Cannon, the famous psychophysiologist, once wrote about the phenomenon as follows:

> There are many systems in the body which, because of misuse or misfortune, may have their services to the organism as a whole so altered as to be actually harmful. Thus vicious circles of causation become established which may lead to death . . . The development of pathological functions in a system is quite consistent with its usual performance of normal functions.
>
> (Cannon, 1953)

Notes

1 An exception, I could (immodestly!) claim, is a linked group of early experiments by me and my colleagues showing a common theme in the psychophysiology of schizophrenics, high P subjects, and LSD drug-induced effects (Claridge, 1972; Claridge & Chappa, 1973; Claridge & Clark, 1982). A slightly unfortunate combination of strategies, given the eventual marginalisation of P and criminalisation of LSD, and the difficulty in finding first-episode drug-free psychotic patients.
2 Raine (2006) is one writer who disagrees, however. In an attempt, seemingly, to avoid incorporating healthy personality traits into his construction of schizotypy, he has proposed the notion of 'pseudoschizotypy'. He claims that this mimics true schizotypy but has no connection to the aetiology of schizophrenia. The idea seems a redundant addition to theory: one wonders whatever happened to Occam's razor (the principle of parsimony)!

Commentary

One more comment to end my narrative. All of the research reported in this collection was done on a shoestring, in my spare time taken out from a full teaching job: in collaboration with equally busy colleagues; or postgraduate students under my supervision; or in two cases – the inspiration for my first schizotypy scale and later my interest in comedy – by undergraduates. Recently Dr Anna Scarna, a good friend and colleague of mine, wonderfully styled it 'socialist' research – as distinct from the 'corporate' variety, fuelled by large grants driving big research teams. I am in no position to compare the two, having only experienced the former. But I hope I have persuaded some of my readers at least that a communal dish consumed on the hoof is as tasty as a full banquet.

References

Abraham, K. R., & Kulhara, P. (1987). The efficacy of electroconvulsive therapy in the treatment of schizophrenia: A comparative study. *British Journal of Psychiatry, 151*, 152–155.

Ackner, B., & Pampiglione, G. (1958). Discussion on physiological measurements of 'emotional tension'. *Proceedings of the Royal Society of Medicine, 51*, 76–81.

Adey, W. R., Bell, F. R., & Dennis, B. J. (1962). Effects of LSD-25, psilocybin and psilocin on temporal lobe EEG patterns and learned behavior in the cat. *Neurology, 12*, 591–602.

Akiskal, H. S. (1996). The prevalent clinical spectrum of bipolar disorders: Beyond DSM-IV. *Journal of Clinical Psychopharmacology, 16*, Supplement 1, 4–14.

Akiskal, H. S., Mendlowicz, M. V., Jean-Louis, G., Rapaport, M. H., Kelsoe, J. R., Gillin, J., & Smith, T. L. (2005). TEMPS-A: Validation of a short version of a self-rated instrument designed to measure variations in temperament. *Journal of Affective Disorders, 85*, 45–52.

Alminhana, L. O., Farias, M., Moreira-Almeida, A., Menezes Jr., A., Zanini, A., Claridge, G., & Cloninger, R. C. (submitted). Psychobiological model of temperament and character: Criterion to mental health and schizotypy in individuals with anomalous experiences.

American Psychiatric Association (1980). *Diagnostic and statistical manual of mental disorders (DSM-III)* (3rd ed.). Washington, DC: APA.

American Psychiatric Association. (1987). *Diagnostic and statistical manual of mental disorders (DSM-IIIR)* (3rd ed., rev.). Washington, DC: Author.

American Psychiatric Association. (1994). *Diagnostic and statistical manual* (4th ed.). Washington, DC: APA.

American Psychiatric Association. (2013). *Diagnostic and statistical manual of mental disorders (DSM-V)* (5th ed.). Arlington, VA: Author.

Ando, V., Claridge., G., & Clark, K. (2014). Psychotic traits in comedians. *British Journal of Psychiatry, 204*, 341–345.

Andreasen, N. J. C., & Powers, P. S. (1974). Overinclusive thinking in mania and schizophrenia. *British Journal of Psychiatry, 125*, 452–456.

Andreassi, J. L., Mayzner, M. S., Davidovics, S., & Beyda, D.R. (1971). Visual evoked potentials at, above, and below two-flash thresholds. *Psychonomic Science, 22*, 185–187.

Annett, M. (1970). A classification of hand preference by association analysis. *British Journal of Psychology, 61*, 303–321.

Annett, M. (1985). Left, right, hand and brain: The right shift theory. Hove, UK: Lawrence Erlbaum Associates Ltd.

Annett, M. (1991). Right hemisphere costs of right handedness. In J. F. Stein (Ed.), *Vision and visual dyslexia: Vol 13, Vision and visual dysfunction* (pp. 84–93). London: Macmillan.

Annett, M. (1992). Spatial ability in subgroups of left- and right-handers. *British Journal of Psychology, 83*, 493–515.

Annett, M. (1993). Disadvantages of dextrality for intelligence: Corrected findings. *British Journal of Psychology, 84*, 511–516.

Annett, M. (1995). The right shift theory of a genetic balanced polymorphism for cerebral dominance and cognitive processing. *Current Psychology of Cognition, 14*, 1–54.

Annett, M., & Manning, M. (1989). The disadvantages of dextrality for intelligence. *British Journal of Psychology, 80*, 213–226.

Annett, M., & Manning, M. (1990). Arithmetic and laterality. *Neuropsychologia, 28*, 61–69.

Anthony, E. J. (1987). Children at high risk for psychosis growing up successfully. In E. J. Anthony & B.J. Cohler (Eds.), *The invulnerable child*. New York: The Guilford Press.

Arduini, A., & Arduini, M. G. (1954). Effect of drugs and metabolic alterations on brainstem arousal mechanism. *Journal of Pharmacology and Experimental Therapeutics, 110*, 76.

Artaud, A. (1992). Van Gogh, the man suicided by society. In S. Sontag (Ed.), *Antonin Artaud: Selected writings*. Berkeley, CA: University of California Press.

Auster, P. (2006). *The notebooks of Joseph Joubert: A selection*. New York Review of Books Classics [Joseph Joubert 1754–1824, no original work published during his life].

Avons, S. E., Nunn, J. A., Chan, L., & Armstrong, H. (2003). Executive function assessed by memory updating and random generation in schizotypal individuals. *Psychiatry Research, 120*, 145–154.

Baron, M., & Gruen, R. S. (1991). Schizophrenia and affective disorder: Are they genetically linked? *British Journal of Psychiatry, 159*, 267–270.

Barrantes-Vidal, N. (1997). The relationship of schizotypal and hypomanic traits with creativity in normal subjects. Unpublished Masters thesis. Autonomous University of Barcelona.

Barrantes-Vidal, N. (2004). Creativity and madness revisited from current psychological perspectives. *Journal of Consciousness Studies, 11*, 58–78.

Beauchaine, T. P., Lenzenweger, N. F., & Waller, N. G. (2008). Schizotypy, taxometrics, and disconfirming theories in soft science: Comment on Rawlings, Williams, Haslam, and Claridge. *Personality and Individual Differences, 44*, 1652–1662.

Beckley Foundation. www.beckleyfoundation.org

Bendall, S., Jackson, H. J., Hulbert, C. A., & McGorry, P. D. (2008). Childhood trauma and psychotic disorders: A systematic, critical review of the evidence. *Schizophrenia Bulletin, 34*, 568–579.

Bentall, R. P., Claridge, G. S., & Slade, P. D. (1989). The multidimensional nature of schizotypal traits: A factor analytic study with normal subjects. *British Journal of Clinical Psychology, 28*, 363–375.

Berrettini, W. (2003). Evidence for shared susceptibility in bipolar disorder and schizophrenia. *American Journal of Medical Genetics, 123C*, 59–64.

Berrios, G. E. (1995). Conceptual problems in diagnosing schizophrenic disorders. In J. A. Den Boer, H. G. M. Westenberg, & H. M. van Praag (Eds.), *Advances in the neurobiology of schizophrenia* (pp. 7–25). Chichester: Wiley.

Birchall, P. M. A., & Claridge, G. S. (1979). Augmenting-reducing of the visual evoked potential as a function of changes in skin conductance level. *Psychophysiology*, 16, 482.

Bishop, D. V. M. (1990). *Handedness and developmental disorder*. Hove, UK: Lawrence Erlbaum Associates Ltd.

Bleich, A., Brown, S.-L., Kaan, R., & van Praag, H. M. (1988). The role of serotonin in schizophrenia. *Schizophrenia Bulletin*, 14, 297–315.

Bleuler, E. P. (1950). *Dementia praecox or the group of schizophrenias* (J. Zinkin, Trans.). New York: International Universities Press. (Original work published in 1911.)

Bleuler, M. (1978). *The schizophrenic disorders* (S. M. Clemens, Trans.). New Haven, CT: Yale University Press.

Bradley, P. B. (1957). The central action of certain drugs in relation to the reticular formation of the brain. In H. H. Jasper, L. D. Proctor, R. S. Knighton, W. C. Noshay, & R. T. Costello (Eds.), *Reticular formation of the brain* (pp. 123–149). London: Churchill.

Bradley, P. B., & Elkes, J. (1957). The effect of some drugs on the electrical activity of the brain. *Brain*, 80, 77–117.

Brezinova, V., & Kendell, R. E. (1977). Smooth pursuit eye movements of schizophrenics and normal people under stress. *British Journal of Psychiatry*, 130, 59–63.

Broadbent, D. E. (1958). *Perception and communication*. London: Pergamon Press.

Broadhurst, P. L., & Broadhurst, A. (1964). An analysis of the pursuit rotor learning of chronic psychotics. *British Journal of Psychology*, 55, 321–331.

Brockington, I. F., Kendell, R. E., Wainwright, S., Hillier, V. F., & Walker, J. (1979). The distinction between the affective psychoses and schizophrenia. *British Journal of Psychiatry*, 135, 243–248.

Brod, J. H. (1997). Creativity and schizotypy. In G. Claridge (Ed.), *Schizotypy: Implications for illness and health* (pp. 274–299). Oxford: Oxford University Press.

Brune, M. (2011). Evolutionary aspects in medicine. In B. D. Kirkcaldy (Ed.), The art and science of health care: Psychology and human factors for practitioners. Cambridge, MA: Hogrefe.

Buchanan, R. D. (2010). Playing with fire: The controversial career of Hans J. Eysenck. Oxford: Oxford University Press.

Buchsbaum, M. S., Post, R. M., & Bunney, W. E. (1977). Average evoked responses in a rapidly cycling manic-depressive patient. *Biological Psychiatry*, 12, 83–99.

Buchsbaum, M. S., & Silverman, J. (1968). Stimulus intensity control and the cortical evoked response. *Psychosomatic Medicine*, 30, 12–22.

Buckley, P., Walshe, D., Colohan, H. A., & O'Callaghan, E. (1990). A study of the occurrence and clinical correlates of violence among schizophrenic patients. *Irish Journal of Psychological Medicine*, 7, 102–108.

Burch, G. S., Steel, C., & Hemsley, D. R. (1988). Oxford-Liverpool Inventory of Feelings and Experiences: Reliability in an experimental population. *British Journal of Clinical Psychology*, 37, 107–108.

Buss, A. H., & Plomin, R. (1984). *Temperament: Early developing personality traits*. Hillsdale, NJ: Lawrence Erlbaum Associates.

Butcher, H. J. (1968). Human intelligence: Its nature and assessment. London: Methuen.

Callaway, E., III, & Dembo, E. (1958). Narrowed attention: A psychological phenomenon that accompanies a certain physiological change. *Archives of Neurology and Psychiatry*, 79, 74–90.

Callaway, E., & Jones, R. T. (1975). Evoked responses for the study of complex cognitive functions. In M. L. Kietzman, S. Sutton, & J. Zubin (Eds.), *Experimental approaches to psychopathology* (pp. 177–186). New York: Academic Press, Inc.

Callaway, E., Jones, R. T., & Layne, R. S. (1965). Evoked responses and segmental set in schizophrenia. *Archives of General Psychiatry*, *12*, 83–89.

Cameron, N. (1938). Reasoning, regression and communication in schizophrenics. *Psychological Monographs*, 50, 1–34.

Cameron, N. (1944). The functional psychoses. In JMcV Hunt (Ed.), *Personality and the behavior disorders* (Vol. 2, pp. 861–921). Ronald Press.

Cannon, M., Byrne, M., Cassidy, B., Larkin, C., Horgan, R., Sheppard, N. P., & O'Callaghan, E. (1995). Prevalence and correlates of mixed-handedness in schizophrenia. *Psychiatry Research*, *59*, 119–125.

Cannon, W. B. (1953). *Bodily changes in pain, hunger, fear, and rage*. Boston, MA: Charles C. Branford.

Canter, S. (1972). Conceptual thinking and selective attention in acute schizophrenics. Ph.D. thesis, University of Glasgow.

Cardinal, R. (2009). Outsider art and the autistic creator. *Philosophical Transactions of the Royal Society B*, *364*, 1459–1466.

Carhart-Harris, R. L, Muthukumaraswamy, S., Roseman, L., Kaelen, M., Droog, W., Murphy, K., Tagliazucchi, E., Schenberg, E. E., Nest, T., Orban, C., Leech, R., Williams, L. T., Williams, T. M., Bolstridge, M., Sessa, B., McGonigle, J., Sereno, M. I., Nichols, D., Hellyere, P. J., Hobden, P., Evans, J., Krish, D., Singh, K. D., Wise, R. G., Curran, H. V., Feilding., A., & Nutt, D. J. (2016) Neural correlates of the LSD experience revealed by multimodal neuroimaging. *Proceedings of the National Academy of Sciences of the United States of America (PNAS)*, *113*, 4853–4858.

Carson, S. H. (2011). Creativity and psychopathology: A shared vulnerability model. *Canadian Journal of Psychiatry*, *56*, 144–153.

Carter, M., & Watts, C. A. H. (1971). Possible biological advantages among schizophrenics' relatives. *British Journal of Psychiatry*, *118*, 453–460.

Cassaday, H. J., Hodges, H., & Gray, J. A. (1993). The effects of ritanserin, RU 24969 and 8-OH-DPAT on latent inhibition in the rat. *Journal of Psychopharmacology*, 7, 63–71.

Cattell, R. B., & Butcher, H. J. (1968). *The prediction of achievement and creativity*. Indianapolis, IN: Bobbs-Merrill.

Cattell, R. B., & Drevdahl, J. E. (1955). A comparison of the personality profile of eminent researchers with that of eminent teachers and administrators and of the general population. *British Journal of Psychiatry*, *46*, 248–261.

Chadwick, P. (2001). *Personality as art: Artistic approaches in psychology*. Ross-on-Wye: PCCS Books.

Chamove, A. S., Eysenck, H. J., & Harlow, H. F. (1972). Personality in monkeys: Factor analyses of rhesus social behaviour. *Quarterly Journal of Experimental Psychology*, *24*, 496–504.

Chapman, A. J., & Foot, H. C. (Eds) (1976). *Humour and laughter: Theory, research and applications*. Pitman.

Chapman, J. (1966). The early symptoms of schizophrenia. *British Journal of Psychiatry*, *121*, 225–253.

Chapman, J. P., & Chapman, L. J. (1987). Handedness in hypothetically psychosis-prone subjects. *Journal of Abnormal Psychology*, *96*, 89–93.

Chapman, J. P., Chapman, L. J., & Kwapil, T. R. (1995). Scales for the measurement of schizotypy. In A. Raine, T. Lencz, & S. A. Mednick (Eds.), *Schizotypal personality* (pp. 79–106). Cambridge: Cambridge University Press.

Chapman, L. J., Chapman, J. P., & Miller, E. N. (1982). Reliabilities and intercorrelations of eight measures of proneness to psychosis. *Journal of Consulting and Clinical Psychology, 50*, 187–195.

Chapman, L. J., Chapman, J. P., & Raulin, M. L. (1976). Scales for physical and social anhedonia. *Journal of Abnormal Psychology, 85*, 374–382.

Chapman, L. J., Chapman, J. P., & Raulin, M. L. (1978). Body image aberration in schizophrenia. *Journal of Abnormal Psychology, 87*, 399–407.

Chapman, L. J., Edell, W. S., & Chapman, J. P. (1980). Physical anhedonia, perceptual aberration, and psychosis proneness. *Schizophrenia Bulletin, 6*, 639–653.

Chaugule, V. B., & Master, R. S. (1981). Impaired cerebral dominance and schizophrenia. *British Journal of Psychiatry, 139*, 23–24.

Claridge, G. S. (1956). *Factors affecting the motivation and performance of imbeciles.* Ph.D. thesis, University of London.

Claridge, G. S. (1960). The excitation-inhibition balance in neurotics. In H. J. Eysenck (Ed.), *Experiments in personality.* London: Routledge and Kegan Paul.

Claridge, G. S. (1961a) Arousal and inhibition as determinants of the performance of neurotics. *British Journal of Psychology, 52*, 53–63.

Claridge, G. S. (1961b) The effects of meprobamate on the performance of a five-choice serial reaction time task. *Journal of Mental Science, 107*, 590–602.

Claridge, G. S. (1967). Personality and arousal: A psychophysiological study of psychiatric disorder. Oxford: Pergamon Press.

Claridge, G. S. (1970a). *Drugs and human behaviour.* London: Allen Lane the Penguin Press.

Claridge, G. S. (1970b). Psychophysiological techniques. In P. Mittler (Ed.), *The psychological assessment of mental and physical handicaps.* London: Methuen.

Claridge, G. S. (1972). The schizophrenias as nervous types. *British Journal of Psychiatry, 121*, 1–17.

Claridge, G. S. (1976). The schizophrenias as nervous types. Paper presented to the Annual Conference of the British Psychological Society, York.

Claridge, G. (1978). Animal models of schizophrenia: The case for LSD-25. *Schizophrenia Bulletin, 4*, 186–209.

Claridge, G. (1981). Psychoticism. In R. Lynn (Ed.), *Dimensions of personality: Papers in honour of H. J. Eysenck* (pp. 79–109). Oxford: Pergamon Press.

Claridge, G. (1983). The Eysenck psychoticism scale. In J. N. Butcher & C. D. Spielberger (Eds.), *Advances in personality assessment* (Vol. 2, pp. 71–114). Hillsdale, NJ: Lawrence Erlbaum Associates.

Claridge, G. (1987). 'The schizophrenias as nervous types' revisited. *British Journal of Psychiatry, 151*, 735–743.

Claridge, G. (1994a). Single indicator of risk for schizophrenia: Probable fact or likely myth? *Schizophrenia Bulletin, 20*, 151–168.

Claridge, G. (1994b). Psychobiological models and issues. In S. Strack & M. Lorr (Eds.), *Differentiating normal and abnormal personality.* New York: Springer.

Claridge, G. (1995). *Origins of mental illness* (new impression). Cambridge, MA: Malor Books.

Claridge, G. (1997a). Eysenck's contribution to understanding psychopathology. In H. Nyborg (Ed.), *The scientific study of human nature: Tribute to Hans Eysenck at eighty* (pp. 364–387). Oxford: Pergamon Press.

Claridge, G. (Ed.) (1997b). *Schizotypy: Implications for illness and health*. Oxford: Oxford University Press.

Claridge, G. (1997c). Theoretical background and issues. In G. Claridge (Ed.), *Schizotypy: Implications for illness and health* (pp. 3–18). Oxford: Oxford University Press.

Claridge, G. (2006). Psychobiological models and issues. In S. Strack (Ed.), *Differentiating normal and abnormal personality* (2nd ed., pp. 137–164). New York: Springer.

Claridge, G. (2009a). Personality and psychosis. In P. J. Corr & G. Matthews (Eds.), *The Cambridge handbook of personality* (pp. 631–648). Cambridge: Cambridge University Press.

Claridge, G. (Ed.) (2009b). Personality, psychopathology, and original minds. *Personality and Individual Differences, 46* (special issue), 749–838.

Claridge, G. (2015). Old thoughts: New ideas: Future directions. In O. J. Mason & G. Claridge (Eds.), *Schizotypy: New dimensions* (pp. 217–227). London: Routledge.

Claridge, G., & Barrantes-Vidal, N. (2013). Creativity: A healthy side of madness. In B. Kirkaldy (Ed.) *Chimes of time: Essays by wounded professionals* (pp. 115–130). Leiden, Netherlands: Sidestone.

Claridge, G. S., & Birchall, P. M. A. (1973). The biological basis of psychoticism: A study of individual differences in response to dexamphetamine. *Biological Psychology, 1*, 125–137.

Claridge, G. S., & Birchall, P. M. A. (1978). Bishop, Eysenck, Block, and psychoticism. *Journal of Abnormal Psychology, 87*, 664.

Claridge, G., & Broks, P. (1984). Schizotypy and hemisphere function – I: Theoretical considerations and the measurement of schizotypy. *Personality and Individual Differences, 5*, 633–648.

Claridge, G. S., & Chappa, H. J. (1973). Psychoticism: A study of its biological basis in normal subjects. *British Journal of Social and Clinical Psychology, 12*, 175–187.

Claridge, G., & Clark, K. (1982). Covariation between two-flash threshold and skin conductance level in first-breakdown schizophrenics: Relationships in drug-free patients and effects of treatment. *Psychiatry Research, 6*, 371–380.

Claridge, G., & Davis, C. (2003). *Personality and psychological disorders*. London: Arnold.

Claridge, G. S., Donald, J. R., & Birchall, P. M. A. (1981). Drug tolerance and personality: Some implications for Eysenck's theory. *Personality and Individual Differences, 2*, 153–166.

Claridge, G., & Healy, D. (1994). The psychopharmacology of individual differences. *Human Psychopharmacology, 9*, 1–14.

Claridge, G. S., & Herrington, R. N. (1960). Sedation threshold, personality and the theory of neurosis. *Journal of Mental Science, 106*, 1568–1583.

Claridge, G. S., & Hume, W. I. (1966). Comparison of effects of dexamphetamine and LSD-25 on perceptual and autonomic function. *Perceptual and Motor Skills, 23*, 456–458.

Claridge, G., & McDonald, A. (2009). An investigation into the relationships between convergent and divergent thinking, schizotypy, and autistic traits. *Personality and Individual Differences, 46*, 794–799.

Claridge, G., McCreery, C., Mason, O., Bentall, R., Boyle, G., Slade, P., & Popplewell, D. (1996). The factor structure of 'schizotypal' traits: A large replication study. *British Journal of Clinical Psychology*, *35*, 103–115.

Claridge, G., Pryor, R., & Watkins, G. (1990). *Sounds from the bell jar: Ten psychotic authors.* London: MacMillan.

Claridge, G., Robinson, D. L., & Birchall, P. M. A. (1983). Characteristics of schizophrenics' and neurotics' relatives. *Personality and Individual Differences*, *4*, 651–664.

Claridge, G., Robinson, D. L., & Birchall, P. M. A. (1985). Psychophysiological evidence of 'psychotic' in schizophrenics' relatives. *Personality and Individual Differences*, *6*, 1–10.

Claridge, G., & Ross, E. (1973). Sedative drug tolerance in twins. In G. S. Claridge, S. Canter, & W. I. Hulme (Eds.), *Personality differences and biological variations* (pp. 115–131). Oxford: Pergamon Press.

Claridge, G., Stein, J., & Wingate, B. Psychophysiological effects of LSD-25 in the monkey, similar to human psychosis (unpublished report).

Clarke, I. (Ed.) (2010). *Psychosis and spirituality: Consolidating the new paradigm* (2nd ed.). Chichester: Wiley-Blackwell.

Clementz, B. A., Iacono, W. G., & Beiser, M. (1994). Handedness in first-episode psychotic patients and their first-degree biological relatives. *Journal of Abnormal Psychology*, *103*, 400–403.

Cloninger, C. R. (2006). Differentiating personality deviance, normality and well-being by the seven-factor psychobiological model. In A. Strack (Ed.), *Differentiating normal and abnormal personality* (2nd ed., pp. 65–81). New York: Springer.

Coid, J. W. (1992). DSM-III diagnoses in criminal psychopaths: A way forward. *Criminal Behaviour and Mental Health*, *2*, 78–94.

Coren, S. (1995). Family patterns in handedness: Evidence for indirect inheritance mediated by birth stress. *Behavior Genetics*, *25*, 517–524.

Corr, P. J. (2010). The psychoticism-psychopathy continuum. *Personality and Individual Differences*, *48*, 695–703.

Corr, P. J. (2016). *Hans Eysenck: A contradictory psychology* (Mind Shapers series). London: Palgrave.

Costa, P. T., Jr., & McCrae, R. R. (1992). Four ways five factors are basic. *Personality and Individual Differences*, *13*, 653–665.

Cross, P., Cattell, R. B., & Butcher, H. J. (1967). The personality pattern of creative artists. *British Journal of Educational Psychology*, *37*, 292–299.

Crow, T. J. (1986). The continuum of psychosis and its implication for the structure of the gene. *British Journal of Psychiatry*, *149*, 419–429.

Crow, T. J. (1990). Temporal lobe asymmetries as the key to the etiology of schizophrenia. *Schizophrenia Bulletin*, *16*, 434–443.

Crow, T. J. (1991). The failure of the Kraepelinian binary concept and the search for the psychosis gene. In A. Kerr and H. McClelland (Eds.), *Concepts of mental disorder: A continuing debate* (pp. 31–47). London: Gaskell.

Cutting, J. (1985). *The psychology of schizophrenia.* Edinburgh: Churchill Livingstone.

Davison, K. (1976). Drug-induced psychoses and their relationship to schizophrenia. In D. Kemali, G. Bartholini, & D. Richter (Eds.), *Schizophrenia today* (pp. 105–125). Oxford: Pergamon Press Ltd.

Day, D., & Peters, E. (1999). The incidence of schizotypy in new religious movements. *Personality and Individual Differences*, *27*, 55–67.

Dell, P. C. (1958). Some basic mechanisms of the translation of bodily needs into behaviour. In *The Neurological Basis of Behaviour*. Ciba Symposium.

Delva, N. J., & Letemendia, F. J. J. (1982). Lithium treatment in schizophrenia and schizoaffective disorders. *British Journal of Psychiatry, 141*, 387–400.

Dolan, R. J., Calloway, S. P., & Mann, A. H. (1985). Cerebral ventricular size in depressed subjects. *Psychological Medicine, 15*, 873–878.

Douglas, R. J. (1967). The hippocampus and behavior. *Psychological Bulletin, 67*, 416–442.

Douglas, R. J., & Pribram, K. H. (1966). Learning and limbic lesions. *Neuropsychologia, 4*, 197–200.

Drevdahl, J. E. (1956). Factors of importance for creativity. *Journal of Clinical Psychology, 12*, 21–26.

Duffy, E. (1934). Emotion: An example of the need for reorientation in psychology. *Psychological Review, 41*, 239–243.

Duffy, E. (1957). The psychological significance of the concept of 'arousal' or 'activation'. *Psychological Review, 64*, 265–275.

Duffy, E. (1962). *Activation and behaviour*. New York: Wiley.

Easterbrook, J. A. (1959). The effect of emotion on cue utilization and the organization of behaviour. *Psychological Review, 66*, 183–201.

Eccles, J. C. (1958). *The physiology of nerve cells*. Oxford: Clarendon Press.

Eckblad, M., & Chapman, L. J. (1983). Magical ideation as an indicator of schizotypy. *Journal of Consulting and Clinical Psychology, 51*, 215–225.

Eckblad, M., & Chapman, L. J. (1986). Development and validation of a scale for hypomanic personality. *Journal of Abnormal Psychology, 95*, 214–222.

Ellinwood, E. H., Jr., Sudilovsky, A., & Nelson, L. M. (1973). Evolving behavior in the clinical and experimental amphetamine (model) psychosis. *American Journal of Psychiatry, 130*, 1088–1093.

Eysenck, H. J. (1947). *Dimensions of personality*. London: Kegan Paul.

Eysenck, H. J. (1952a). Schizothymia-cyclothymia as a dimension of personality. II. Experimental. *Journal of Personality, 20*, 345–384.

Eysenck, H. J. (1952b). *The scientific study of personality*. London: Routledge and Kegan Paul.

Eysenck, H. J. (1953). *The structure of human personality*. London: Methuen.

Eysenck, H. J. (1955a). A dynamic theory of anxiety and hysteria. *Journal of Mental Science, 101*, 28–51.

Eysenck, H. J. (1955b). Psychiatric diagnosis as a psychological and statistical problem. *Psychological Reports, 1*, 3–17.

Eysenck, H. J. (1957a). Drugs and personality. I. Theory and methodology. *Journal of Mental Science, 103*, 119–131.

Eysenck, H. J. (1957b). *The dynamics of anxiety and hysteria*. London: Routledge and Kegan Paul.

Eysenck, H. J. (1960). Classification and the problem of diagnosis. In H. J. Eysenck (Ed.), *Handbook of abnormal psychology* (pp. 1–31). London: Pitman.

Eysenck, H. J. (1961). Psychosis, drive and inhibition: A theoretical and experimental account. *American Journal of Psychiatry, 118*, 198–204.

Eysenck, H. J. (1963). *Experiments with drugs*. Oxford: Pergamon Press.

Eysenck, H. J. (1967). *The biological basis of personality*. Springfield, IL: Charles C. Thomas.

Eysenck, H. J. (Ed.) (1973). *Handbook of abnormal psychology* (2nd ed.). London: Pitman.

Eysenck, H. J. (1992a). A reply to Costa and McCrae: P or A and C – the role of theory. *Personality and Individual Differences, 13,* 867–868.
Eysenck, H. J. (1992b). The definition and measurement of psychoticism. *Personality and Individual Differences, 13,* 757–785.
Eysenck, H. J., & Barrett, P. (1993). The nature of schizotypy. *Psychological Reports, 73,* 59–63.
Eysenck, H. J., & Eysenck, S. B. G. (1968). The measurement of psychoticism: A study of factor stability and reliability. *British Journal of Social and Clinical Psychology, 7,* 286–294.
Eysenck, H. J., & Eysenck, S. B. G. (1975). *Manual of the Eysenck Personality Questionnaire.* London: Hodder & Stoughton.
Eysenck, H. J., & Eysenck, S. B. G. (1976). *Psychoticism as a dimension of personality.* London: Hodder & Stoughton.
Eysenck, M. (2013). Lost in shadows. In B. D. Kirkcaldy (Ed.), *Chimes of time* (pp. 245–258). Leiden: Sidestone Press.
Eysenck, S. B. G. (1956). Neurosis and psychosis: An experimental analysis. *Journal of Mental Science, 102,* 517–529.
Farias, M., Claridge, G., & Lalljee, M. (2005) Personality and cognitive predictors of New Age practices and beliefs. *Personality and Individual Differences, 39,* 979–989.
Féré, C. (1899). *The pathology of emotions* (English edition, R. Park, Trans.). London: The University Press.
Fischman, L. G. (1983). Dreams, hallucinogenic states, and schizophrenia: A psychological and biological comparison. *Schizophrenia Bulletin, 9,* 73–94.
Fish, F. A. (1961). A neurophysiological theory of schizophrenia. *Journal of Mental Science, 107,* 828–838.
Fleminger, J. J., Dalton, R., & Standage, K. F. (1977). Handedness in psychiatric patients. *British Journal of Psychiatry, 131,* 448–452.
Flint, J., & Mufano, M. R. (2007). The endophenotypic concept in psychiatric genetics. *Psychological Medicine, 37,* 163–180.
Flor-Henry, P. (1969). Psychosis and temporal lobe epilepsy: A controlled investigation. *Epilepsia, 10,* 365–395.
Forabosco, G. (1998). The ill side of humour: Pathological conditions and sense of humour. In W. Ruch (Ed.), *The sense of humour: Explorations of a personality characteristic* (pp. 271–292). Berlin: Walter de Gruyter.
Foulds, G. A. (1965). *Personality and personal illness.* London: Tavistock.
Foulds, G. A., & Bedford, A. (1975). Hierarchy of classes of personal illness. *Psychological Medicine, 5,* 181–192.
Frankenhaeuser, M., Post, B., Hagdahl, R., & Wrangsjoe, B. (1964). Effects of a depressant drug as modified by experimenter-induced expectation. *Perceptual and Motor Skills, 18,* 513–522.
Freedman, B. J. (1974). The subjective experience of perceptual and cognitive disturbance in schizophrenia. *Archives of General Psychiatry, 30,* 333–340.
Freedman, R., Adams, C. E., Adler, L. E., Bickford, P. C., Gault, J., Harris J. G., Nagamoto, H. T., Olincy, A., Ross, R. G., Stevens, K. E., Waldo, M., & Leonard, S. (2000). Inhibitory neurophysiological deficit as a phenotype for genetic investigation of schizophrenia. *American Journal of Medical Genetics, 97,* 58–64.
French, J. D., Verzeano, M., & Magoun, H. W. (1953). A neural basis for the anaesthetic state. *Archives of Neurology and Psychiatry (Chicago), 69,* 519.

Fuxe, K., Everitt, B. J., Agnati, L., Fredholm, B., & Jonsson, G. (1976). On the biochemistry and pharmacology of hallucinogens. In D. Kemali, G. Bartholini, & D. Richter (Eds.), *Schizophrenia today* (pp. 135–155). Oxford: Pergamon Press Ltd.

Galloway, J. (1989). *The trick is to keep breathing*. London: Polygon.

Gardner, L. P. (1945). The learning of low-grade aments. *American Journal of Mental Deficiency, 50*, 59–80.

Gellhorn, E. (1957) *Autonomic imbalance and the hypothalamus*. Minneapolis: University of Minnesota Press.

George, A., & Soloff, P. H. (1986). Schizotypal symptoms in patients with borderline personality disorders. *American Journal of Psychiatry, 143*, 212–215.

Gerlach, J. (1991). New antipsychotics. *Schizophrenia Bulletin, 17*, 289–309.

Geyer, M. A., & Braff, D. L. (1987). Startle habituation and sensorimotor gating in schizophrenia and related animal models. *Schizophrenia Bulletin, 13*, 643–668.

Glass, H. B. (1954) Genetic aspects of adaptability. In *Genetics and the inheritance of integrated neurological and psychiatric patterns: Proceedings for research in nervous and mental disease, vol 33*. Baltimore, MD: Williams & Wilkins.

Golden, R. R., & Meehl, P. E. (1979). Detection of the schizoid taxon with MMPI indicators. *Journal of Abnormal Psychology, 88*, 217–233.

Gordon, S. (1953) *Some effects of incentives on the behaviour of imbeciles*. Ph.D. thesis, University of London.

Gottesman, I. I., & Shields, J. (1968). In pursuit of the schizophrenic genotype. In S. G. Vandenberg (Ed.), *Progress in human behaviour genetics*. Baltimore, MD: The Johns Hopkins Press.

Gottesman, I. I., & Shields, J. (1973). Genetic theorising and schizophrenia. *British Journal of Psychiatry, 122*, 15–30.

Gottesman, I. I., & Shields, J. (1976). A critical review of recent adoption, twin, and family studies of schizophrenia: Behavioral genetics perspectives. *Schizophrenia Bulletin, 2*, 360–398.

Goulding, A. (2004). Schizotypy models in relation to subjective health and paranormal beliefs and experiences. *Personality and Individual Differences, 37*, 157–167.

Gray, J. A. (1964). *Pavlov's typology*. Oxford: Pergamon.

Gray, J. A. (1967). Strength of the nervous system, introversion-extraversion, conditionability and arousal. *Behaviour Research and Therapy, 5*, 151–169.

Gray, J. A. (1970). The psychophysiological basis of introversion-extraversion. *Behaviour Research and Therapy, 8*, 249–266.

Gray, J. A. (1973). Causal theories of personality and how to test them. In J. R. Royce (Ed.), *Multivariate analysis and psychological theory* (pp. 409–451). New York: Academic Press.

Gray, J. A. (1981). A critique of Eysenck's theory of personality. In H. J. Eysenck (Ed.), *A model for personality* (pp. 246–276). Berlin: Springer-Verlag.

Gray, J. A., Feldon, J., Rawlins, J. N. P., Hemsley, D. R., & Smith, A. D. (1991). The neuropsychology of schizophrenia. *Behavioral and Brain Sciences, 14*, 1–84.

Gray, N. S., Fernandez, M., Williams, J., Ruddle, R. A., & Snowden, R. J. (2000). Which schizotypal dimensions abolish latent inhibition? *British Journal of Clinical Psychology, 41*, 271–284.

Green, M., Satz, P., Smith, C., & Nelson, L. (1989). Is there atypical handedness in schizophrenia? *Journal of Abnormal Psychology, 98*, 57–61.

Greengross, G., & Miller, G. F. (2009). The Big Five personality traits of professional comedians compared to amateur comedians, comedy writers and college students. *Personality and Individual Differences, 47*, 79–83.

Gruzelier, J. H. (1994). Syndromes of schizophrenia and schizotypy, hemisphere imbalance and sex differences: Implications for developmental psychopathology. *International Journal of Psychophysiology*, *18*, 167–178.

Gruzelier, J., Burgess, A., Stygall, J., Irving, G., & Raine, A. (1995). Patterns of cerebral asymmetry and syndromes of schizotypal personality. *Psychiatry Research*, *56*, 71–79.

Gruzelier, J. H., & Corballis, M. C. (1970). Effects of instructions and drug administration on temporal resolution of paired flashes. *Quarterly Journal of Experimental Psychology*, *22*, 115.

Gruzelier, J., Lykken, D., & Venables, P. (1972). Schizophrenia and arousal revisited. *Archives of General Psychiatry*, *26*, 427–432.

Gruzelier, J., & Richardson, A. (1994). Patterns of cognitive asymmetry and psychosis proneness. *International Journal of Psychophysiology*, *18*, 217–225.

Gruzelier, J. H., & Venables, P. H. (1975). Relations between two-flash discrimination and electrodermal activity, re-examined in schizophrenics and normals. *Journal of Psychiatric Research*, *12*, 73–85.

Gur, R. E. (1977). Motoric laterality imbalance in schizophrenia: A possible concomitant of left hemisphere dysfunction. *Archives of General Psychiatry*, *34*, 33–37.

Haier, R. J., Buchsbaum, M. S., Murphy, D. L., Gottesman, I. I., & Coursey, R. D. (1980). Psychiatric vulnerability, monoamine oxidase, and the average evoked potential. *Archives of General Psychiatry*, *37*, 340.

Hare, R. D. (1993). *Without conscience*. New York: Guilford Press.

Hay, D. A. (1985) *Essentials of behaviour genetics*. Oxford: Blackwell.

Healy, D. (1990). Schizophrenia: Basic, release, reactive, and defect processes. *Human Psychopharmacology*, *5*, 105–122.

Hebb, D. O. (1949). *The organisation of behaviour: A neuropsychological theory*. New York: Wiley.

Hebb, D. O. (1955). Drives and the CNS (conceptual nervous system). *Psychological Review*, *62*, 243–254.

Hermelin B., & O'Connor N. (1983). The idiot savant: flawed genius or clever Hans? *Psychological Medicine*, *13*, 479–481.

Heron, J., Jones, I., Williams, J., Owen, M. J., Craddock, N., & Jones, L. A. (2003). Self-reported schizotypy and bipolar disorder: Demonstration of a lack of specificity of the Kings Schizotypy Questionnaire. *Schizophrenia Research*, *65*, 153–158.

Herrington, R. N., & Claridge, G. S. (1965). Sedation threshold and Archimedes' spiral after-effect in early psychosis. *Journal of Psychiatric Research*, *3*, 159–170.

Hershmann, D. J., & Lieb, J. (1998). *Manic depression and creativity*. New York: Prometheus Books.

Hill, H. E., Belleville, R. E., & Wikler, A. (1957). Motivational determinants in modification of behaviour by morphine and pentobarbital. *Archives of Neurology and Psychiatry*, *77*, 28–35.

Hirschfeld, R. M. A. (2000). Development and validation of a screening instrument for bipolar spectrum disorder: The Mood Disorder Questionnaire. *American Journal of Psychiatry*, *157*, 1873–1875.

Holzman, P. S., Proctor, L. R., Levy, D. L., Yasillo, N. J., Meltzer, H. Y., & Hurt, S. W. (1974). Eye-tracking dysfunctions in schizophrenic patients and their relatives. *Archives of General Psychiatry*, *31*, 143–151.

Howell, D. (1992). *Statistical methods for psychology* (3rd ed.). Belmont, CA: Duxbury Press.

Hugelshofer D. S., Kwon, P., Reff, R. C., & Olson, M. L. (2006). Humour's role in the relation between attributional style and dysphoria. *European Journal of Personality*, *20*, 325–336.

Hume, W. I. (1970). *An experimental analysis of 'arousal'*. Ph.D. thesis, University of Bristol.

Hume, W. I. (1973). Physiological measures in twins. In G. Claridge, S. Canter, & W. I. Hume (Eds.), *Personality differences and biological variations: A study of twins* (pp. 87–114). Oxford: Pergamon Press.

Hume, W. I., & Claridge, G. S. (1965). A comparison of two measures of 'arousal' in normal subjects. *Life Sciences*, *4*, 545–553.

Huxley, J., Mayr, E., Osmond, H., & Hoffer, A. (1964). Schizophrenia as a genetic morphism. *Nature*, *204*, 220–221.

Iacono, W. G., Peloquin, L. J., Lumry, A., Valentine, B. H., & Tuason, V. B. (1982). Eye tracking in patients with unipolar and bipolar affective disorder in remission. *Journal of Abnormal Psychology*, *91*, 35–44.

Ingraham, L. J. (1995). Family-genetic research and schizotypal personality. In A. Raine, T. Lencz, & S. A. Mednick (Eds.), *Schizotypal personality* (pp. 19–42). Cambridge: Cambridge University Press.

Isard, M., & Claridge, G. (unpublished study). Psychotic traits and creativity in adults reporting childhood imaginary friends.

Ivanov-Smolensky, A. G. (1954). *Essays on the pathophysiology of the higher nervous activity*. Moscow: Foreign Languages Publishing House.

Jackson, M. (1997). Benign schizotypy? The case of spiritual experience. In G. Claridge (Ed.), *Schizotypy: Implications for illness and health* (pp. 227–250). Oxford: Oxford University Press.

Jacobs, B. L., & Trulson, M. E. (1979). Mechanisms of action of LSD. *American Scientist*, *67*, 396–404.

Jamison, K. R. (1993). *Touched with fire: Manic-depressive illness and the artistic temperament*. New York: Free Press.

Jaspers, K. (1913). *General psychopathology* (J. Hoenig & M. W. Hamilton, Trans, 1963). Manchester: Manchester University Press.

Johns, L. C., & van Os, J. (2001). The continuity of psychotic experiences in the general population. *Clinical Psychology Review*, *21*, 1125–1141.

Jolley, S., Jones, S. H., & Hemsley, D. R. (1999). Causal processing and schizotypy. *Personality and Individual Differences*, *27*, 277–291.

Journal of Mental Health (1993). Perspectives on schizophrenia. What is schizophrenia? (Special section featuring articles by E. C. Johnstone, A. Farmer *et al.*, R. P. Bentall, and P. K. Chadwick; and commentaries by G. Claridge), *2*, 193–253.

Jung, C. G. (1960). *The psychogenesis of mental disease*, Vol. 3 of *The collected works of C. G. Jung* (R. F. C. Hull, Trans.). London: Routledge and Kegan Paul.

Jung, C. G. (1963). *Memories, dreams, reflections*. London: Collins and Routledge Kegan Paul.

Kaysen, S. (1995). *Girl interrupted*. London: Virago Press.

Kelley, M. P., & Coursey, R. D. (1992a). Factor structure of schizotypy scales. *Personality and Individual Differences*, *13*, 723–731.

Kelley, M. P., & Coursey, R. D. (1992b). Lateral preference and neuropsychological correlates of schizotypy. *Psychiatry Research*, *41*, 115–135.

Kelly, D. H. W. (1966). Measurement of anxiety by forearm blood flow. *British Journal of Psychiatry*, 112, 789–798.

Kelly, P. H., & Iversen, L. L. (1975). LSD as an agonist of mesolimbic dopamine receptors. *Psychopharmacologia, 45*, 221–224.

Kendell, R. E. (1991). The major functional psychoses: Are they independent entities or part of a continuum? Philosophical and conceptual issues underlying the debate. In A. Kerr & H. McClelland (Eds.), *Concepts of mental disorder* (pp. 1–16). London: Gaskell.

Kendell, R. E., & Brockington, I. F. (1980). The identification of disease entities and the relationship between schizophrenic and affective psychoses. *British Journal of Psychiatry, 137*, 324–331.

Kendler, K. S. (1985). Diagnostic approaches to schizotypal personality disorder: A historical perspective. *Schizophrenia Bulletin, 11*, 538–553.

Kendler, K. S. (2005). Toward a philosophical structure for psychiatry. *American Journal of Psychiatry, 162*, 433–440.

Kendler, K. S. (2012). The dappled nature of causes of psychiatric illness: Replacing the organic-functional/hardware-software dichotomy with empirically based pluralism. *Molecular Psychiatry, 17*, 377–388.

Kendler, K. S., & Hewitt, J. (1992). The structure of self-report schizotypy in twins. *Journal of Personality Disorders, 6*, 1–17.

Kesey, K. (1962). *One flew over the cuckoo's nest*. London: Methuen.

Kessler, P., & Neale, J. M. (1974). Hippocampal damage and schizophrenia: A critique of Mednick's theory. *Journal of Abnormal Psychology, 83*, 91–96.

Kety, S. S. (1960). Recent biochemical theories of schizophrenia. In D. D. Jackson (Ed.), *The aetiology of schizophrenia*. New York: Basic Books.

Key, B. J. (1961). The effect of drugs on discrimination and sensory generalisation of auditory stimuli in cats. *Psychopharmacologia, 2*, 352–363.

Key, B. J. (1964). Alterations in the generalisation of visual stimuli induced by lysergic acid diethylamide in cats. *Psychopharmacologia, 6*, 327–337.

Key, B. J. (1965). Effect of LSD-25 on potentials evoked in specific sensory pathways. *British Medical Bulletin, 21*, 30–35.

Killam, E. K., Killam, K. F., & Shaw, T. (1957). The effects of psychotherapeutic compounds on central afferent and limbic pathways. *Annals of the New York Academy of Sciences, 64*, 784–805.

Kim, D., Raine, A., Triphon, N., & Green, M. F. (1992). Mixed handedness and features of schizotypal personality in a nonclinical sample. *Journal of Nervous and Mental Disease, 180*, 133–135.

Kimble, D. P. (1968). Hippocampus and internal inhibition. *Psychological Bulletin, 70*, 285–295.

Kimble, G. A. (1949). An experimental test of a two-factor theory of inhibition. *Journal of Experimental Psychology, 39*, 15–23.

King, E. E. (1956). Differential action of anaesthetics and interneuron depressants on EEG arousal and recruiting responses. *Journal of Pharmacology and Experimental Therapeutics, 116*, 404.

Klein, D. F., & Fink, M. (1963). Multiple item factors as change measures in psychopharmacology. *Psychopharmacologia, 4*, 43–52.

Klein, M. (1940). Mourning and its relation to manic-depressive states. *International Journal of Psychoanalysis, 21*, 125–153.

Klerman, G. L., DiMascio, A., Greenblatt M., & Rinkel, M. (1959). The influence of specific personality patterns on the reactions to psychotropic agents. In J. H. Masserman (Ed.), *Biological psychiatry*. New York: Grune & Stratton.

Knopik, V. S., Neiderhiser, J. M., DeFries, J. C., & Plomin, R. (2016). *Behavioral genetics* (7th ed., pp. 272–273). New York: Worth.

Koestler, A. (1964). *The act of creation.* London: Hutchinson.

Kornetsky, C., & Markowitz, R. (1975). Animal models and schizophrenia. In D. J. Ingle & H. M. Shein (Eds.), *Model systems in biological psychiatry* (pp. 26–50). Cambridge, MA: MIT Press.

Kraepelin, E. (1919). *Dementia praecox and paraphrenia* (R. M. Barclay, Trans.). Edinburgh: Churchill Livingstone.

Kravetz, S., Faust, M., & Edelman, A. (1998). Dimensions of schizotypy and lexical decision in the two hemispheres. *Personality and Individual Differences, 2,* 857–871.

Kretschmer, E. (1925). *Physique and character* (W. J. H. Sprott, Trans.). London: Kegan, Trench, and Trubner.

Kretschmer, E. (1927). *Der Sensitive Beziehungswahn* (3rd ed., 1950). Berlin: Springer.

Krishnamoorti, S. R., & Shagass, C. (1964). Some psychological test correlates of sedation threshold. In J. Wortis (Ed.), *Recent advances in biological psychiatry.* New York: Plenum.

Lader, M. H., & Wing, L. (1964). Habituation of the psychogalvanic reflex in patients with anxiety states and in normal subjects. *Journal of Neurology, Neurosurgery and Psychiatry, 27,* 210–218.

Laing, R. D. (1960). *The divided self.* London: Tavistock.

Landau, S. G., Buchsbaum, M. S., Carpenter, W., Strauss, J., & Sacks, M. (1975). Schizophrenia and stimulus intensity control. *Archives of General Psychiatry, 32,* 1239–1245.

Launay, G., & Slade, P. (1981). The measurement of hallucinatory predisposition in male and female prisoners. *Personality and Individual Differences, 2,* 221–234.

Laverty, S. G. (1958). Sodium amytal and extraversion. *Journal of Neurology, Neurosurgery and Psychiatry, 21,* 50–54.

Leavitt, F. (1974). *Drugs and behavior.* Philadelphia: W. B. Saunders.

Lefcourt H. M., & Martin, R. A. (1986). *Humor and life stress: Antidote to adversity.* New York: Springer.

Lenzenweger, M. F. (1994). Psychometric high-risk paradigm, perceptual aberrations, and schizotypy: An update. *Schizophrenia Bulletin, 20,* 121–135.

Lenzenweger, M. F., & Korfine, L. (1995). Tracking the taxon: On the latent structure and base rate of schizotypy. In A. Raine, T. Lencz, & S. A. Mednick (Eds.), *Schizotypal personality* (pp. 135–167). Cambridge: Cambridge University Press.

Leonard, B. E. (1994). Serotonin receptors: Where are they going? *International Clinical Psychopharmacology, 9* Suppl. 1, 7–17.

Levinson, D. F., & Mowry, B. J. (1991). Defining the schizophrenia spectrum. *Schizophrenia Bulletin, 17,* 491–514.

Lichtenstein, P., Yip, B. J., Björk, C., Pawitan, Y., Cannon, T. D., Sullivan, P. F., & Hultman, C. M. (2009). Common genetic determinants of schizophrenia and bipolar disorder in Swedish families: A population-based study. *The Lancet, 373,* 234–239.

Liddle, P. (1987). The symptoms of chronic schizophrenia: A re-examination of the positive negative dichotomy. *British Journal of Psychiatry, 151,* 221–234.

Lidz, T., Wild, C., Schafer, S., Rosman, B., & Fleck, S. (1963). Thought disorders in the parents of schizophrenic patients: A study utilizing the object sorting test. *Journal of Psychiatric Research, 1,* 193–200.

Lieberman, J. A., & Koreen, A. R. (1993). Neurochemistry and neuroendocrinology of schizophrenia: A selective review. *Schizophrenia Bulletin, 19,* 371–429.

Lindsley, D. B. (1951). Emotion. In S. S. Stevens (Ed.), *Handbook of experimental psychology*. London: Chapman & Hall.

Lindsley, D. B. (1957). The reticular system and perceptual discrimination. In H. H. Jasper, L. D. Proctor, R. S. Knighton, W. C. Noshay, & R. T. Costello (Eds.), *Reticular formation of the brain* (pp. 513–534). London: Churchill.

Linney, Y., Murray, R., Peters, E., MacDonald, A., & Rijsdijk, S. (2003). A quantitative genetic analysis of schizotypal personality traits. *Psychological Medicine, 33*, 803–816.

Lishman, W. A., & McMeekan, E.R.L.T. (1976). Hand preference patterns in psychiatric patients. *British Journal of Psychiatry, 129*, 158–166.

Lovibond, S. H. (1954). The object sorting test and conceptual thinking in schizophrenia. *Australian Journal of Psychology, 6*, 52–70.

Lykken, D. T. (1975). The role of individual differences in psychophysiological research. In P. H. Venables & M. J. Christie (Eds.), *Research in psychophysiology* (p. 3). London: Wiley.

Lykken, D. T., & Maley, M. (1968). Autonomic versus cortical arousal in schizophrenics and non-psychotics. *Journal of Psychiatric Research, 6*, 21–32.

Lykken, D. T., Rose, R., Luther, B., & Maley, M. (1966). Correcting psychophysiological measures for individual differences in range. *Psychological Bulletin, 66*, 481–484.

MacDonald, N. (1960). Living with schizophrenia. *Canadian Medical Association Journal, 82*, 219–221.

Mace, C. A. (1935). *Incentives: Some experimental studies*. M.R.C. Report No. 72. Industrial Health Research Board. London: H.M.S.O.

MacKinnon, D. W. (1962). The personality correlates of creativity. In *Proceedings of the Fourteenth Congress on Applied Psychology*, Vol. 2, Munksgaard.

Malamud, N. (1967). Psychiatric disorders with intracranial tumors of the limbic system. *Archives of Neurology, 17*, 113–123.

Malesu, R. R., Cannon, M., Jones, P. B., McKenzie, K., Gilvarry, K., Rifkin, L., Toone, B. K., & Murray, R. M. (1996). Mixed-handedness in patients with functional psychosis. *British Journal of Psychiatry, 168*, 234–236.

Malmo, R. B. (1957). Anxiety and behavioural arousal. *Psychological Review, 64*, 276–287.

Malmo, R. B. (1959). Activation: A neuropsychological dimension. *Psychological Review, 66*, 367–386.

Marjoram, D., Tansley, H., Miller, P., MacIntyre, D., Owens, D. G., Johnstone, E. C., & Lawrie, S. (2005). A theory of mind investigation into the appreciation of visual jokes in schizophrenia. *BMC Psychiatry, 5*, 12.

Marneros, A., & Akiskal, H. S. (Ed.) (2007). *The overlap of affective and schizophrenic spectra*. London: Cambridge University Press.

Marshall, D. L. (1973). Cognitive functioning in schizophrenia. *British Journal of Psychiatry, 123*, 413–433.

Marziali, E., Munroe-Blum, H., & Links, P. (1994). Severity as a diagnostic dimension of borderline personality disorder. *Canadian Journal of Psychiatry, 39*, 540–544.

Mason, C. F. (1956). Pre-illness intelligence of mental hospital patients. *Journal of Consulting and Clinical Psychology, 20*, 297–300.

Mason, O. (1995). A confirmatory factor analysis of the structure of schizotypy. *European Journal of Personality, 9*, 271–283.

Mason, O. J. (2014). The duality of schizotypy: Is it both dimensional and categorical? *Frontiers in Psychiatry*, *5*, 1–4.

Mason, O., & Claridge, G. (1994). Individual differences in schizotypy and reduced asymmetry using the chimeric faces task. *Cognitive Neuropsychiatry*, *4*, 289–301.

Mason, O., & Claridge, G. (2006). The Oxford-Liverpool Inventory of Feelings and Experiences (O-LIFE): Further description and extended norms. *Schizophrenia Research*, *82*, 203–211.

Mason, O. J., & Claridge, G. (Eds.). (2015). *Schizotypy: New dimensions*. London: Routledge.

Mason, O., Claridge, G., & Clark, K. (1997). Electrodermal relationships with personality measures of psychosis-proneness in psychotic and normal subjects. *International Journal of Psychophysiology*, *27*, 137–146.

Mason, O., Claridge, G., & Jackson, M. (1995). New scales for the assessment of schizotypy. *Personality and Individual Differences*, *18*, 7–13.

Mason, O., Claridge, G., & Williams, L. (1997). Questionnaire measurement. In G. Claridge (Ed.), *Schizotypy: Implications for illness and health* (pp. 19–37). Oxford: Oxford University Press.

Mason, O., Linney, Y., & Claridge, G. (2005). Short scales for measuring schizotypy. *Schizophrenia Research*, *78*, 293–296.

Mason, O. J., Mort, H., & Woo, J. (2015). Research letter: Investigating psychotic traits in poets. *Psychological Medicine*, *45*, 667–669.

Mason, O., Olivers, C., & Booth, H. (2004). Proneness to psychosis and selecting objects of visual attention: Individual differences in visual marking. *Personality and Individual Differences*, *36*, 1771–1779.

Matthews, S. M., Roper, M. T., Mosher, L. R., & Menn, A. Z. (1979). A non-neuroleptic treatment for schizophrenia. *Schizophrenia Bulletin*, *5*, 322–333.

Matthysse, S., & Haber, S. (1975). Animal models of schizophrenia. In D. J. Ingle & H. M. Shein (Eds.), *Model systems in biological psychiatry* (pp. 4–25). Cambridge, MA: MIT Press.

McAllister, J. (1968). Foulds' 'Continuum of personal illness' and the 16PF. *British Journal of Psychiatry*, *114*, 53–56.

McBride, A. J. (2004). Comedians: Fun and dysfunctionality. *British Journal of Psychiatry*, *185*, 177.

McConaghy, N. (1959). The use of an object sorting test in elucidating the hereditary factor in schizophrenia. *Journal of Neurology, Neurosurgery and Psychiatry*, *22*, 243–246.

McConaghy, N. (1960). Modes of abstract thinking and psychosis. *American Journal of Psychiatry*, *117*, 106–110.

McConaghy, N. (1961). The measurement of inhibitory processes in human higher nervous activity: Its relation to allusive thinking and fatigue. *American Journal of Psychiatry*, *118*, 125–132.

McConaghy, N., & Clancy, M. (1968). Familial relationships of allusive thinking in university students and their parents. *British Journal of Psychiatry*, *114*, 1079–1087.

McCreery, C. A. S. (1993). *Schizotypy and out-of-the-body experiences*. DPhil thesis, University of Oxford.

McDougall, W. (1929). The chemical theory of temperament applied to introversion and extra-version. *Journal of Abnormal Psychology*, *24*, 293–309.

McGhie, A. (1969). *Pathology of Attention*. London: Penguin.

McGhie, A., & Chapman, J. (1961). Disorders of attention and perception in early schizophrenia. *British Journal of Medical Psychology, 34*, 103–116.

McGrath, M. E. (1984). First person account: Where did I go? *Schizophrenia Bulletin, 10*, 638–640.

McGuffin, P., Farmer, A., & Gottesman, I. I. (1987). Is there really a split in schizophrenia? The genetic evidence. *British Journal of Psychiatry, 150*, 581–592.

McGuire, R. J., Mowbray, R. M., & Vallance, R. C. (1963). The Maudsley personality inventory used with psychiatric inpatients. *British Journal of Psychology, 54*, 157–166.

McManus, I. C., Shergill, S., & Bryden, M. P. (1993). Annett's theory that individuals heterozygous for the right shift gene are intellectually advantaged: Theoretical and empirical problems. *British Journal of Psychology, 84*, 517–537.

McNeil, T. F. (1988). Obstetric factors and perinatal injuries. In M. T. Tsuang & J. C. Simpson (Eds.), *Handbook of schizophrenia* (Vol. 3, pp. 319–344). Amsterdam: Elsevier.

McPeake, J. D., & DiMascio, A. (1965). Drug-personality interaction in the learning of a nonsense syllable task. *Journal of Psychiatric Research, 3*, 105–111.

McPherson, M. W. (1948). A survey of experimental studies of learning in individuals who achieve subnormal ratings on standardised psychometric measures. *American Journal of Mental Deficiency, 52*, 232–254.

Mednick, S. A. (1958). A learning theory approach to research in schizophrenia. *Psychological Bulletin, 55*, 316–327.

Mednick, S. A. (1970). Breakdown in individuals at high risk for schizophrenia: Possible predispositional perinatal factors. *Mental Hygiene, 54*, 50–63.

Mednick, S. A. (1974). Electrodermal recovery and psychopathology. In S. A. Mednick, F. Schulsinger, J. Higgins, & B. Bell, B. (Eds.), *Genetics, environment and psychopathology* (pp. 89–102). New York: American Elsevier Publishing Company, Inc.

Mednick, S. A., & Schulsinger, F. (1968). Some premorbid characteristics related to breakdown in children with schizophrenic mothers. In D. Rosenthal & S. S. Kety (Eds.), *The transmission of schizophrenia*. Oxford: Pergamon.

Mednick, S. A., & Schulsinger, F. (1973). A learning theory of schizophrenia: Thirteen years later. In M. Hammer, K. Salzinger, & S. Sutton (Eds.), *Psychopathology: Contributions from the social, behavioral, and biological sciences* (pp. 343–360). New York: John Wiley & Sons, Inc.

Meehl, P. E. (1962). Schizotaxia, schizotypy, schizophrenia. *American Psychologist, 17*, 827–838.

Meehl, P. E. (1990). Toward an integrated theory of schizotaxia, schizotypy, and schizophrenia. *Journal of Personality Disorders, 4*, 1–99.

Meltzer, H. Y. (1991). The mechanism of action of novel antipsychotic drugs. *Schizophrenia Bulletin, 17*, 263–287.

Meltzer, H. Y., & Stahl, S. M. (1976). The dopamine hypothesis of schizophrenia: A review. *Schizophrenia Bulletin, 2*, 19–76.

Millett, K. (1991).*The loony bin trip*. London: Virago Press.

Milligan, S., & Clare A. (1993). *Depression and how to survive it*. London: Ebury Press.

Mirdal, G. M., Rosenthal, D., Wender, P. H., & Schulsinger, F. (1977). Perinatal complications in offspring of schizophrenics. *British Journal of Psychiatry, 130*, 495–505.

Moran, P. M., Al-Uzri, M. M., Watson, J., & Reveley, M. A. (2003). Reduced Kamin blocking in non-paranoid schizophrenia: Associations with schizotypy. *Journal of Psychiatric Research, 37*, 155–163.

240 References

Müller-Hill, B. (1988). *Murderous science* (G. R. Fraser, Trans.). Oxford: Oxford University Press.

Muntaner, C., Garcia-Sevilla, L., Fernandez, A., & Torrubia, R. (1988). Personality dimensions, schizotypal and borderline personality traits and psychosis proneness. *Personality and Individual Differences*, 9, 257–268.

NAP5 (2014) *Accidental awareness during general anaesthesia in the United Kingdom and Ireland: Report and findings.* Edited by J. J. Pandit & T. M. Cook. Royal College of Anaesthetists/Association of Anaesthetists of Great Britain and Ireland.

Nasrallah, H. A., McCalley, W. M., & Kuperman, S. (1982). Neurological differences between paranoid and nonparanoid schizophrenics: I. Sensory-motor lateralization. *Journal of Clinical Psychiatry*, 43, 305–306.

Nebylitsyn, V. D., & Gray, J. A. (Eds.) (1973). *Biological bases of individual behaviour.* New York: Academic Press.

Nelson, L. D., Satz., P., Green, M., & Cicchetti, D. (1993). Re-examining handedness in schizophrenia: Now you see it—now you don't. *Journal of Clinical and Experimental Neuropsychology*, 15, 149–158.

Nettle, D. (2001). *Strong imagination.* Oxford: Oxford University Press.

Nettle, D. (2006). Schizotypy and mental health amongst poets, visual artists, and mathematicians. *Journal of Research in Personality*, 40, 876–890.

Nias, D. K. B. (1997). Psychology and medicine. In H. Nyborg (Ed.), *The scientific study of human nature: Tribute to Hans Eysenck at eighty* (pp. 92–108). Oxford: Pergamon Press.

Nielsen, T. C., & Petersen, N. E. (1976). Electrodermal correlates of extraversion, trait anxiety, and schizophrenism. *Scandinavian Journal of Psychology*, 17, 73–80.

Nunn, J., & Peters, E., 2001. Schizotypy and patterns of lateral asymmetry on hemisphere-specific language tasks. *Psychiatry Research*, 103, 179–192.

Nymgaard, K. (1959). Studies on the sedation threshold. A: Reproducibility and effect of drugs. B: Sedation threshold in neurotic and psychotic depression. *Archives of General Psychiatry*, 1, 530–536.

O'Brien, B. (1976). *Operators and things: The inner life of a schizophrenic.* London: Sphere Books.

O'Connor, N., & Claridge, G. S. (1955). The effect of goal-setting and encouragement on the performance of imbecile men. *Quarterly Journal of Experimental Psychology*, 7, 37–45 (Part 1).

O'Quin, K., & Derks, P. (1999). Humor. In M. Runco & S. R. Pritzker (Eds.), *Encyclopedia of creativity* (Vol. 1, pp. 845–852). Cambridge, MA: Academic Press.

Overall, J. E., Hollister, L. E., & Meyer, F. (1964). Imipramine and thioridazine in depressed and schizophrenic patients. *Journal of the American Medical Association*, 189, 605–608.

Overby, L. A. (1993). Handedness patterns of psychosis-prone college students. *Personality and Individual Differences*, 15, 261–265.

Paris, J. (1994). *Borderline personality disorder: A multidimensional approach.* Washington, DC: APA.

Parnas, J., Schulsinger, F., Neasdale, T. W., Schulsinger, H., Feldman, P. M., & Mednick, S. A. (1982). Perinatal complications and clinical outcome within the schizophrenia spectrum. *British Journal of Psychiatry*, 140, 416–420.

Pavlov, I. P. (1927). *Conditioned reflexes* (G. V. Anrep, Trans.). London: Oxford University Press.

Pavlov, I. P. (1955). Experimental pathology of the higher nervous activity. In *Selected Works*. Moscow: Foreign Languages Publishing House.

Payne, R. W. (1960). Cognitive abnormalities. In H. J. Eysenck (Ed.), *Handbook of abnormal psychology*. London: Pitman.

Payne, R. W. (1962). An object classification test as a measure of overinclusive thinking in schizophrenic patients. *British Journal of Social and Clinical Psychology, 1*, 213–221.

Payne, R.W. (1971). Cognitive deficits in schizophrenia: Overinclusive thinking. In J. Hellmuth (Ed.), *Cognitive studies, Vol. 2, Deficits in Cognition* (pp. 53–89). New York: Brunner/Maze.

Payne, R. W., & Hewlett, J. H. G. (1960). Thought disorder in psychotic patients. In H. J. Eysenck (Ed.), *Experiments in personality* (pp. 3–104). London: Routledge and Kegan Paul.

Payne, R. W., Hochberg, A. C., & Hawks, D. V. (1970). Dichotic stimulation as a method of assessing disorder of attention in overinclusive schizophrenic patients. *Journal of Abnormal Psychology, 76*, 185–193.

Payne, R. W., Mattusek, P., & George, E. I. (1959). An experimental study of schizophrenia thought disorder. *Journal of Mental Science, 105*, 627–652.

Perelle, I. B., & Ehrman, L. (1982). What is a lefthander? *Experientia, 38*, 1257–1258.

Perez-Reyes, M., Shands, H. C., & Johnson, G. (1962). Galvanic skin reflex inhibition threshold: A new psychophysiologic technique. *Psychosomatic Medicine, 24*, 274.

Perkins, S. L., & Allen, R. (2006). Childhood physical abuse and differential development of paranormal belief systems. *Journal of Nervous and Mental Disease, 194*, 349–355.

Perry, W., Minassian, A., Feifel, D., & Braff, D. L. (2001). Sensorimotor gating deficits in bipolar disorder patients with acute psychotic mania. *Biological Psychiatry, 50*, 418–424.

Perugi, G., Fornaro, I., & Akiskal, H. S. (2011) Are atypical depression, borderline personality disorder and bipolar II overlapping manifestations of a common cyclothymic diathesis? *World Psychiatry, 10*, 45–51.

Peterson, D. (1982). *A mad people's history of madness*. Pittsburgh: University of Pittsburgh Press.

Phillips, J. E., Jacobsen, N., & Turner, W. M. (1965). Conceptual thinking in schizophrenics and their relatives. *British Journal of Psychiatry, 111*, 823–839.

Pickering, A. D., Corr, P. J., Powell, J. H., Kumari, V., Thornton, J. C., & Gray, J. A. (1997). Individual differences in reactions to reinforcing stimuli are neither black nor white: To what extent are they Gray? In H. Nyborg (Ed.), *The scientific study of human nature: Tribute to Hans Eysenck at eighty* (pp. 36–67). Oxford: Pergamon Press.

Poreh, A. M. (1994). Reexamination of mixed handedness in psychosis-prone college students. *Personality and Individual Differences, 17*, 445–448.

Poreh, A.M., Levin, J., Teves, H., & States, J. (1997). Mixed handedness and schizotypal personality in a nonclinical sample: The role of task demand. *Personality and Individual Differences, 23*, 501–507.

Previc, F. H. (1996). Nonright-handedness, central nervous system and related pathology, and its lateralization: A reformulation and synthesis. *Developmental Neuropsychology, 12*, 443–515.

Rado, S. (1953). Dynamics and classification of disordered behavior. *American Journal of Psychiatry, 110*, 406–416.

Raine, A. (1991). The SPQ: A scale for the assessment of schizotypal personality based on DSM-III-R criteria. *Schizophrenia Bulletin, 17*, 555–564.

Raine, A. (2006). Schizotypal personality: Neurodevelopmental and psychosocial trajectories. *Annual Review of Clinical Psychology, 2*, 291–326.

Raine, A., & Allbutt, J. (1989). Factors of schizoid personality. *British Journal of Clinical Psychology, 28*, 31–40.

Raine, A., Lencz, T., & Mednick, S. (Eds.) (1995). *Schizotypal personality*. Cambridge: Cambridge University Press.

Raine, A., Reynolds, C., Lencz, T., Scerbo, A., Triphon, N., & Kim, D. (1994). Cognitive-perceptual, interpersonal, and disorganized features of schizotypal personality. *Schizophrenia Bulletin, 20*, 191–201.

Randrup, A., & Munkvad, I. (1975). Pharmacology and physiology of stereotyped behaviour. In S. Matthysse & S. S. Kety (Eds.), *Catecholamines and schizophrenia*. Oxford: Pergamon Press Ltd.

Rapaport, D. (1945). *Diagnostic psychological testing*. Chicago: Year Book Publ.

Rappaport, M., Hopkins, K., Hall, K., & Belleze, T. (1975). Schizophrenia and evoked potentials: Maximum amplitudes, frequency of peaks, variability and phenothiazine effects. *Psychophysiology, 12*, 196–206.

Rawlings, D. (1983). *An enquiry into the nature of psychoticism as a dimension of personality*. DPhil thesis. University of Oxford.

Rawlings, D. R. (2008). Relating humor preference to schizotypy and autism scores in a student sample. *Humor, 21*, 197–219.

Rawlings, D., & Freeman, J. L. (1997). Measuring paranoia/suspiciousness. In G. Claridge (Ed.), *Schizotypy: Implications for illness and health* (pp. 38–60). Oxford: Oxford University Press.

Rawlings, D., & Goldberg, M. (2001). Correlating a measure of sustained attention with a multi-dimensional measure of schizotypal traits. *Personality and Individual Differences, 31*, 421–431.

Rawlings, D., Williams, B., Haslam, N., & Claridge, G. (2008a). Taxometric analysis supports a dimensional latent structure for schizotypy. *Personality and Individual Differences, 44*, 1640–1651.

Rawlings, D., Williams, B., Haslam, N., & Claridge, G. (2008b). Is schizotypy taxonic? Response to Beauchaine, Lenzenweger, and Waller. *Personality and Individual Differences, 44*, 1663–1672.

Read, J., Bentall, R. P., & Fosse, R. (2009). Time to abandon the bio-bio-bio model of psychosis: Exploring the epigenetic and psychological mechanisms by which adverse life events lead to psychotic symptoms. *Epidemiologia e Psichiatria Sociale, 18*, 299–310.

Read, J., Fink, P. J., Rudegeair, T., Felitti, V., & Whitfield, C. L. (2008). Child maltreatment and psychosis: A return to a genuinely integrated bio-psycho-social model. *Clinical Schizophrenia & Related Psychoses, 2*, 235–254.

Redding, F. K. (1967). Modification of sensory cortical evoked potentials by hippocampal stimulation. *Electroencephalography and Clinical Neurophysiology, 22*, 74–83.

Reich, W. (1975). The spectrum concept of schizophrenia. *Archives of General Psychiatry, 32*, 489–498.

Reichenstein, S. (1976). *A pilot study into the incidence of schizophrenic symptoms in a normal population*. Undergraduate research dissertation, University of Oxford.

Richards, R. L. (1981). Relationship between creativity and psychopathology: An evaluation and interpretation of the evidence. *Genetic Psychology Monographs, 103*, 261–324.

Richardson, A. J. (1994). Dyslexia, handedness and syndromes of psychosis-proneness. *International Journal of Psychophysiology, 18*, 251–263.

Richardson, A. J., Mason, O., & Claridge, G. (1997). Schizotypy and cerebral lateralisation. In G. Claridge (Ed.), *Schizotypy: Implications for illness and health*. Oxford: Oxford University Press.

Roberts, D., & Claridge, G. (1991). A genetic model compatible with a dimensional model of schizophrenia. *British Journal of Psychiatry, 158*, 451–456.

Robinson, T. N., & Zahn, T. P. (1979). Covariation of two-flash threshold and autonomic arousal for high and low scorers on a measure of psychoticism. *British Journal of Social and Clinical Psychology, 18*, 431.

Rodnick, E. H., & Shakow, D. (1940). Set in the schizophrenic as measured by a composite reaction time index. *American Journal of Psychiatry, 97*, 214–225.

Rodnight, E., & Gooch, R. N. (1963). A new method for determination of individual differences in susceptibility to a depressant drug. In H. J. Eysenck (Ed.), *Experiments with drugs* (pp. 169–193). Oxford: Pergamon Press.

Romney, D. (1969). Psychometrically assessed thought disorder in schizophrenic and control patients and in their parents and siblings: Part I—Patients; Part II—Relatives. *British Journal of Psychiatry, 115*, 999–1002.

Rosman, B., Wild, C., Ricci, J., Fleck, S., & Lidz, T. (1964). Thought disorders in the parents of schizophrenic patients: A further study utilizing the object sorting test. *Journal of Psychiatric Research, 2*, 211–221.

Roth, T. L., & Sweatt, J. D. (2011). Annual research review: Epigenetic mechanisms and environmental shaping of the brain during sensitive periods of development. *Journal of Child Psychology & Psychiatry, 52*, 398–408.

Rushton, J. P., & Irwing, P. (2008). A General Factor of Personality (GFP) from two meta-analyses of the Big Five: Digman (1997) and Mount, Barrick, Scullen, and Rounds (2005). *Personality and Individual Differences, 45*, 679–683.

Sass, L. A., & Schuldberg, D. (2000–1) (Eds.) *Special Issue*. Creativity and the schizophrenia spectrum. *Creativity Research Journal, 13*, 1–132.

Satz, P., & Green, M. F. (1999). Atypical handedness in schizophrenia. *Schizophrenia Bulletin, 25*, 63–78.

Schizophrenia Bulletin (1989). Issue theme: Subjective experiences of schizophrenia and related disorders. *15*, 177–324.

Schizophrenia Bulletin (2015). Proceedings, international workshop on schizotypy: Integration, development, and future research. *41* suppl. 2. Geneva, Switzerland, 12–2013.

Schneider, K. (1959). *Clinical psychopathology* (M. W. Hamilton, Trans.). New York: Grune and Stratton.

Sedman, G., & Kenna, J. C. (1965). The use of LSD-25 as a diagnostic aid in doubtful cases of schizophrenia. *British Journal of Psychiatry, 111*, 96–111.

Seligman, M. E. P. (1975). *Helplessness*. San Francisco, CA: W. H. Freeman and Company, Publishers.

Sellen, J. L., Oaksford, M., & Gray, N. S. (2005). Schizotypy and conditioning reasoning. *Schizophrenia Bulletin, 31*, 1–12.

Servais, J., & Hubin, P. (1964). Étude psychopharmacologique de l'amphetamine et du meprobamate chez l'homme normal. *International Journal of Neuropharmacology, 3*, 517–540.

Shagass, C. (1954). The sedation threshold: A method for estimating tension in psychiatric patients. *EEG Clinical Neurophysiology, 6*, 221–233.

Shagass, C. (1956). The sedation threshold as an objective index of manifest anxiety in psychoneurosis. *Journal of Psychosomatic Research, 1*, 49–57.

Shagass, C. (1958). Neurophysiological studies of anxiety and depression. *APA Psychiatric Research Reports, 8*.

Shagass, C., & Jones, A. L. (1958). A neurophysiological test for psychiatric diagnosis: Results in 750 patients. *American Journal of Psychiatry, 114*, 1002–1009.

Shagass, C., & Kerenyi, A. B. (1958). Neurophysiologic studies of personality. *Journal of Nervous and Mental Disease, 126*, 141–147.

Shagass, C., & Naiman, J. (1955). The sedation threshold, manifest anxiety, and some aspects of ego function. *Archives of Neurology and Psychiatry, 74*, 397–406.

Shagass, C., Straumanis, S. J. J., & Overton, D. A. Psychiatric diagnoses and EEG-evoked response relationships. *Neuropsychobiology, 1*, 1–15.

Shakow, D. (1963). Psychological deficit in schizophrenia. *Behavioral Science, 8*, 275–305.

Shaw, J., Claridge, G., & Clark, K. (1999). Schizotypy and the shift from dextrality: A study of handedness in a large non-clinical population. *Schizophrenia Research, 50*, 181–189.

Sherwin, A. (2013, 6 June). Stephen Fry reveals he attempted suicide in 2012. *The Independent*.

Sigal, J. J., Star, K. H., & Franks, C. M. (1958). Hysterics and dysthymics as criterion groups in the study of introversion-extraversion. *Journal of Abnormal and Social Psychology, 57*, 143–148.

Silverman, J. (1964a). The problem of attention in research and theory in schizophrenia. *Psychological Review, 71*, 352–379.

Silverman, J. (1964b). Scanning-control mechanism and 'cognitive filtering' in paranoid and non-paranoid schizophrenia. *Journal of Consulting and Clinical Psychology, 28*, 385–393.

Silverman, J. (1967). Variations in cognitive control and psychophysiological defense in the schizophrenias. *Psychosomatic Medicine, 29*, 225–251.

Silverman, J. (1973). Perceptual and neurophysiological analogues of 'experience' in schizophrenia and LSD reactions. In J. Fadiman & D. Kewman (Eds.), *Exploring madness* (pp. 151–173). Monterey, CA: Brooks/Cole Publishing Company.

Silvia, P., & Kaufman, J. (2010). Creativity and mental illness. In J. C. Kaufman & R. J. Sternberg (Eds.), *The Cambridge handbook of creativity* (pp. 381–394). Cambridge: Cambridge University Press.

Slater, E., & Beard, A. W. The schizophreniclike psychoses of epilepsy. 1. Psychiatric aspects. *British Journal of Psychiatry, 109*, 95–105.

Slater, E., & Roth, M. (1969). *Clinical psychiatry* (Mayer-Gross, Slater and Roth). 3rd ed. London: Baillière, Tindall and Cassell.

Slater, P. (1956). Weighting responses to items in attitude scales. *British Journal of Mathematical and Statistical Psychology, 9* (Part 1, 41–48).

Slater, P. (1960). A re-examination of some data collected by H. P. Hildebrand. In H. J. Eysenck (Ed.), *Experiments in personality* (pp. 271–299). London: Routledge & Kegan Paul.

Snyder, S. H. (1973). Amphetamine psychosis: A model schizophrenia mediated by catecholamines. *American Journal of Psychiatry, 130*, 61–67.

Solovay, M. R., Shenton, M. E., & Holzman, P. S. (1987). Comparative studies of thought disorder: I. Mania and schizophrenia. *Archives of General Psychiatry*, 44: 13–20.

Sommer, R., & Osmond, H. (1960). Autobiographies of former mental patients. *Journal of Mental Science, 106*, 648–662.

Sommer, R. & Osmond, H. (1961). Autobiographies of former mental patients. Addendum. *Journal of Mental Science, 107*, 1030–1032.

Spitzer, R. L., Endicott, J., & Gibbon, M. (1979). Crossing the border into borderline personality and borderline schizophrenia: The development of criteria. *Archives of General Psychiatry, 36*, 17–24.

Spohn, H. E., Thetford, P. E., & Woodham, F. L. (1970). Span of apprehension and arousal in schizophrenia. *Journal of Abnormal Psychology, 75*, 113.

Starkweather, J. A. (1959). Individual and situational influences on drug effects. In R. M. Featherstone & A. Simon (Eds.), *A pharmacologic approach to the study of the mind.* Springfield: C. C. Thomas.

Startup, M., (1999). Schizotypy, dissociative experiences and childhood abuse: Relationships among self-report measures. *British Journal of Clinical Psychology, 38*, 333–344.

Steel, C., Hemsley, D. R., & Pickering, A.D. (2002). Distractor cueing effects on choice reaction time and their relationship with schizotypal personality. *British Journal of Clinical Psychology, 41*, 143–156.

Steel, C., Marzillier, S., Fearon, B., & Ruddle, A. (2009). Child abuse and schizotypal personality. *Social Psychiatry and Psychiatric Epidemiology, 44*, 917–923.

Stein, L., & Wise, C. D. (1971). Possible etiology of schizophrenia: Progressive damage of the noradrenergic reward mechanisms by endogenous 6-hydroxydopamine. *Science, 171*, 1032–1036.

Stevens, J. M., & Derbyshire, A. J. (1958). Shifts along the alert-repose continuum during remission of catatonic 'stupor' with amobarbital. *Psychosomatic Medicine, 20*, 99–107.

Stip, E., & Letourneau, G. (2009). Psychotic symptoms as a continuum between normality and pathology. *Canadian Journal of Psychiatry, 54*, 140–151.

Stone, M. H. (1977). The borderline syndrome: Evaluation of the term, genetic aspects, and prognosis. *American Journal of Psychotherapy, 31*, 345–365.

Stone, M. H. (1980). *The borderline syndromes.* New York: McGraw Hill.

Storms, L. H., & Sigal, J. J. (1958). Eysenck's personality theory with special reference to 'the dynamics of anxiety and hysteria'. *British Journal of Medical Psychology, 31*, 228–246.

Storr, A. (1972). *The dynamics of creation.* London: Secker and Warburg.

Storr, A. (1988a). *Solitude: A return to the self.* New York: Free Press.

Storr, A. (1988b). *The school of genius.* London: André Deutsch.

Strahan, R. A. (1966). *A coefficient of directional correlation for time series analyses.* Psychiatric Research Reports, No PR-66–10, University of Minnesota.

Strassman, R. J. (1992). Human hallucinogen interactions with drugs affecting serotonergic neurotransmission. *Neuropsychopharmacology, 7*, 241–243.

Strelau, J., & Zawadzki, B. (1997). Temperament and personality: Eysenck's three superfactors as related to temperamental dimensions. In H. Nyborg (Ed.), *The scientific study of human nature: Tribute to Hans Eysenck at Eighty* (pp. 68–91). Oxford: Pergamon Press.

Taylor, M. A. (1992). Are schizophrenia and affective disorder related? A selective literature review. *American Journal of Psychiatry, 149*, 22–32.

Taylor, M. (1999). *Imaginary companions and the children who create them.* Oxford: Oxford University Press.

Taylor, M. A., & Amir, N. (1995). Sinister psychotics: Left-handedness in schizophrenia and affective disorder. *Journal of Nervous and Mental Disease, 183*, 3–9.

Taylor, P., Dalton, R., & Fleminger, J. J. (1980). Handedness in schizophrenia. *British Journal of Psychiatry, 136*, 157–183.

Taylor, P., Dalton, R., & Fleminger, J. J. (1982). Handedness and schizophrenic symptoms. *British Journal of Medical Psychology, 55,* 287–291.

Teicher, M. H., Samson, J. A., Sheu, Y. S., Polcari, A., & McGreenery, C. E. (2010). Hurtful words: Association of exposure to peer verbal abuse with elevated psychiatric symptom scores and corpus callosum abnormalities. *American Journal of Psychiatry, 167,* 1464–1471.

Thorpe, J. G., & Barker, J. C. (1957). Objectivity of the sedation threshold. *Archives of Neurology and Psychiatry, 78,* 194–196.

Torgersen, S. (1994). Personality deviations within the schizophrenia spectrum. *Acta Psychiatrica Scandinavica, 90* (suppl. 384), 40–44.

Tredgold, A. F. (1952). *A textbook of mental deficiency* (8th ed.). London: Balliere, Tindall and Cox.

Trouton, D. S., & Maxwell, A. E. (1956). The relation between neurosis and psychosis. *Journal of Mental Science, 102,* 1–21.

Tsakanikos, E., & Reed, P. (2003). Visuo-spatial processing and dimensions of schizotypy: Figure–ground segregation as a function of psychotic-like features. *Personality and Individual Differences, 35,* 703–712.

Tsakanikos, E., Sverdrup-Thygenson, L., & Reed, P. (2003). Latent inhibition and psychosis-proneness: Visual search as a function of pre-exposure to the target and schizotypy level. *Personality and Individual Differences, 34,* 575–589.

Tyrer, P. (1994). What are the borders of borderline personality disorder? *Acta Psychiatrica Scandinavica, 89,* 38–44.

Uhr, L., & Miller, J. G. (Eds.) (1960). *Drugs and behavior.* New York: John Wiley.

Van der Merwe, A. B. (1948). The diagnostic value of peripheral vasomotor reactions in the psychoneuroses. *Psychosomatic Medicine, 10,* 347–354.

Van Praag, H. M. (1977). The significance of dopamine for the mode of action of neuroleptics and the pathogenesis of schizophrenia. *British Journal of Psychiatry, 130,* 463–474.

Vardy, M. M., & Kay, S. R. (1983). LSD psychosis or LSD-induced schizophrenia? *Archives of General Psychiatry, 40,* 877–883.

Varma, S. L., & Sharma, I. (1993). Psychiatric morbidity in the first degree relatives of schizophrenic patients. *British Journal of Psychiatry, 162,* 672–678.

Vaughan, H. G. (1966). The perceptual and physiologic significance of visual evoked responses recorded from the scalp in man. In *Electroretinography.* Supplement to *Vision Research* (pp. 203–233). New York: Pergamon Press Ltd.

Venables, P. H. (1959). Factors in the motor behaviour of functional psychotics. *Journal of Abnormal Social Psychology, 58,* 153–156.

Venables, P. H. (1963). The relationship between level of skin potential and fusion of paired light flashes in schizophrenic and normal subjects. *Journal of Psychiatric Research, 1,* 279–287.

Venables, P. H. (1964). Input dysfunction in schizophrenia. In B. Maher (Ed.), *Progress in experimental personality research* (pp. 1–47). New York: Academic Press.

Venables, P. H. (1967). The relation of two flash and two click thresholds to withdrawal in paranoid and non-paranoid schizophrenics. *British Journal of Social and Clinical Psychology, 6,* 60–62.

Venables, P. H. (1973). Input regulation and psychopathology. In M. Hammer, K. Salzinger, & S. Sutton (Eds.), *Psychopathology: Contributions from the social, behavioural and biological sciences* (pp. 261–284). New York: Wiley.

Venables, P. H. (1977). The electrodermal psychophysiology of schizophrenics and children at risk for schizophrenia: Controversies and developments. *Schizophrenia Bulletin, 3*, 28–48.

Venables, P. H., & Martin, I. (Eds.) (1967). *Manual of psychophysiological methods.* Amsterdam: Elsevier/North-Holland.

Venables, P. H., & Rector, N. A. (2000). The content and structure of schizotypy. *Schizophrenia Bulletin, 26*, 587–602.

Venables, P. H., Wilkins, S., Mitchell, D. A., Raine, A., & Bailes, K. (1990). A scale for the measurement of schizotypy. *Personality and Individual Differences, 11*, 481–495.

Venables, P. H., & Wing, J. K. (1962). Level of arousal and the subclassification of schizophrenia. *Archives of General Psychiatry, 7*, 114–119.

Viding, E. (2004). Annotation: Understanding the development of psychopathy. *Journal of Child Psychology and Psychiatry, 45*, 1329–1337.

Vinogradova, O. S. (1975). Functional organization of the limbic system in the process of registration of information: Facts and hypotheses. In R. L. Isaacson & K. H. Pribram (Eds.), *The Hippocampus, Vol. 2, Neurophysiology and Behavior* (pp. 3–69). New York: Plenum Press Ltd.

Vollema, M. G., & Hoijtinkm, H. (2000). The multidimensionality of self-report schizotypy in a psychiatric population. *Schizophrenia Bulletin, 26*, 565–575.

Vollema, M. G., & van den Bosch, R. J. (1995). The multidimensionality of schizotypy. *Schizophrenia Bulletin, 21*, 19–31.

Walker, R. (1974). *Personality and thinking styles in a delinquent and a student sample.* M.Phil. dissertation, Glasgow University.

Wallace, C. M. (1965). *Portrait of a schizophrenic nurse.* London: Hammond & Hammond.

Wallace, D. B. (1989). Stream of consciousness and reconstruction of self in Dorothy Richardson's *Pilgrimage.* In D. B. Wallace & H. E. Gruber (Eds.), *Creative people at work.* Oxford: Oxford University Press.

Watt, N. F., Anthony, J., Wynne, L. C., & Rolf, J. E. (Eds.) (1984). *Children at risk for schizophrenia: A longitudinal perspective.* Cambridge: Cambridge University Press.

Weckowicz, T. E. (1958). Autonomic activity as measured by the mecholyl test and size constancy in schizophrenic patients. *Psychosomatic Medicine, 20*, 66–71.

Weil-Malherbe, H. (1955). The concentration of adrenaline in human plasma and its relation to mental activity. *Journal of Mental Science, 101*, 733–755.

West, L. J. (1975). A clinical and theoretical overview of hallucinatory phenomena. In R. K. Siegel & L. J. West (Eds.), *Hallucinations* (pp. 187–311). London: John Wiley & Sons, Inc.

Wikipedia (2016, 29 August). Intellectual disability.

Wikler, A., Haertzen, C. A., Chessick, R. D., Hill, E. H., & Pescor, F. T. (1965). Reaction time ('mental set') in control and chronic schizophrenic subjects and in post-addicts under placebo, LSD-25, morphine, pentobarbital and amphetamine. *Psychopharmacologia, 7*, 423–443.

Wingate, B. (1982). *A psychophysiological study of an animal model of schizophrenia in the monkey.* DPhil thesis, University of Oxford.

Wolff, S. (1995). *Loners: The life path of unusual children.* London: Routledge.

Woodrow, H. (1940). The interrelation of measures of learning. *Journal of Psychology, 10*, 49–73.

Woody, E. Z., & Claridge, G. S. (1977). Psychoticism and thinking. *British Journal of Social and Clinical Psychology, 16*, 241–248.

Woolley, D. W., & Shaw, E. (1954). A biochemical and pharmacological suggestion about certain mental disorders. *Proceedings of the National Academy of Sciences, 40*, 228–231.

World Health Organization (1992). *ICD: The ICD-10 classification of mental and behavioural disorders—clinical descriptions and diagnostic guidelines.* Geneva: WHO.

Wyatt, S., & Langdon, J. N. (1937). *Fatigue and boredom in repetitive work.* M. R. C. Report No. 77. Industrial Health Research Board. London: H.M.S.O.

Yeo, R. A., Gangestad, S. W., & Daniel, W. F. (1993). Hand preference and developmental instability. *Psychobiology, 21*, 161–168.

Yerkes, R. M., & Dodson, J. D. (1908). The relation of strength of stimulus to rapidity of habit formation. *Journal of Comparative Neurology and Psychology, 18*, 459–482.

Young, B. J. (1974). A phenomenological comparison of LSD and schizophrenic states. *British Journal of Psychiatry, 124*, 64–73.

Zarroug, E. A. (1975). The frequency of visual hallucinations in schizophrenic patients in Saudia Arabia. *British Journal of Psychiatry, 127*, 553–555.

Zuckerman, M. (1979). *Sensation seeking.* New York: Wiley.

Zuckerman, M. (1989). Personality in the third dimension: A psychobiological approach. *Personality and Individual Differences, 10*, 391–418.

Index

16 Personality Factor (16PF) questionnaire 12, 102, 104, 127–128

aberrant perceptions and beliefs 164, 165, 166, 168
absence of feeling 201
accidental awareness during general anaesthesia (AAGA) 63
Ackner, B. 30
activity level 18, 24
actors 208–210, 212–213
aetiology 153
age 32; *O-LIFE* 173–177
aggressiveness 10, 18, 19, 24, 73, 155, 168
alcohol 53
Allbutt, J. 159
allusive thinking 128–129; *see also* overinclusive thinking
alpha index 67–69
altered feedback model 134–135
Alzheimer's disease 145, 146
amenability 18, 25
Amir, N. 184
amobarbital 60
amphetamine 55, 89, 90, 92; group-interaction effects 50–51, 52; vs LSD in schizophrenia research 112–115
amphetamine psychosis 73
amphotonics 55
amygdala 95
amylobarbitone sodium 62–69
anaesthesia 62–63
Andersen, H.C. 196–197
Ando, V. 219
anhedonia 159; introvertive *see* introvertive anhedonia
animals 118; animal models of schizophrenia 72–97; research using LSD 93–94, 116–118

Annett, M. hand preference questionnaire 182, 184, 185, 188–189; theory of handedness 189–190
Anthony, E.J. 196–197
antisociality 10, 142, 155, 217
anxiety 7, 9, 126–127, 151, 196; sedation threshold and 29, 30–32; Taylor Manifest Anxiety Scale (MAS) 33, 37–38
apathy 18, 20, 21, 22
Archimedes Spiral 35–36, 41–42, 66–69, 80, 131–132, 135, 136–138, 139
arousal 116–118, 123; covariation studies of perception and 80–87; mediating variable in experimental psychopathology of schizophrenia 78–80; nervous typological model of schizophrenia 131–136; sedation threshold and the theory of neurosis 31–32, 38–41, 42–44
arousal modulating system 96
Artaud, A. 206
asocial behaviour 164, 165, 166, 167, 168, 170
attention 76–78, 135–136; narrowed 79–80, 136, 139; selective 75, 77, 135
atypical antipsychotic drugs 114
auditory vigilance 67–69
augmenting-reducing phenomenon 91–92
autobiographical novels 198–200
autonomic nervous system 55

barbiturates 5–6, 26, 27; nervous typology, weight and the tolerance of 62–69
Barker, J.C. 30
Barrett, P. 160
Beauchaine, T.P. 220
beliefs, aberrant perceptions and 164, 165, 166, 168
belle indifference 11
Bentall, R.P. 159

Bethlem Royal Hospital ('Bedlam') 200
Bidwell's ghost 12
'Big 5' OCEAN questionnaire 12
bipolar disorder 10, 146–147, 198, 206, 211–212
birth stress/trauma 95, 190
bisociation 206
Bleuler, E. 144–145, 148, 151, 214–215
Bleuler, M. 148, 151
body type 52–53
borderline 147–150
borderline borderline 218–219
borderline personality (disorder) (BPD) 150, 218–219, 220
Borderline Personality Scale (STB) 156, 160, 167, 218
Bradley, P.B. 92
brain disease 192–193, 216
brainstem reticular formation 43, 95
British Journal of Anaesthesia 62
British Psychological Society 1
Brod, J. 195
broken brain theory 192–193, 216
Broks, P. 218
Burt, C. 3
Buss, A.H. 8

caffeine 53, 59, 60
Callaway, E. 77
Cannon, W.B. 221
Carter, M. 126
catatonia 79
cats 93
Cattrell 16 Personality Factor questionnaire 12, 102, 104, 127–128
central nervous system: homeostasis failure 107, 134; organisation and schizophrenias 135–136, 139
cerebral asymmetry 202
Chadwick, P. 202–203
Chamove, A.S. 73
Chapman, J. 72, 90
Chapman, J.P. 159, 169
Chapman, L.J. 159, 169
character 8
child abuse 196
chlorpromazine 55, 56, 92, 93
Clancy, M. 129
Clark, K. 219
Cloninger, C.R. 8
cognitive disorganisation (Cog-Dis) 169, 170, 179–180, 194, 217–218; with anxiety 164, 165–166; comedians 207, 208–212; extended normative data for *O-LIFE* 171, 172, 173–177
combinatorial thinking 206
comedians 191, 203, 205–213, 219
conceptual nervous system model 7, 14
conditioned generalization 93, 94
continuous motor performance task 75
conversion hysteria 5, 11
Costa, P.T. 12
Coursey, R.D. 159, 160
covariation 70–71, 94; arousal and perception 80–87; nervous typological model of schizophrenias 131–135, 136; two-flash threshold and skin conductance level 83–84, 86, 88, 97–108
creativity 120, 127–128, 191, 219; mad thought and 191, 192–204; psychotic traits in comedians 191, 205–213
criminalisation of LSD 109–110
criterion groups 4–7, 11
critical flicker fusion 132
critical level 40–41
Cross, P. 128
Crow, T.J. 147
CSTQ 159–168
cyclothymia-schizothymia dimension 9, 152, 197–198, 216, 220

Dalton, R. 184
Davison, K. 91
delusional scales 160, 161
delusions, systematic 202
dementia praecox 145
depressant drugs 49–51, 52
depression 73, 206
dexamphetamine 138, 140
Diagnostic and Statistical Manual (*DSM*) 112, 219
DiMascio, A. 54, 55, 56
disease, schizophrenias as 124–130
dissociation 116–118, 135, 136
divergent thinking 206
dizygotic twins 45, 46, 60, 61
dopamine 89, 90, 112–114
Drevdahl, J.E. 127–128
drug-free patients 97–108
drug techniques 5–7, 123–124, 139–140; LSD *see* LSD; sedation threshold *see* sedation threshold; variation in drug response 45–62

drug tolerance index 66–69
dysthymia 4–6, 136; sedation threshold 30–31, 32–45

EAS scheme 8
ecological validity 112–113
EEG changes 29, 30
Einheitpsychose theory *see* unitary model
'either' responses 188
electrodermal activity 27, 81; covariation with two-flash threshold 82–87, 88, 97–108; *see also* skin conductance, skin potential
electroencephalograph alpha index 67–69
emotionality level 18, 19, 24
endophenotypes 62
environmental social adversity 193
EPQ 82, 160, 164, 167–168
errors/gaps in performance 35, 39, 40–41
evoked response 77, 92–93, 94
excitability 18–23; rating scale 18–21, 23, 24–25
excitation-inhibition balance 31, 32, 41–43, 44, 123
expectations 48–49
experimental pathology of schizophrenia 76–87
extraversion 122–123; Eysenck 4–7, 17, 53–54, 216; sedation threshold and 30–31, 37–38; variation in drug response 53–54, 57, 58
Eysenck, H.J. 15, 16, 22, 23, 26, 28, 115, 121, 215, 216; contribution to our understanding of personality and psychological disorders 1–13; drug response variation 53–54; *Einheitpsychose* theory 9, 10, 154, 167, 216; excitation-inhibition theory 31, 44, 123; fully dimensional model 154–155; inhibition hypothesis for schizophrenia 130–131; and Laing 120; P scale 9–10, 82, 158, 168, 217; PEN inventory 102, 104, 125, 137; psychoticism 4, 5, 9–10, 11, 73, 125, 142, 154–155, 194, 216, 217, 219; sedation threshold 5–7, 29–30
Eysenck Personality Questionnaire (EPQ) 82, 160, 164, 167–168

face validity 90
factor structure of psychotic traits 156–157, 158–168, 169–170
fantasy 196–197

filtering 77–78, 202; *see also* overinclusive thinking
first-breakdown schizophrenics 97–108
Fischman, L.G. 111
five-choice serial reaction time test 34–35, 38–41
Fleminger, J.J. 184
Foulds, G. 154
Foulds delusional scales 160, 161
four factor structure of psychosis-proneness 164–168
Frankenhaeuser, M. 48
Freedman, B.J. 72
Fry, S. 211–212
fully dimensional model 152–154, 170–171, 193–194, 203, 214, 220–221

galvanic skin response (GSR) 82
gaps/errors in performance 35, 39, 40–41
Gardner, L.P. 17
Gellhorn, E. 43
gender differences: excitability score 19; handedness 187–188; *O-LIFE* 173–178, 208–210
General Paralysis of the Insane (GPI) 192
genetics 126, 147, 149; differences in drug response 45–46, 59–62; right shift (rs) gene 189–190; and sedative threshold 59–61, 62
Glass, B. 59, 60
Gooch, R.N. 56–57, 58
Gordon, S. 17
Gottesman, I.I. 126, 140
Gray, J.A. 7, 10, 73, 95, 123
group-interaction effects 13; drug reponses 49–51, 52
group learning experiments 17, 18–19, 20
Gruzelier, J.H. 99

Haber, S. 72
hallucinations 201; visual 90
Handbook of Abnormal Psychology (Eysenck) 13
handedness 182–190
happy schizotype 154
Harlow, H.F. 73
Haslam, N. 220
Hebb, D.O. 22, 23, 43
Hermelin, B. 14
Heron, J. 170
Herrington, R.N. 27, 58, 97, 131

heterogeneity of psychosis 73–74, 144–147
hippocampus 95–96
Holzman, P.S. 77
Hubin, P. 55
Hugelshofer, D.S. 206
Hume, W.I. 132
humour 202–203, 205–206; comedians 191, 203, 205–213, 219
Huxley, J. 126
hydroxydopamine 75
Hypomanic Personality Scale 160, 167
hysteria 4–6, 136; conversion hysteria 5, 11; sedation threshold 29–31, 32–45

illness, schizophrenias as 124–130
imaginary friends 196
imbeciles *see* intellectual disability
improvement in performance 14–25
impulsive nonconformity (ImpCon) 170, 181, 194, 218, 219, 220; comedians 207, 208–212; extended normative data for *O-LIFE* 171, 172, 173–177
impulsivity 7
incentives: improvement of intellectually disabled adults under incentive conditions 21, 22; and reversing the effects of drugs 48–49
incongruity theories 205–206
individual differences 13; variation in drug responses 45–62
inhibition 23, 130–131; excitation-inhibition balance 31, 32, 41–43, 44, 123; latent 118; reactive 130–131; sedation threshold 31–32, 35, 36, 38–41, 43–44; transmarginal inhibition principle *see* inverted-U
injection of drugs 47–48
input dysfunction 78, 91, 95–96
institutions for the 'mentally deficient' 14–15
intellectual disability 14–25
intelligence 130
intelligence tests 14, 17, 26
interior monologue 199
inter-personal response 18, 25
intra-individual drug response variability 51–52
introversion 4–7, 9, 17, 30–31, 53–54, 216
introvertive anhedonia (IntAn) 164, 165, 166, 167, 180, 194, 218; comedians 207, 208–212; extended normative data for *O-LIFE* 171, 172, 173–177

inverted-U 79–80, 99–100, 108, 127, 136, 139
IQ 14
Isard, M. 196

Jacobs, B.L. 113
Jones, A.L. 29
Jung, C.G. 151, 197

Kelley, M.P. 159, 160
Kempe, M. 200
Kendell, R.E. 146, 147
Kendler, K.S. 148–149
Kenna, J.C. 140
Kerenyi, A.B. 29
Key, B.J. 92–93, 94, 113
Kimble, G.A. 40
Koestler, A. 206
Kornetsky, C. 75
Kraepelin, E. 144–145, 146, 214–215
Kretschmer, E. 9, 151–152, 215–216

labels for intellectual disability 14
Laing, R.D. 110–111, 120, 192
language 125
latent inhibition 118
Launay, G. 169
Laverty, S.G. 30
learning, in intellectually impaired adults 14–25
Leavitt, F. 110
left handedness 185–190
Lenzenweger, N.F. 220
Liddle, P. 159
long delay patients 103–104, 105, 106, 107
loosened thinking 128–129
LSD 70–71, 96, 108–120, 124, 140; alternative construction of psychosis 115–116; amphetamine vs 112–115; animal research using 93–94, 116–118; covariation between two-flash threshold and skin potential 84, 85, 87, 100; criminalisation 109–110; effect in the monkey 116–118; nervous typological model and schizophrenias 132–134, 137–138; 'psychotic' symptoms 74; as a psychotomimetic 87–93
Lykken, D.T. 99, 132

MacDonald, N. 202
Mace, C.A. 22
MacKinnon, D.W. 127
Maley, M. 132

manic thinking 206
Manifest Anxiety Scale (MAS) 33, 37–38
marker behaviour for LSD-induced states in animals 94
Mason, O.J. 219
Matthysse, S. 72
Maudsley Personality Inventory (MPI) 33, 37–38
McAllister, J. 128
McConaghy, N. 128–129
McCreery, C. 154, 160
McDougall, W. 29, 53
McGrath, M.E. 203–204
McPeake, J.D. 56
McPherson, M.W. 17
medical model 3–4, 150
medical tradition 214–215, 216–217
Mednick, S.A. 79, 93, 95
Meehl, P. 148, 153, 158, 214–215, 216, 220
Meltzer, H.Y. 89
mental age 17
mental deficiency *see* intellectual disability
mental set 91
meprobamate 55
Miller, J.G. 110
Milligan, S. 203, 206
mixed handedness 185–190
MMPI 12, 126, 127
monkey 116–118
monozygotic twins 45, 46, 59–61, 126
Mort, H. 219
motivation 22–23
MPI 33, 37–38
MRC Social Psychiatry Research Unit 14–16

nail-frame task 20
Naiman, J. 29
narrowed attention 79–80, 136, 139
negative schizotypy (social impairment) 169
Neidpath, A. 119–120
nervous typology 17, 53–54, 121–141; model of schizophrenias 130–138; weight and the tolerance of amylobarbitone sodium 62–69
Netley Royal Victoria Military Hospital 5–6
Nettle, D. 219
neuroleptic drugs 113
neurosis, theory of 27–45
neuroticism 4, 6–7, 57, 58, 216

Nielsen, T.C. 82
nitrous oxide 6, 56–57, 58
non-incentive conditions, improvement under 20–21
nonsense syllable learning 55, 56
Nutt, D. 119

occupational therapy 15
O'Connor, N. 14–15, 17
oral administration of drugs 47–48
organic phase of psychiatry 111–112
Outsider Art (*Art Brut*) 198
Overby, L.A. 184
overinclusive thinking 77–78, 128–129, 136, 147, 206
Overton, D.A. 81
Oxford-Liverpool Inventory of Feelings and Experiences (*O-LIFE*) 157, 194, 215, 217–218, 219; extended normative data 169–181; psychotic traits in comedians 191, 205–213

P scale 9–10, 82, 158, 168, 217
Pampiglione, G. 30
Pavlov, I. 7, 17, 29, 53, 123, 130
Payne, R.W. 77–78
PEN inventory 102, 104, 125, 137
pentobarbital 48–49
perception 76–78; aberrant perceptions and beliefs 164, 165, 166, 168; covariation studies of arousal and 80–87
performance improvement 14–25
performance tests 33–36, 38–42
personality disorders 149–150, 152
personality tradition 215–217
Petersen, N.E. 82
Peterson, D. 200
phenobarbital 50–51, 52
phentolamine response 67–69
phenyltoloxamine 54
Plomin, R. 8, 62
poets 219
polygenic theory 126
positive schizotypy 169
predictability 18, 25
primary psychopathy 8
psychedelic drugs 109, 124; LSD *see* LSD
psychobiological view 115–116
psychomotor tasks 54
psychophysiology 26, 27, 96, 122; drug techniques *see* drug techniques
psychosis 11; borderline 147–150; creativity and 191, 192–204;

dimensions of 150–155, 193; varieties of 73–74, 144–147
psychosis-proneness 115, 170; four factor structure 164–168
psychotic traits questionnaires *see* questionnaires
psychoticism 73, 152, 215, 219; Eysenck 4, 5, 9–10, 11, 73, 125, 142, 154–155, 194, 216, 217, 219; P scale 9–10, 82, 158, 168, 217; PEN inventory 102, 104, 125, 137; schizophrenias and nervous types 136, 137–138, 139; two-flash threshold and electrodermal level 82–84, 85, 86, 100, 107
psychotomimetics 124, 140; LSD as a psychotomimetic 87–93

quasi-dimensional model 152–153, 170–171, 214–215, 220–221
questionnaires 156, 217; Eysenck's contribution 11–12; factor structure of psychotic traits 156–157, 158–168; sedation threshold and 33, 37–38; *see also under individual questionnaires*

radical psychiatry 110–111
Rado, S. 148, 158
Raine, A. 159, 169, 221
Rapaport, D. 128
Rappaport, M. 77
rate of fall-off 35, 38–39, 39–40
Rawlings, D. 220
reaction time task 34–35, 38–41, 67–69
reactive inhibition 130–131
Reichenstein, S. 82
reinforcement theory 7
religious experiences 195
reminiscence 35, 39
reserpine 54
reticular formation 43, 95
reward system defect 75
Richardson, D. 199–200
right handedness 185–190
right shift (rs) gene 189–190
Robinson, T.N. 107
Rodnight, E. 56–57, 58
Ross, E. 60
Royal Victoria Military Hospital, Netley 5–6

schizoidness 148–149, 151
schizophrenia 10, 70–71, 120, 143, 145–147, 156, 206; animal models of 72–97; changing viewpoints in research on 110–112; covariation between two-flash threshold and skin conductance level in first-breakdown schizophrenics 97–108; dimensional view of 81–82, 124–130; experimental psychopathology of 76–87; illness vs dimension 124–130; LSD as a psychotomimetic 87–93; nervous typological model 130–138; physiological speculations 94–96; risk and handedness 182–190; schizophrenias as nervous types 121–141
schizotaxia 148, 153
schizothymia-cyclothymia dimension 9, 152, 197–198, 216, 220
schizotypal borderline/schizotypal personality disorder (SPD) 149, 150, 218–219
Schizotypal Personality Questionnaire (SPQ) 169
Schizotypal Personality Scale (STA) 156, 185–188, 218
schizotypy 9–10, 115–116, 142, 143, 194, 214; factor structure of 'schizotypal' traits 156–157, 158–168, 169–170; Meehl 148–149, 153
scientists 198
secobarbital 55, 56
sedation threshold 26–27, 80, 124; differences in drug response 45–62; Eysenck 5–7, 29–30; group differences 36; nervous typology model of schizophrenias 131–132, 135, 136–138; performance tests and 33–36, 38–42; and personality 37–38; personality and the theory of neurosis 27–45; weight, nervous typology and the tolerance of amylobarbitone sodium 62–69
Sedman, G. 140
selective attention 75, 77, 135
Seligman, M.E.P. 73
sensory generalization 113; in cats 93
sensory sensitivity 116–118
serial reaction time task 34–35, 38–41, 67–69
serotonin 89, 112, 114
Servais, J. 55
seven-class analysis of handedness 185, 186–190

severely intellectually impaired adults 14–25
Shagass, C. 6, 26, 29, 43, 64, 81
Shields, J. 124, 140
short delay patients 103–104, 105, 106, 107
Silverman, J. 77, 91–92
size constancy 77, 79
skin conductance 86, 132; covariation between two-flash threshold and skin conductance level 83–84, 86, 88, 97–108; LSD and skin conductance level in the monkey 117–118
skin potential 80–81, 84, 85, 86, 87, 131–134
Slade, P.D. 159, 169
slurred speech 29, 30
sociability 18, 24
social impairment 169
sociopsychological account of schizophrenia 110–111
sodium amytal 33–45
solitude 198
spatial ability 188–189
spectrum disorders 81
spiral after-effect 35–36, 41–42, 66–69, 80, 131–132, 135, 136–138, 139
spiritual experiences 195
SPQ 169
STA 156, 185–188, 218
Stahl, S.M. 89
Starkweather, J.A. 49–51, 52
starting level 35, 38, 39
startle habituation 118
STB 156, 160, 167, 218
Stein, L. 75
stimulant drugs 49–51, 52
Storr, A. 197–198
STQ 156, 160
Strassman, R.J. 119
Straumanis, S.J.J. 81
stream of consciousness writing 199
susceptibility, index of 56–57
sympathicotonics 55
symptoms, traits and 220–221
systematic delusions 202

target-aiming task 59, 60
Taylor, M.A. 184
Taylor Manifest Anxiety Scale (MAS) 33, 37–38
temperament 8

Teplov, B.M. 123
theoretical issues 142–156
therapeutic use of LSD 119–120
thinking 76–78, 125
thinking styles 127–128
thiopentone 92
Thorpe, J.G. 30
thought disorder 72–73, 128–129
three-class analysis of handedness 185, 186, 188
thymotypy 219, 220
tonic arousal system 96
trail-marking test 49–51
traits, and symptoms 220–221
transmarginal inhibition principle *see* inverted-U
Tredgold, A.F. 18
trifluoperazine 55, 56
Trulson, M.E. 113
twin studies 45–46, 59–61, 126
'two faces of psychology' 13
two-flash threshold 82–87, 94; covariation with skin conductance level 83–84, 86, 88, 97–108; covariation with skin potential 80–81, 84, 85, 86, 87, 131–134
Type A and Type B personalities 54, 55, 56

U-shaped function 100, 104–105, 106–107
Uhr, L. 110
'unbalanced' nervous type 107–108
unitary model (*Einheitpsychose* model) 142, 146–147, 170, 193, 194, 219; Eysenck 9, 10, 154, 167, 216
University College London Psychology Department 3
unusual experiences (UnEx) 170, 178–179, 194, 196, 217–218; comedians 207, 208–212; extended normative data for *O-LIFE* 171, 172, 173–177

vagotonics 55
variability of work activity 18, 24
variation in drug responses 45–62
varieties of psychosis 73–74, 144–147
Venables, P.H. 80–81, 95, 99, 131, 134
verbal activity 18, 24
visual evoked potential (VEP) amplitude 116–118
visual hallucinations 90

Wallace, C.M. 199
Waller, N.G. 220
wash-out effect 49–51, 52
Watts, C.A.H. 126
weight 52, 58–59; nervous typology and the tolerance of amylobarbitone sodium 62–69
West, L.J. 90
White, A. 200
Wikler, A. 91
Williams, B. 220
Wise, C.D. 75
Woo, J. 219
Woodrow, H. 17
Woolf, V. 199
workshops for intellectually-disabled adults 15
writing: about mental illness 200–201; autobiographical novels 198–200

Yerkes-Dodson principle *see* inverted-U
Young, B.J. 90, 91

Zarroug, E.A. 90
zone analysis 7